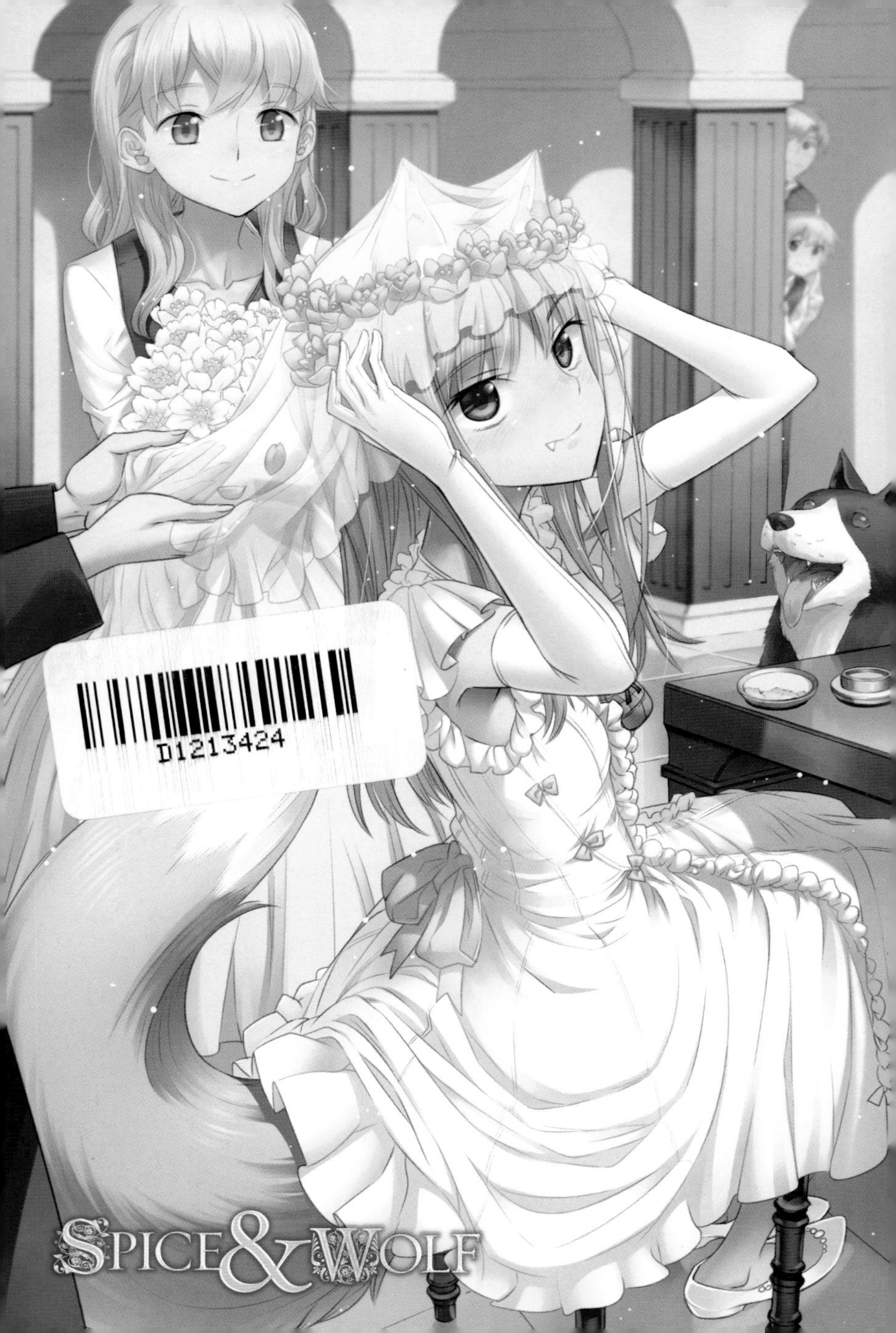
SPICE & WOLF

Spice & Wolf

CONTENTS

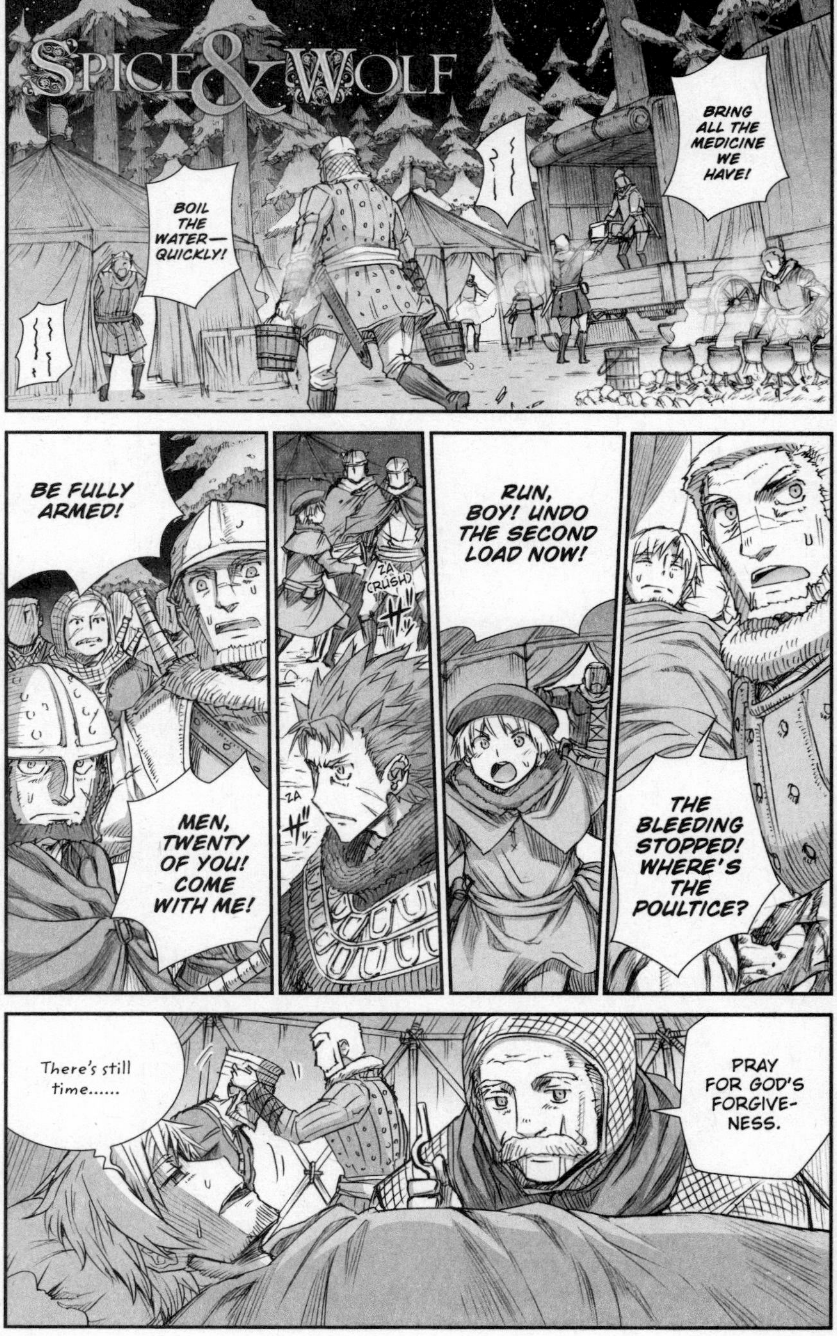
SPICE & WOLF
BRING ALL THE MEDICINE WE HAVE!
BOIL THE WATER— QUICKLY!
THE BLEEDING STOPPED! WHERE'S THE POULTICE?
RUN, BOY! UNDO THE SECOND LOAD NOW!
ZA (CRUSH)
ZA
BE FULLY ARMED!
MEN, TWENTY OF YOU! COME WITH ME!
PRAY FOR GOD'S FORGIVE-NESS.
There's still time......

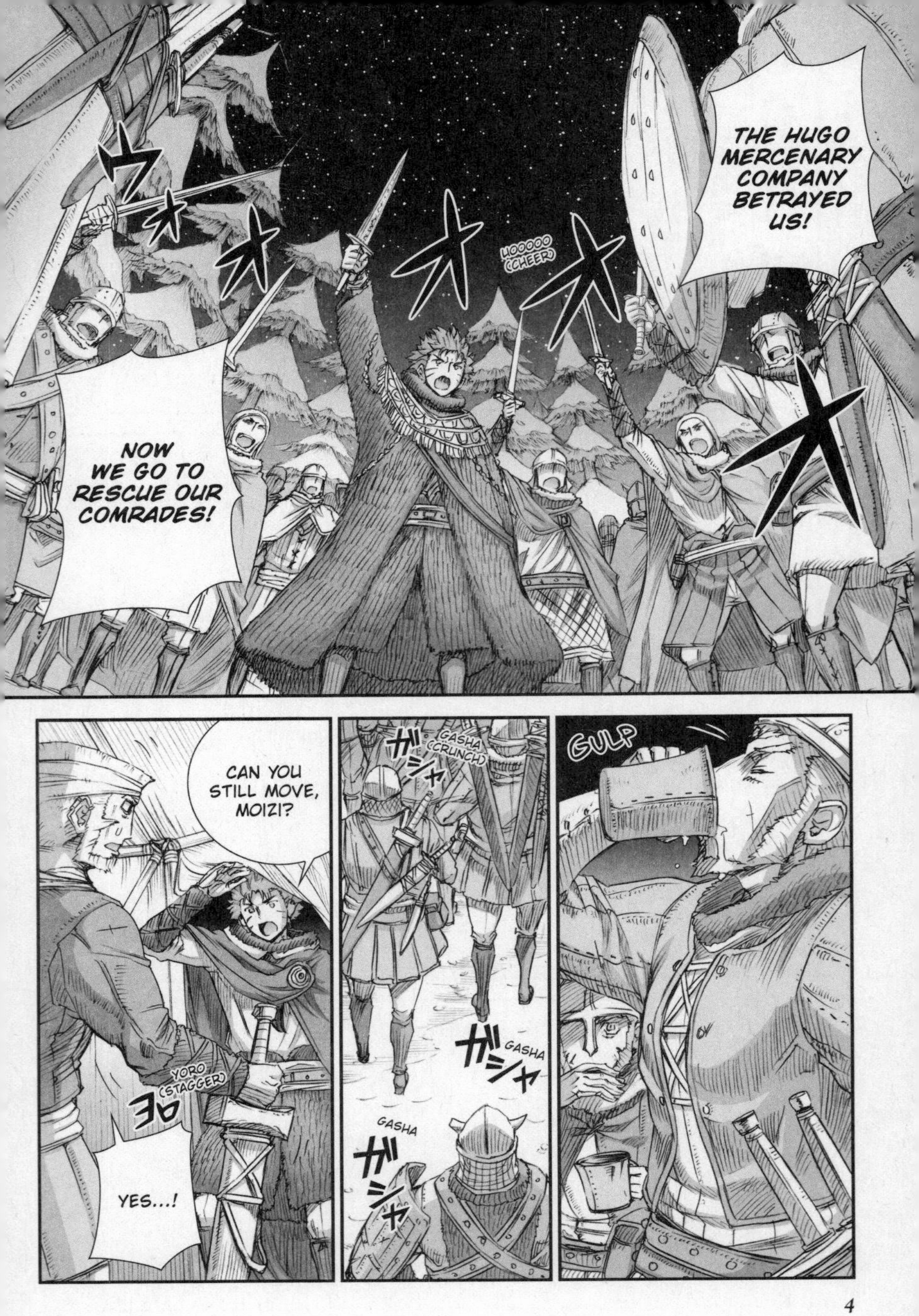
THE HUGO MERCENARY COMPANY BETRAYED US!
UOOOOO (CHEER)
NOW WE GO TO RESCUE OUR COMRADES!
GULP
ガシャ GASHA (CRUNCH)
ガシャ GASHA
ガシャ GASHA
CAN YOU STILL MOVE, MOIZI?
ヨロ YORO (STAGGER)
YES...!

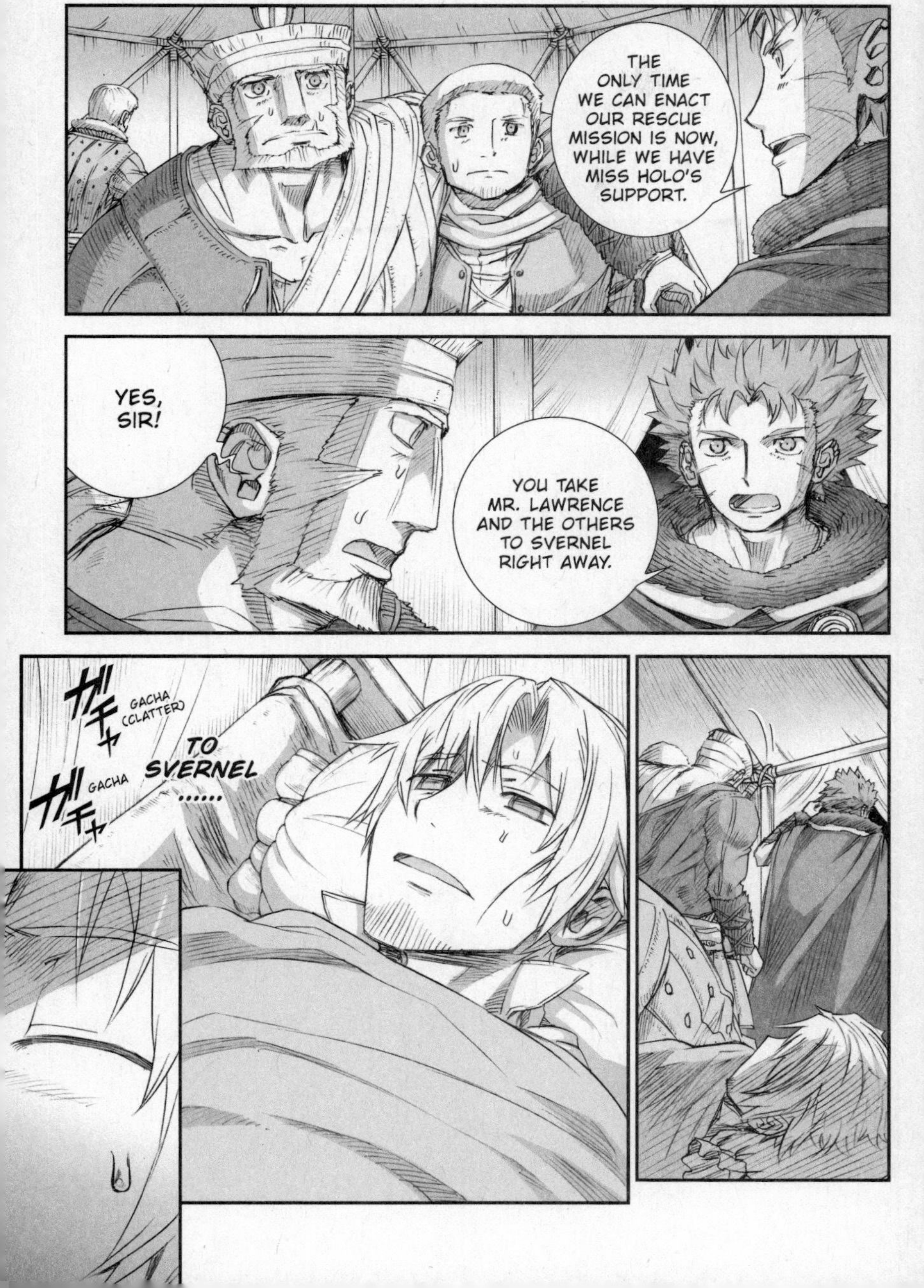
THE ONLY TIME WE CAN ENACT OUR RESCUE MISSION IS NOW, WHILE WE HAVE MISS HOLO'S SUPPORT.
YOU TAKE MR. LAWRENCE AND THE OTHERS TO SVERNEL RIGHT AWAY.
YES, SIR!
TO SVERNEL ......
ガチャ
GACHA (CLATTER)
ガチャ
GACHA

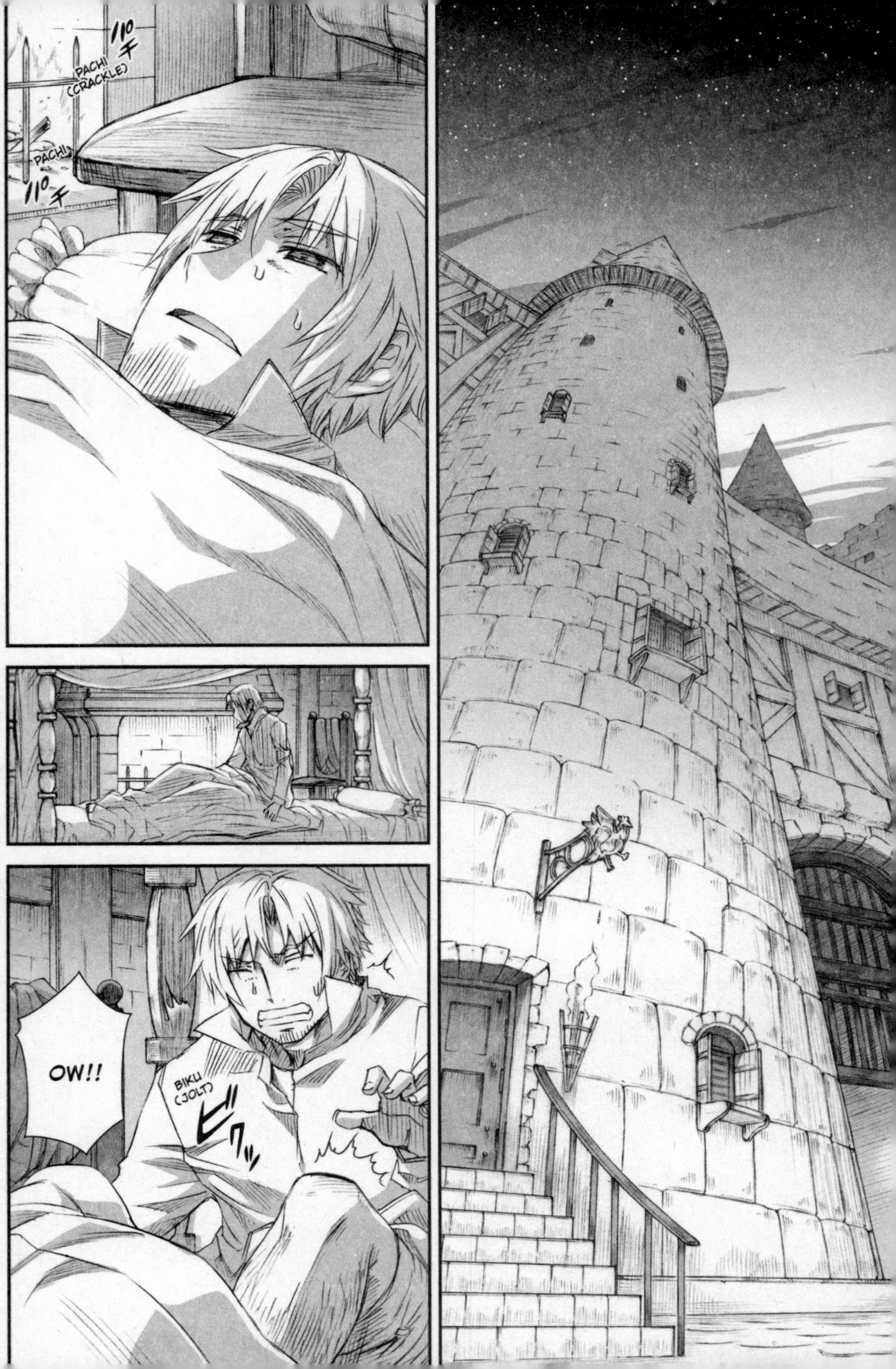
パチ
PACHI (CRACKLE)
PACHI
パチ
OW!!
BIKU (JOLT)
ビクッ

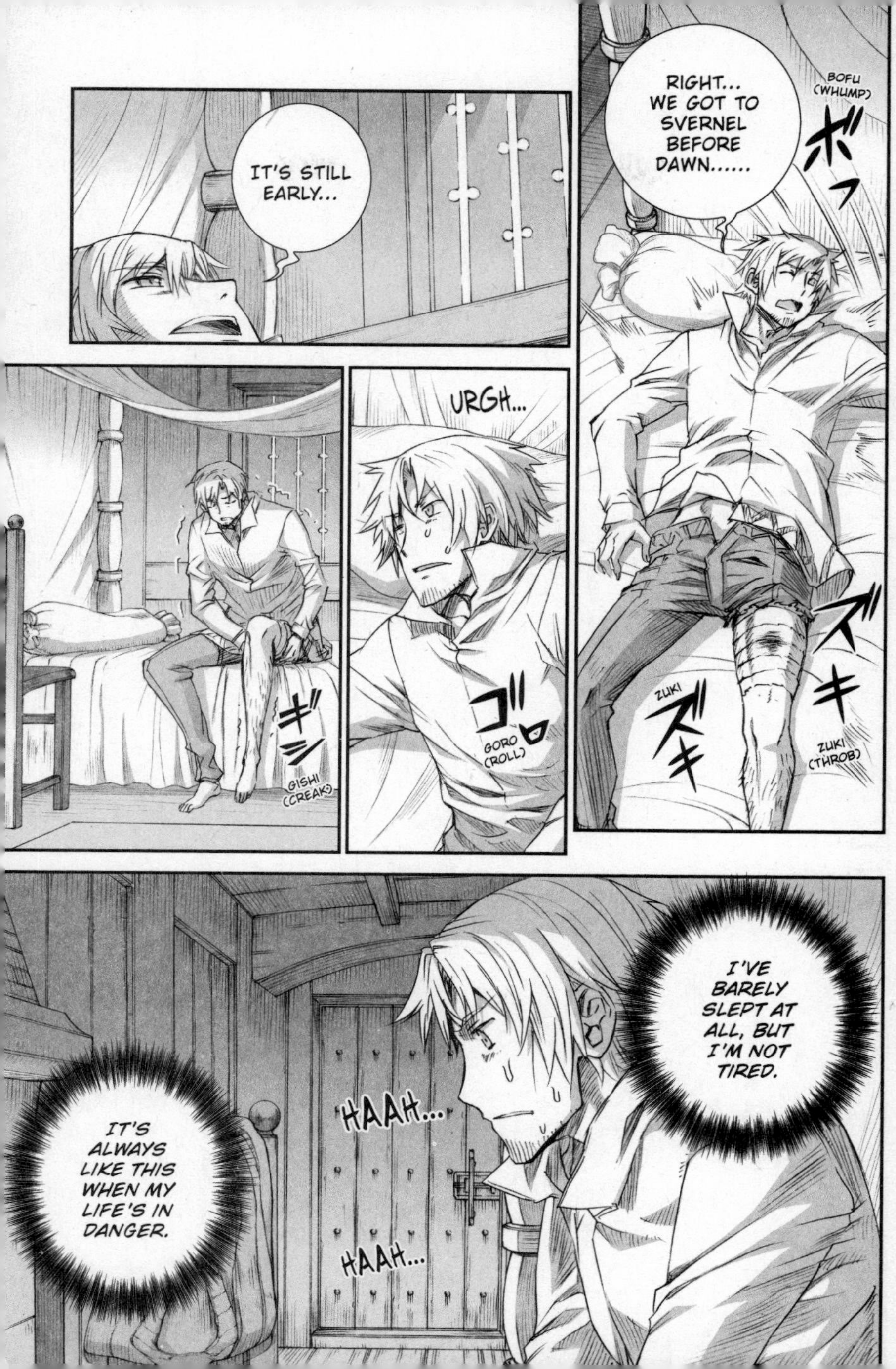
RIGHT... WE GOT TO SVERNEL BEFORE DAWN......
BOFU (WHUMP)
ボフ
ズキ
ZUKI
ズキ
ZUKI (THROB)
IT'S STILL EARLY...
URGH...
ゴロ
GORO (ROLL)
ギシ
GISHI (CREAK)
I'VE BARELY SLEPT AT ALL, BUT I'M NOT TIRED.
HAAH...
IT'S ALWAYS LIKE THIS WHEN MY LIFE'S IN DANGER.
HAAH...

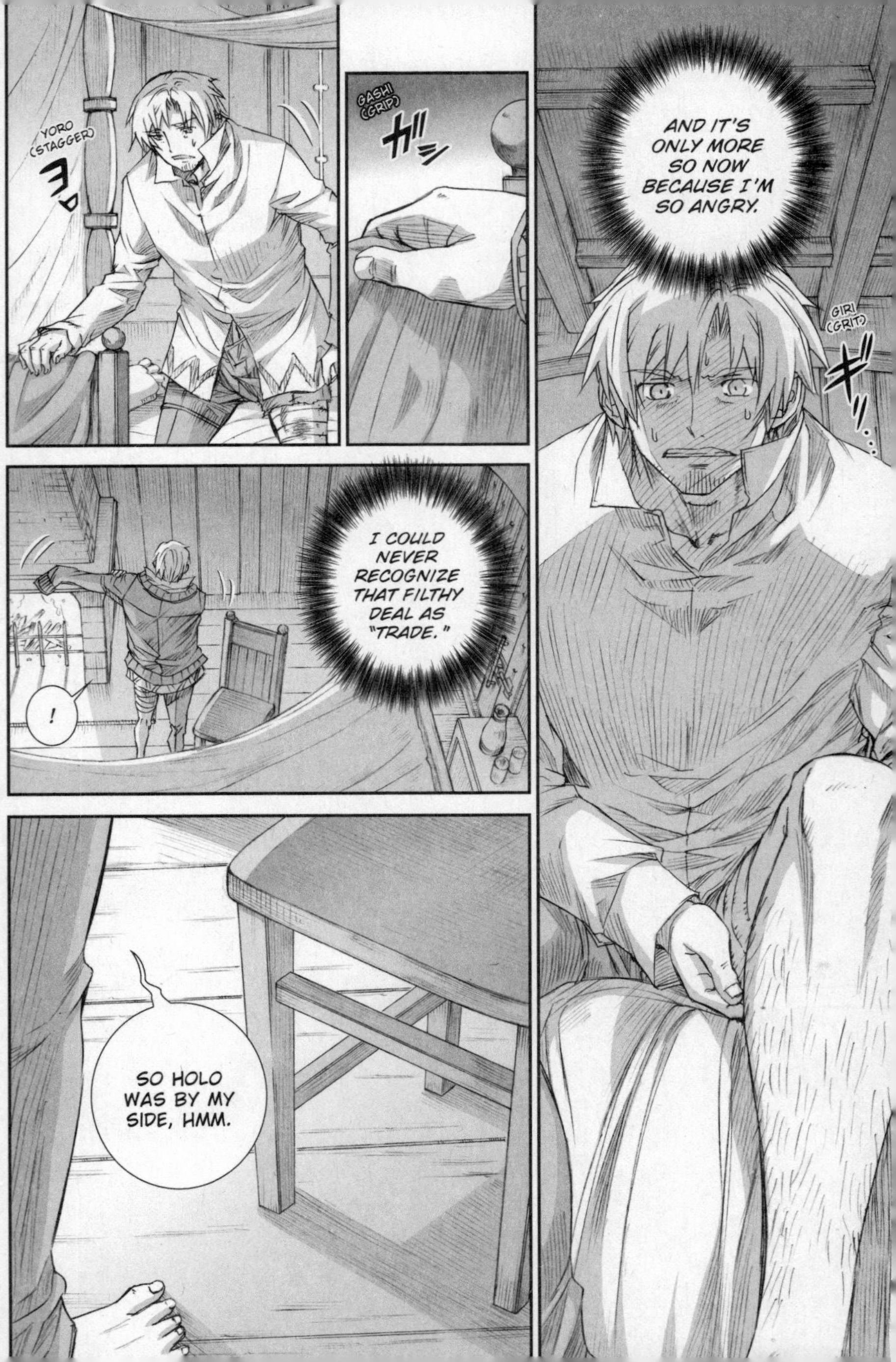
AND IT'S ONLY MORE SO NOW BECAUSE I'M SO ANGRY.
GIRI (GRIT)
GASHI (GRIP)
YORO (STAGGER)
I COULD NEVER RECOGNIZE THAT FILTHY DEAL AS "TRADE."
!
SO HOLO WAS BY MY SIDE, HMM.

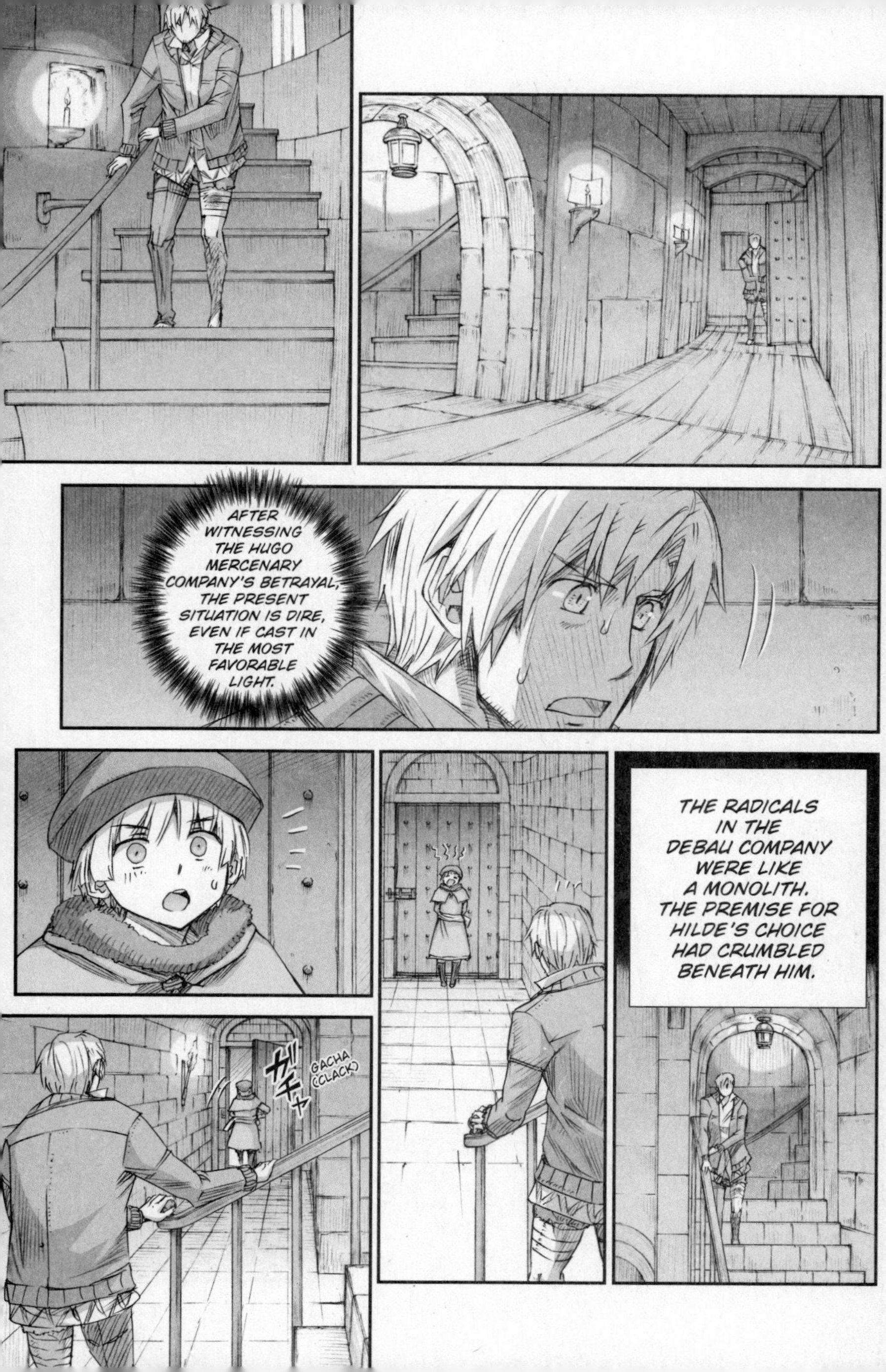
AFTER WITNESSING THE HUGO MERCENARY COMPANY'S BETRAYAL, THE PRESENT SITUATION IS DIRE, EVEN IF CAST IN THE MOST FAVORABLE LIGHT.
THE RADICALS IN THE DEBAU COMPANY WERE LIKE A MONOLITH. THE PREMISE FOR HILDE'S CHOICE HAD CRUMBLED BENEATH HIM.
ガチャ
GACHA (CLACK)

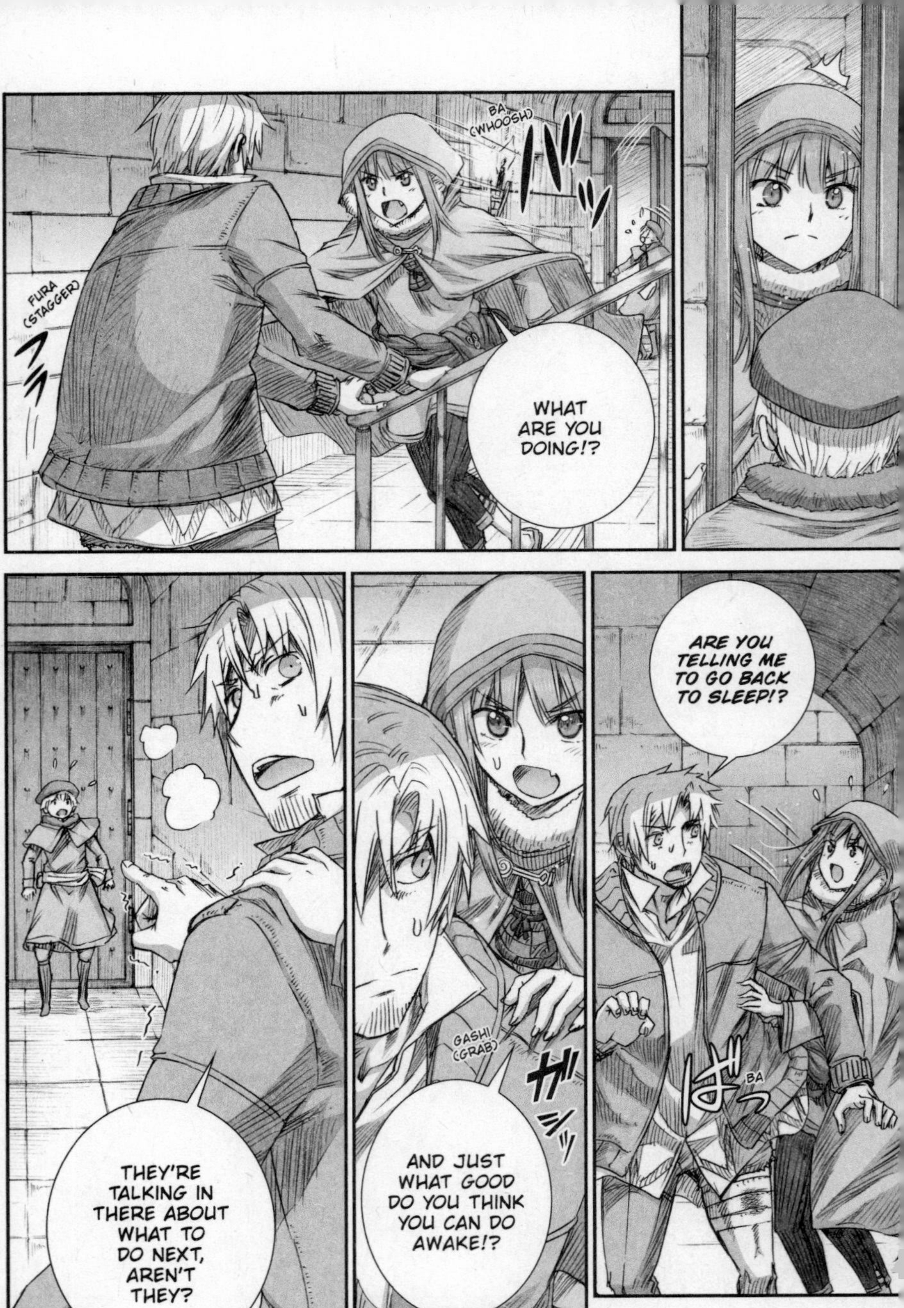
BA (WHOOSH)
WHAT ARE YOU DOING!?
FURA (STAGGER)
ARE YOU TELLING ME TO GO BACK TO SLEEP!?
BA
GASHI (GRAB)
AND JUST WHAT GOOD DO YOU THINK YOU CAN DO AWAKE!?
THEY'RE TALKING IN THERE ABOUT WHAT TO DO NEXT, AREN'T THEY?

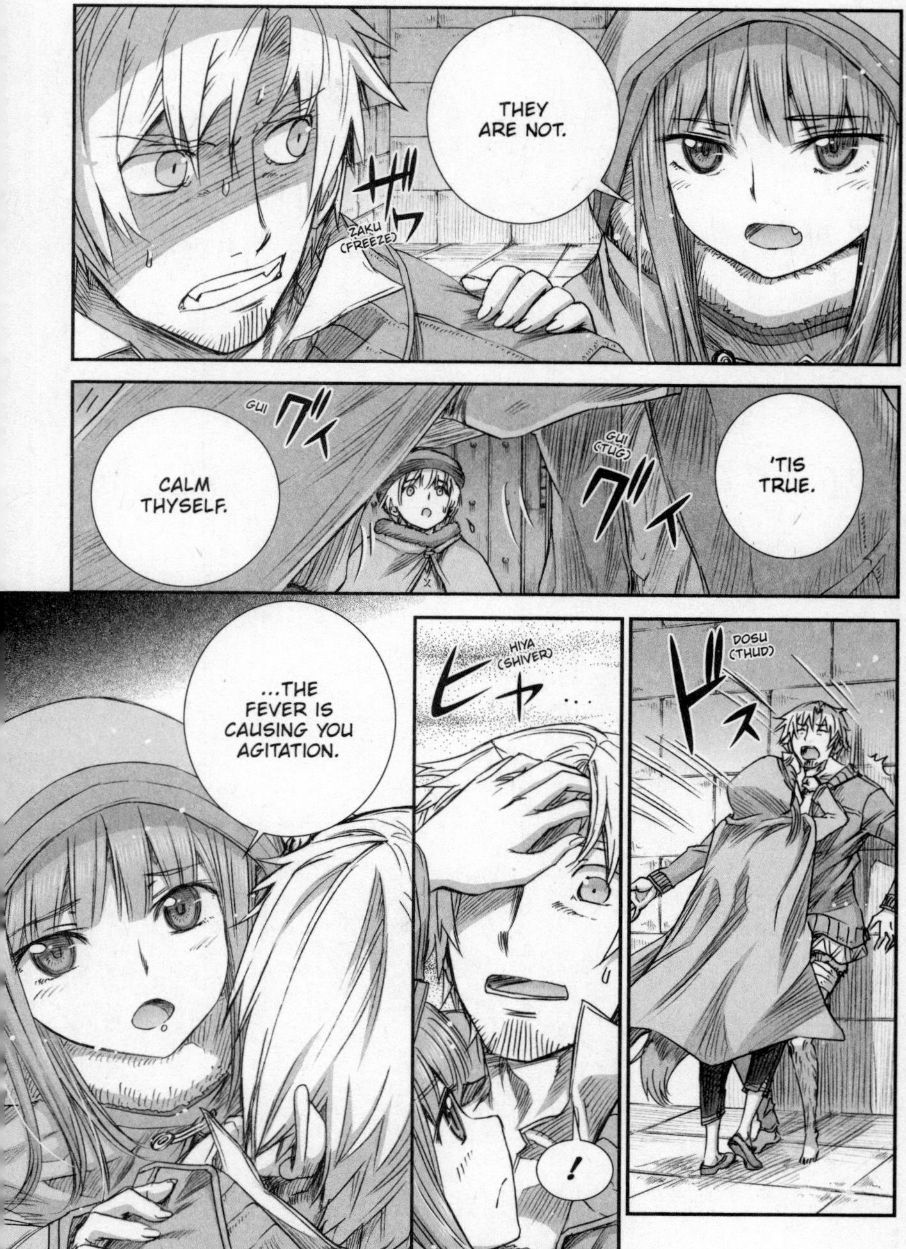
THEY ARE NOT.
ZAKU (FREEZE)
'TIS TRUE.
GUI (TUG)
GUI
CALM THYSELF.
DOSU (THUD)
HIYA (SHIVER)
...
!
...THE FEVER IS CAUSING YOU AGITATION.

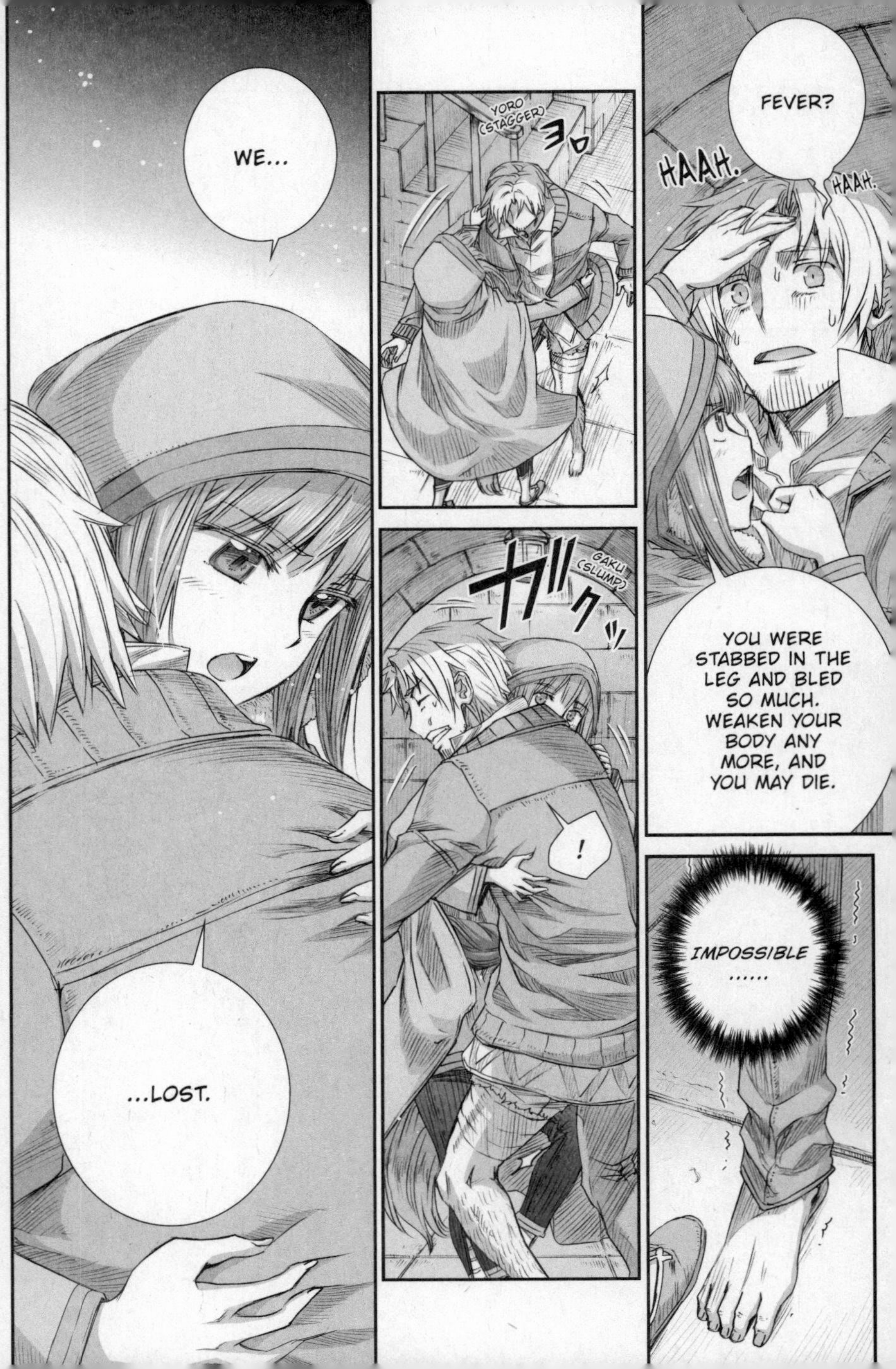
FEVER?
HAAH.
HAAH.
YOU WERE STABBED IN THE LEG AND BLED SO MUCH. WEAKEN YOUR BODY ANY MORE, AND YOU MAY DIE.
IMPOSSIBLE ......
YORO (STAGGER)
ヨロ
GAKU (SLUMP)
ガクッ
!
WE...
...LOST.

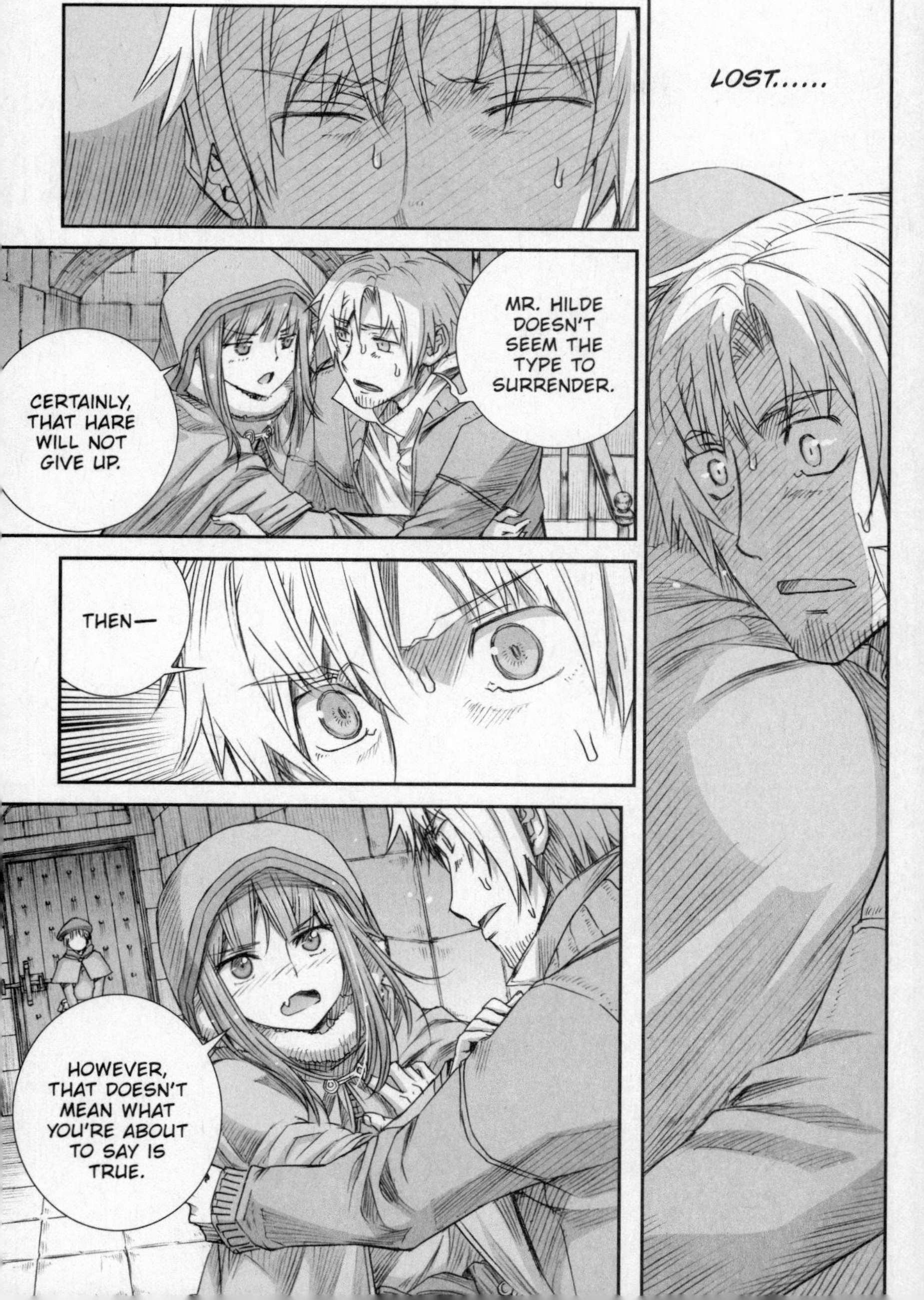
LOST......
MR. HILDE DOESN'T SEEM THE TYPE TO SURRENDER.
CERTAINLY, THAT HARE WILL NOT GIVE UP.
THEN—
HOWEVER, THAT DOESN'T MEAN WHAT YOU'RE ABOUT TO SAY IS TRUE.

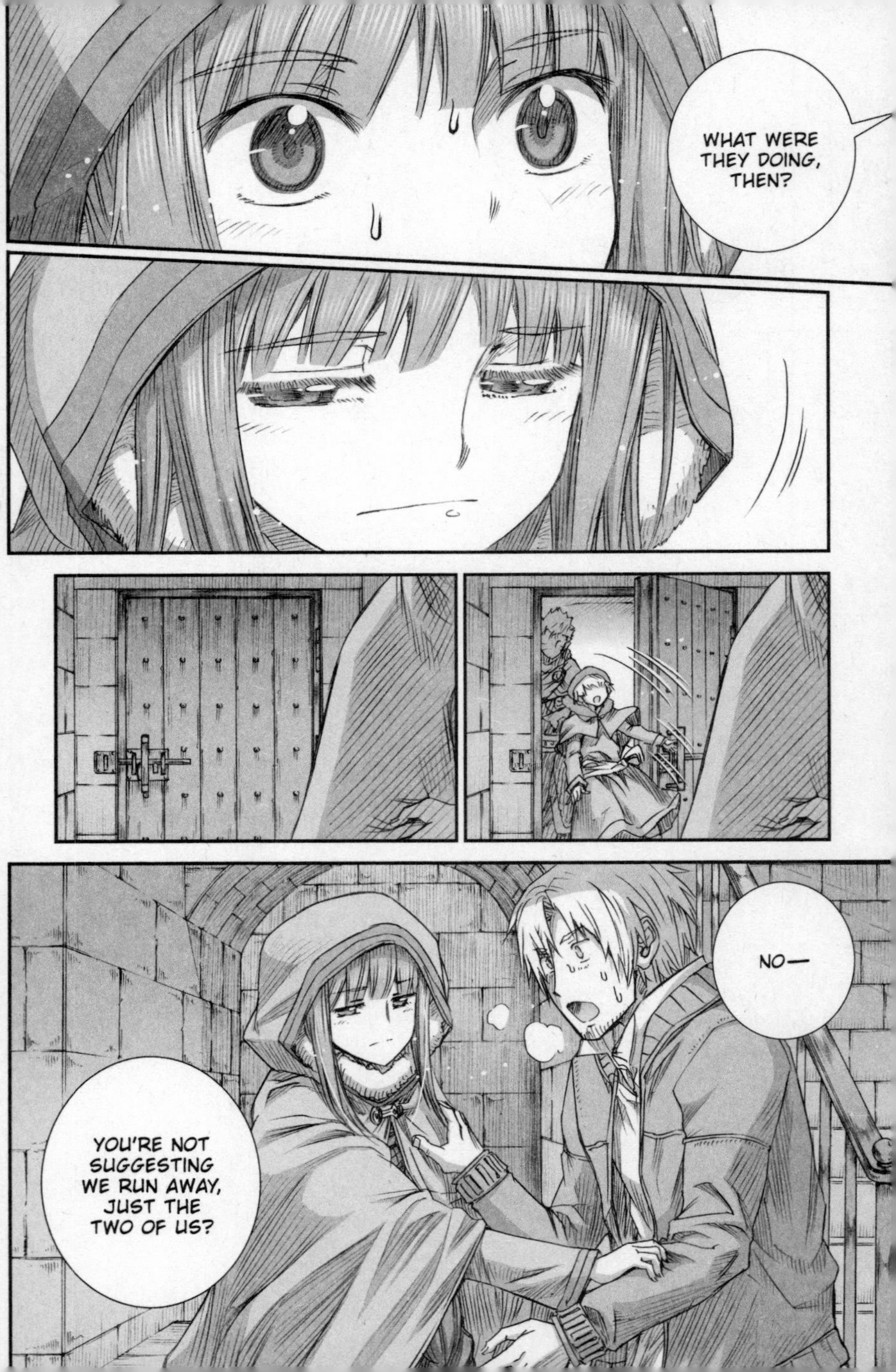
WHAT WERE THEY DOING, THEN?
NO—
YOU'RE NOT SUGGESTING WE RUN AWAY, JUST THE TWO OF US?

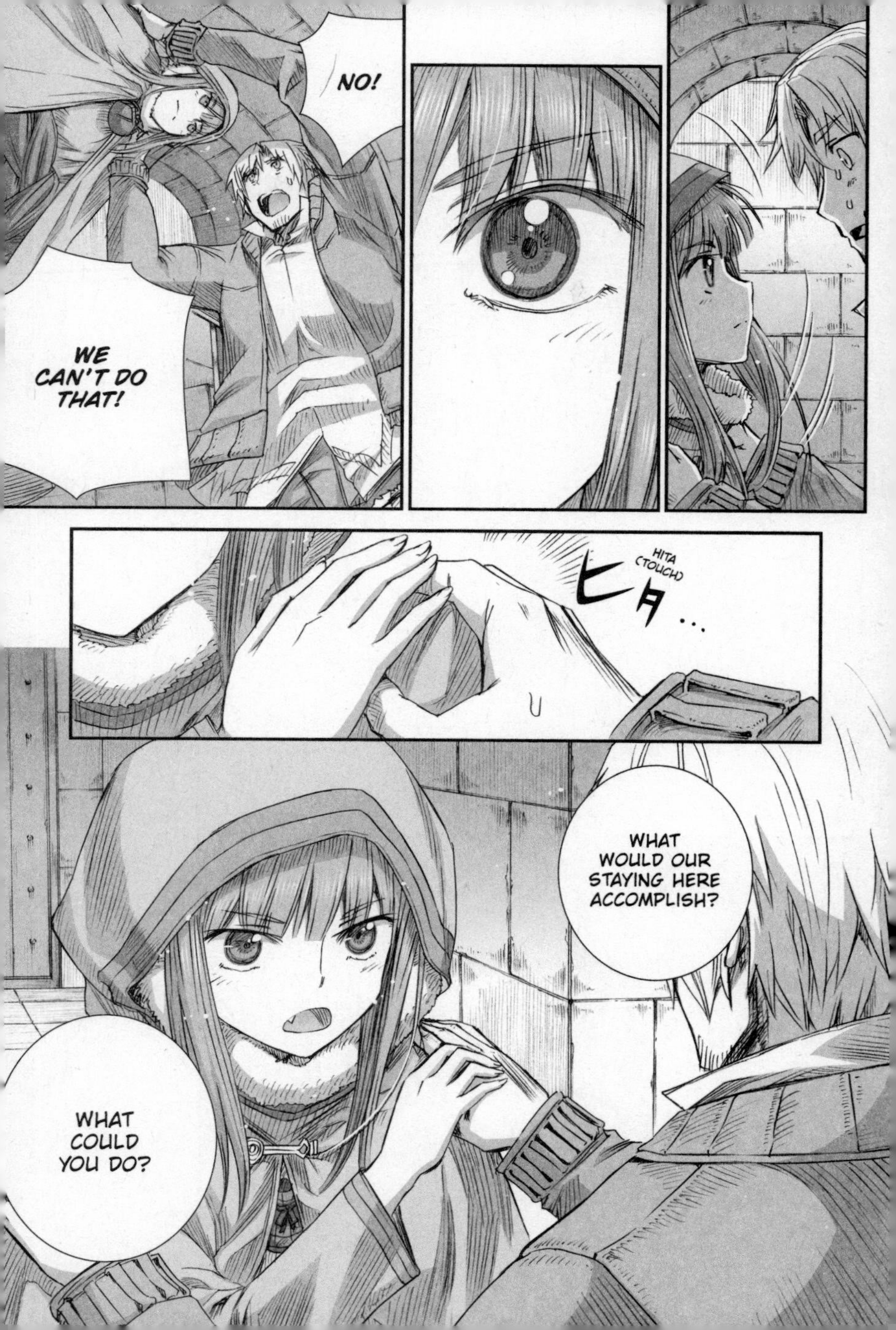
NO!
WE CAN'T DO THAT!
HITA (TOUCH)
ヒタ...
WHAT WOULD OUR STAYING HERE ACCOMPLISH?
WHAT COULD YOU DO?

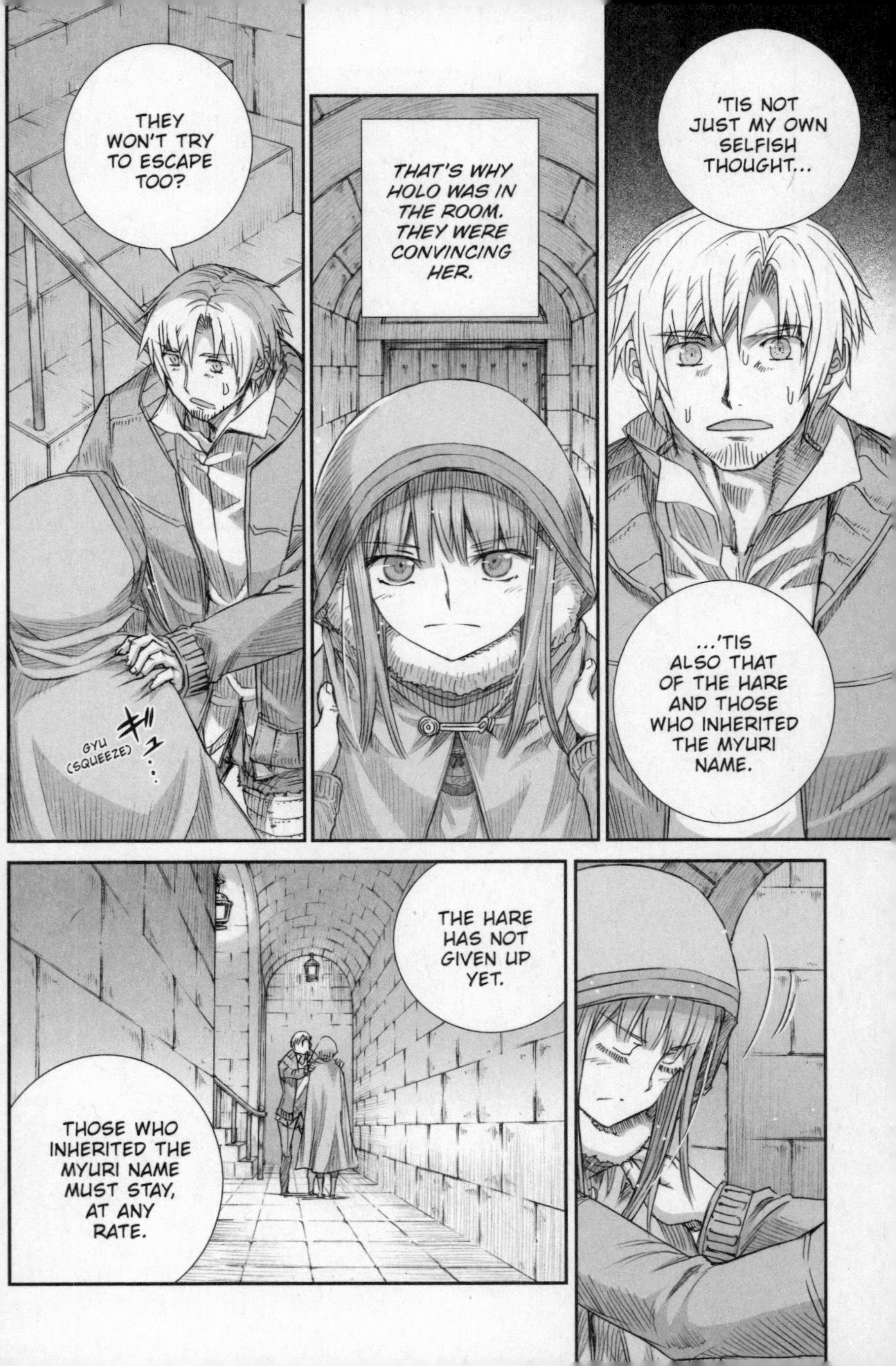
'TIS NOT JUST MY OWN SELFISH THOUGHT...
...'TIS ALSO THAT OF THE HARE AND THOSE WHO INHERITED THE MYURI NAME.
THAT'S WHY HOLO WAS IN THE ROOM. THEY WERE CONVINCING HER.
THEY WON'T TRY TO ESCAPE TOO?
GYU (SQUEEZE)
THE HARE HAS NOT GIVEN UP YET.
THOSE WHO INHERITED THE MYURI NAME MUST STAY, AT ANY RATE.

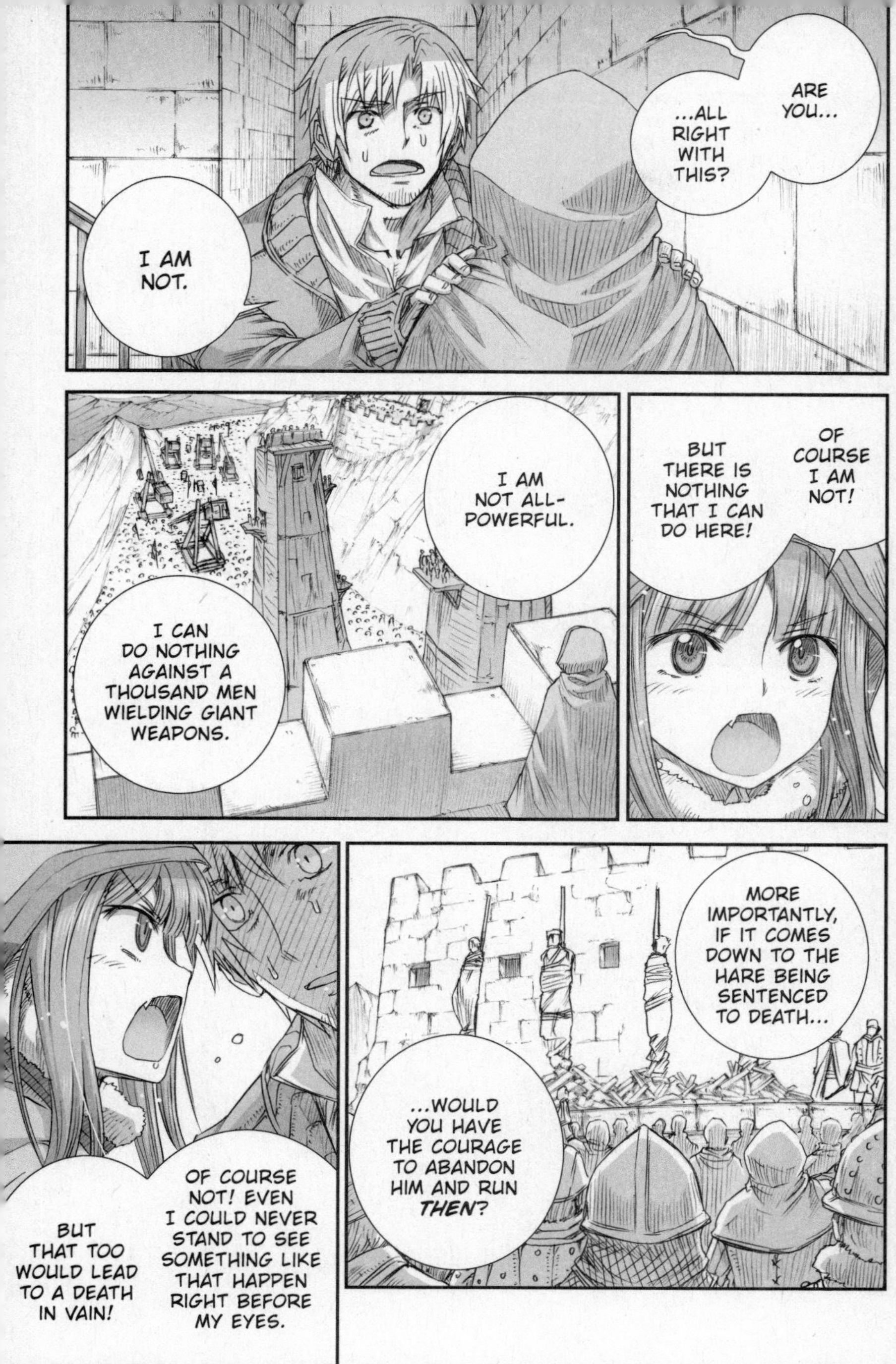
ARE YOU...
...ALL RIGHT WITH THIS?
I AM NOT.
OF COURSE I AM NOT!
BUT THERE IS NOTHING THAT I CAN DO HERE!
I AM NOT ALL-POWERFUL.
I CAN DO NOTHING AGAINST A THOUSAND MEN WIELDING GIANT WEAPONS.
MORE IMPORTANTLY, IF IT COMES DOWN TO THE HARE BEING SENTENCED TO DEATH...
...WOULD YOU HAVE THE COURAGE TO ABANDON HIM AND RUN *THEN*?
OF COURSE NOT! EVEN I COULD NEVER STAND TO SEE SOMETHING LIKE THAT HAPPEN RIGHT BEFORE MY EYES.
BUT THAT TOO WOULD LEAD TO A DEATH IN VAIN!

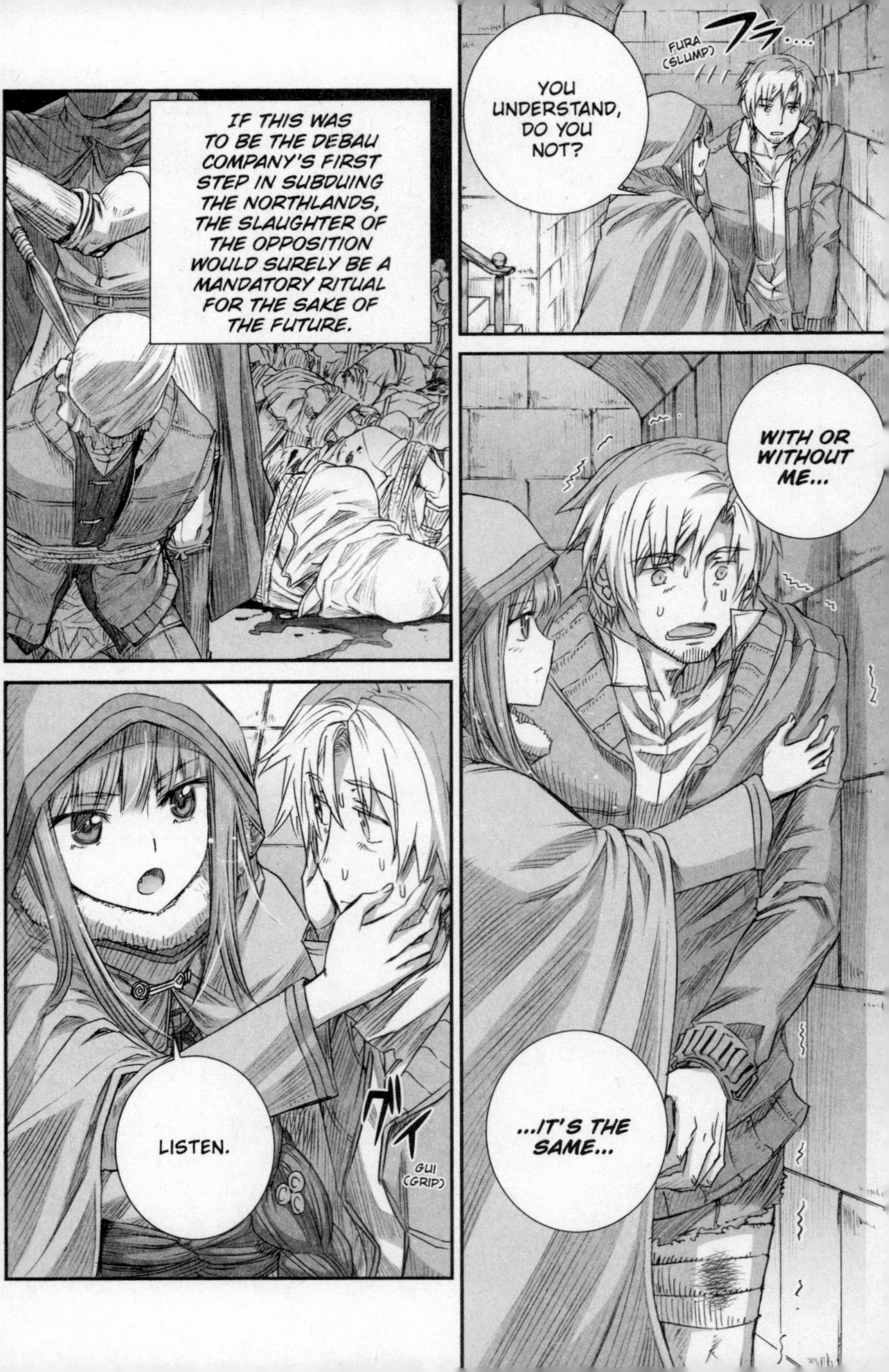
FURA (SLUMP)
YOU UNDERSTAND, DO YOU NOT?
WITH OR WITHOUT ME...
...IT'S THE SAME...
IF THIS WAS TO BE THE DEBAU COMPANY'S FIRST STEP IN SUBDUING THE NORTHLANDS, THE SLAUGHTER OF THE OPPOSITION WOULD SURELY BE A MANDATORY RITUAL FOR THE SAKE OF THE FUTURE.
LISTEN.
GUI (GRIP)

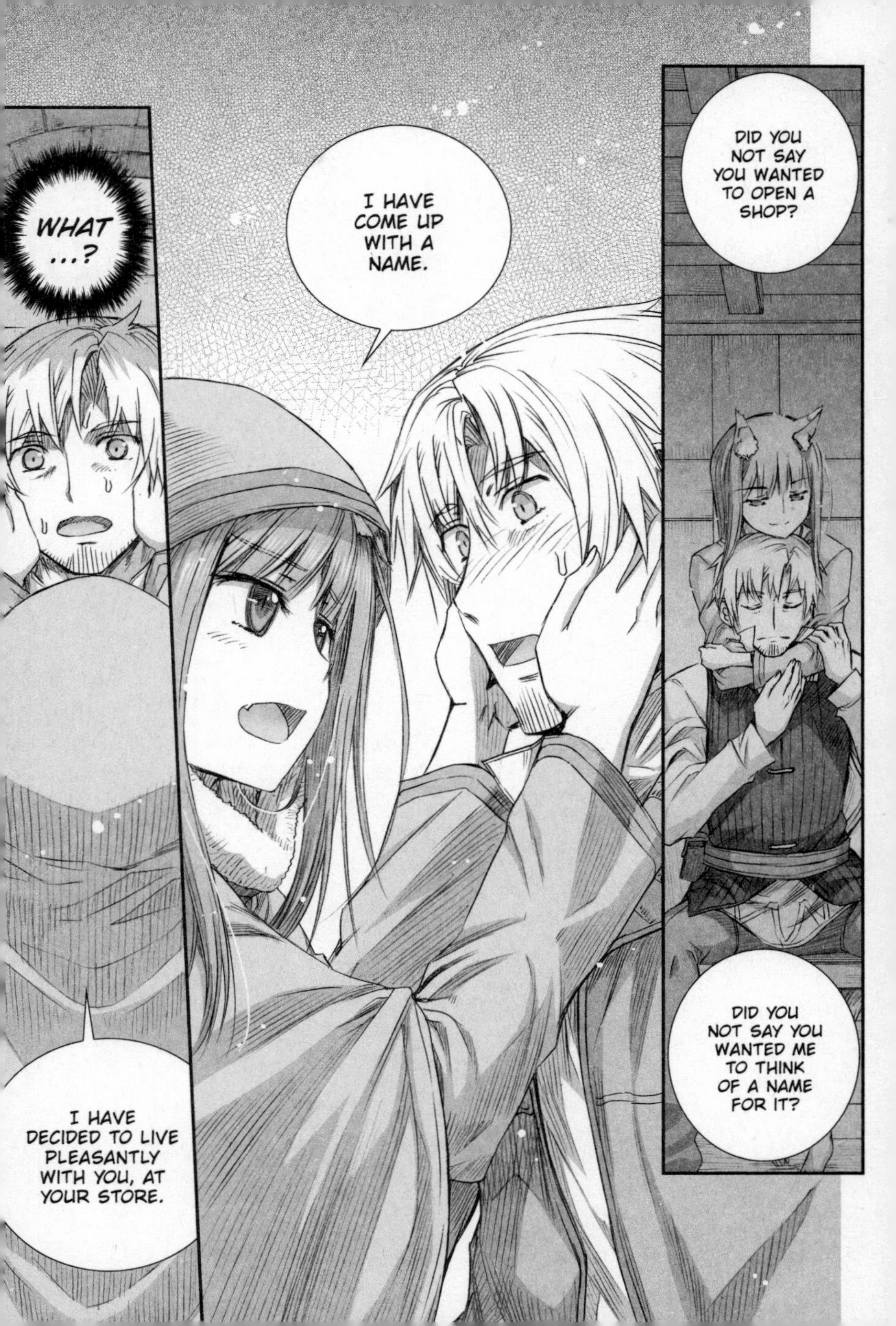
DID YOU NOT SAY YOU WANTED TO OPEN A SHOP?
DID YOU NOT SAY YOU WANTED ME TO THINK OF A NAME FOR IT?
I HAVE COME UP WITH A NAME.
WHAT ...?
I HAVE DECIDED TO LIVE PLEASANTLY WITH YOU, AT YOUR STORE.

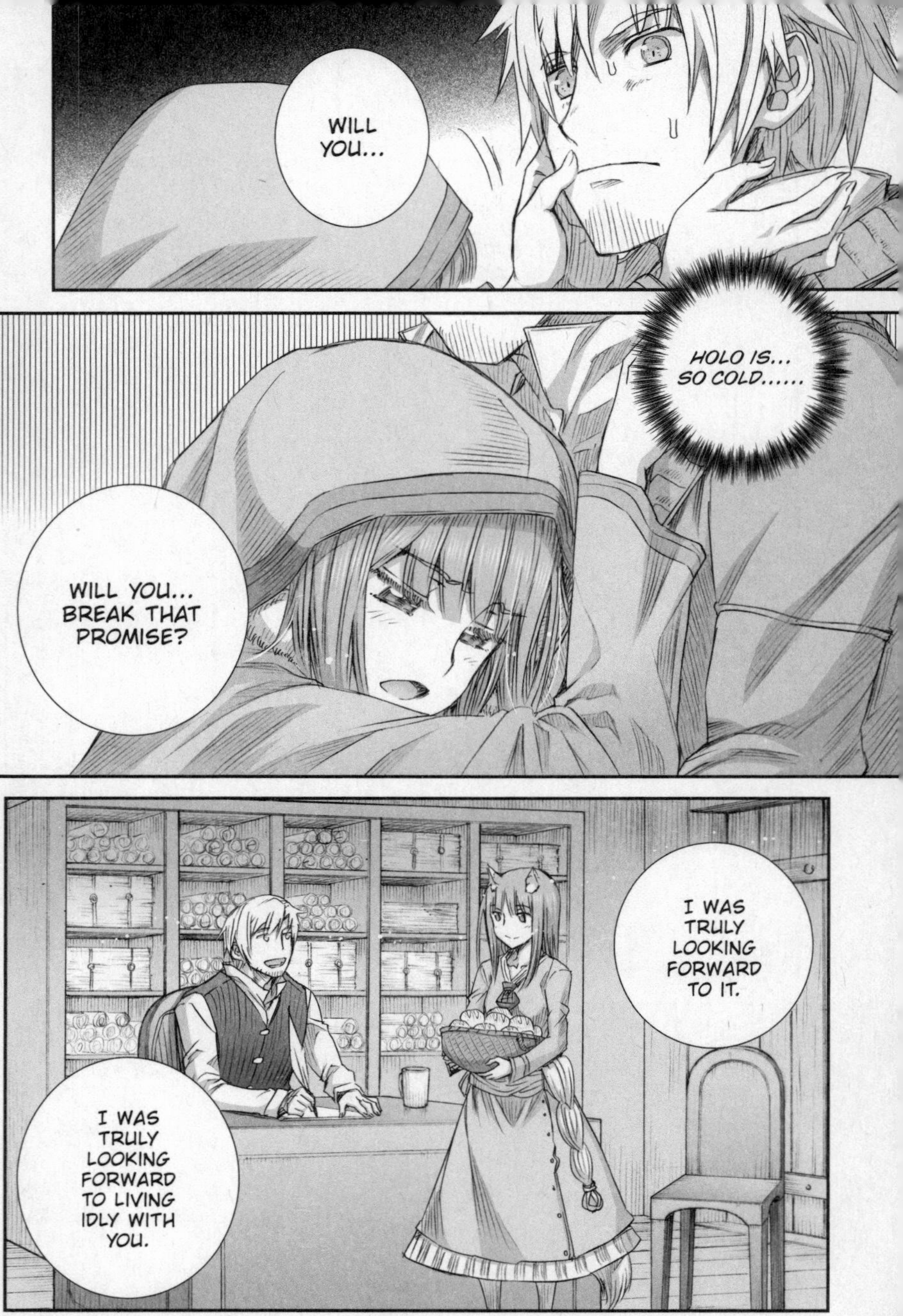
WILL YOU...
HOLO IS... SO COLD......
WILL YOU... BREAK THAT PROMISE?
I WAS TRULY LOOKING FORWARD TO IT.
I WAS TRULY LOOKING FORWARD TO LIVING IDLY WITH YOU.

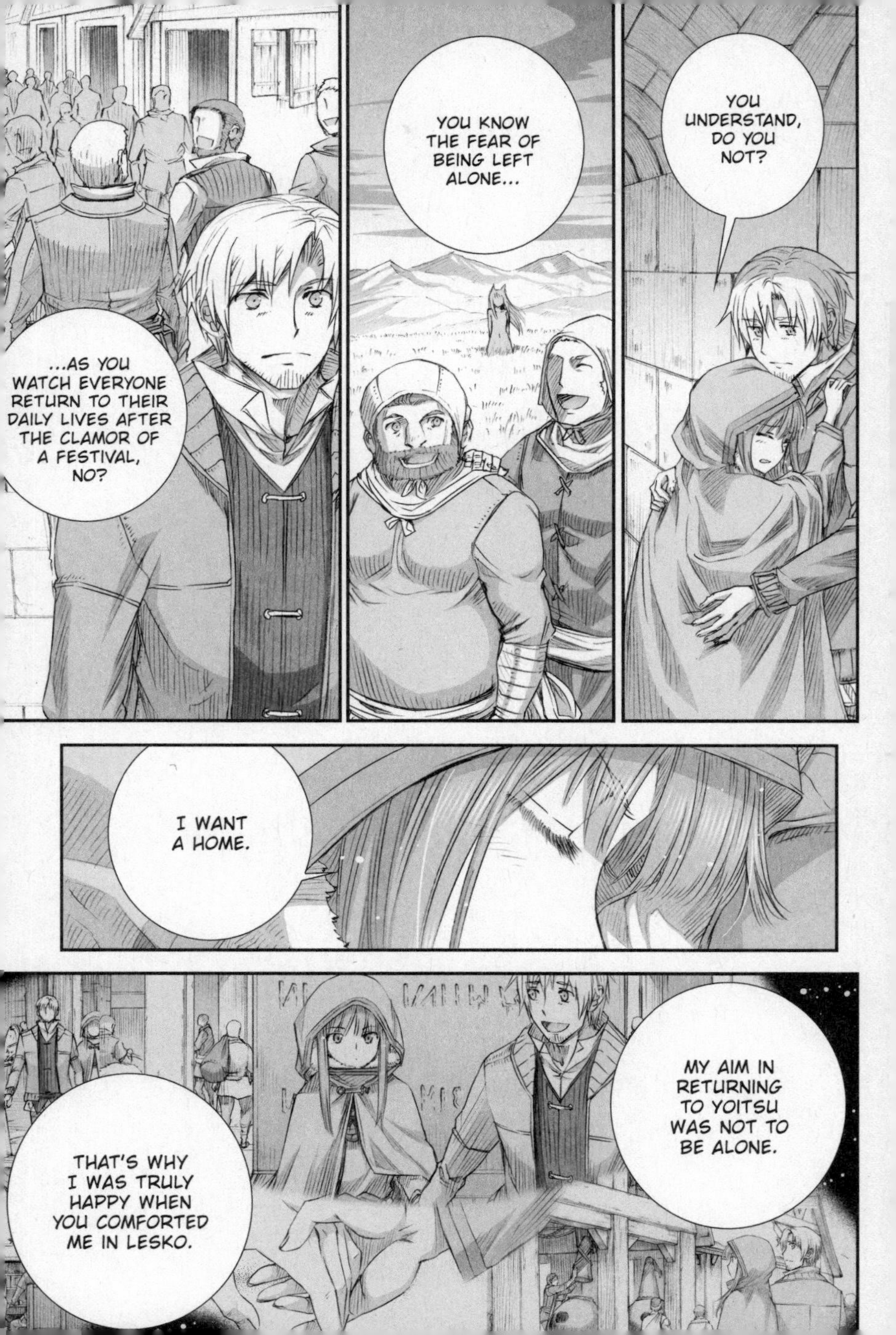
YOU UNDERSTAND, DO YOU NOT?
YOU KNOW THE FEAR OF BEING LEFT ALONE...
...AS YOU WATCH EVERYONE RETURN TO THEIR DAILY LIVES AFTER THE CLAMOR OF A FESTIVAL, NO?
I WANT A HOME.
MY AIM IN RETURNING TO YOITSU WAS NOT TO BE ALONE.
THAT'S WHY I WAS TRULY HAPPY WHEN YOU COMFORTED ME IN LESKO.

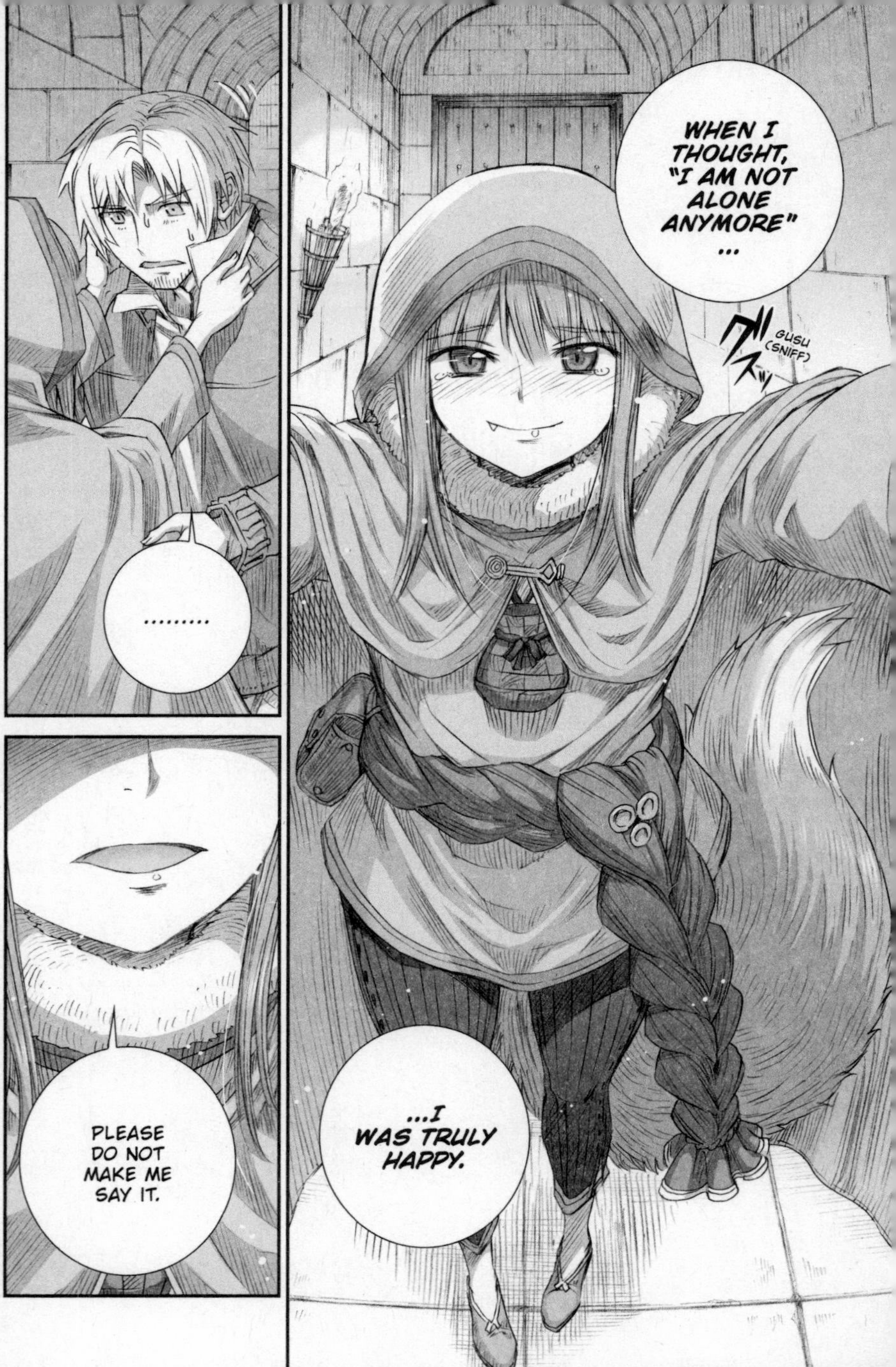
WHEN I THOUGHT, "I AM NOT ALONE ANYMORE"...
GUSU (SNIFF)
...I WAS TRULY HAPPY.
....
PLEASE DO NOT MAKE ME SAY IT.

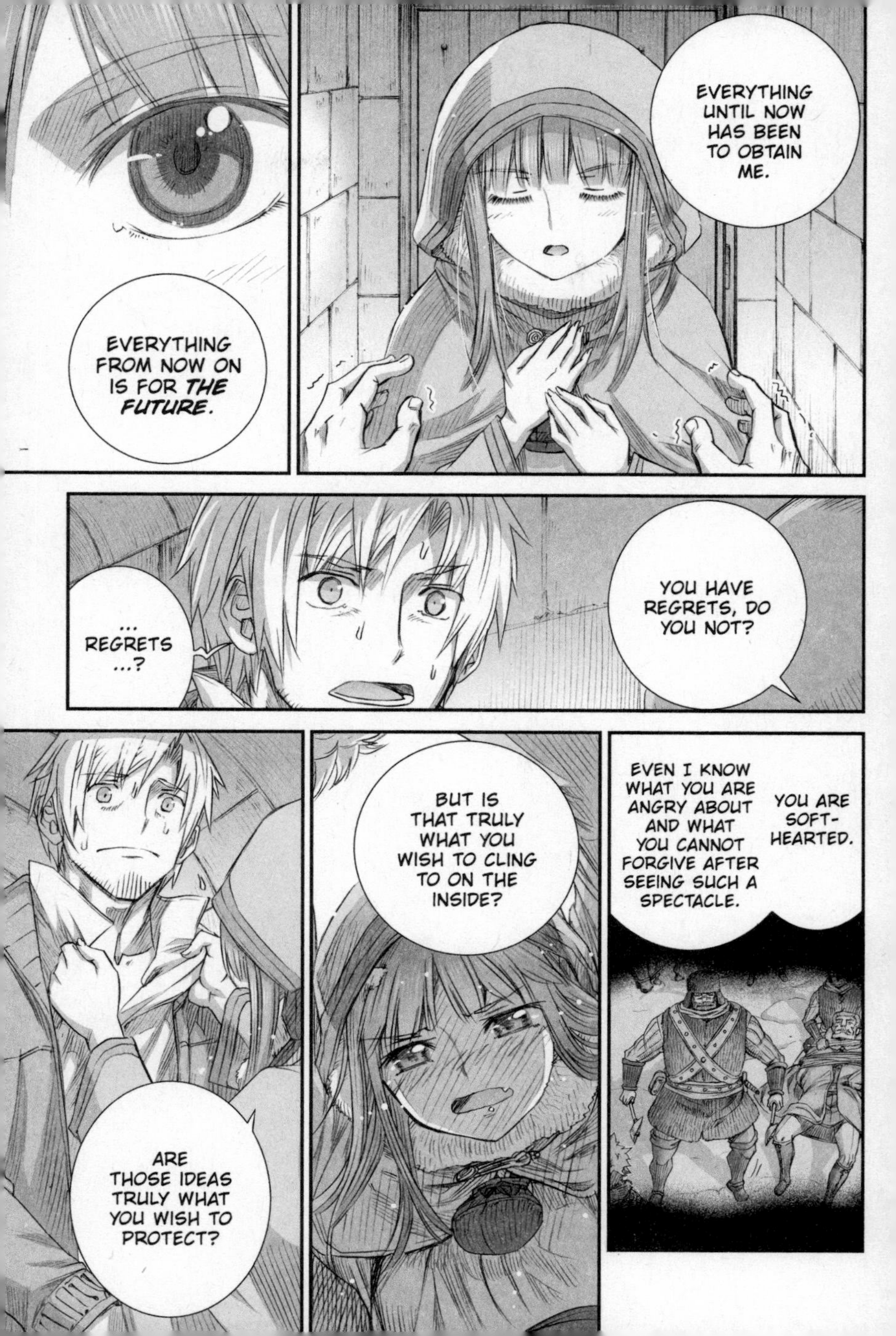
EVERYTHING UNTIL NOW HAS BEEN TO OBTAIN ME.
EVERYTHING FROM NOW ON IS FOR *THE FUTURE*.
YOU HAVE REGRETS, DO YOU NOT?
...REGRETS...?
YOU ARE SOFT-HEARTED.
EVEN I KNOW WHAT YOU ARE ANGRY ABOUT AND WHAT YOU CANNOT FORGIVE AFTER SEEING SUCH A SPECTACLE.
BUT IS THAT TRULY WHAT YOU WISH TO CLING TO ON THE INSIDE?
ARE THOSE IDEAS TRULY WHAT YOU WISH TO PROTECT?

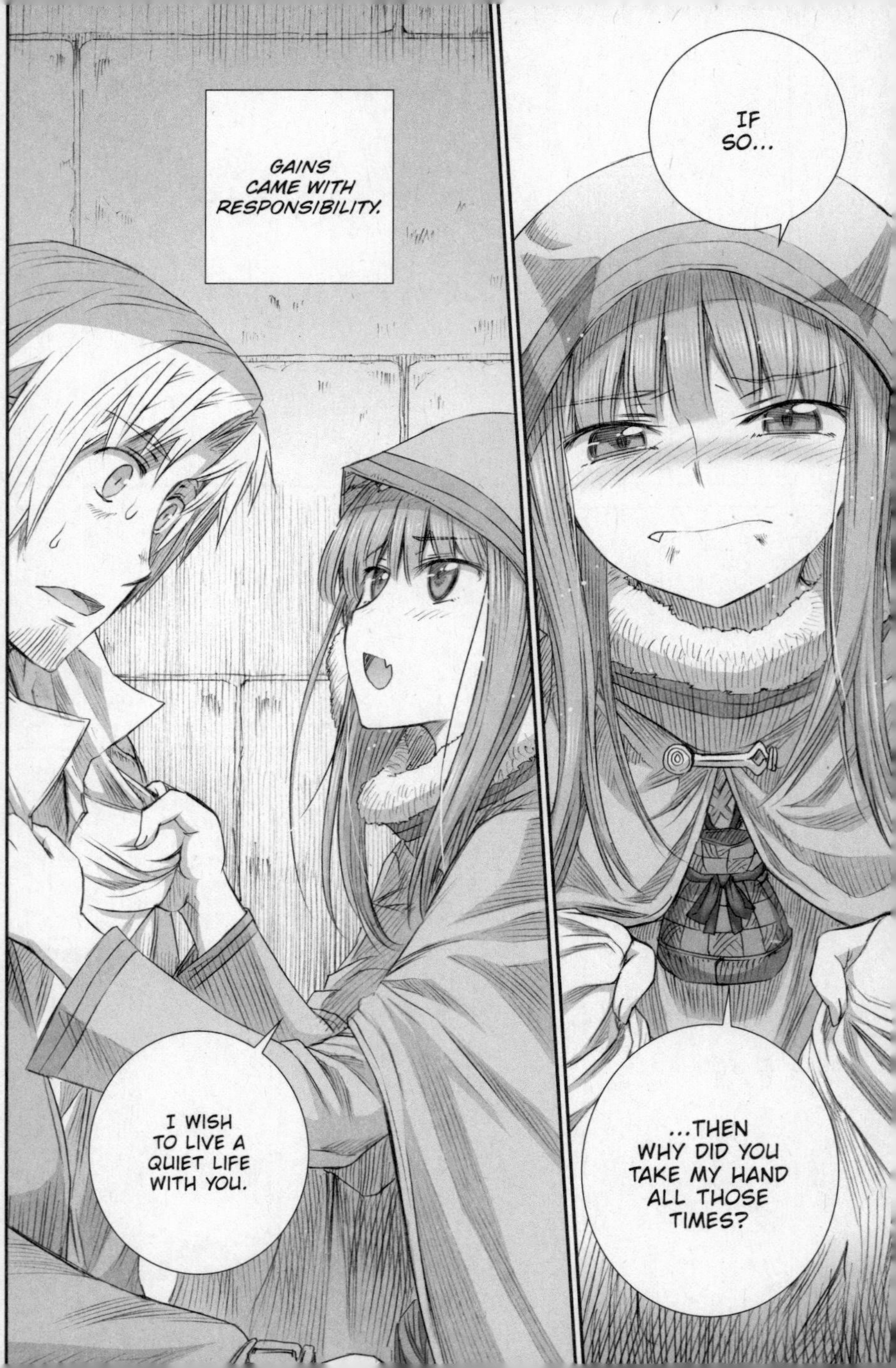
IF SO...
...THEN WHY DID YOU TAKE MY HAND ALL THOSE TIMES?
GAINS CAME WITH RESPONSIBILITY.
I WISH TO LIVE A QUIET LIFE WITH YOU.

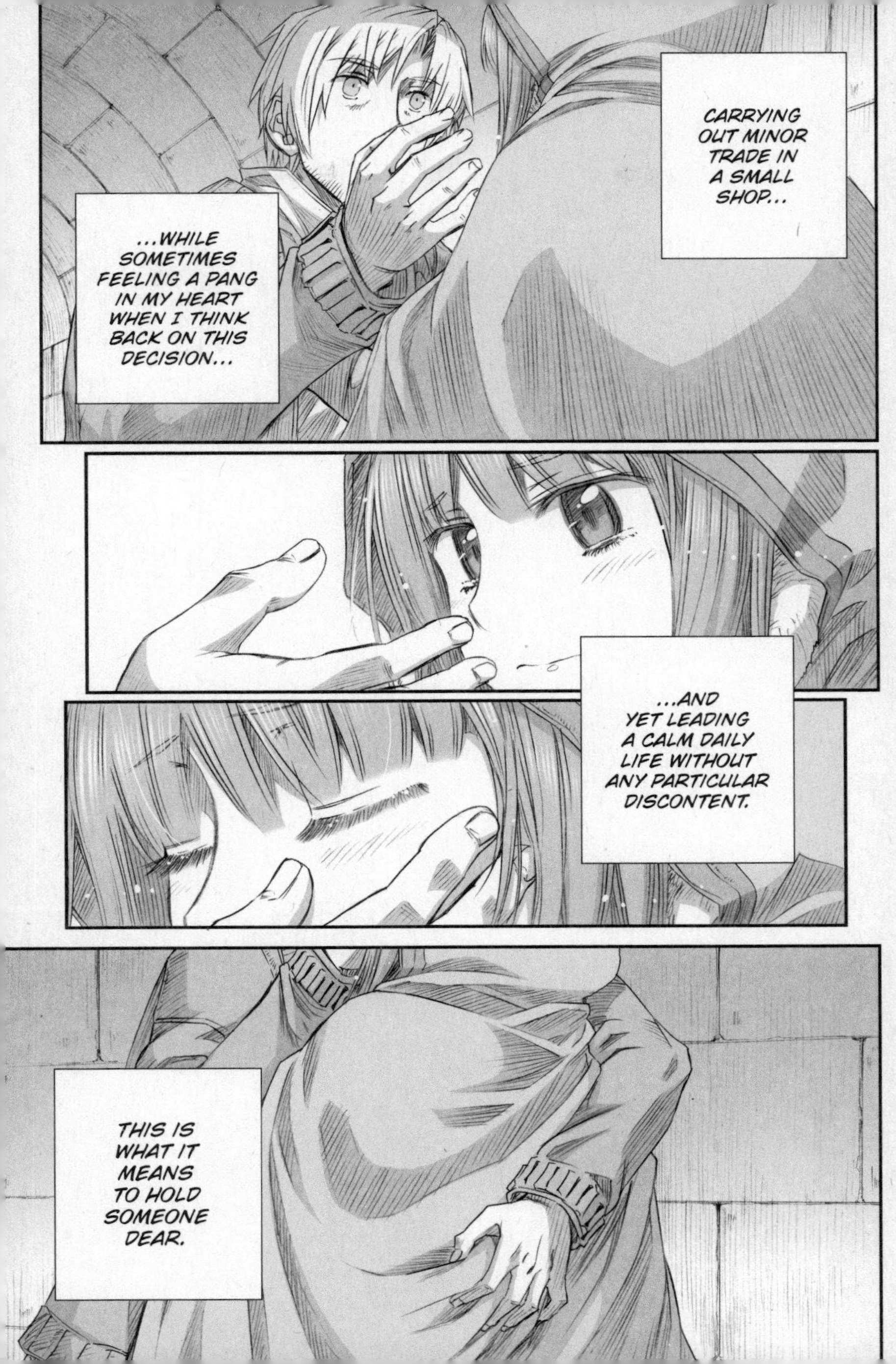
CARRYING OUT MINOR TRADE IN A SMALL SHOP...
...WHILE SOMETIMES FEELING A PANG IN MY HEART WHEN I THINK BACK ON THIS DECISION...
...AND YET LEADING A CALM DAILY LIFE WITHOUT ANY PARTICULAR DISCONTENT.
THIS IS WHAT IT MEANS TO HOLD SOMEONE DEAR.

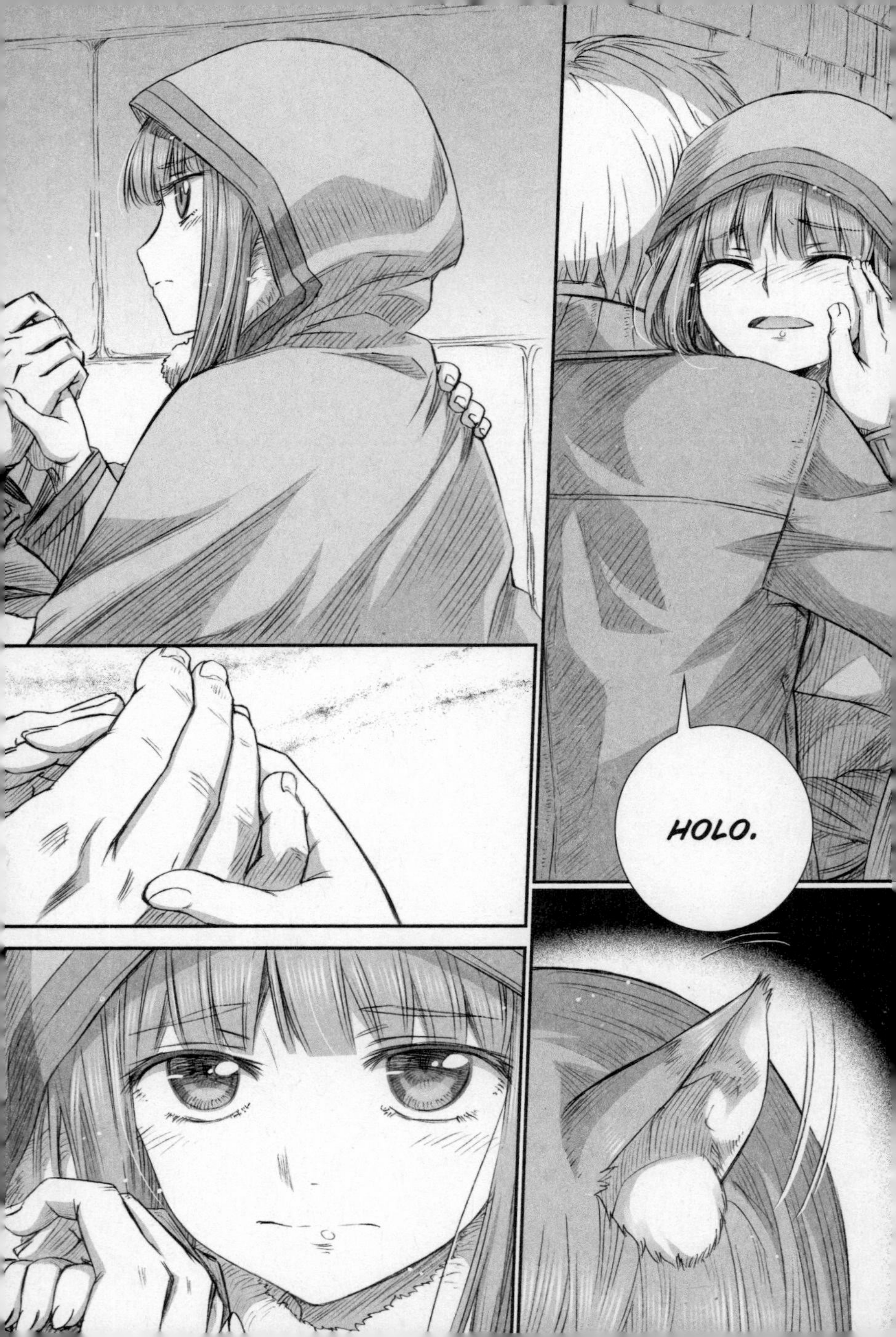
HOLO.

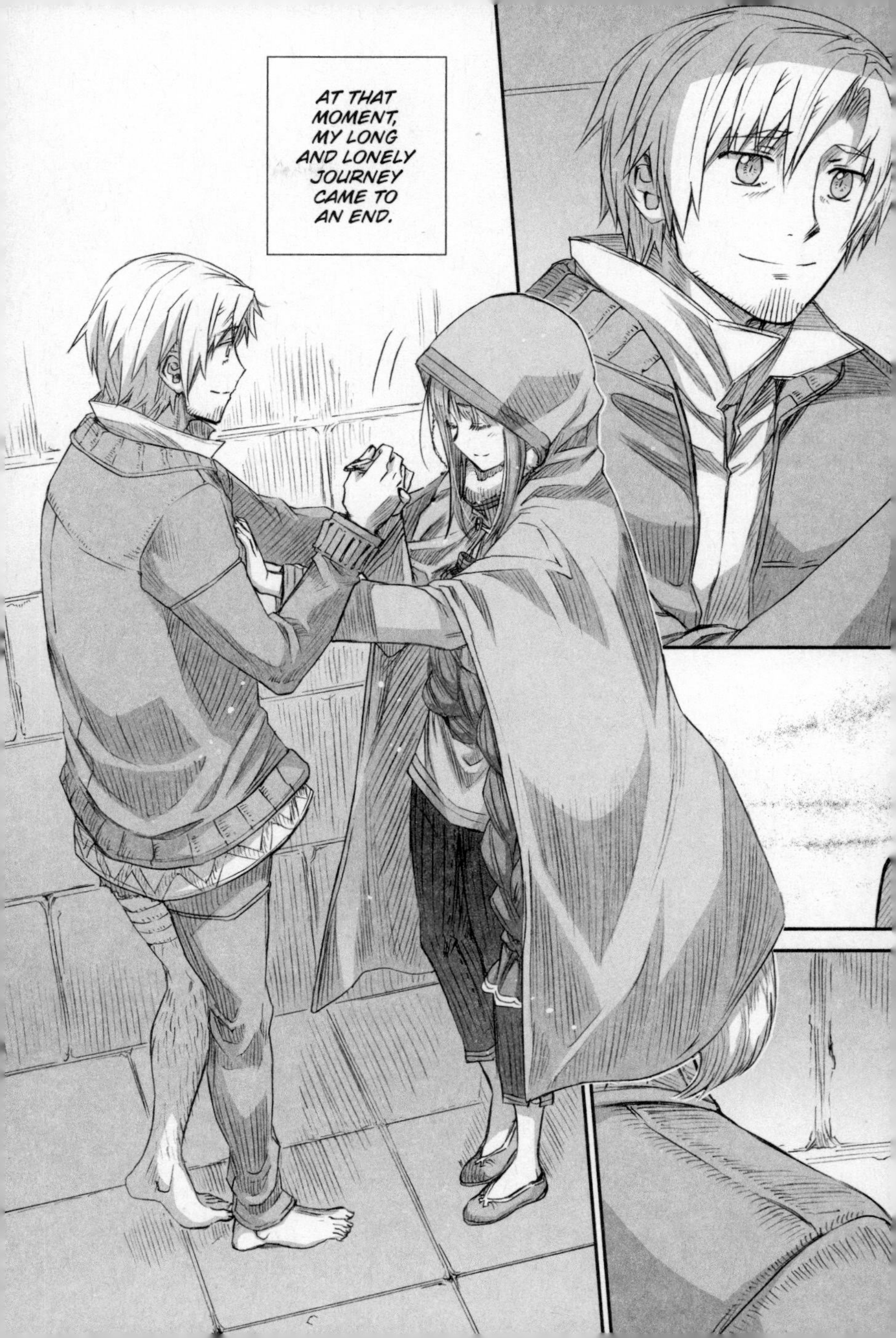
AT THAT MOMENT, MY LONG AND LONELY JOURNEY CAME TO AN END.

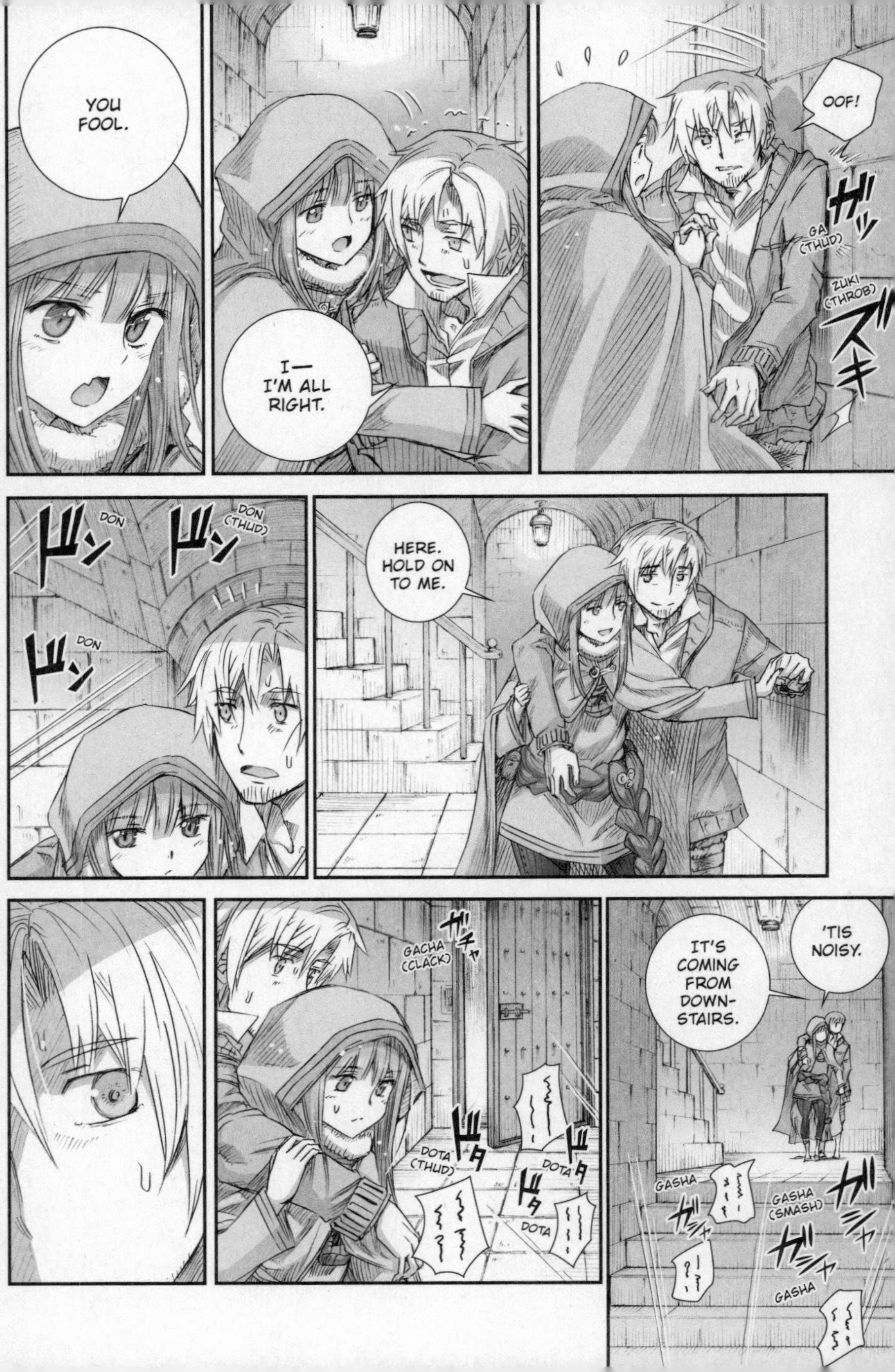
OOF!
GA (THUD)
ZUKI (THROB)
I— I'M ALL RIGHT.
YOU FOOL.
HERE. HOLD ON TO ME.
DON (THUD)
DON
DON
'TIS NOISY.
IT'S COMING FROM DOWN-STAIRS.
GASHA (SMASH)
GASHA
GASHA
GACHA (CLACK)
DOTA (THUD)
DOTA
DOTA

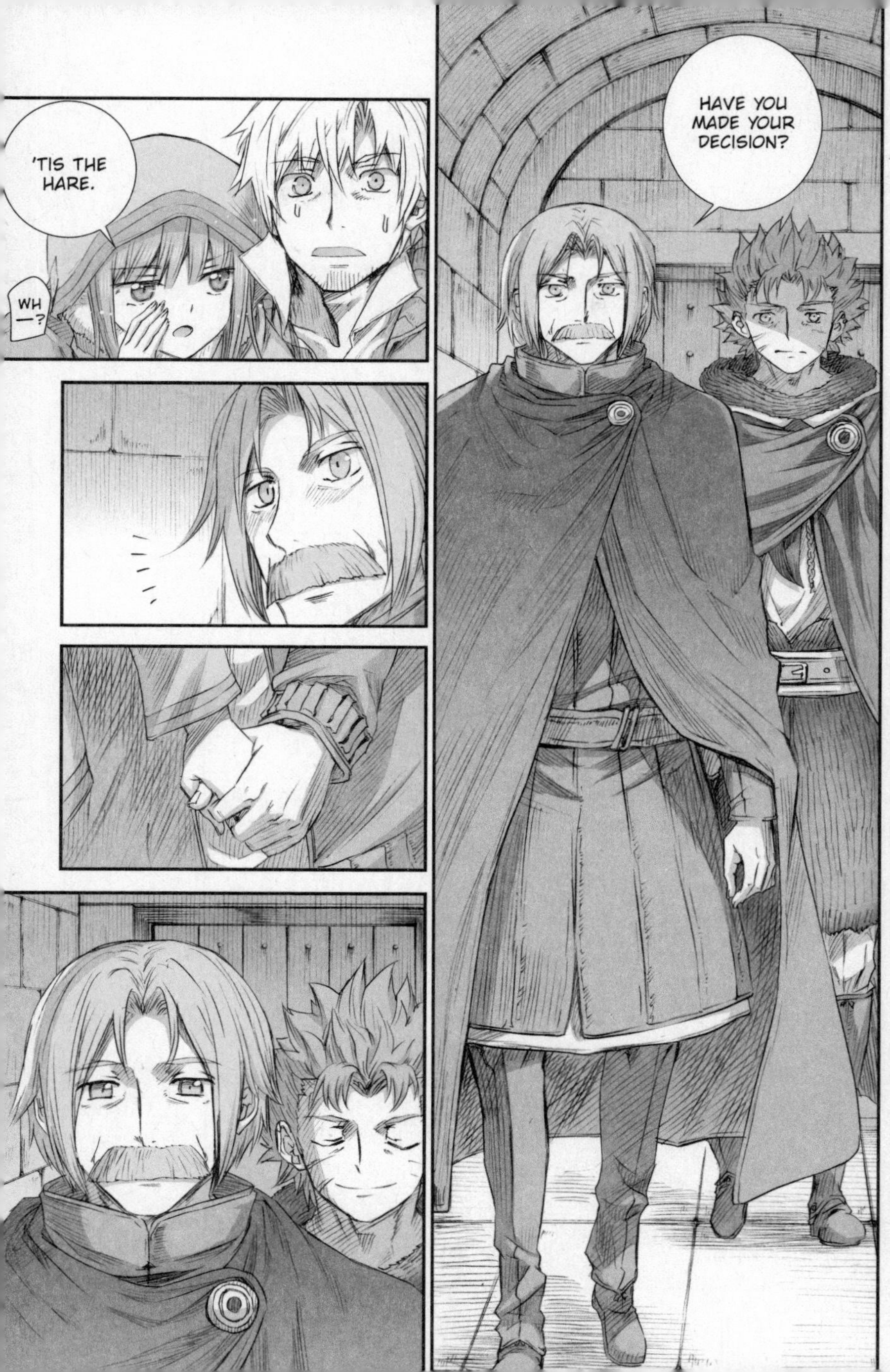
HAVE YOU MADE YOUR DECISION?
'TIS THE HARE.
WH—?

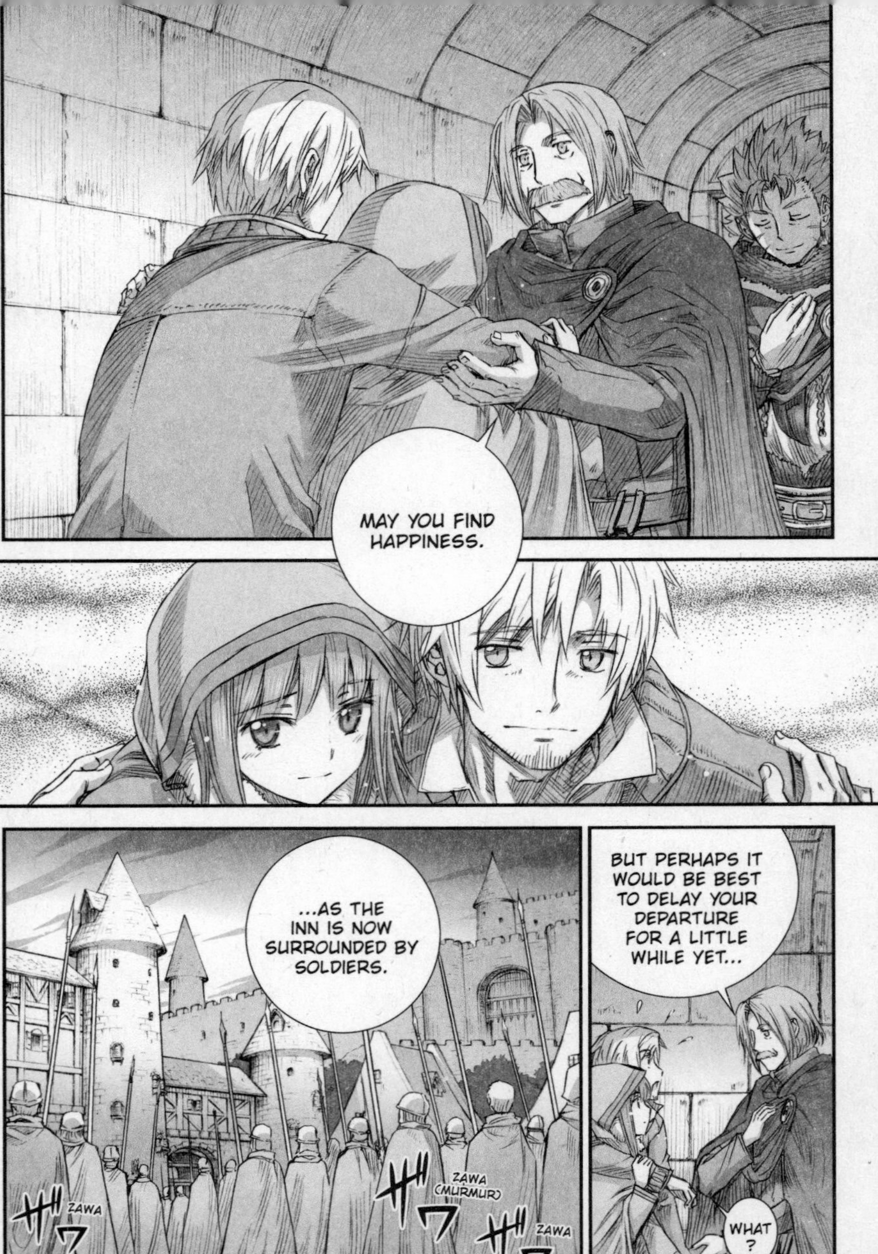
MAY YOU FIND HAPPINESS.
BUT PERHAPS IT WOULD BE BEST TO DELAY YOUR DEPARTURE FOR A LITTLE WHILE YET...
WHAT?
...AS THE INN IS NOW SURROUNDED BY SOLDIERS.
ザワ ZAWA (MURMUR)
ザワ ZAWA
ザワ ZAWA

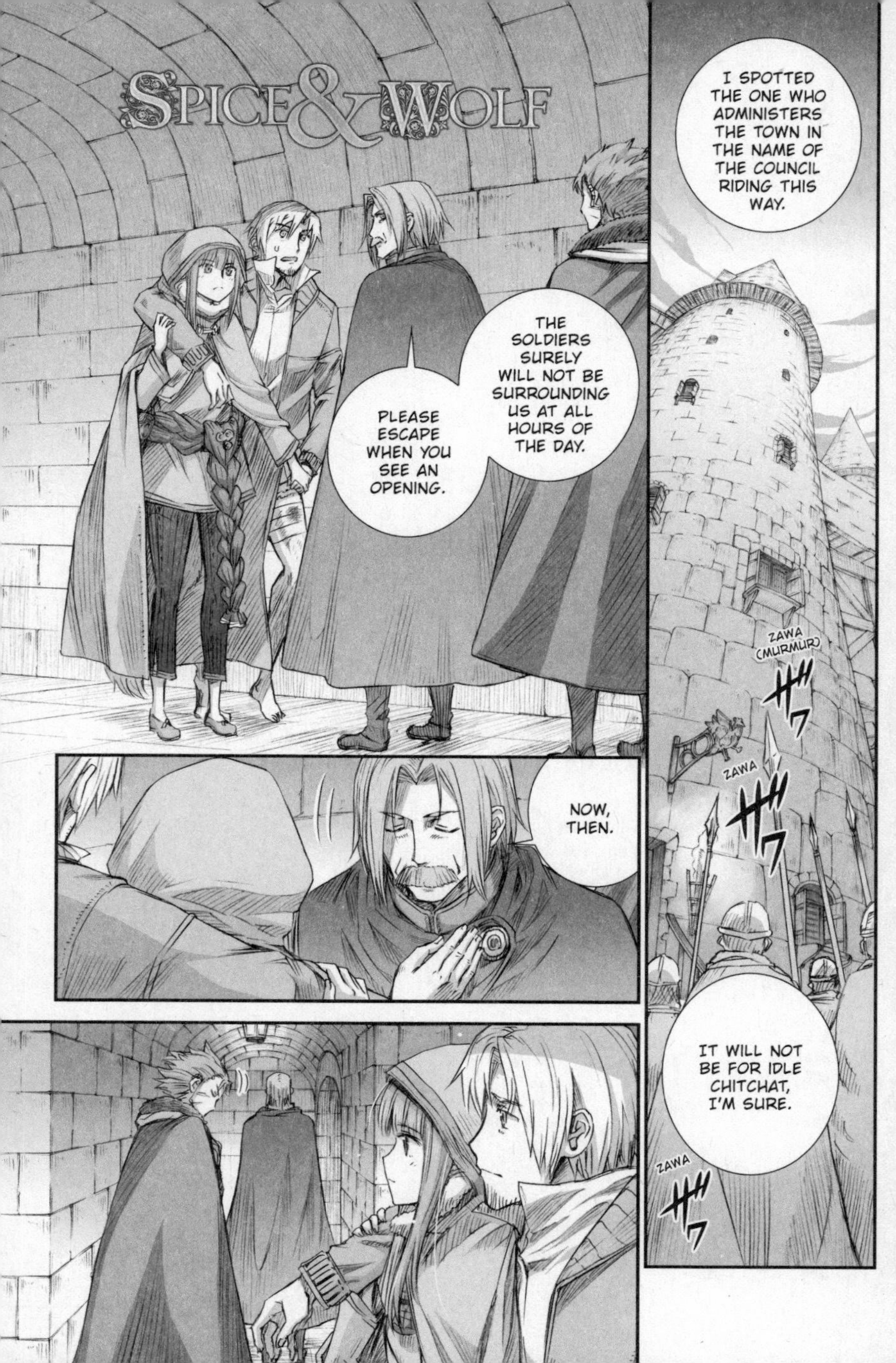
I SPOTTED THE ONE WHO ADMINISTERS THE TOWN IN THE NAME OF THE COUNCIL RIDING THIS WAY.
ZAWA (MURMUR)
ZAWA
IT WILL NOT BE FOR IDLE CHITCHAT, I'M SURE.
ZAWA
SPICE & WOLF
THE SOLDIERS SURELY WILL NOT BE SURROUNDING US AT ALL HOURS OF THE DAY.
PLEASE ESCAPE WHEN YOU SEE AN OPENING.
NOW, THEN.

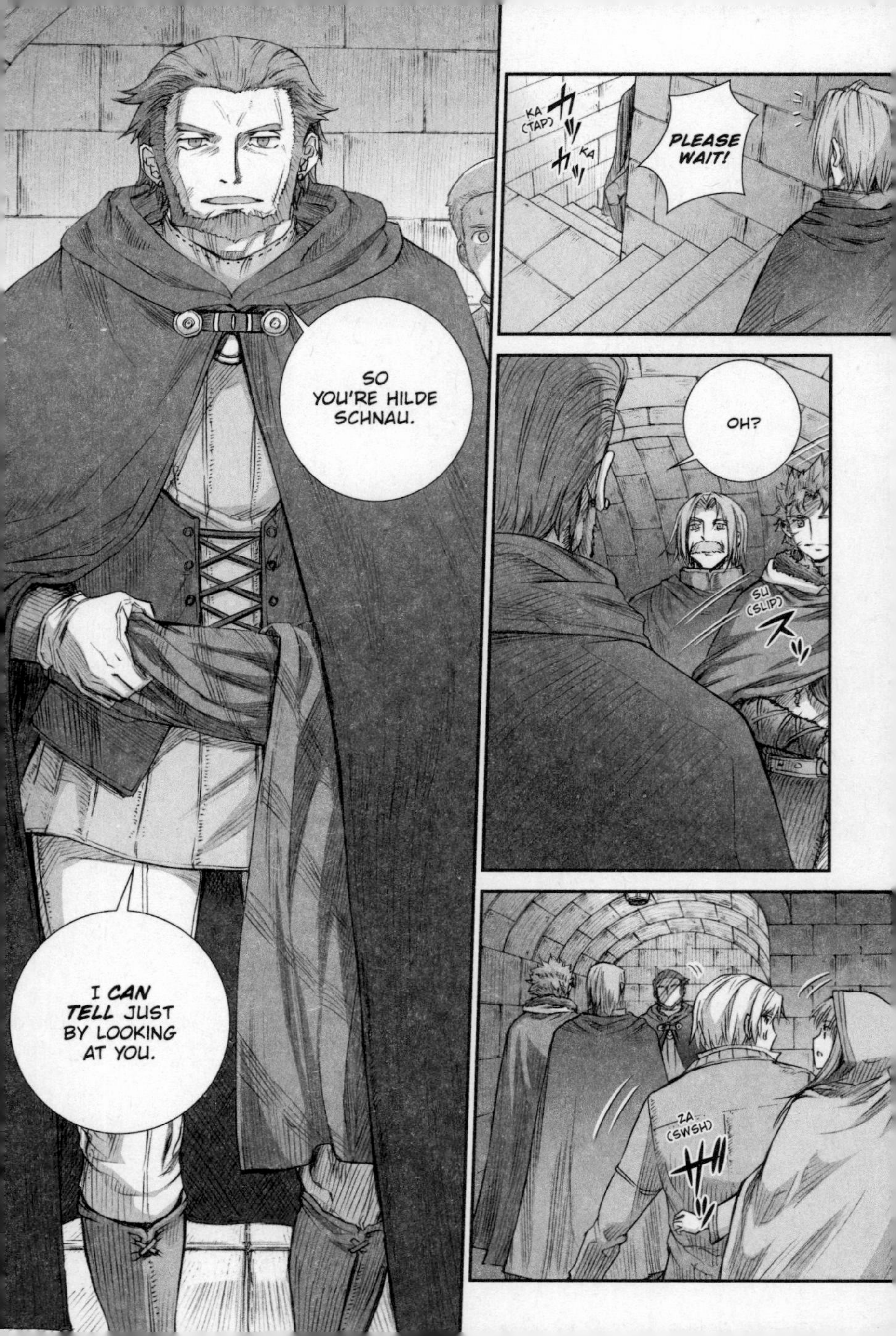

PLEASE WAIT!
KA (TAP)
KA
OH?
SU (SLIP)
ZA (SWSH)
SO YOU'RE HILDE SCHNAU.
I CAN TELL JUST BY LOOKING AT YOU.

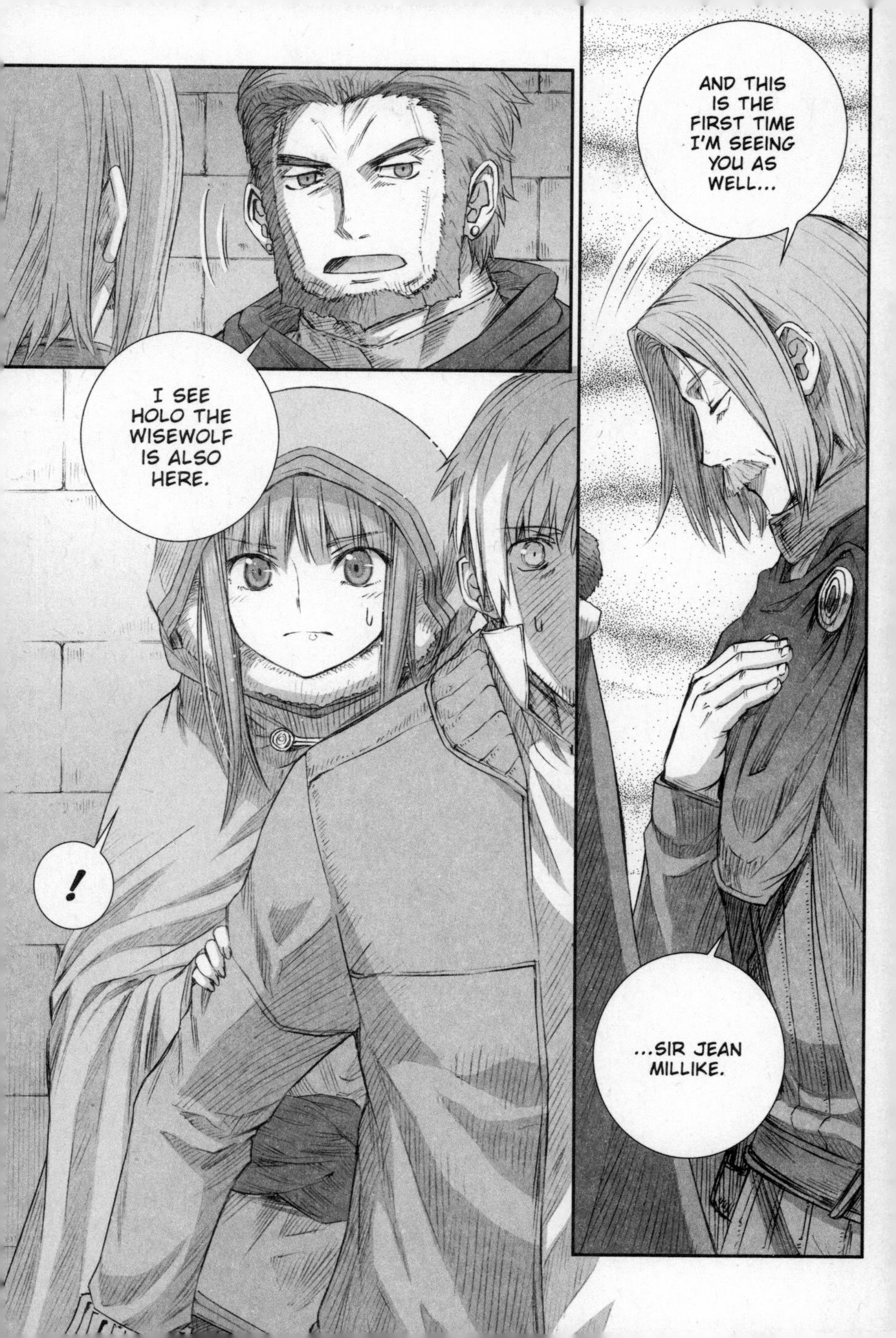
AND THIS IS THE FIRST TIME I'M SEEING YOU AS WELL...
...SIR JEAN MILLIKE.
I SEE HOLO THE WISEWOLF IS ALSO HERE.
!

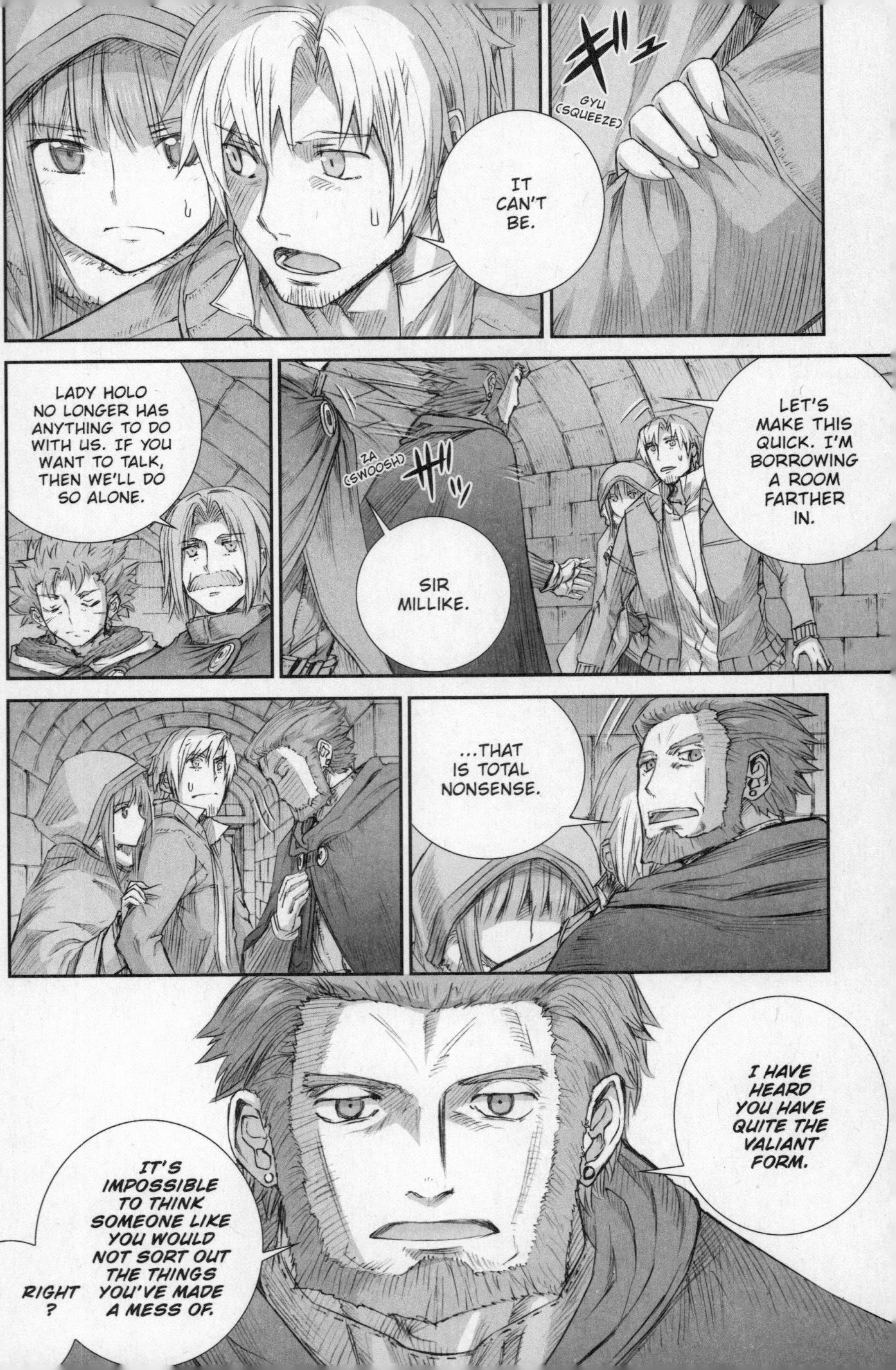
GYU (SQUEEZE)
IT CAN'T BE.
LET'S MAKE THIS QUICK. I'M BORROWING A ROOM FARTHER IN.
ZA (SWOOSH)
SIR MILLIKE.
LADY HOLO NO LONGER HAS ANYTHING TO DO WITH US. IF YOU WANT TO TALK, THEN WE'LL DO SO ALONE.
...THAT IS TOTAL NONSENSE.
I HAVE HEARD YOU HAVE QUITE THE VALIANT FORM.
IT'S IMPOSSIBLE TO THINK SOMEONE LIKE YOU WOULD NOT SORT OUT THE THINGS YOU'VE MADE A MESS OF.
RIGHT?

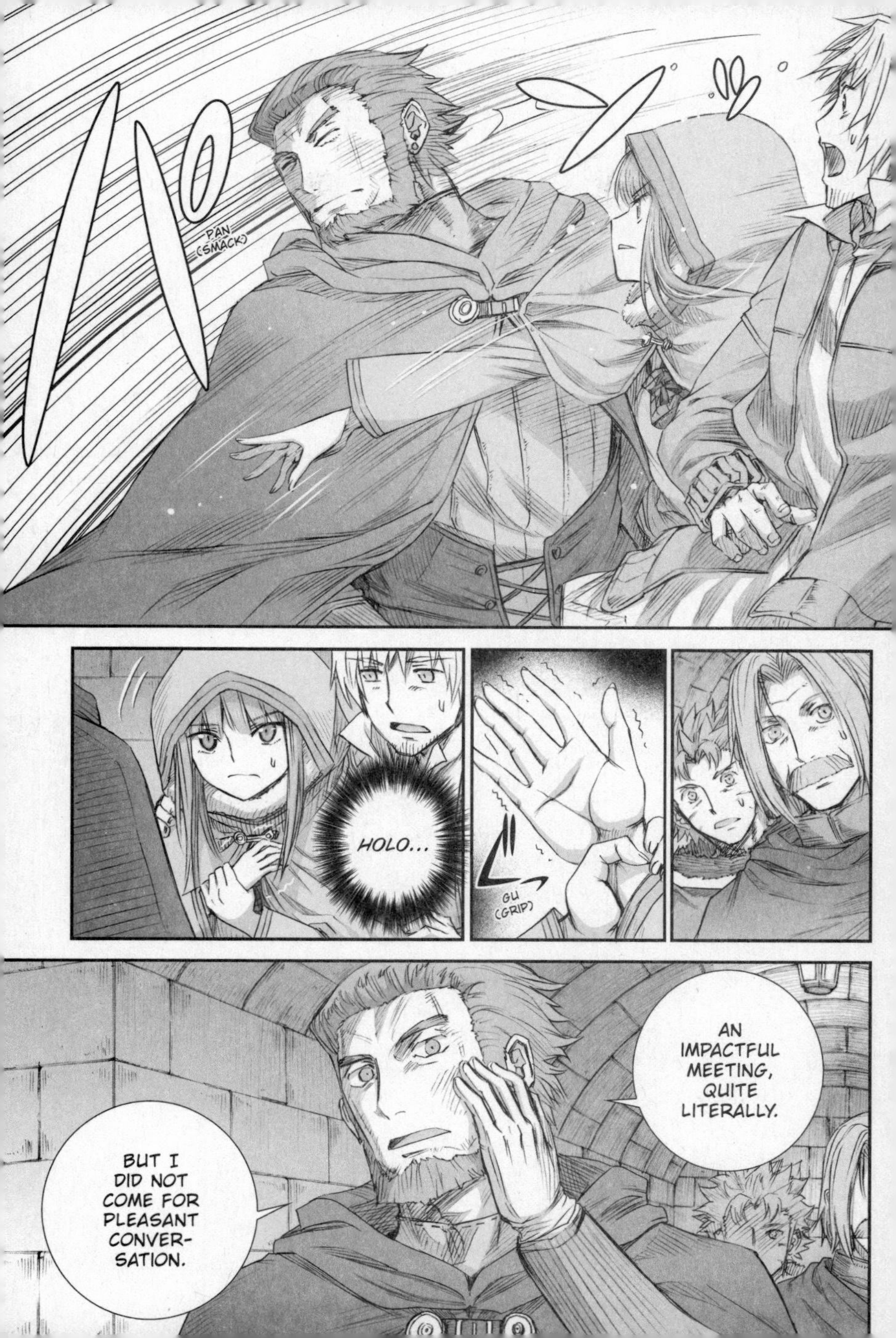
PAN (SMACK)
GU (GRIP)
HOLO...
AN IMPACTFUL MEETING, QUITE LITERALLY.
BUT I DID NOT COME FOR PLEASANT CONVERSATION.

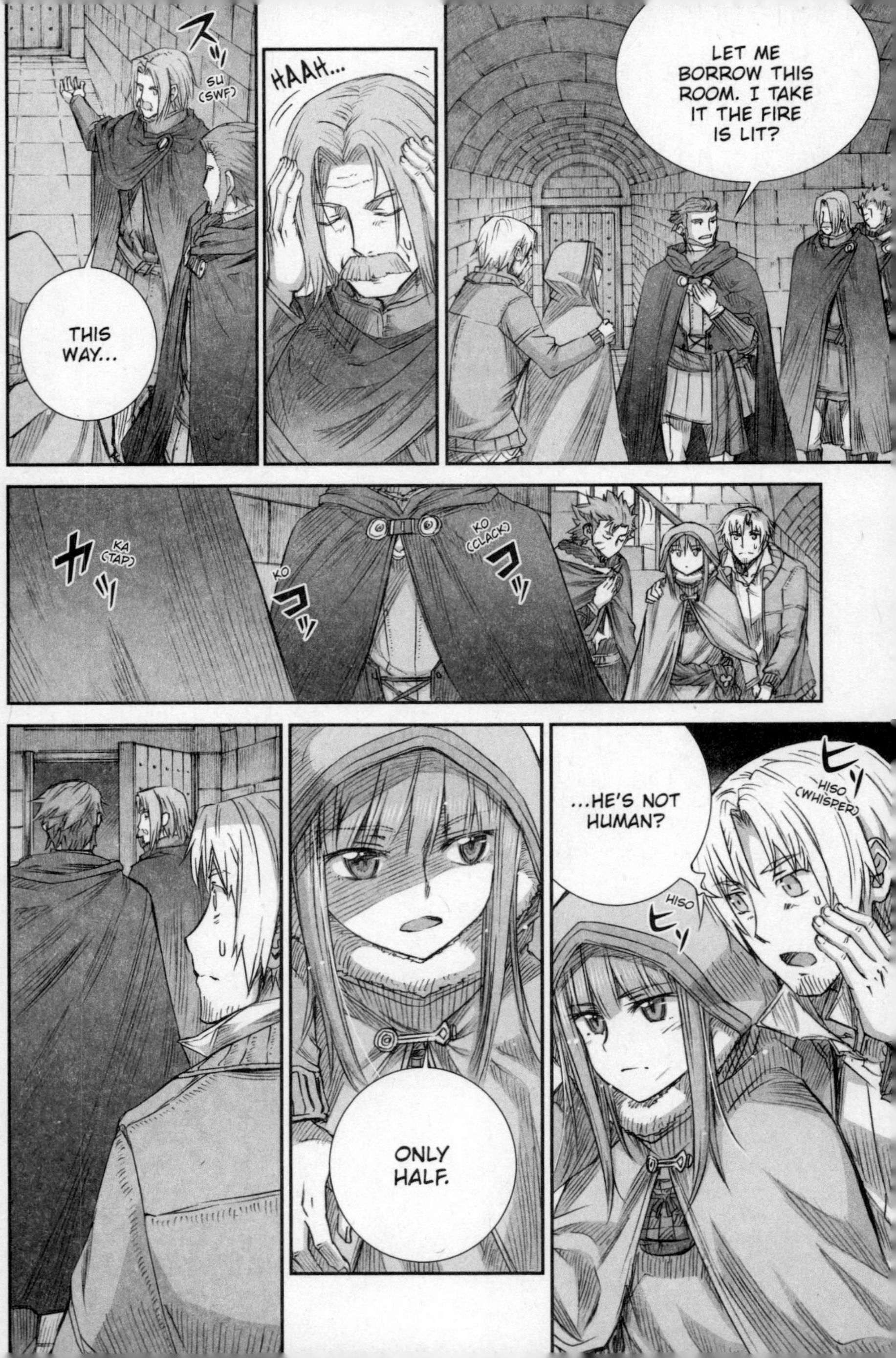
LET ME BORROW THIS ROOM. I TAKE IT THE FIRE IS LIT?
HAAH...
スッ
SU (SWF)
THIS WAY...
コッ
KO (CLACK)
コッ
KO
カッ
KA (TAP)
ヒソ
HISO (WHISPER)
...HE'S NOT HUMAN?
ヒソ
HISO
ONLY HALF.

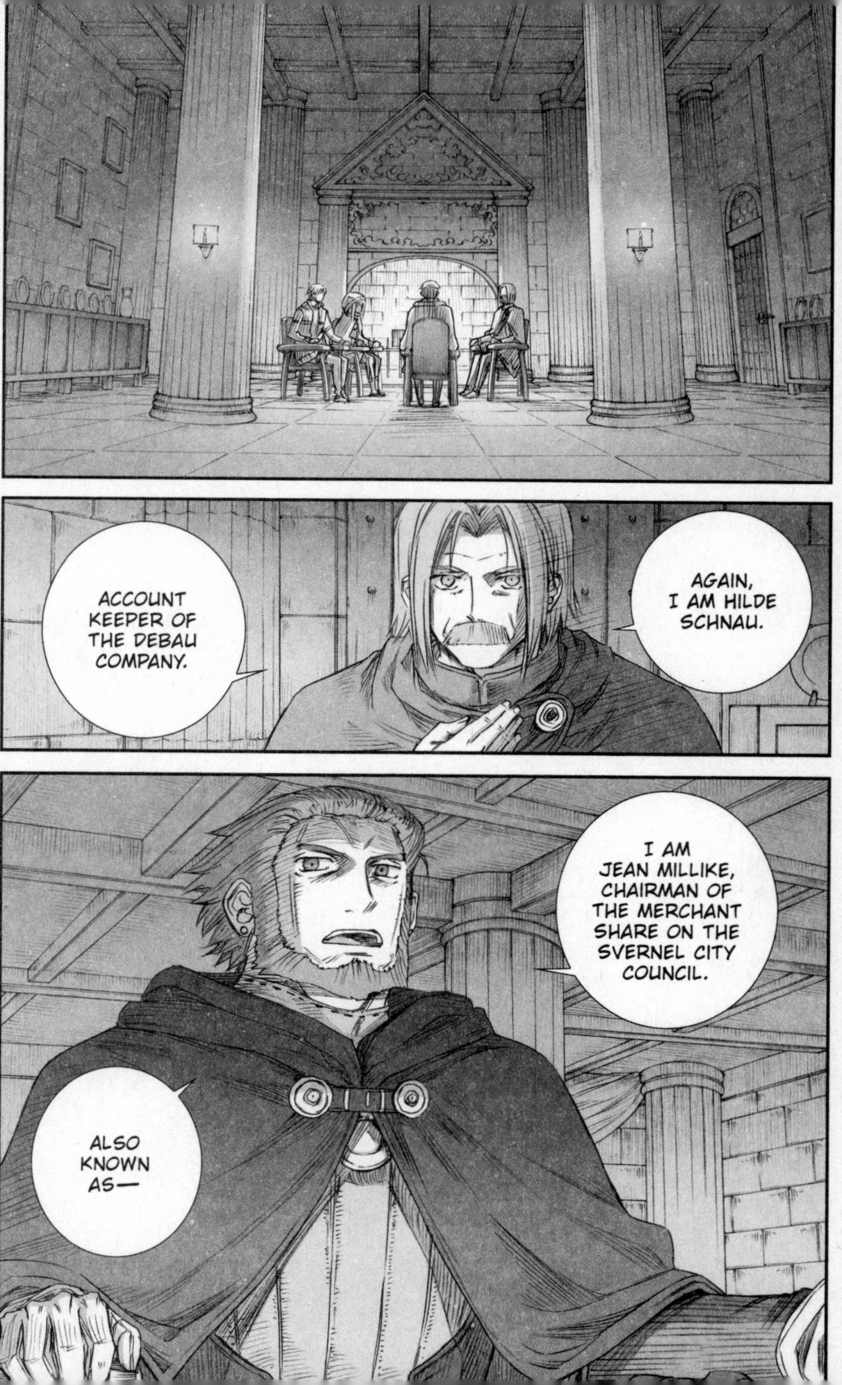
AGAIN, I AM HILDE SCHNAU.
ACCOUNT KEEPER OF THE DEBAU COMPANY.
I AM JEAN MILLIKE, CHAIRMAN OF THE MERCHANT SHARE ON THE SVERNEL CITY COUNCIL.
ALSO KNOWN AS—

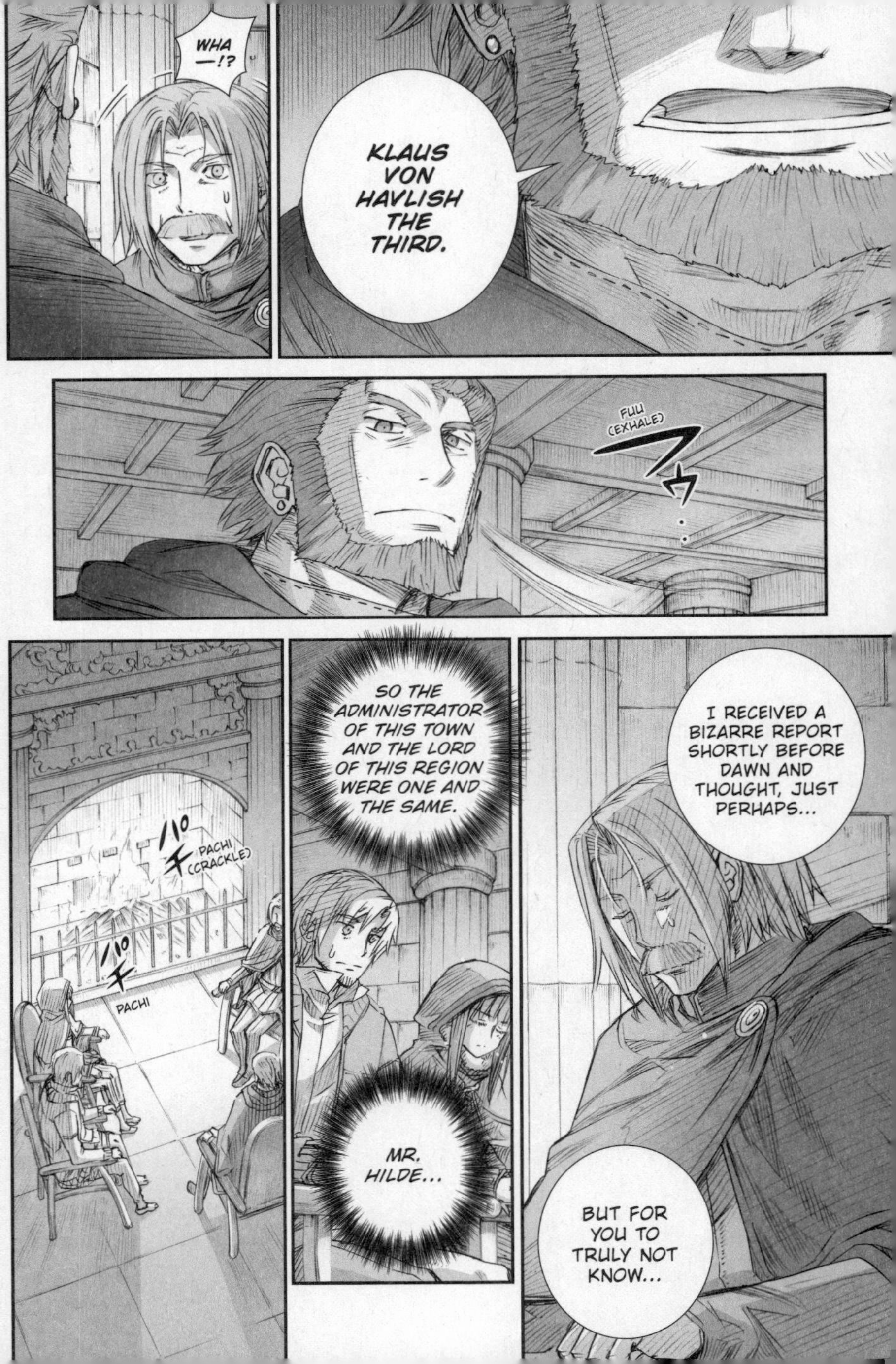
KLAUS VON HAVLISH THE THIRD.
WHA—!?
FUU (EXHALE)
I RECEIVED A BIZARRE REPORT SHORTLY BEFORE DAWN AND THOUGHT, JUST PERHAPS...
BUT FOR YOU TO TRULY NOT KNOW...
SO THE ADMINISTRATOR OF THIS TOWN AND THE LORD OF THIS REGION WERE ONE AND THE SAME.
MR. HILDE...
PACHI (CRACKLE)
PACHI

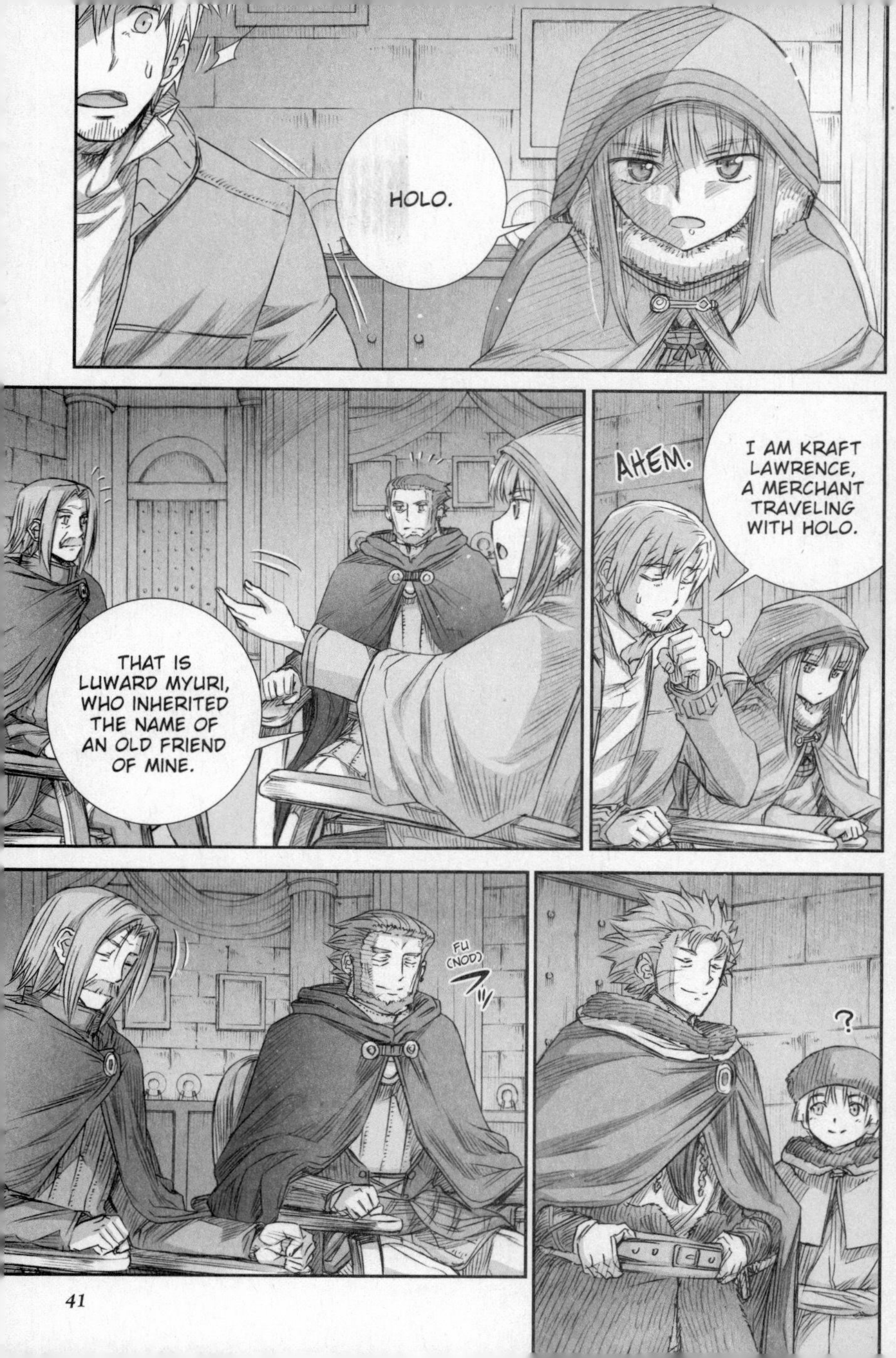
HOLO.
I AM KRAFT LAWRENCE, A MERCHANT TRAVELING WITH HOLO.
AHEM.
THAT IS LUWARD MYURI, WHO INHERITED THE NAME OF AN OLD FRIEND OF MINE.
?
FU (NOD)

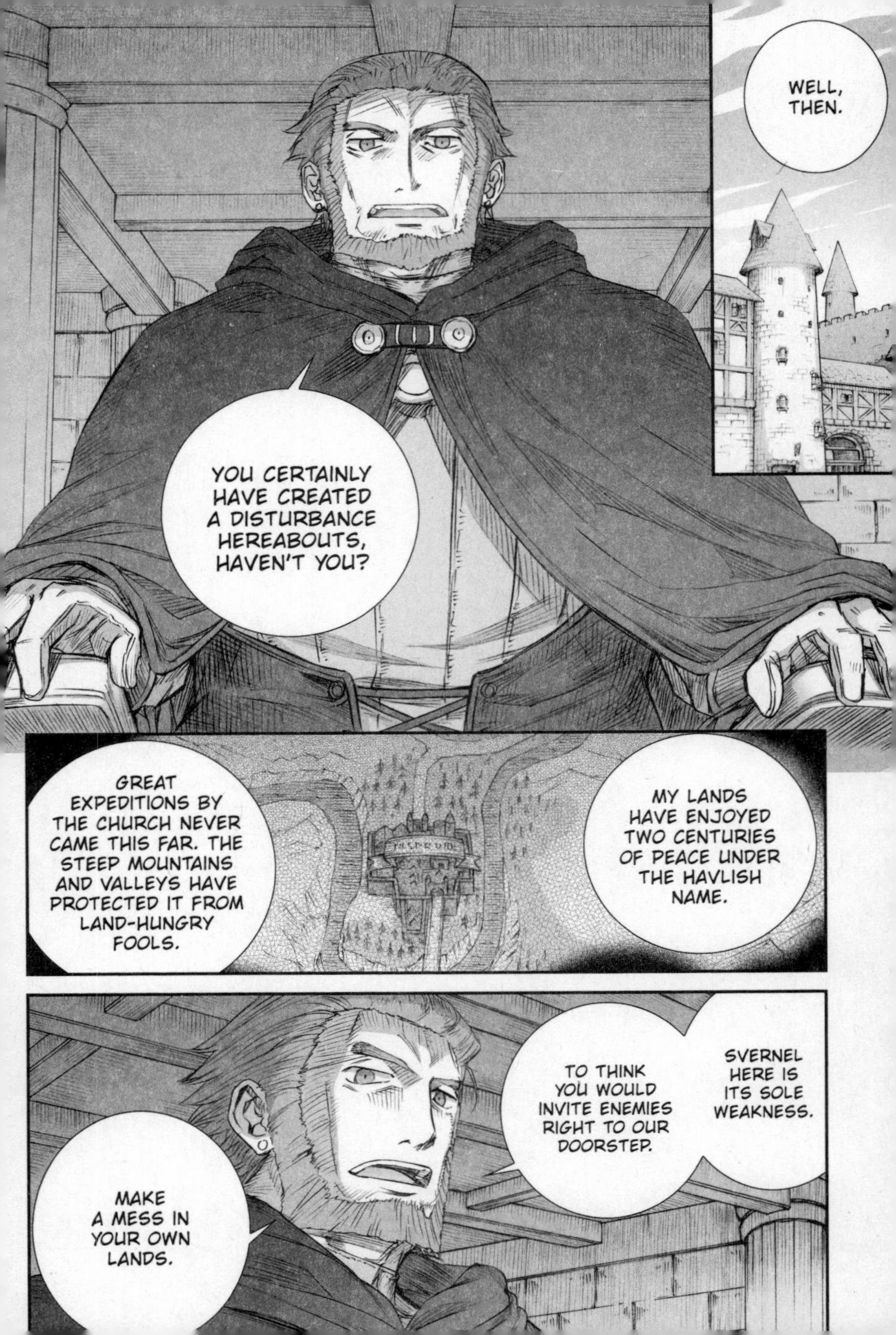
WELL, THEN.
YOU CERTAINLY HAVE CREATED A DISTURBANCE HEREABOUTS, HAVEN'T YOU?
MY LANDS HAVE ENJOYED TWO CENTURIES OF PEACE UNDER THE HAVLISH NAME.
GREAT EXPEDITIONS BY THE CHURCH NEVER CAME THIS FAR. THE STEEP MOUNTAINS AND VALLEYS HAVE PROTECTED IT FROM LAND-HUNGRY FOOLS.
SVERNEL HERE IS ITS SOLE WEAKNESS.
TO THINK YOU WOULD INVITE ENEMIES RIGHT TO OUR DOORSTEP.
MAKE A MESS IN YOUR OWN LANDS.

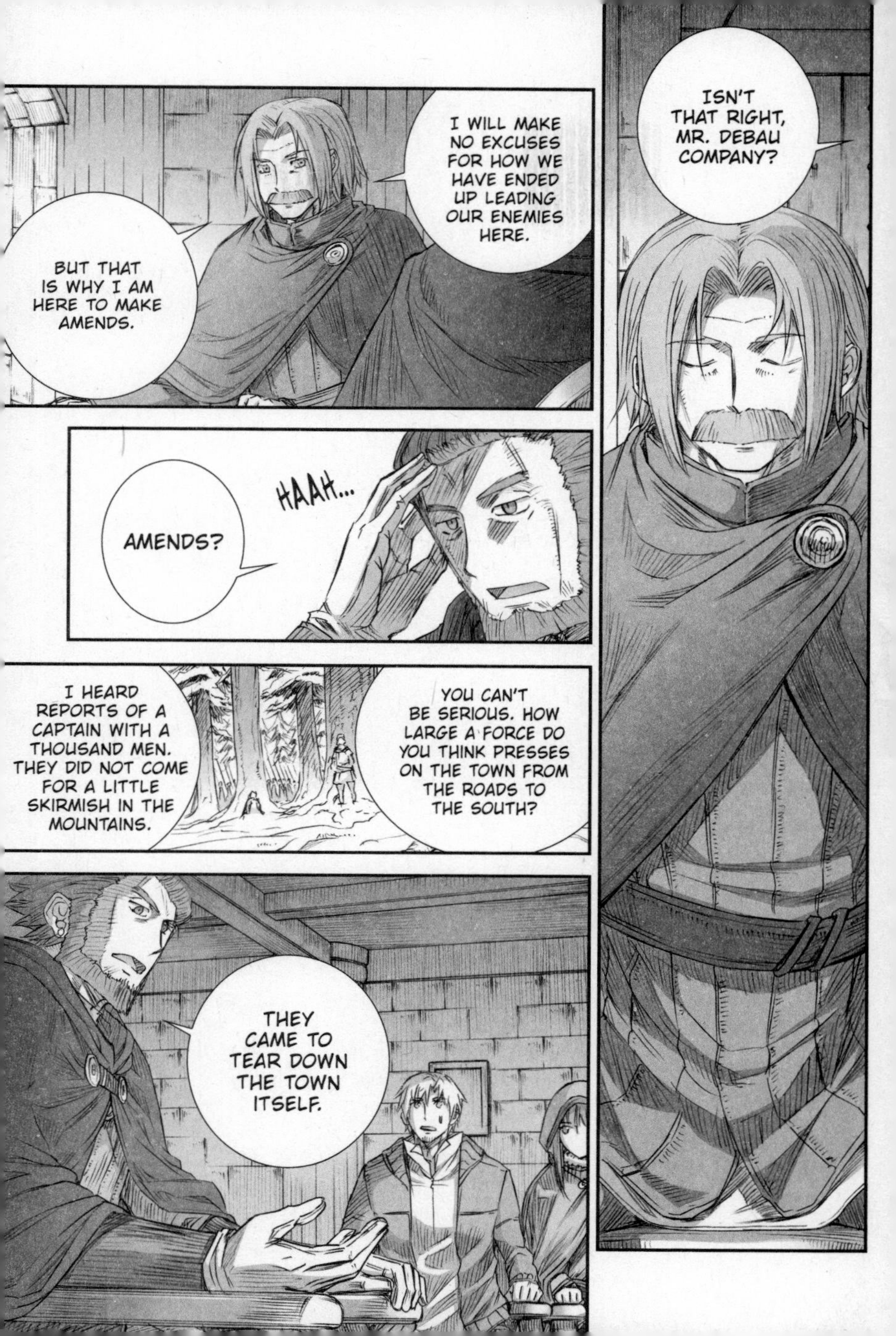
ISN'T THAT RIGHT, MR. DEBAU COMPANY?
I WILL MAKE NO EXCUSES FOR HOW WE HAVE ENDED UP LEADING OUR ENEMIES HERE.
BUT THAT IS WHY I AM HERE TO MAKE AMENDS.
HAAH...
AMENDS?
YOU CAN'T BE SERIOUS. HOW LARGE A FORCE DO YOU THINK PRESSES ON THE TOWN FROM THE ROADS TO THE SOUTH?
I HEARD REPORTS OF A CAPTAIN WITH A THOUSAND MEN. THEY DID NOT COME FOR A LITTLE SKIRMISH IN THE MOUNTAINS.
THEY CAME TO TEAR DOWN THE TOWN ITSELF.

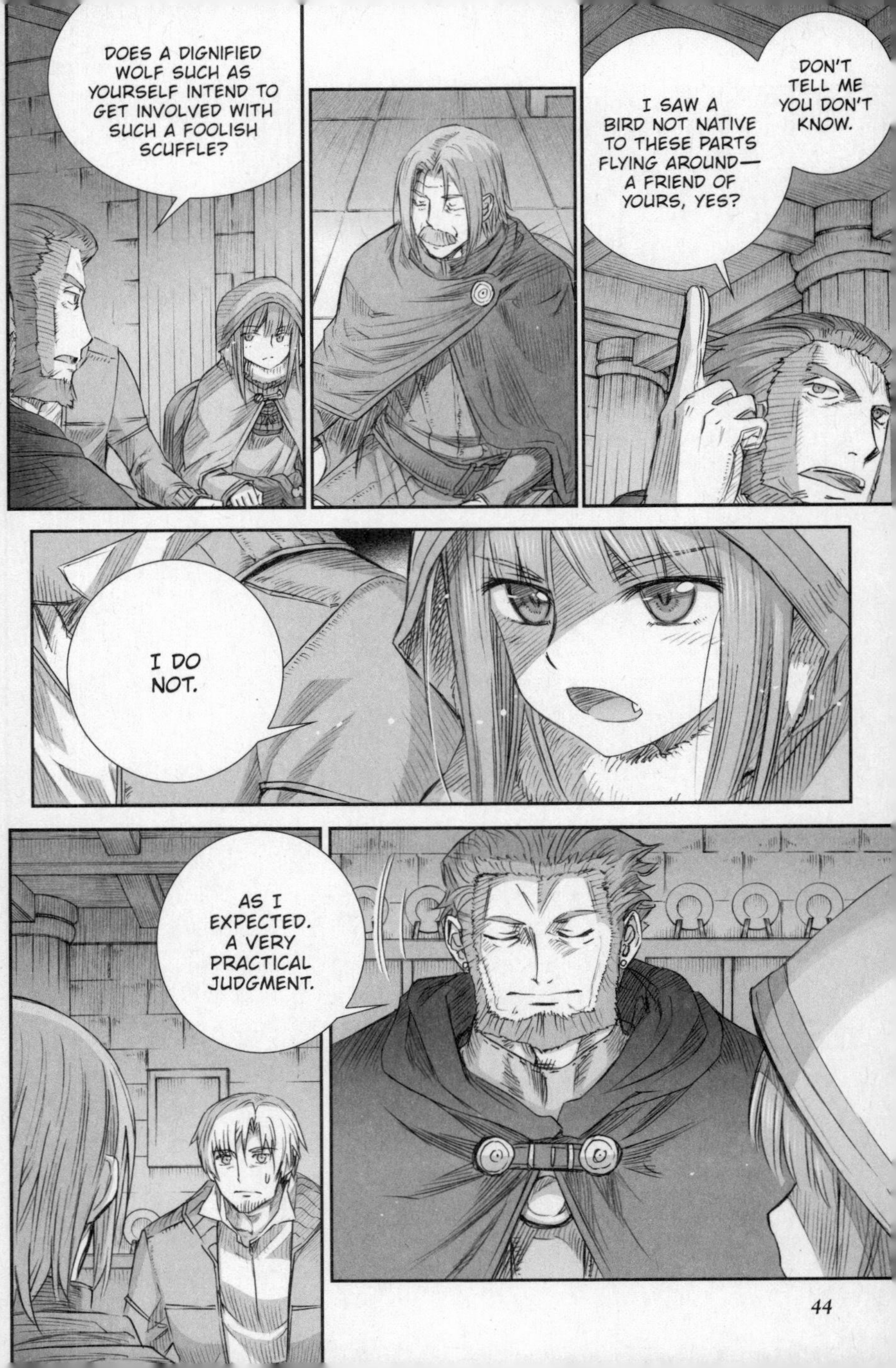
I SAW A BIRD NOT NATIVE TO THESE PARTS FLYING AROUND—A FRIEND OF YOURS, YES? DON'T TELL ME YOU DON'T KNOW.
DOES A DIGNIFIED WOLF SUCH AS YOURSELF INTEND TO GET INVOLVED WITH SUCH A FOOLISH SCUFFLE?
I DO NOT.
AS I EXPECTED. A VERY PRACTICAL JUDGMENT.

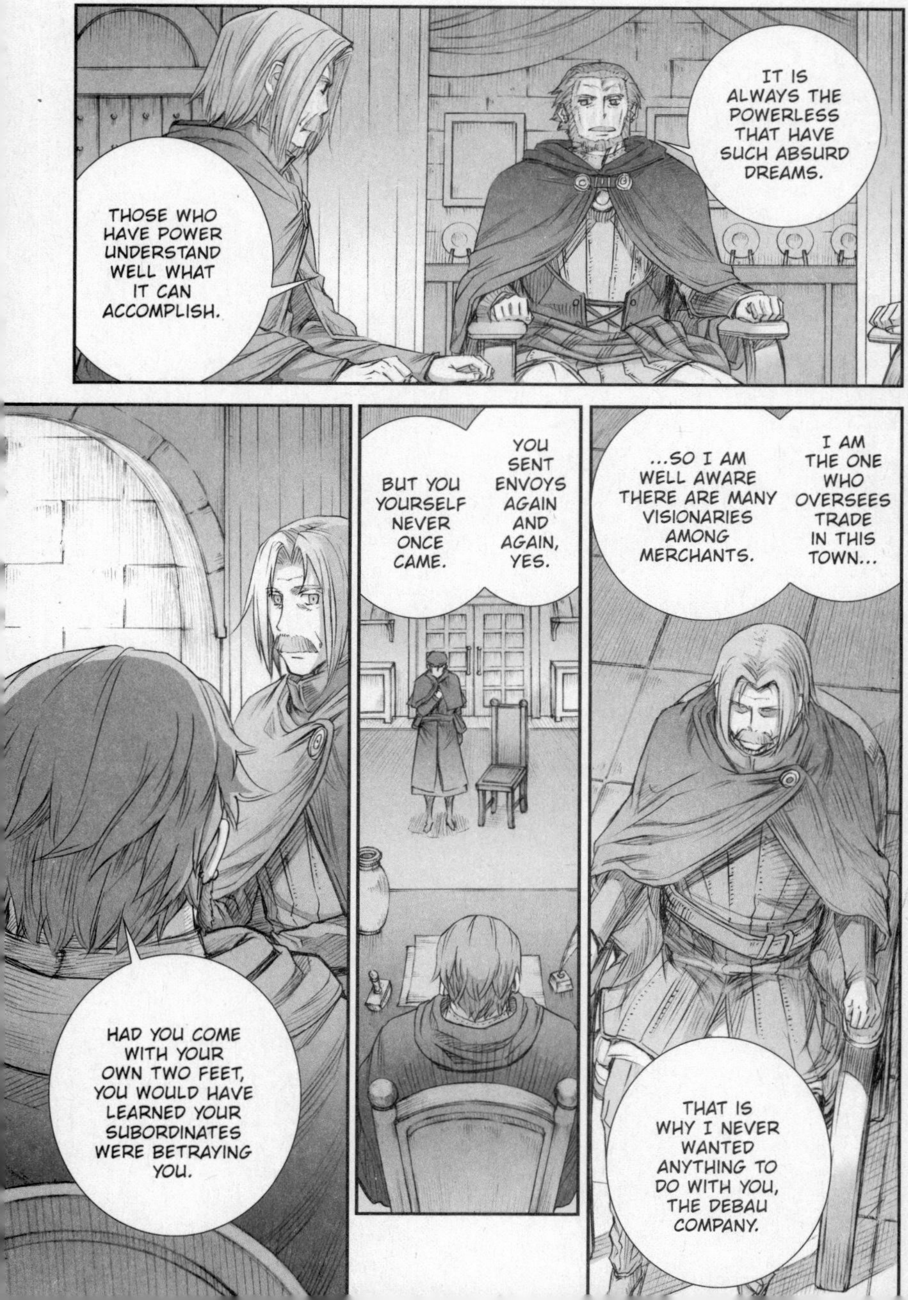
IT IS ALWAYS THE POWERLESS THAT HAVE SUCH ABSURD DREAMS.
THOSE WHO HAVE POWER UNDERSTAND WELL WHAT IT CAN ACCOMPLISH.
I AM THE ONE WHO OVERSEES TRADE IN THIS TOWN...
...SO I AM WELL AWARE THERE ARE MANY VISIONARIES AMONG MERCHANTS.
THAT IS WHY I NEVER WANTED ANYTHING TO DO WITH YOU, THE DEBAU COMPANY.
YOU SENT ENVOYS AGAIN AND AGAIN, YES.
BUT YOU YOURSELF NEVER ONCE CAME.
HAD YOU COME WITH YOUR OWN TWO FEET, YOU WOULD HAVE LEARNED YOUR SUBORDINATES WERE BETRAYING YOU.

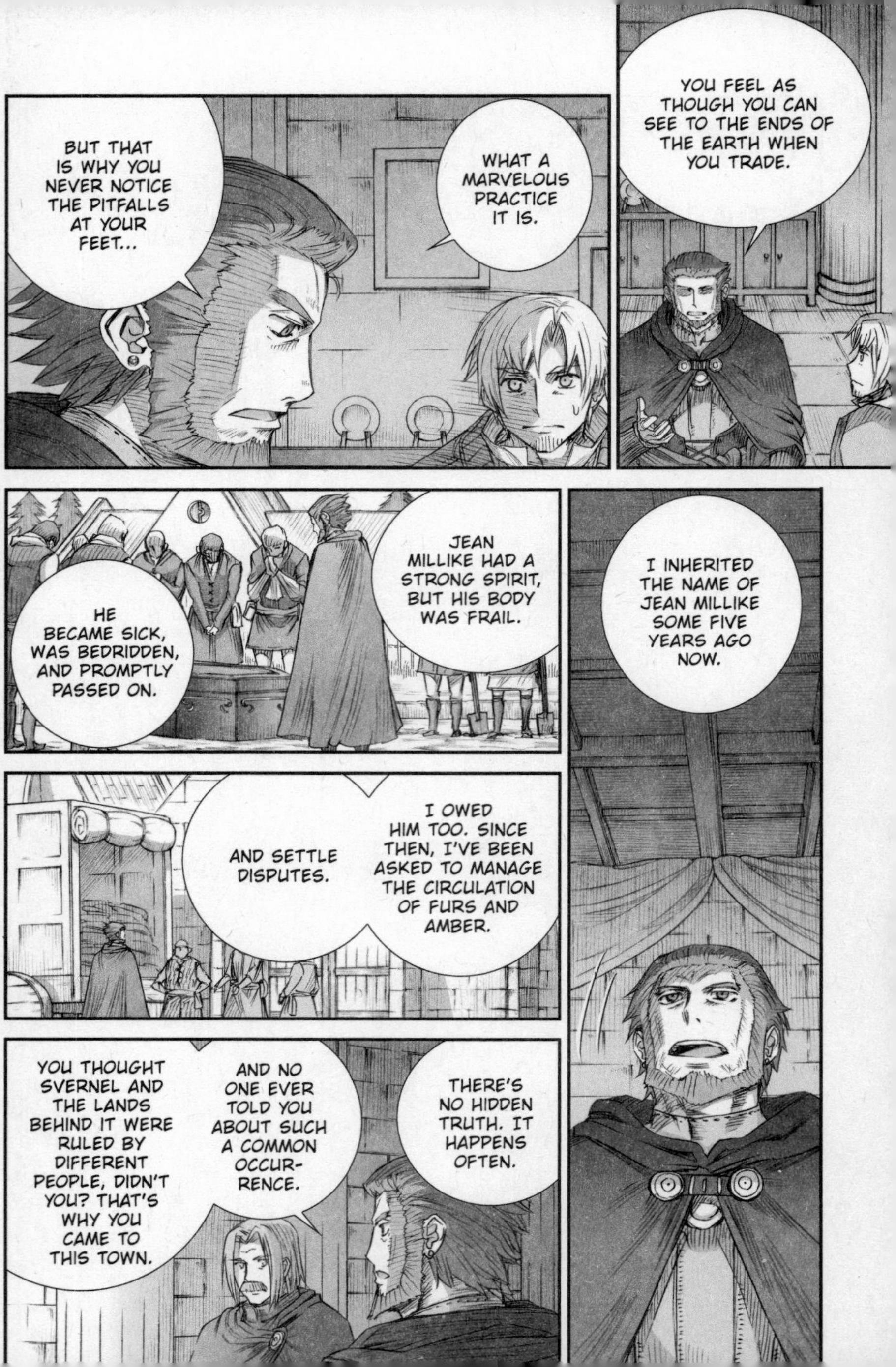
YOU FEEL AS THOUGH YOU CAN SEE TO THE ENDS OF THE EARTH WHEN YOU TRADE.
WHAT A MARVELOUS PRACTICE IT IS.
BUT THAT IS WHY YOU NEVER NOTICE THE PITFALLS AT YOUR FEET...
I INHERITED THE NAME OF JEAN MILLIKE SOME FIVE YEARS AGO NOW.
JEAN MILLIKE HAD A STRONG SPIRIT, BUT HIS BODY WAS FRAIL.
HE BECAME SICK, WAS BEDRIDDEN, AND PROMPTLY PASSED ON.
I OWED HIM TOO. SINCE THEN, I'VE BEEN ASKED TO MANAGE THE CIRCULATION OF FURS AND AMBER.
AND SETTLE DISPUTES.
THERE'S NO HIDDEN TRUTH. IT HAPPENS OFTEN.
AND NO ONE EVER TOLD YOU ABOUT SUCH A COMMON OCCUR-RENCE.
YOU THOUGHT SVERNEL AND THE LANDS BEHIND IT WERE RULED BY DIFFERENT PEOPLE, DIDN'T YOU? THAT'S WHY YOU CAME TO THIS TOWN.

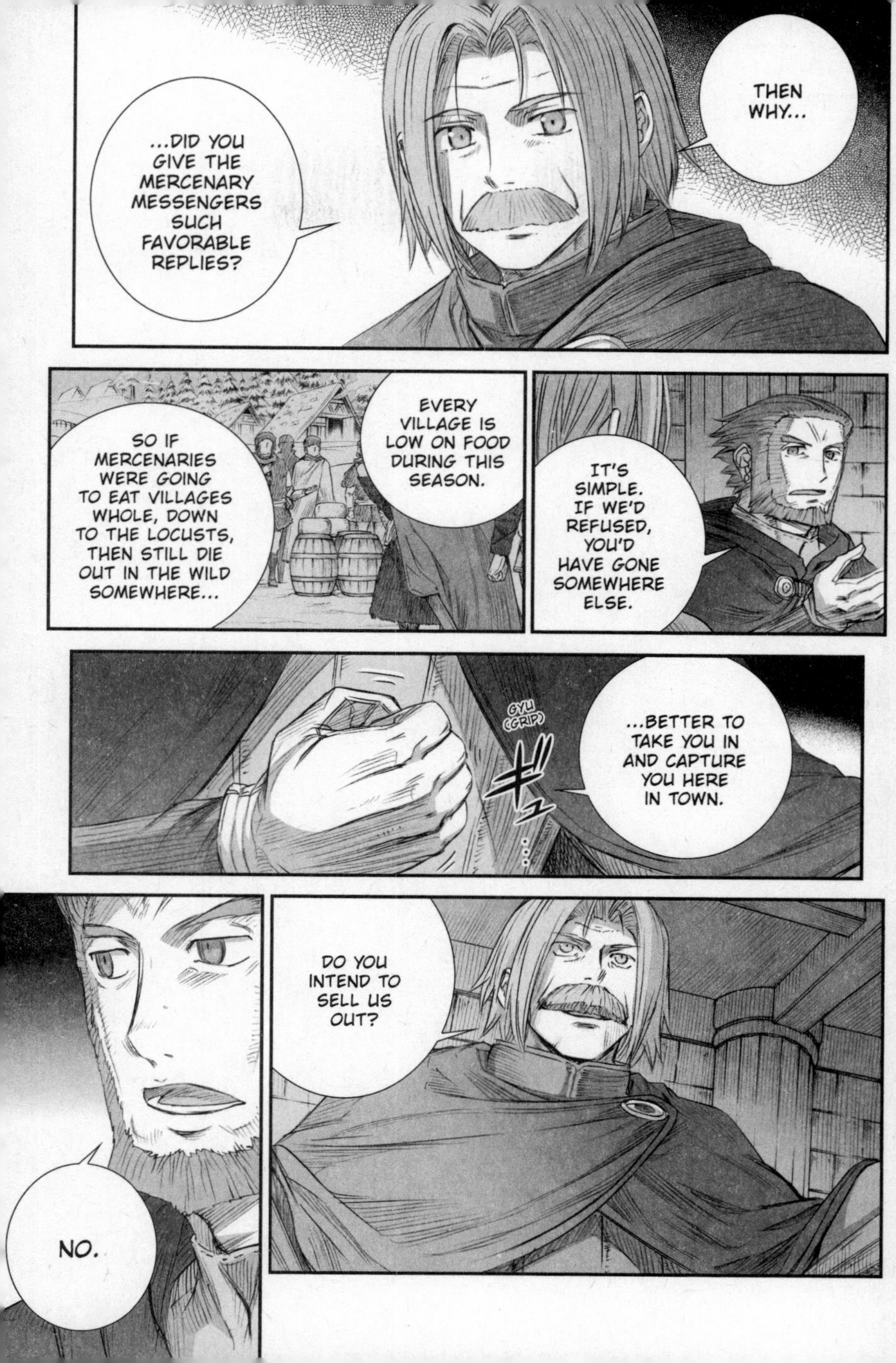
THEN WHY...
...DID YOU GIVE THE MERCENARY MESSENGERS SUCH FAVORABLE REPLIES?
IT'S SIMPLE. IF WE'D REFUSED, YOU'D HAVE GONE SOMEWHERE ELSE.
EVERY VILLAGE IS LOW ON FOOD DURING THIS SEASON.
SO IF MERCENARIES WERE GOING TO EAT VILLAGES WHOLE, DOWN TO THE LOCUSTS, THEN STILL DIE OUT IN THE WILD SOMEWHERE...
...BETTER TO TAKE YOU IN AND CAPTURE YOU HERE IN TOWN.
GYU (GRIP)
DO YOU INTEND TO SELL US OUT?
NO.

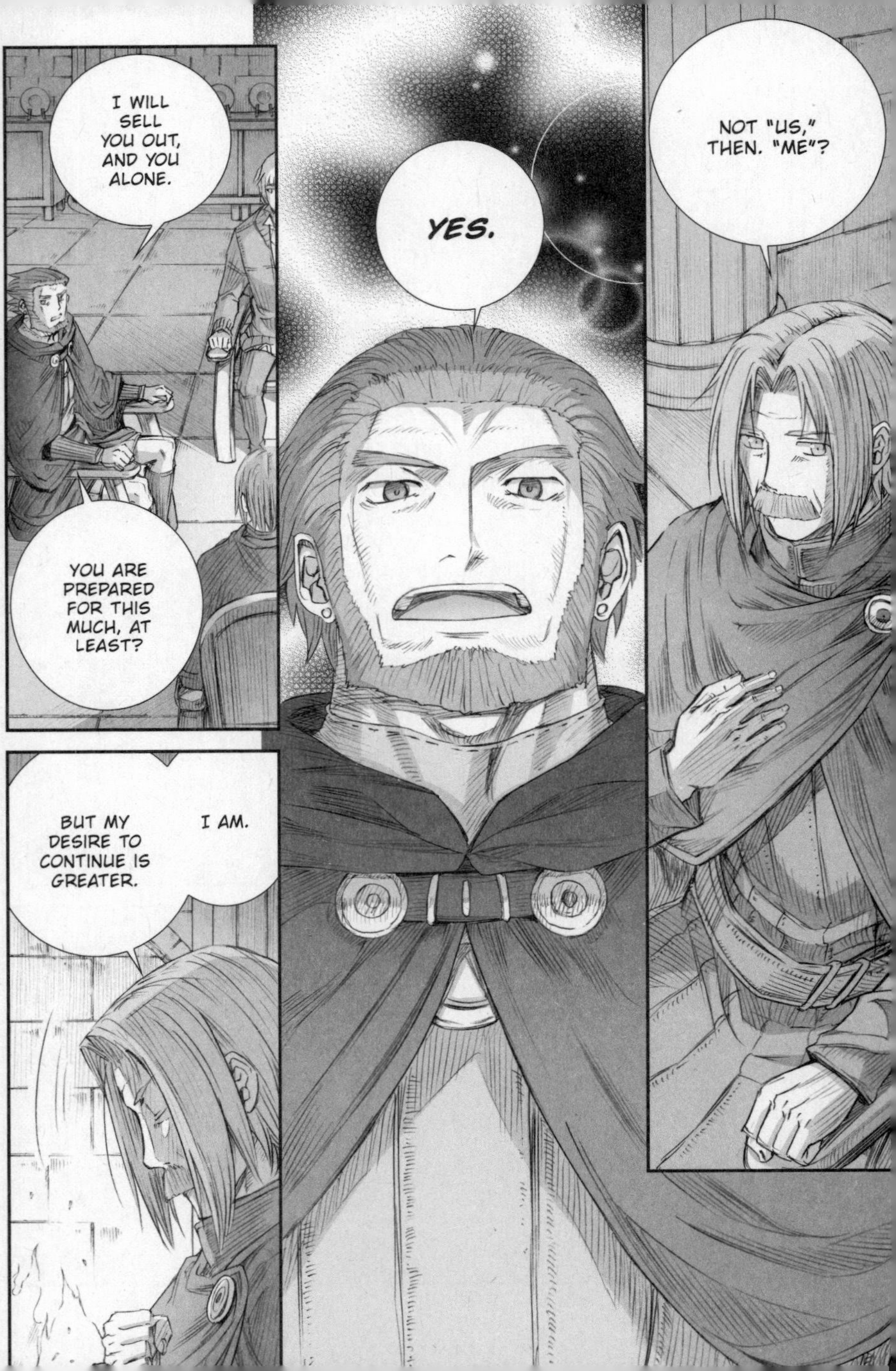
NOT "US," THEN. "ME"?
YES.
I WILL SELL YOU OUT, AND YOU ALONE.
YOU ARE PREPARED FOR THIS MUCH, AT LEAST?
I AM.
BUT MY DESIRE TO CONTINUE IS GREATER.

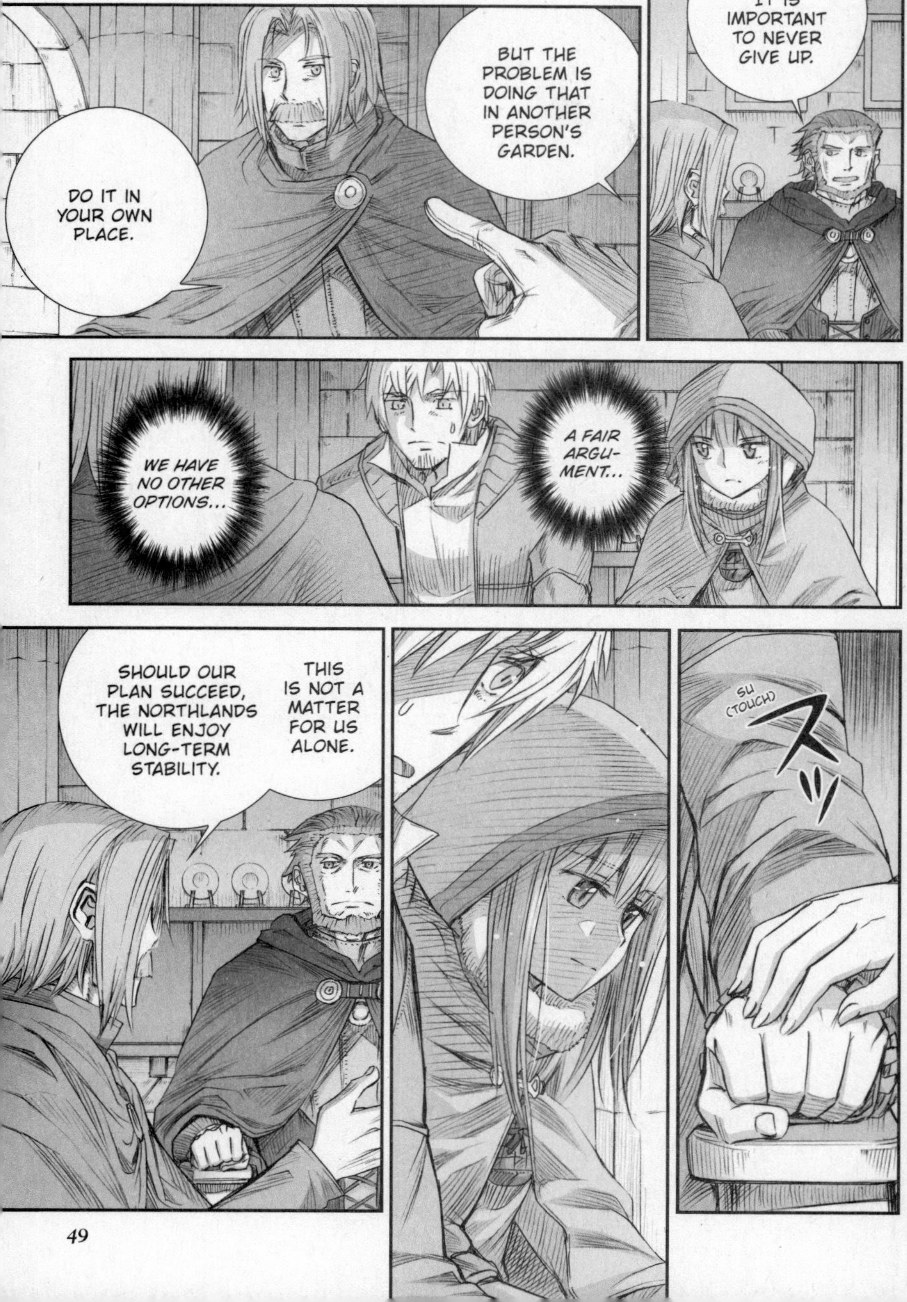
INDEED. IT IS IMPORTANT TO NEVER GIVE UP.
BUT THE PROBLEM IS DOING THAT IN ANOTHER PERSON'S GARDEN.
DO IT IN YOUR OWN PLACE.
A FAIR ARGUMENT...
WE HAVE NO OTHER OPTIONS...
SU (TOUCH)
THIS IS NOT A MATTER FOR US ALONE.
SHOULD OUR PLAN SUCCEED, THE NORTHLANDS WILL ENJOY LONG-TERM STABILITY.

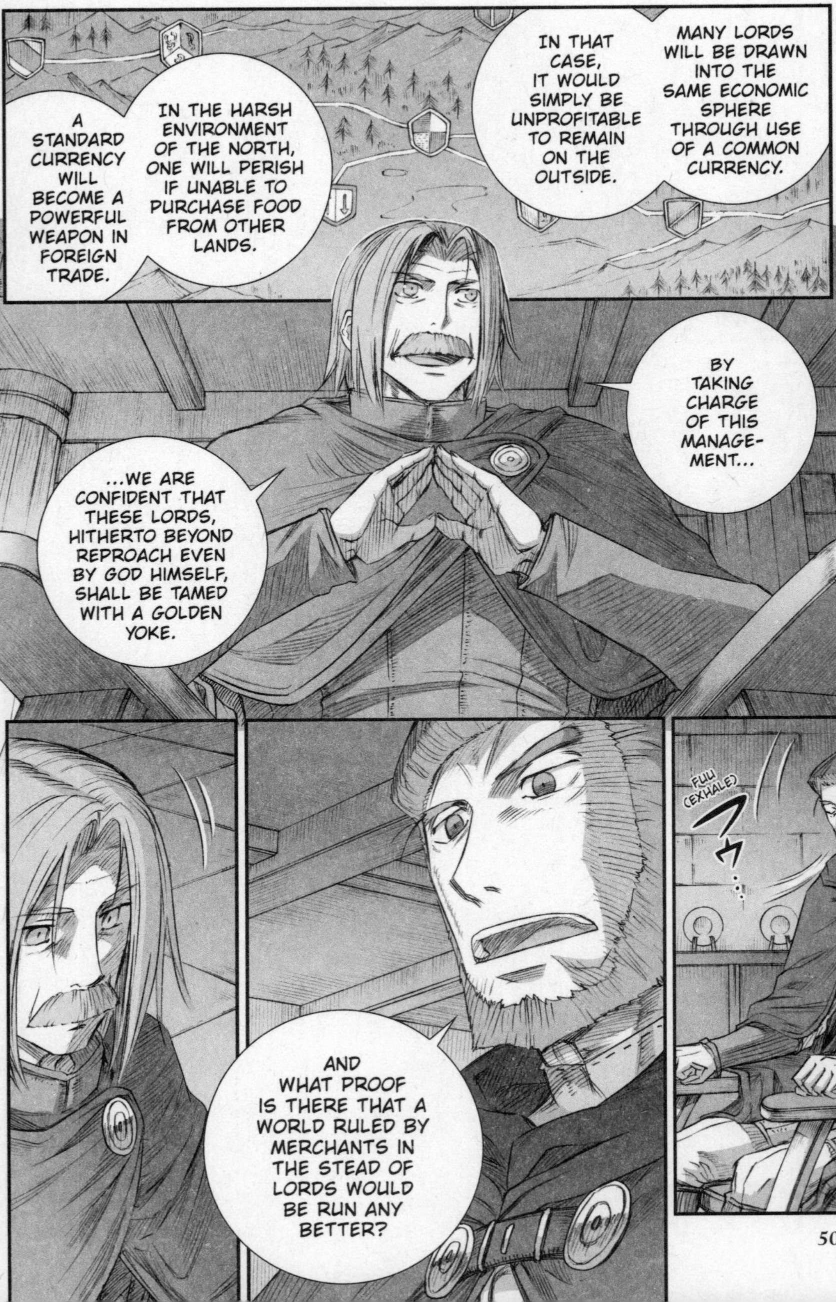
MANY LORDS WILL BE DRAWN INTO THE SAME ECONOMIC SPHERE THROUGH USE OF A COMMON CURRENCY.
IN THAT CASE, IT WOULD SIMPLY BE UNPROFITABLE TO REMAIN ON THE OUTSIDE.
IN THE HARSH ENVIRONMENT OF THE NORTH, ONE WILL PERISH IF UNABLE TO PURCHASE FOOD FROM OTHER LANDS.
A STANDARD CURRENCY WILL BECOME A POWERFUL WEAPON IN FOREIGN TRADE.
BY TAKING CHARGE OF THIS MANAGE-MENT...
...WE ARE CONFIDENT THAT THESE LORDS, HITHERTO BEYOND REPROACH EVEN BY GOD HIMSELF, SHALL BE TAMED WITH A GOLDEN YOKE.
FUU (EXHALE)
AND WHAT PROOF IS THERE THAT A WORLD RULED BY MERCHANTS IN THE STEAD OF LORDS WOULD BE RUN ANY BETTER?

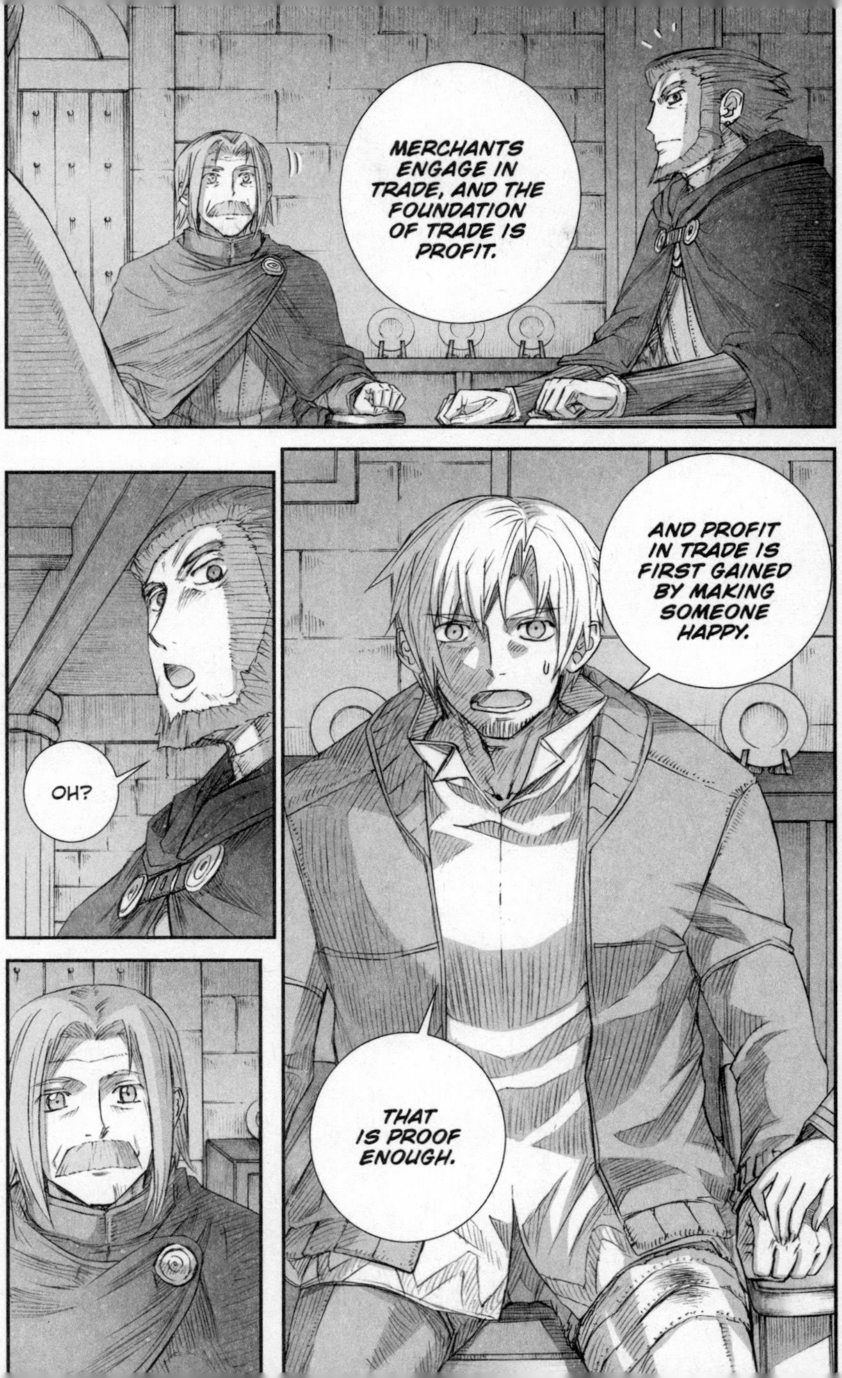
MERCHANTS ENGAGE IN TRADE, AND THE FOUNDATION OF TRADE IS PROFIT.
AND PROFIT IN TRADE IS FIRST GAINED BY MAKING SOMEONE HAPPY.
THAT IS PROOF ENOUGH.
OH?

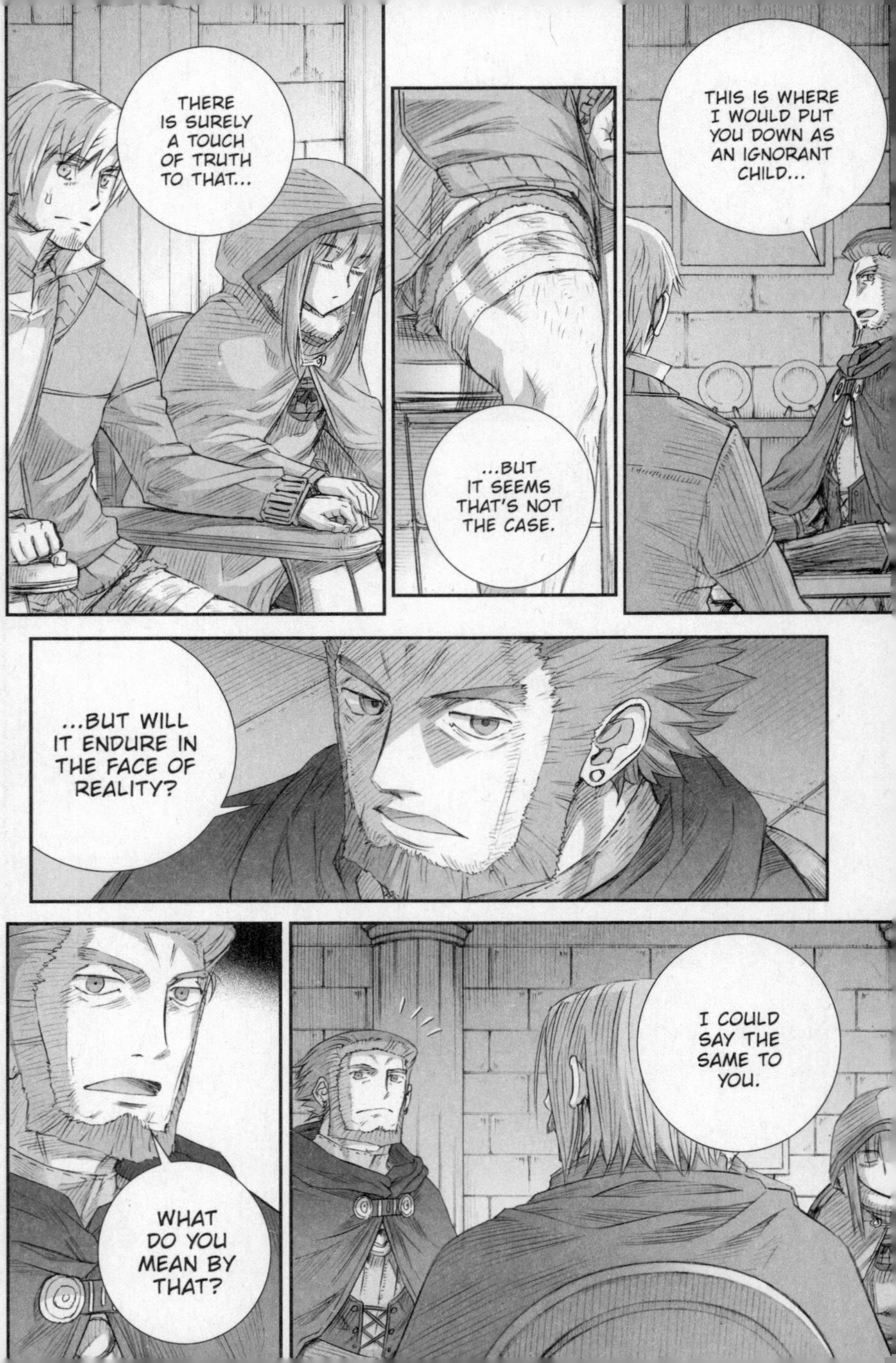
THIS IS WHERE I WOULD PUT YOU DOWN AS AN IGNORANT CHILD...
...BUT IT SEEMS THAT'S NOT THE CASE.
THERE IS SURELY A TOUCH OF TRUTH TO THAT...
...BUT WILL IT ENDURE IN THE FACE OF REALITY?
I COULD SAY THE SAME TO YOU.
WHAT DO YOU MEAN BY THAT?

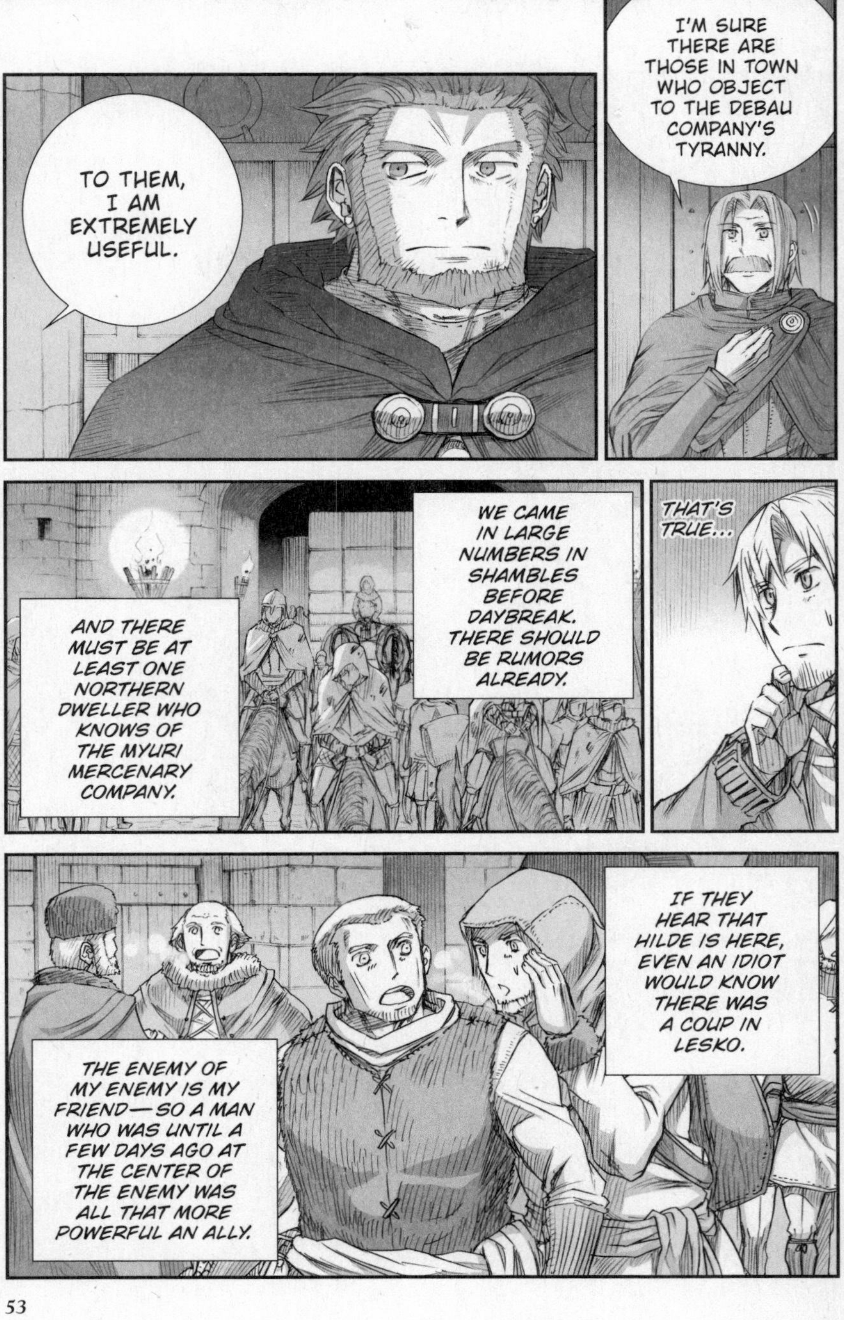
I'M SURE THERE ARE THOSE IN TOWN WHO OBJECT TO THE DEBAU COMPANY'S TYRANNY.
TO THEM, I AM EXTREMELY USEFUL.
THAT'S TRUE...
WE CAME IN LARGE NUMBERS IN SHAMBLES BEFORE DAYBREAK. THERE SHOULD BE RUMORS ALREADY.
AND THERE MUST BE AT LEAST ONE NORTHERN DWELLER WHO KNOWS OF THE MYURI MERCENARY COMPANY.
IF THEY HEAR THAT HILDE IS HERE, EVEN AN IDIOT WOULD KNOW THERE WAS A COUP IN LESKO.
THE ENEMY OF MY ENEMY IS MY FRIEND—SO A MAN WHO WAS UNTIL A FEW DAYS AGO AT THE CENTER OF THE ENEMY WAS ALL THAT MORE POWERFUL AN ALLY.

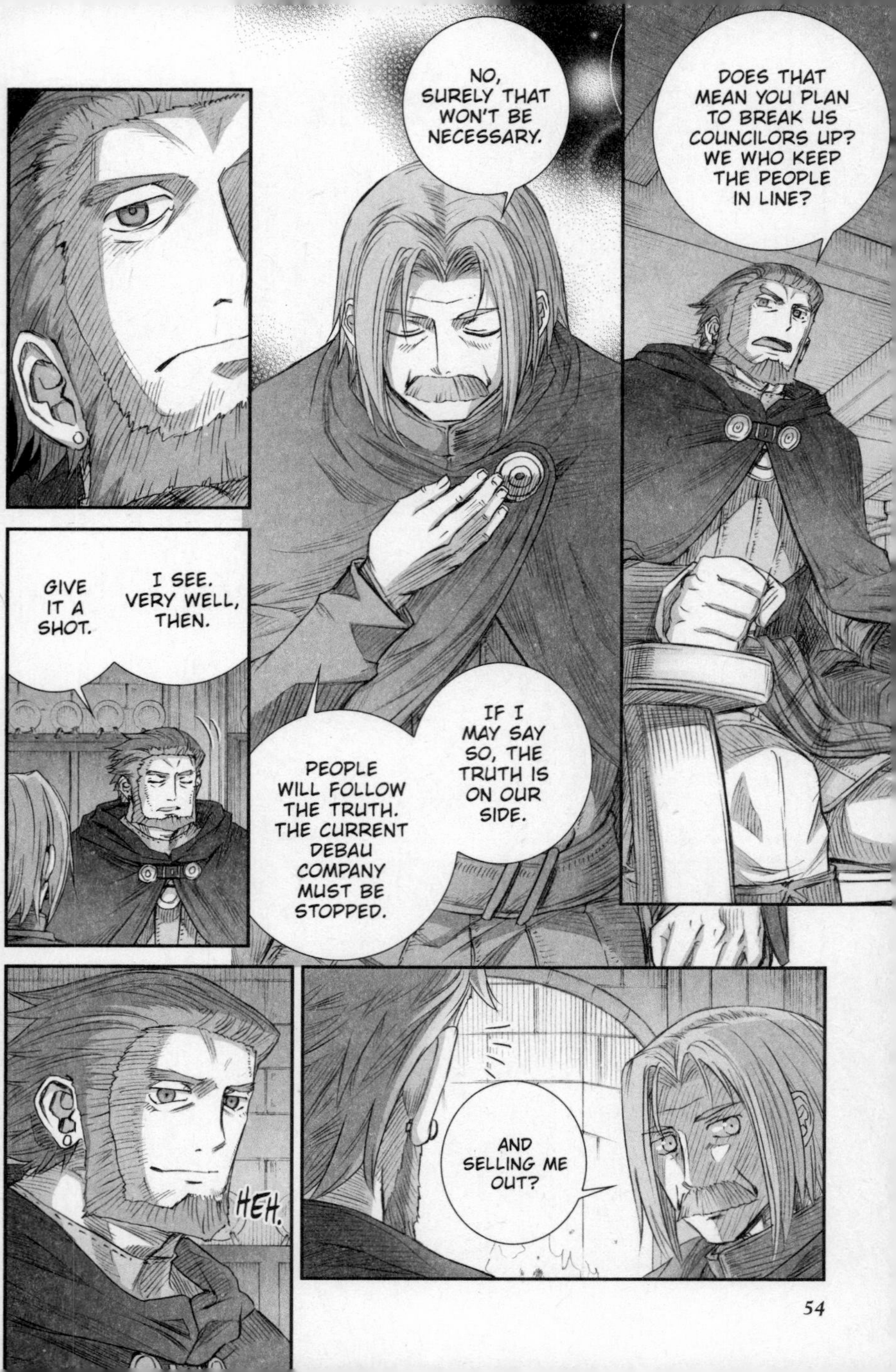
DOES THAT MEAN YOU PLAN TO BREAK US COUNCILORS UP? WE WHO KEEP THE PEOPLE IN LINE?
NO, SURELY THAT WON'T BE NECESSARY.
IF I MAY SAY SO, THE TRUTH IS ON OUR SIDE.
PEOPLE WILL FOLLOW THE TRUTH. THE CURRENT DEBAU COMPANY MUST BE STOPPED.
I SEE. VERY WELL, THEN.
GIVE IT A SHOT.
AND SELLING ME OUT?
HEH.

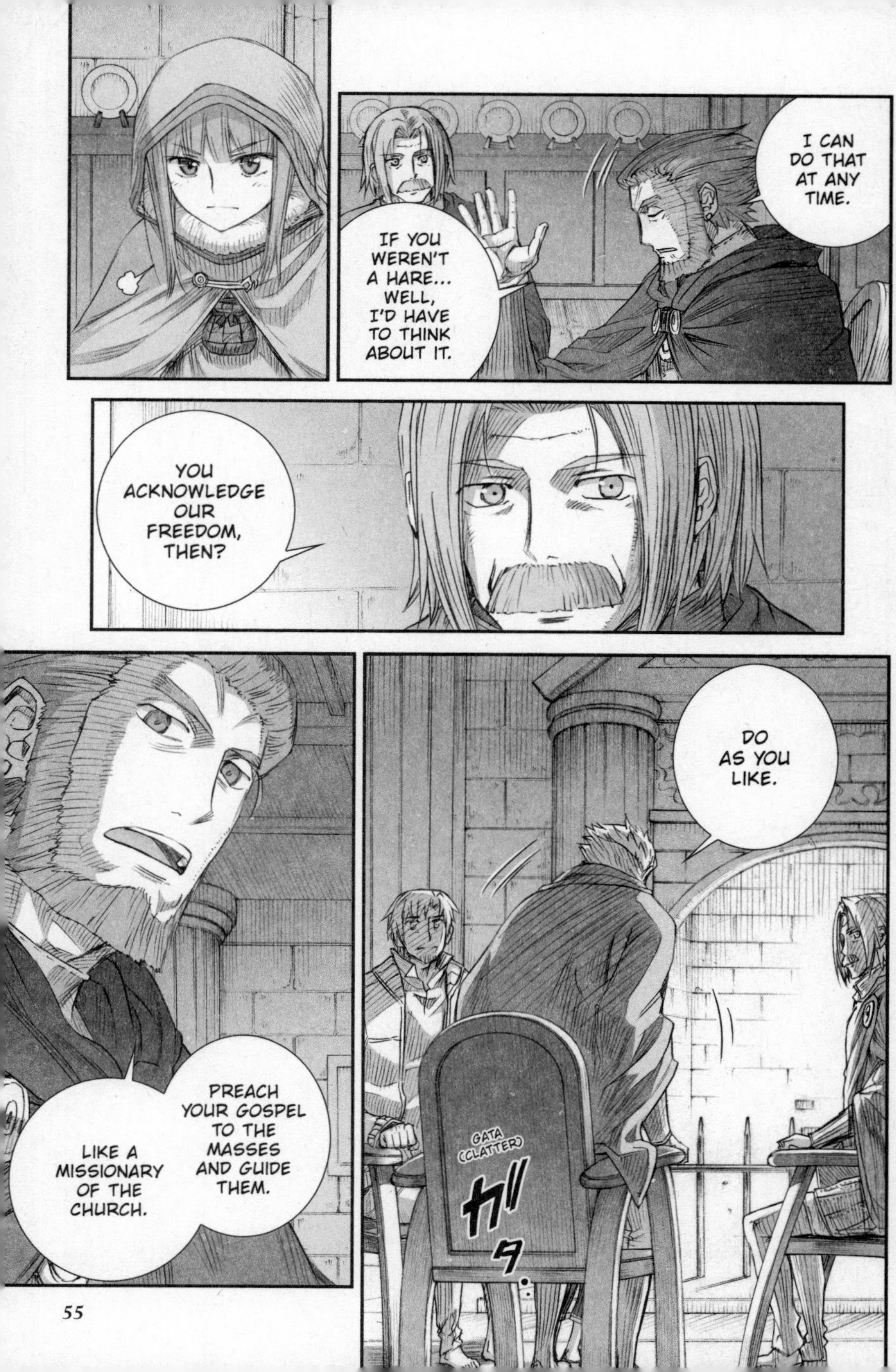
I CAN DO THAT AT ANY TIME.
IF YOU WEREN'T A HARE... WELL, I'D HAVE TO THINK ABOUT IT.
YOU ACKNOWLEDGE OUR FREEDOM, THEN?
DO AS YOU LIKE.
GATA (CLATTER)
ガタ
PREACH YOUR GOSPEL TO THE MASSES AND GUIDE THEM.
LIKE A MISSIONARY OF THE CHURCH.

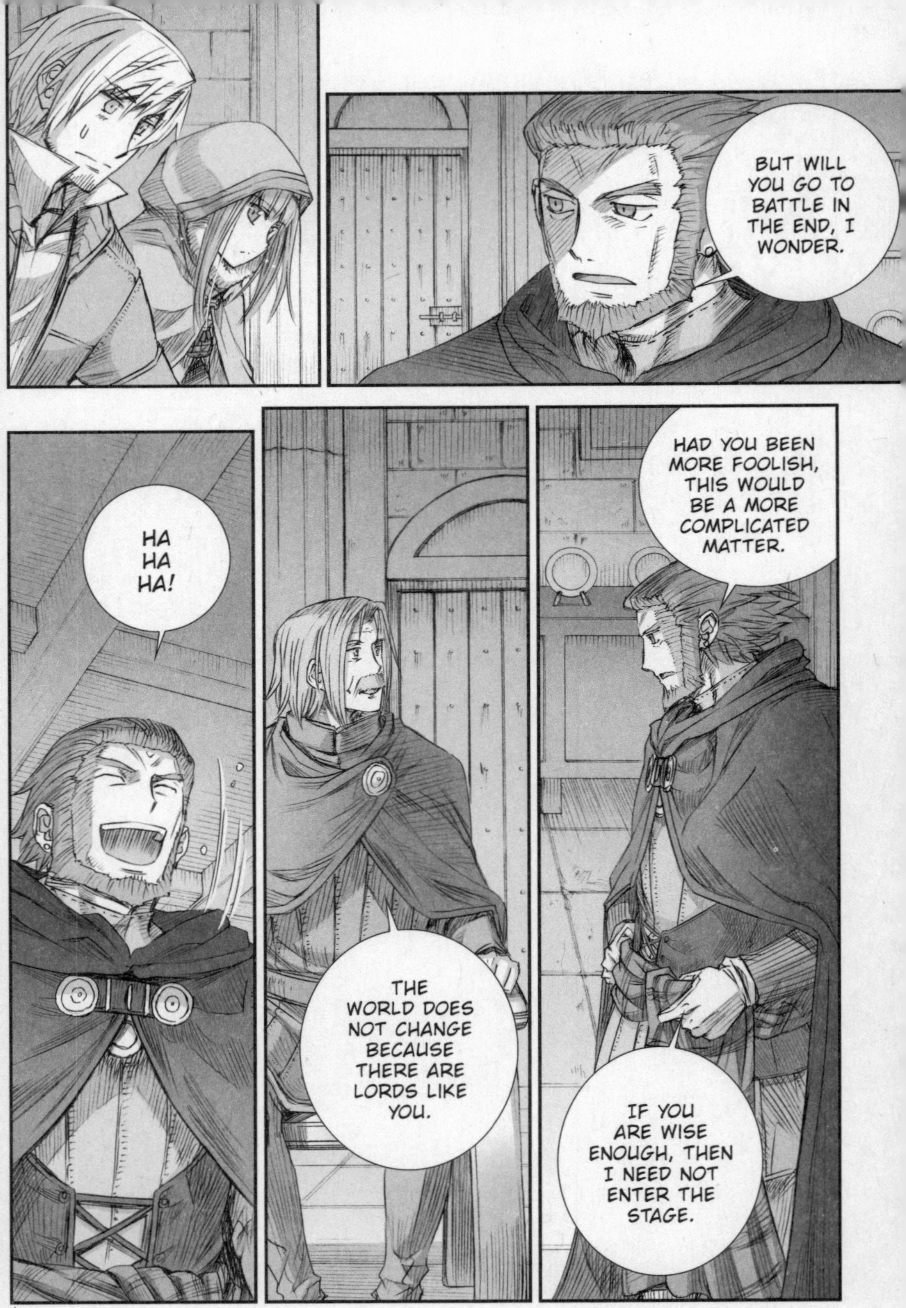
BUT WILL YOU GO TO BATTLE IN THE END, I WONDER.
HAD YOU BEEN MORE FOOLISH, THIS WOULD BE A MORE COMPLICATED MATTER.
IF YOU ARE WISE ENOUGH, THEN I NEED NOT ENTER THE STAGE.
THE WORLD DOES NOT CHANGE BECAUSE THERE ARE LORDS LIKE YOU.
HA HA HA!

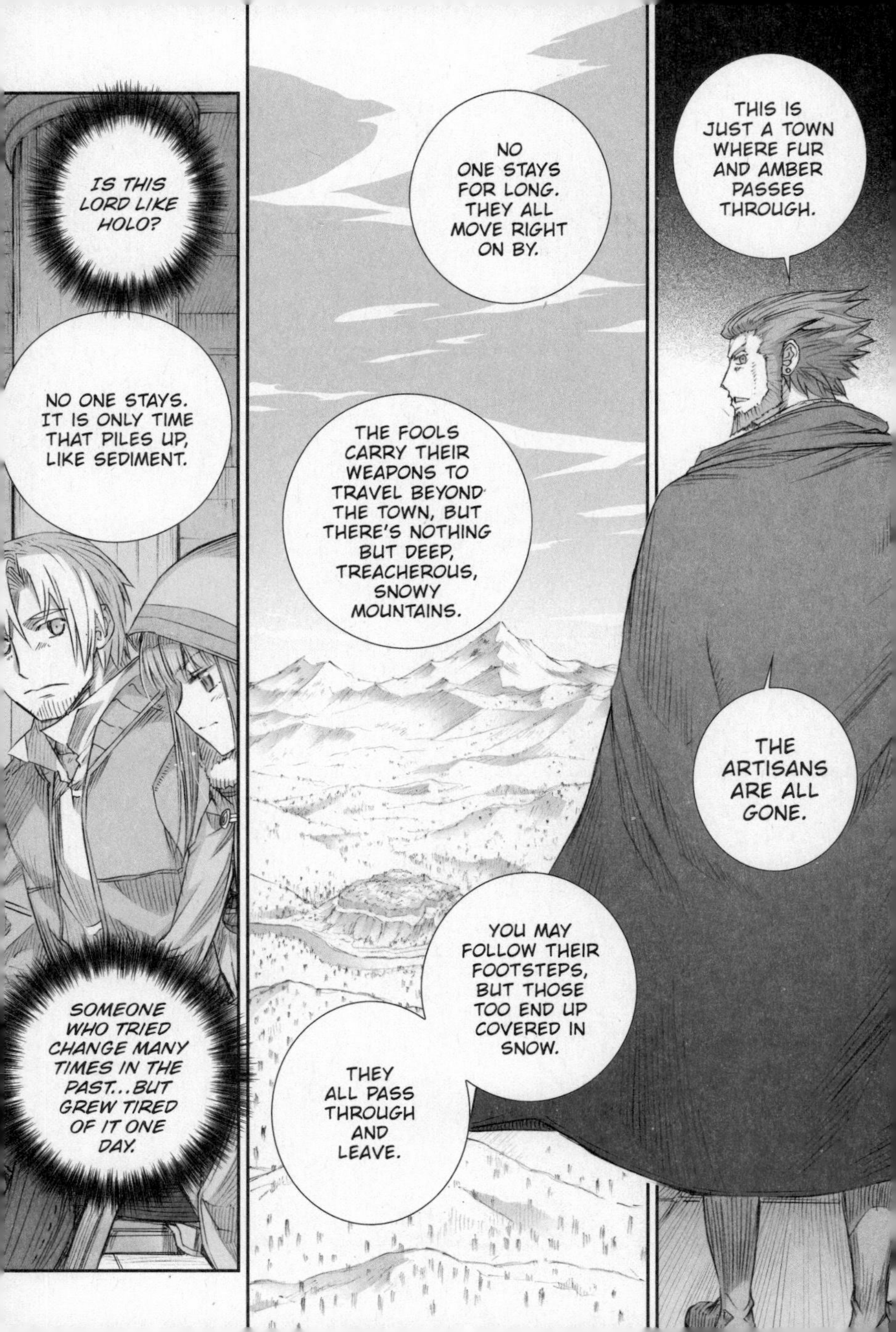
THIS IS JUST A TOWN WHERE FUR AND AMBER PASSES THROUGH.
THE ARTISANS ARE ALL GONE.
NO ONE STAYS FOR LONG. THEY ALL MOVE RIGHT ON BY.
THE FOOLS CARRY THEIR WEAPONS TO TRAVEL BEYOND THE TOWN, BUT THERE'S NOTHING BUT DEEP, TREACHEROUS, SNOWY MOUNTAINS.
YOU MAY FOLLOW THEIR FOOTSTEPS, BUT THOSE TOO END UP COVERED IN SNOW.
THEY ALL PASS THROUGH AND LEAVE.
IS THIS LORD LIKE HOLO?
NO ONE STAYS. IT IS ONLY TIME THAT PILES UP, LIKE SEDIMENT.
SOMEONE WHO TRIED CHANGE MANY TIMES IN THE PAST...BUT GREW TIRED OF IT ONE DAY.

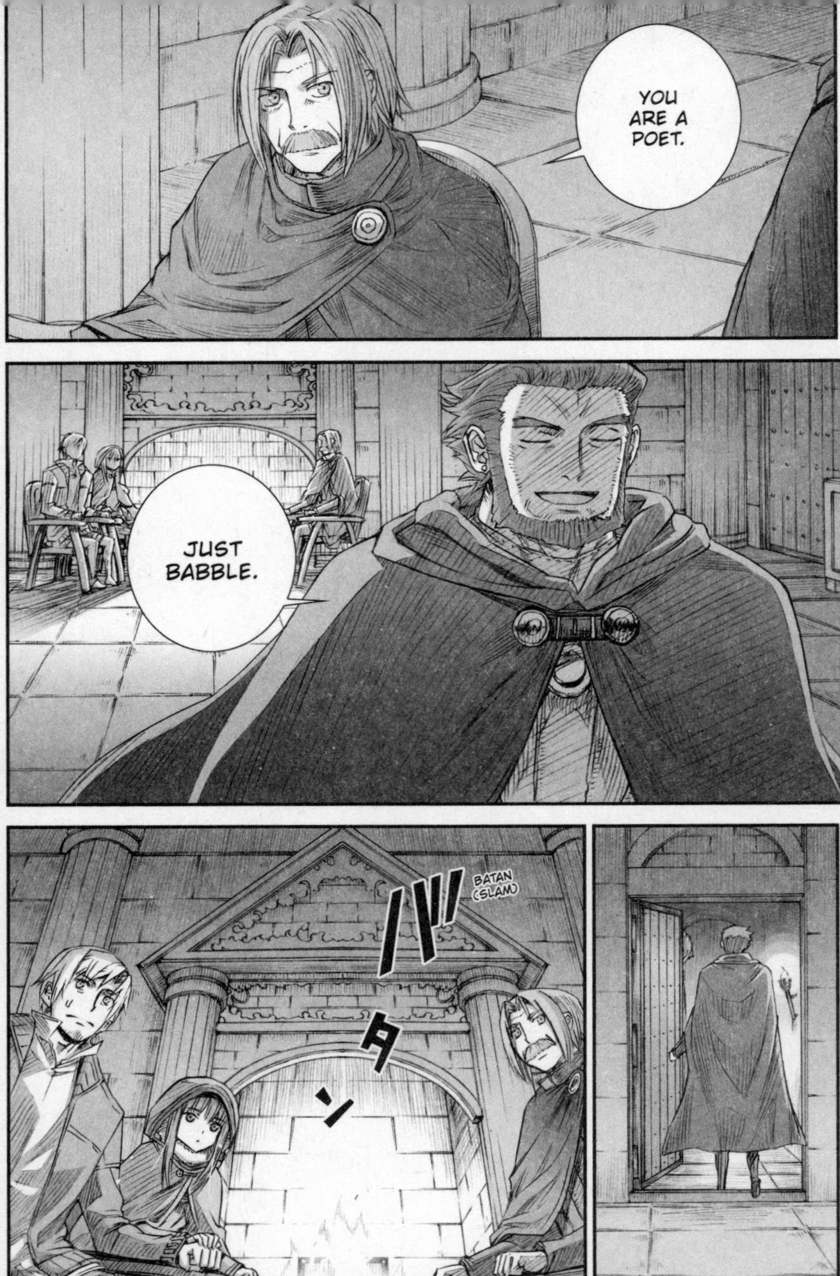
YOU ARE A POET.
JUST BABBLE.
バタン
BATAN (SLAM)

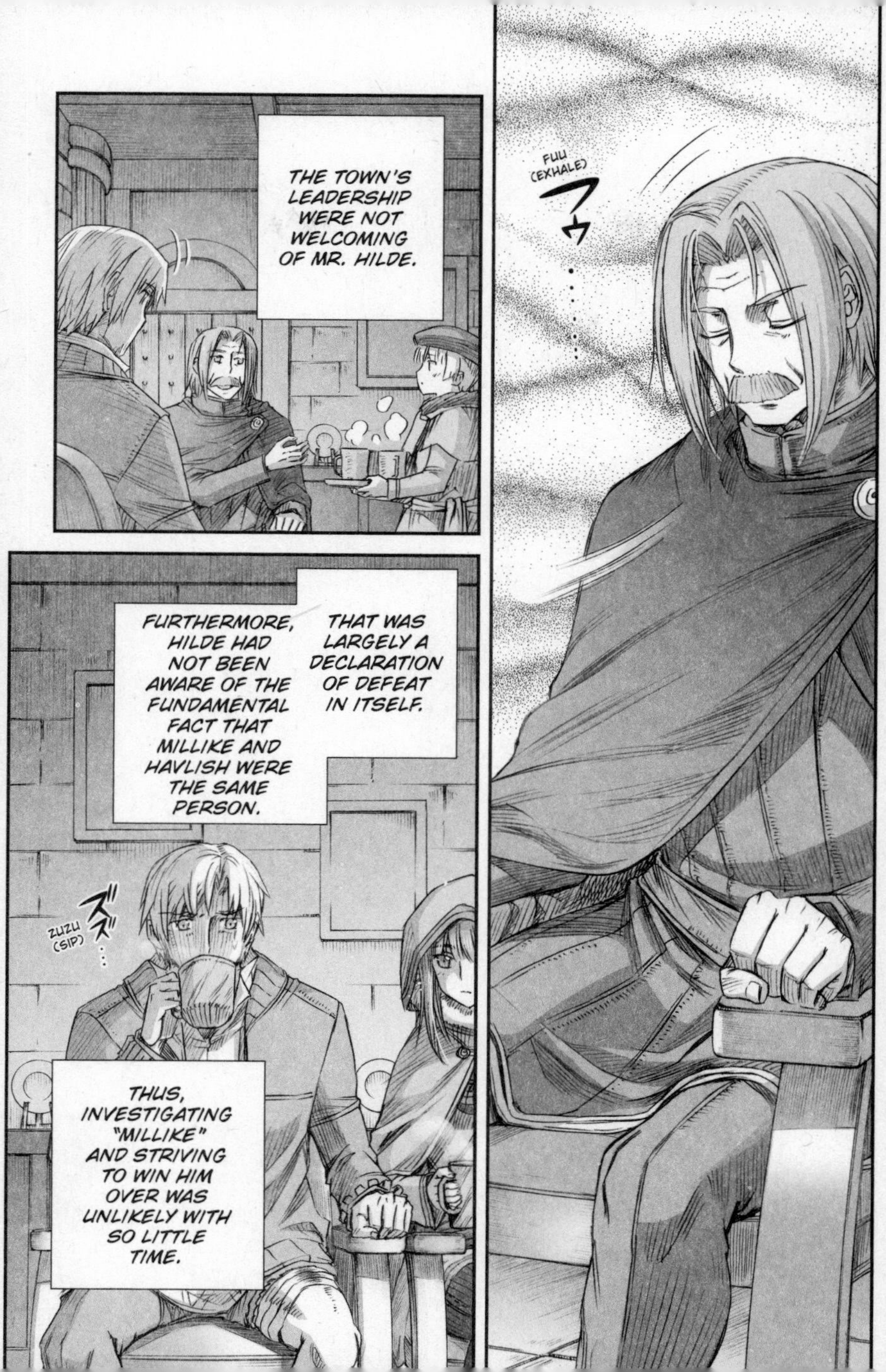
FUU (EXHALE)
THE TOWN'S LEADERSHIP WERE NOT WELCOMING OF MR. HILDE.
FURTHERMORE, HILDE HAD NOT BEEN AWARE OF THE FUNDAMENTAL FACT THAT MILLIKE AND HAVLISH WERE THE SAME PERSON.
THAT WAS LARGELY A DECLARATION OF DEFEAT IN ITSELF.
ZUZU (SIP)
THUS, INVESTIGATING "MILLIKE" AND STRIVING TO WIN HIM OVER WAS UNLIKELY WITH SO LITTLE TIME.

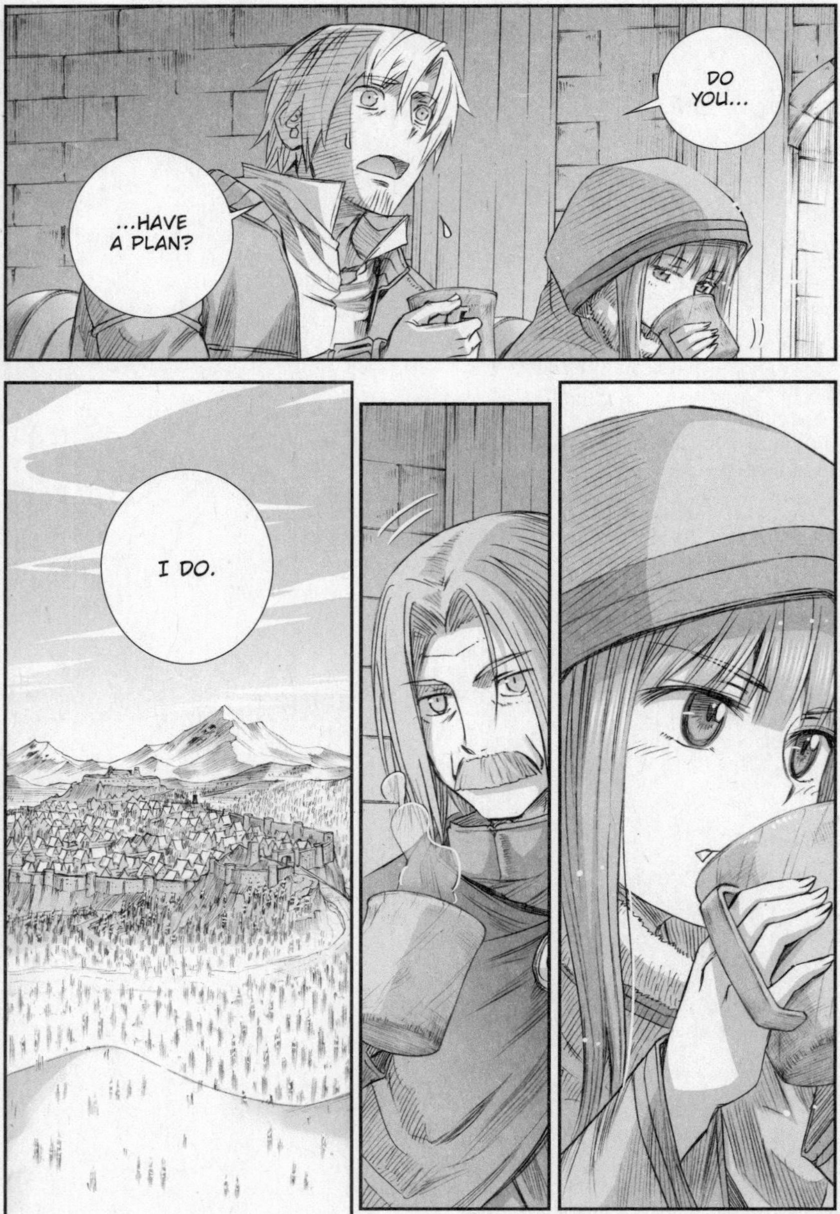
DO YOU...
...HAVE A PLAN?
I DO.

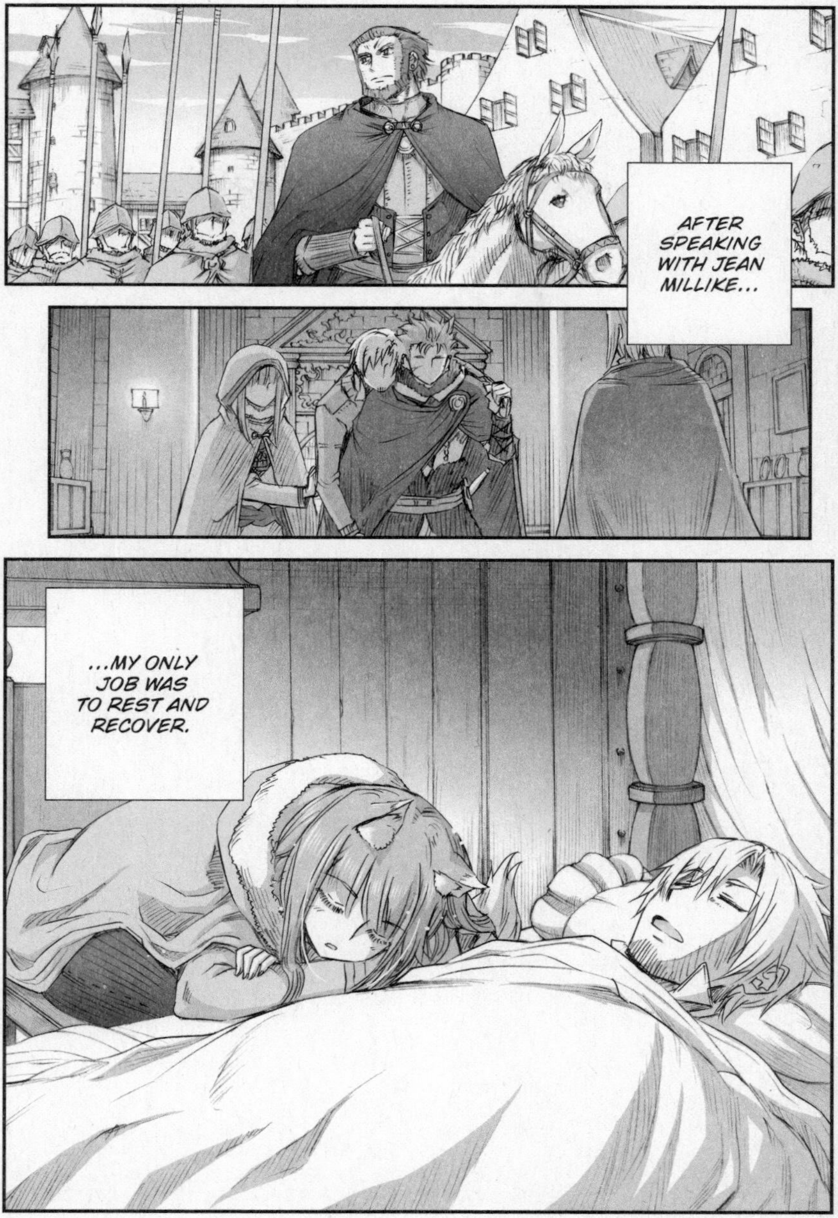
AFTER SPEAKING WITH JEAN MILLIKE...
...MY ONLY JOB WAS TO REST AND RECOVER.

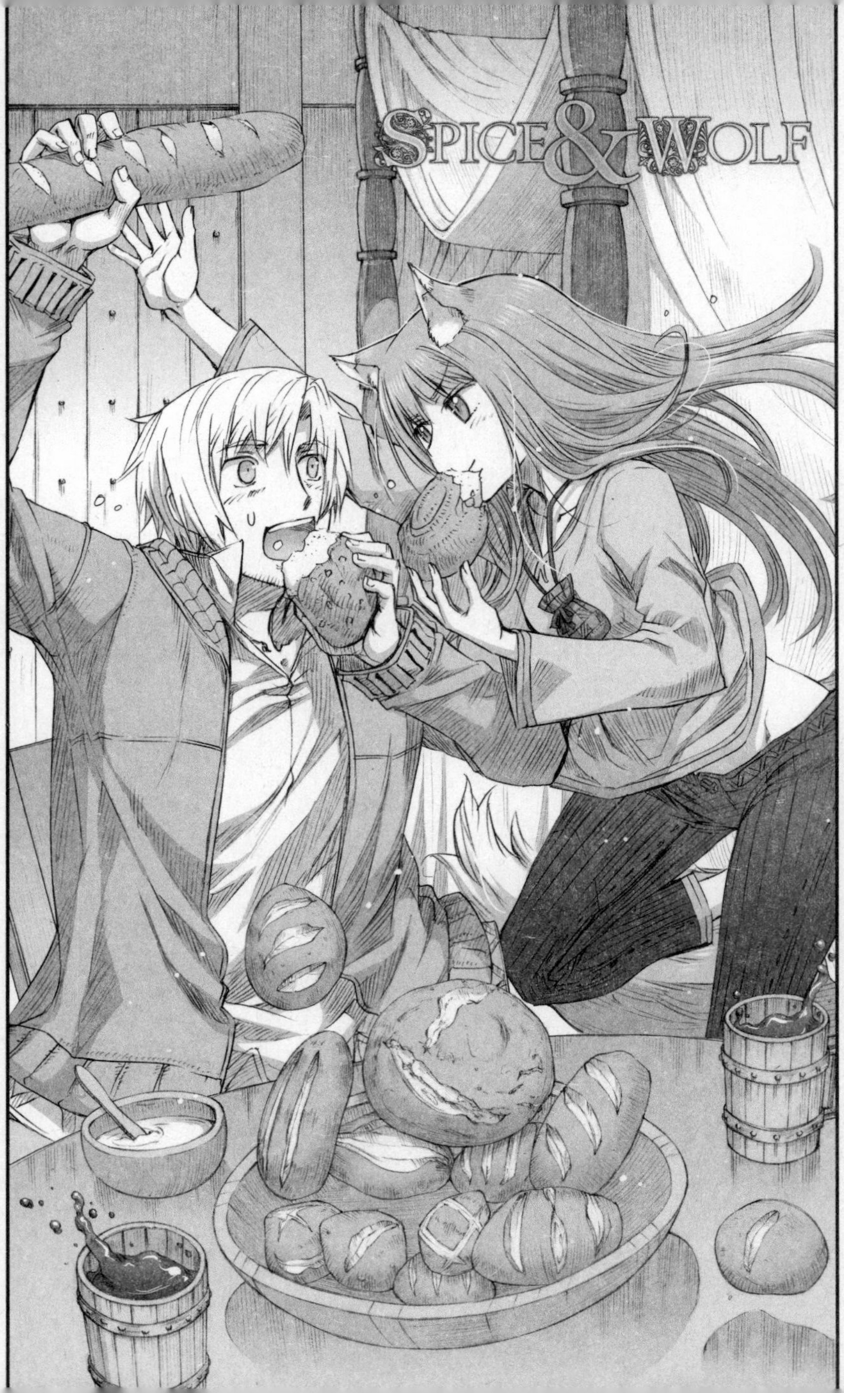
SPICE & WOLF

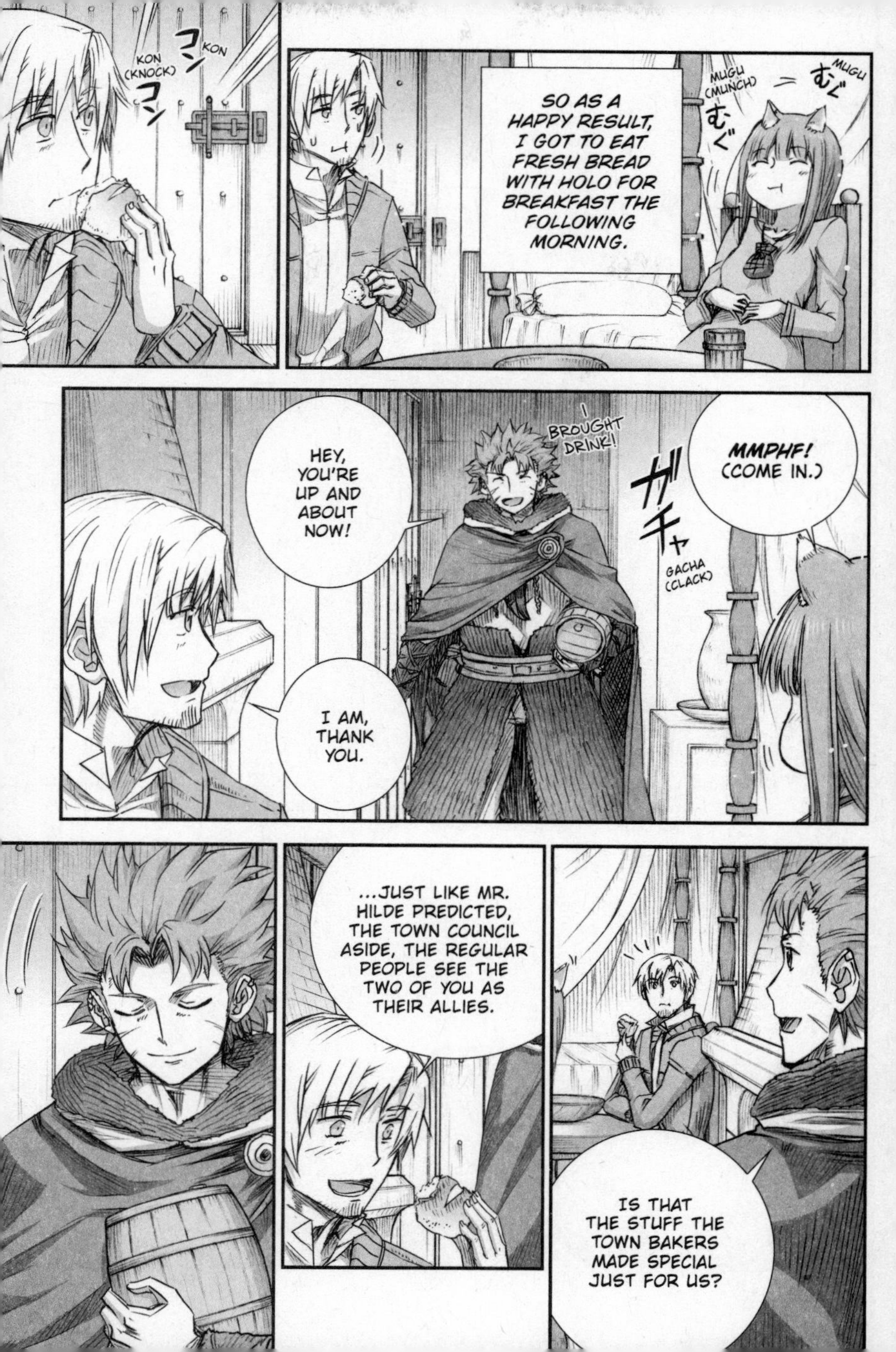
MUGU
むぐ
MUGU (MUNCH)
むぐ
SO AS A HAPPY RESULT, I GOT TO EAT FRESH BREAD WITH HOLO FOR BREAKFAST THE FOLLOWING MORNING.
KON
コン
KON (KNOCK)
コン
MMPHF! (COME IN.)
ガチャ
GACHA (CLACK)
I BROUGHT DRINK!
HEY, YOU'RE UP AND ABOUT NOW!
I AM, THANK YOU.
IS THAT THE STUFF THE TOWN BAKERS MADE SPECIAL JUST FOR US?
...JUST LIKE MR. HILDE PREDICTED, THE TOWN COUNCIL ASIDE, THE REGULAR PEOPLE SEE THE TWO OF YOU AS THEIR ALLIES.

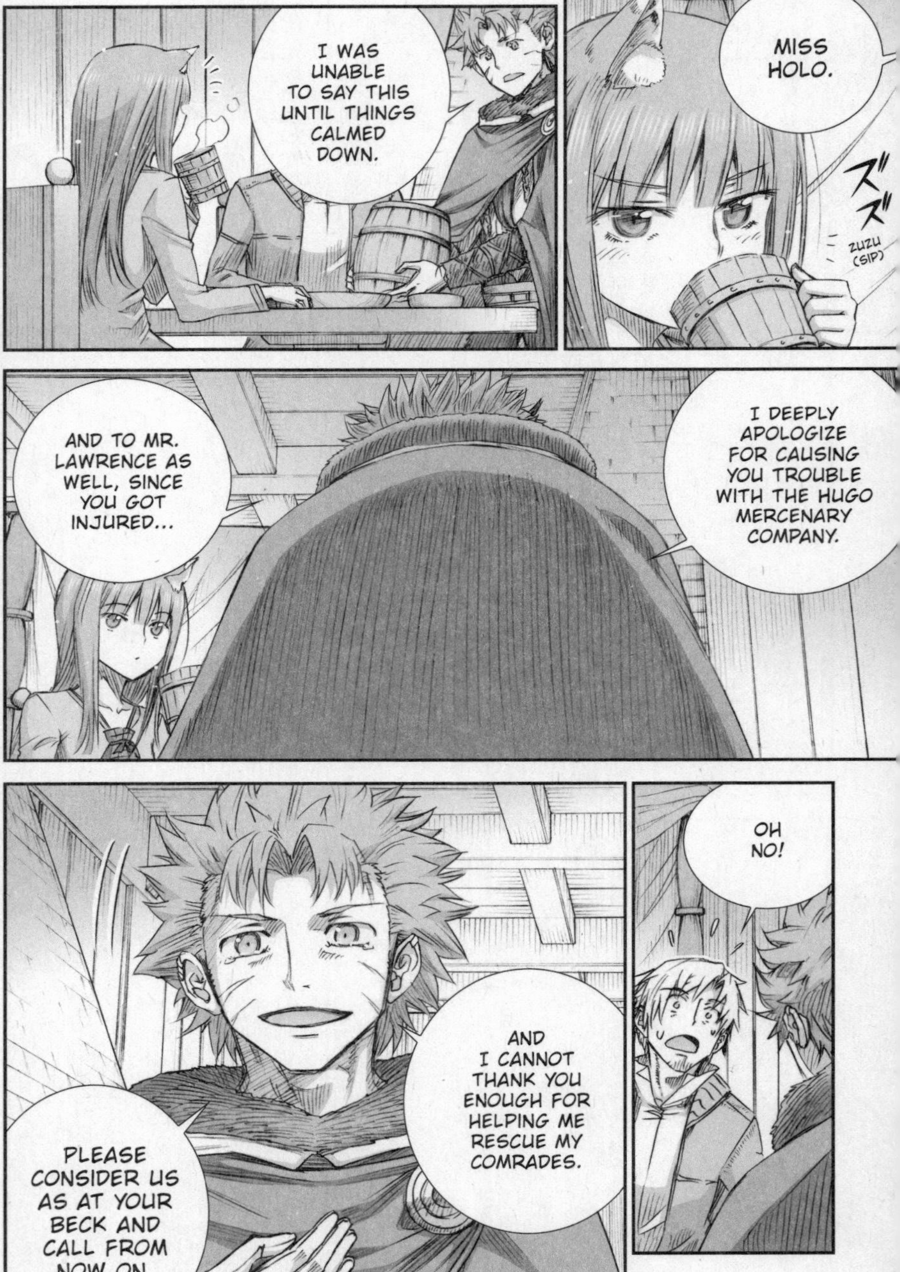
MISS HOLO.
ズズ
ZUZU (SIP)
I WAS UNABLE TO SAY THIS UNTIL THINGS CALMED DOWN.
I DEEPLY APOLOGIZE FOR CAUSING YOU TROUBLE WITH THE HUGO MERCENARY COMPANY.
AND TO MR. LAWRENCE AS WELL, SINCE YOU GOT INJURED...
OH NO!
AND I CANNOT THANK YOU ENOUGH FOR HELPING ME RESCUE MY COMRADES.
PLEASE CONSIDER US AS AT YOUR BECK AND CALL FROM NOW ON.

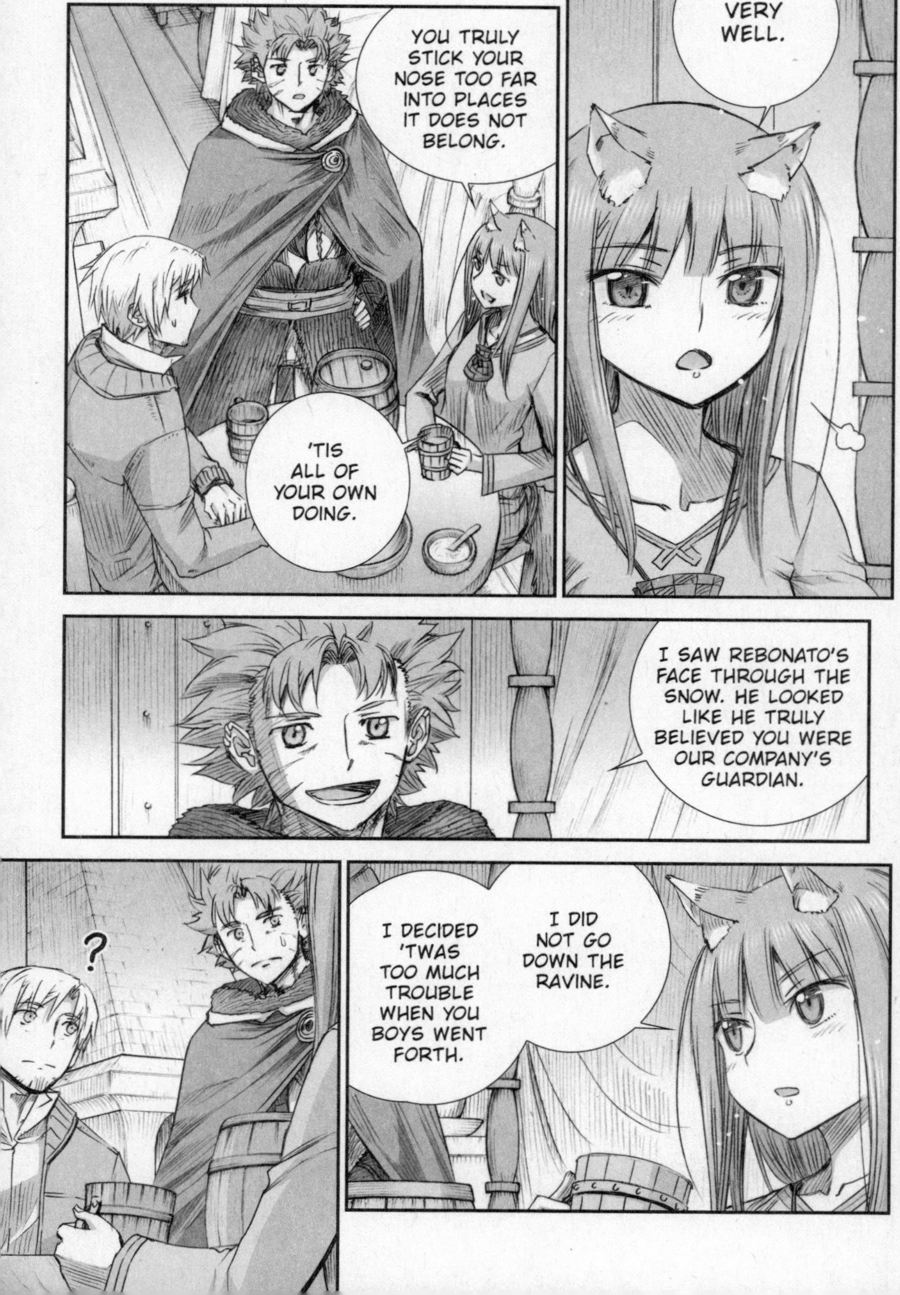
VERY WELL.
YOU TRULY STICK YOUR NOSE TOO FAR INTO PLACES IT DOES NOT BELONG.
'TIS ALL OF YOUR OWN DOING.
I SAW REBONATO'S FACE THROUGH THE SNOW. HE LOOKED LIKE HE TRULY BELIEVED YOU WERE OUR COMPANY'S GUARDIAN.
I DID NOT GO DOWN THE RAVINE.
I DECIDED 'TWAS TOO MUCH TROUBLE WHEN YOU BOYS WENT FORTH.
?

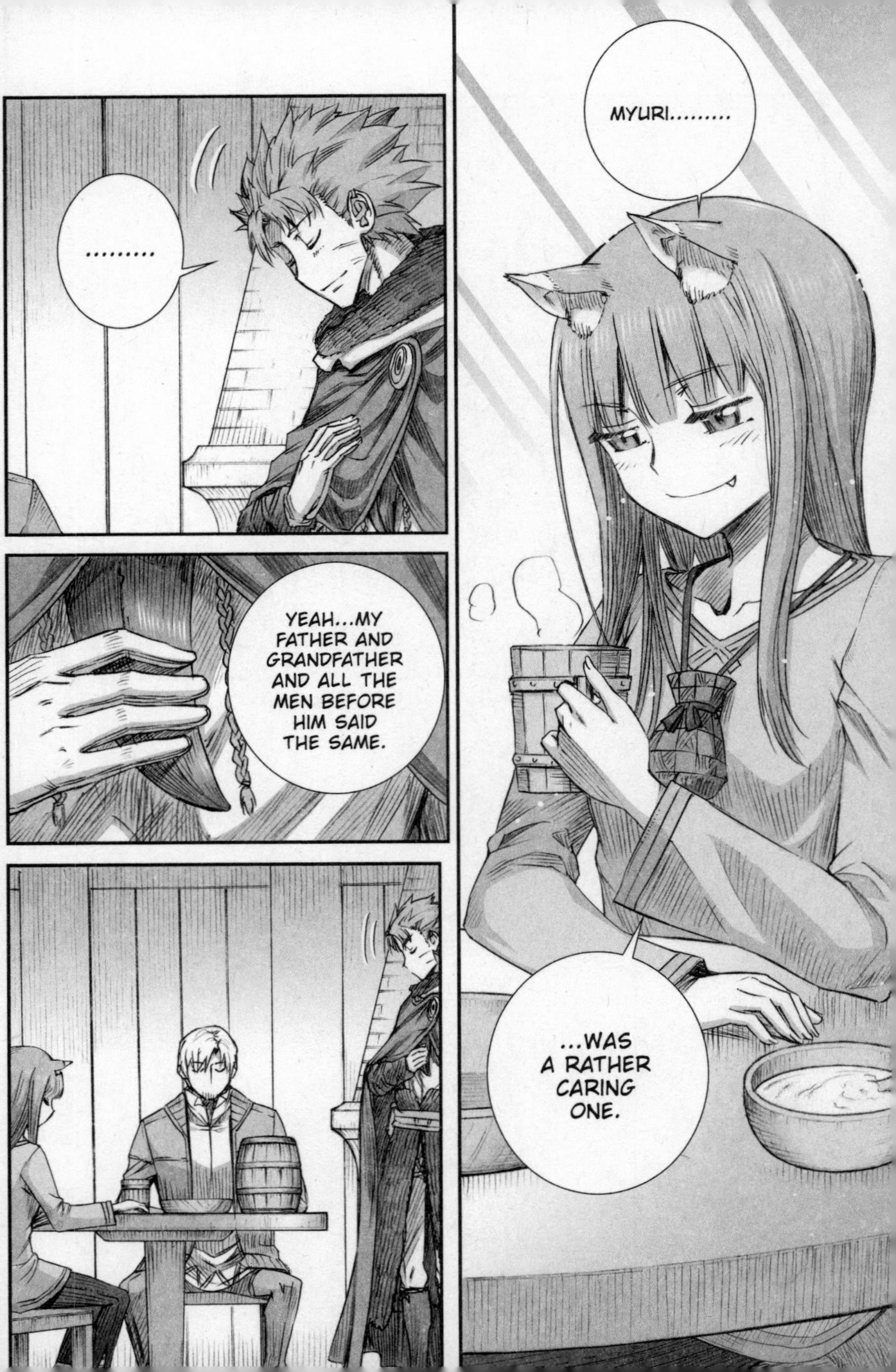
MYURI.........
...WAS A RATHER CARING ONE.
....
YEAH...MY FATHER AND GRANDFATHER AND ALL THE MEN BEFORE HIM SAID THE SAME.

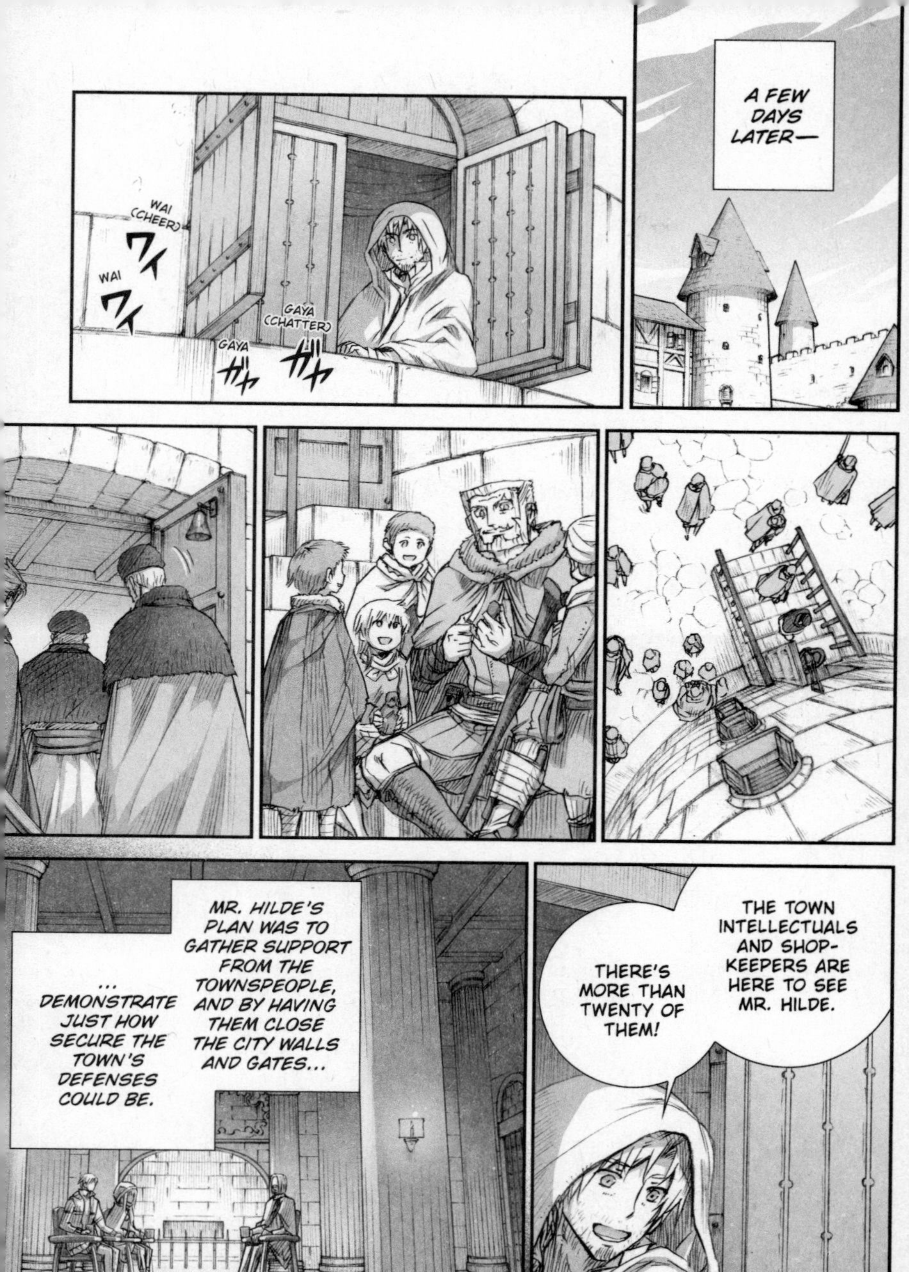
A FEW DAYS LATER—
WAI (CHEER)
ワイ
WAI
ワイ
GAYA (CHATTER)
ガヤ
GAYA
ガヤ
THE TOWN INTELLECTUALS AND SHOP-KEEPERS ARE HERE TO SEE MR. HILDE.
THERE'S MORE THAN TWENTY OF THEM!
MR. HILDE'S PLAN WAS TO GATHER SUPPORT FROM THE TOWNSPEOPLE, AND BY HAVING THEM CLOSE THE CITY WALLS AND GATES...
...DEMONSTRATE JUST HOW SECURE THE TOWN'S DEFENSES COULD BE.

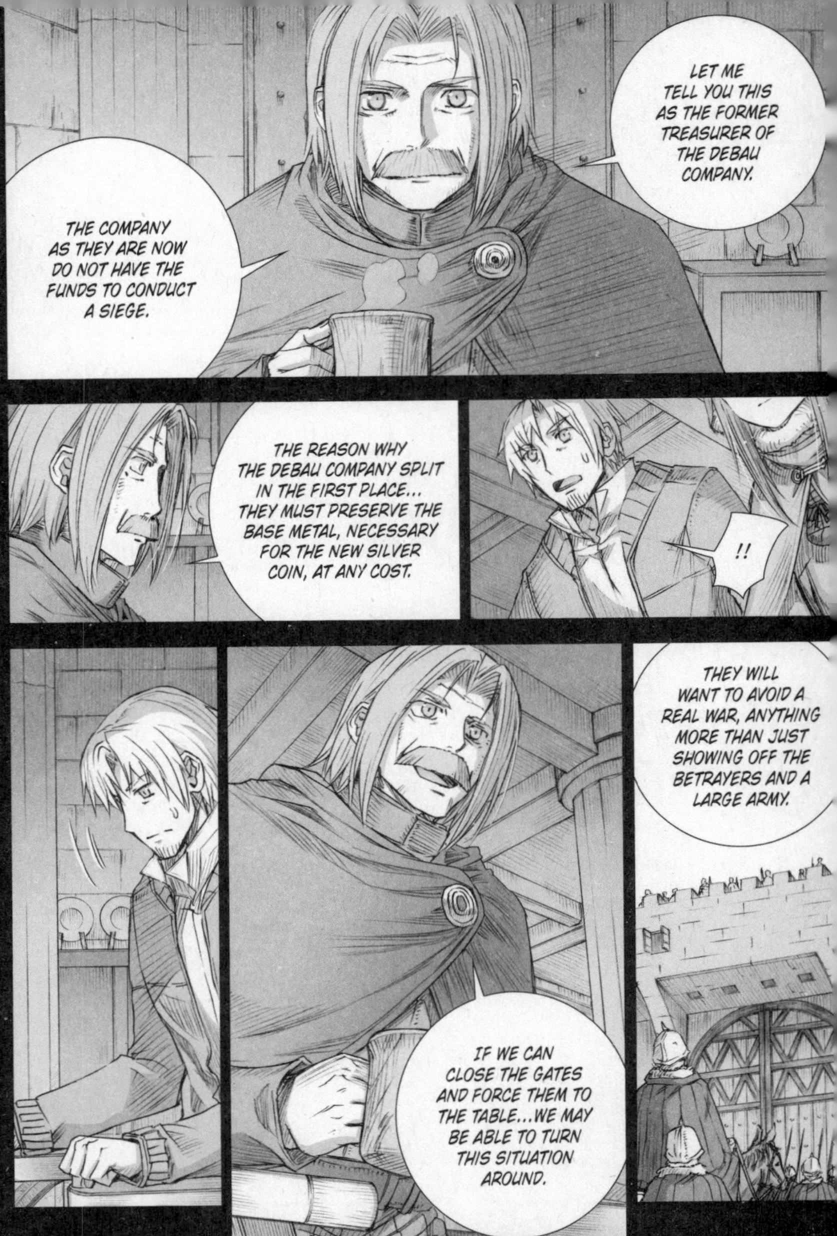
LET ME TELL YOU THIS AS THE FORMER TREASURER OF THE DEBAU COMPANY.
THE COMPANY AS THEY ARE NOW DO NOT HAVE THE FUNDS TO CONDUCT A SIEGE.
!!
THE REASON WHY THE DEBAU COMPANY SPLIT IN THE FIRST PLACE... THEY MUST PRESERVE THE BASE METAL, NECESSARY FOR THE NEW SILVER COIN, AT ANY COST.
THEY WILL WANT TO AVOID A REAL WAR, ANYTHING MORE THAN JUST SHOWING OFF THE BETRAYERS AND A LARGE ARMY.
IF WE CAN CLOSE THE GATES AND FORCE THEM TO THE TABLE...WE MAY BE ABLE TO TURN THIS SITUATION AROUND.

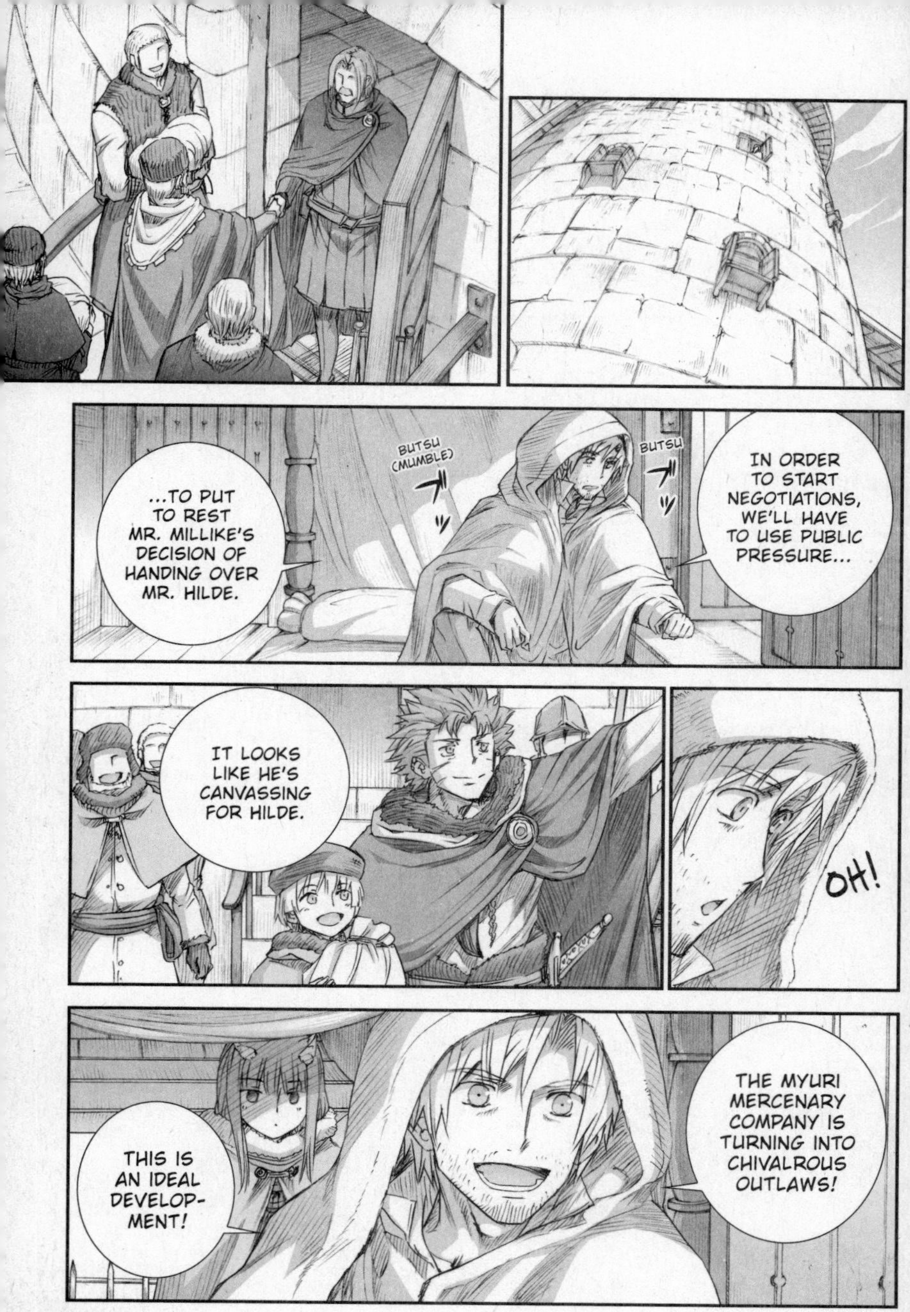
IN ORDER TO START NEGOTIATIONS, WE'LL HAVE TO USE PUBLIC PRESSURE...
BUTSU
BUTSU (MUMBLE)
...TO PUT TO REST MR. MILLIKE'S DECISION OF HANDING OVER MR. HILDE.
OH!
IT LOOKS LIKE HE'S CANVASSING FOR HILDE.
THE MYURI MERCENARY COMPANY IS TURNING INTO CHIVALROUS OUTLAWS!
THIS IS AN IDEAL DEVELOP-MENT!

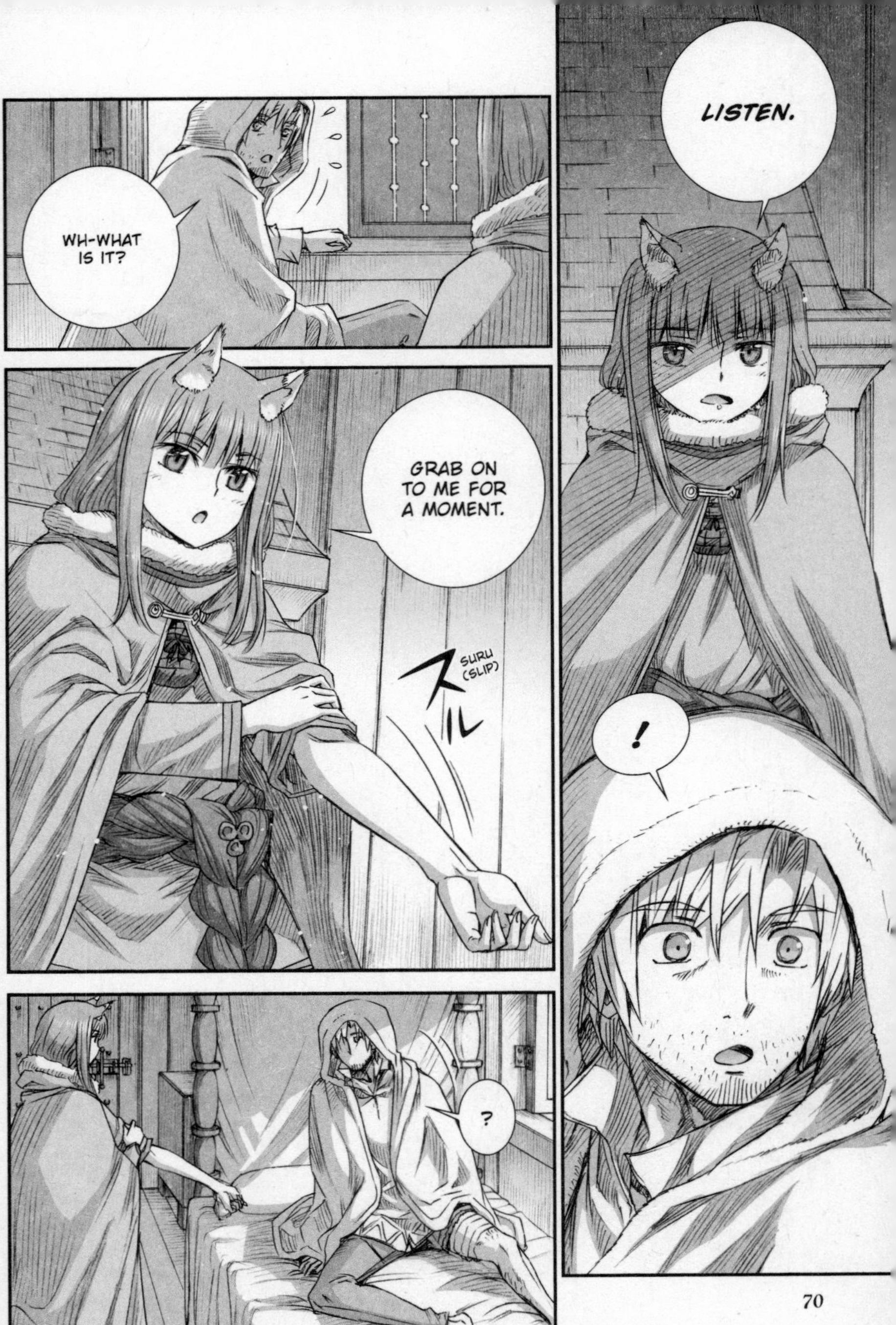
LISTEN.
!
WH-WHAT IS IT?
GRAB ON TO ME FOR A MOMENT.
SURU (SLIP)
?

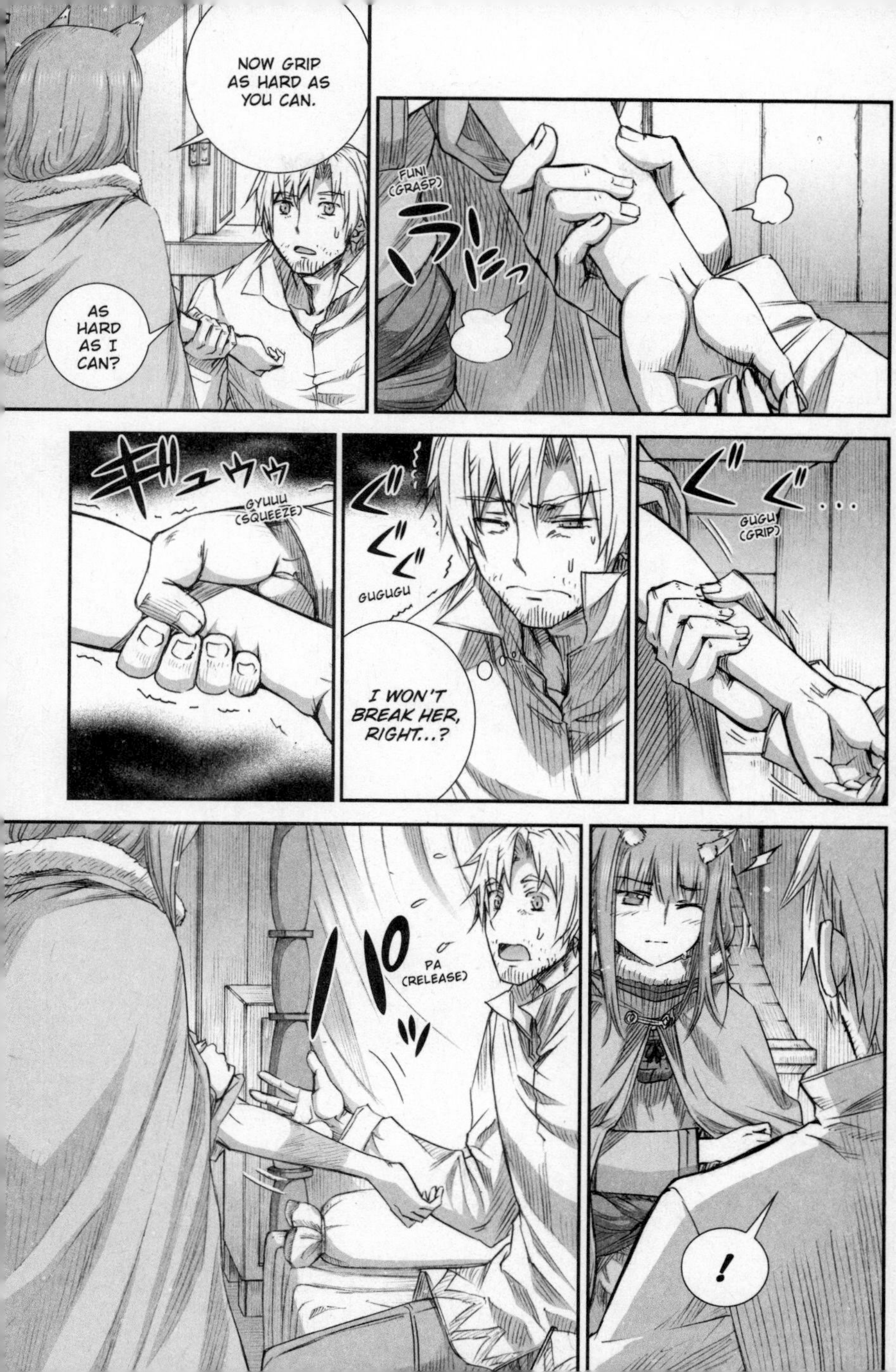
FUNI (GRASP)
NOW GRIP AS HARD AS YOU CAN.
AS HARD AS I CAN?
GUGU (GRIP)
GUGUGU
I WON'T BREAK HER, RIGHT...?
GYUUU (SQUEEZE)
!
PA (RELEASE)

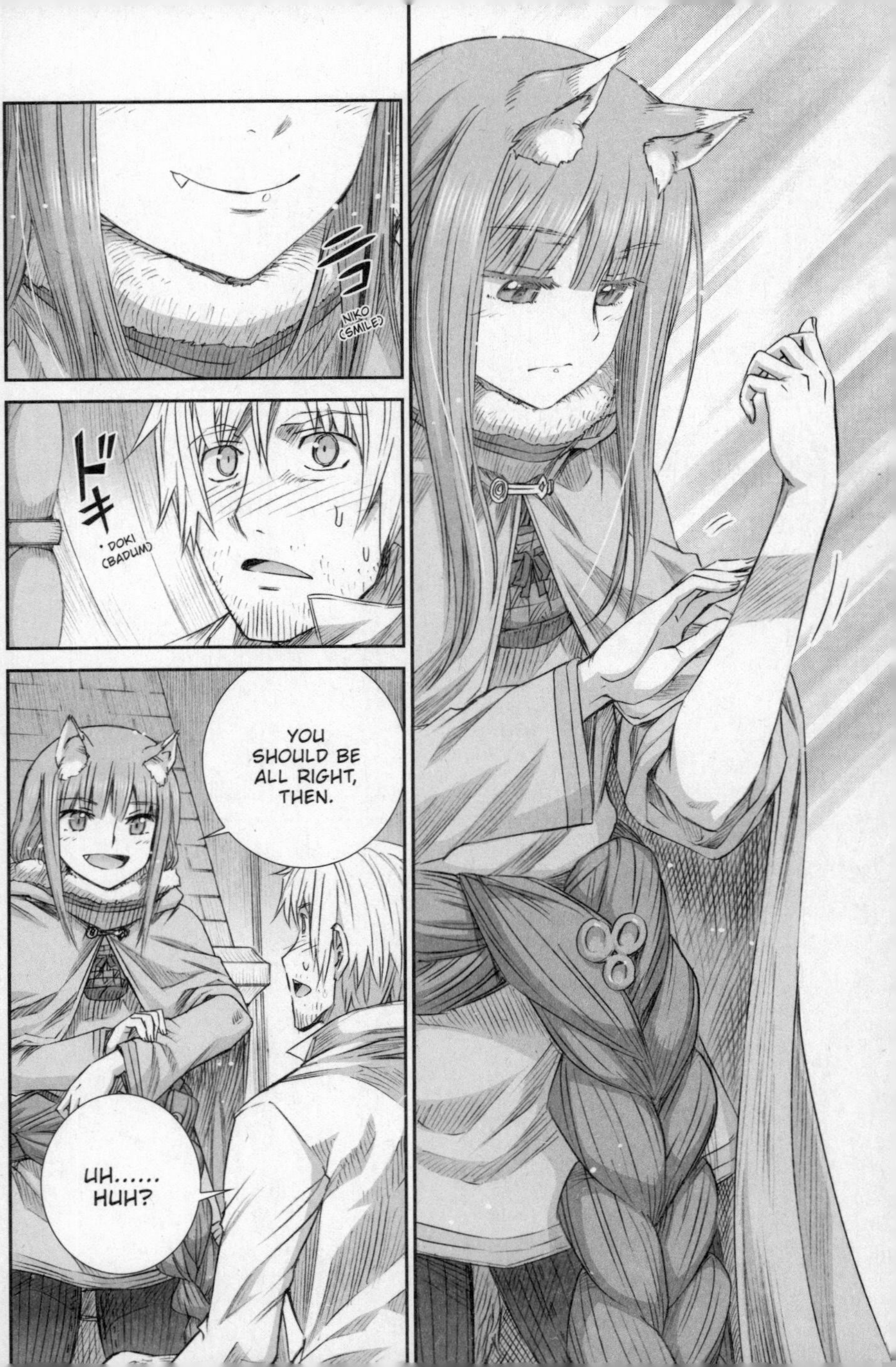
ニコ
NIKO (SMILE)
ドキ
DOKI (BADUM)
YOU SHOULD BE ALL RIGHT, THEN.
UH...... HUH?

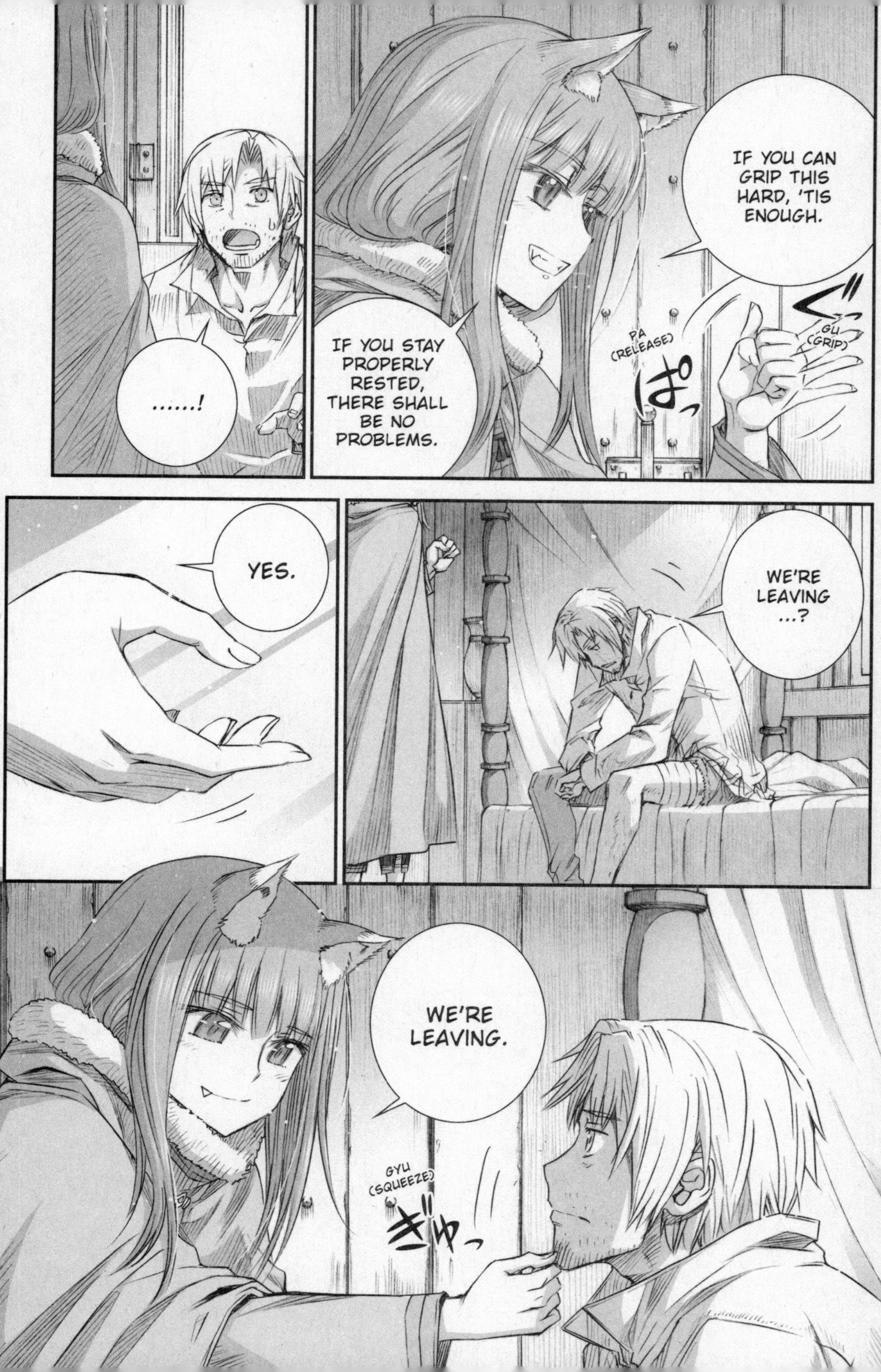
IF YOU CAN GRIP THIS HARD, 'TIS ENOUGH.
ぐっ
GU (GRIP)
PA (RELEASE)
ぱっ
IF YOU STAY PROPERLY RESTED, THERE SHALL BE NO PROBLEMS.
......!
WE'RE LEAVING ...?
YES.
WE'RE LEAVING.
GYU (SQUEEZE)
ぎゅっ

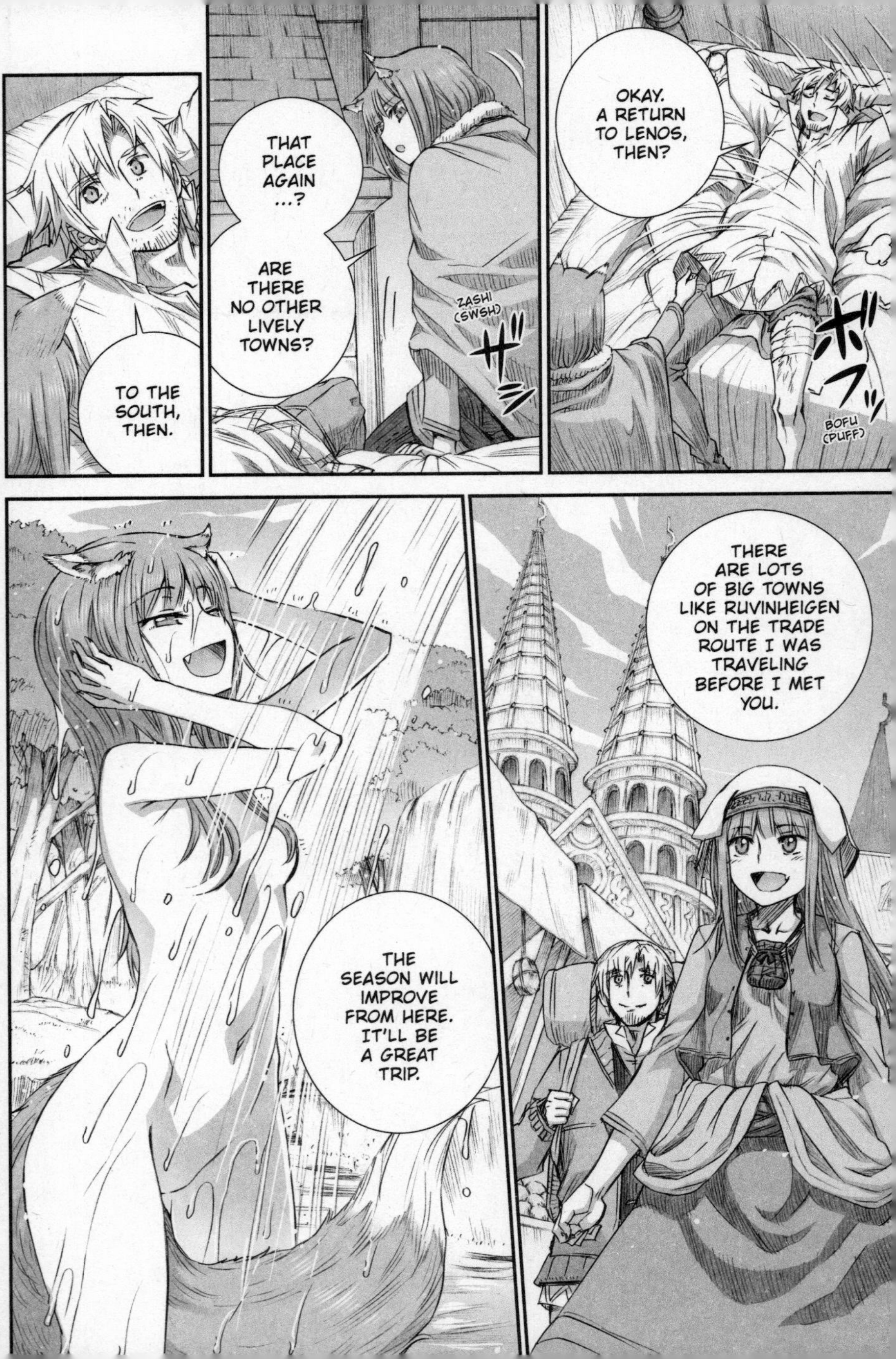
OKAY. A RETURN TO LENOS, THEN?
BOFU (PUFF)
THAT PLACE AGAIN ...?
ARE THERE NO OTHER LIVELY TOWNS?
ZASHI (SWSH)
TO THE SOUTH, THEN.
THERE ARE LOTS OF BIG TOWNS LIKE RUVINHEIGEN ON THE TRADE ROUTE I WAS TRAVELING BEFORE I MET YOU.
THE SEASON WILL IMPROVE FROM HERE. IT'LL BE A GREAT TRIP.

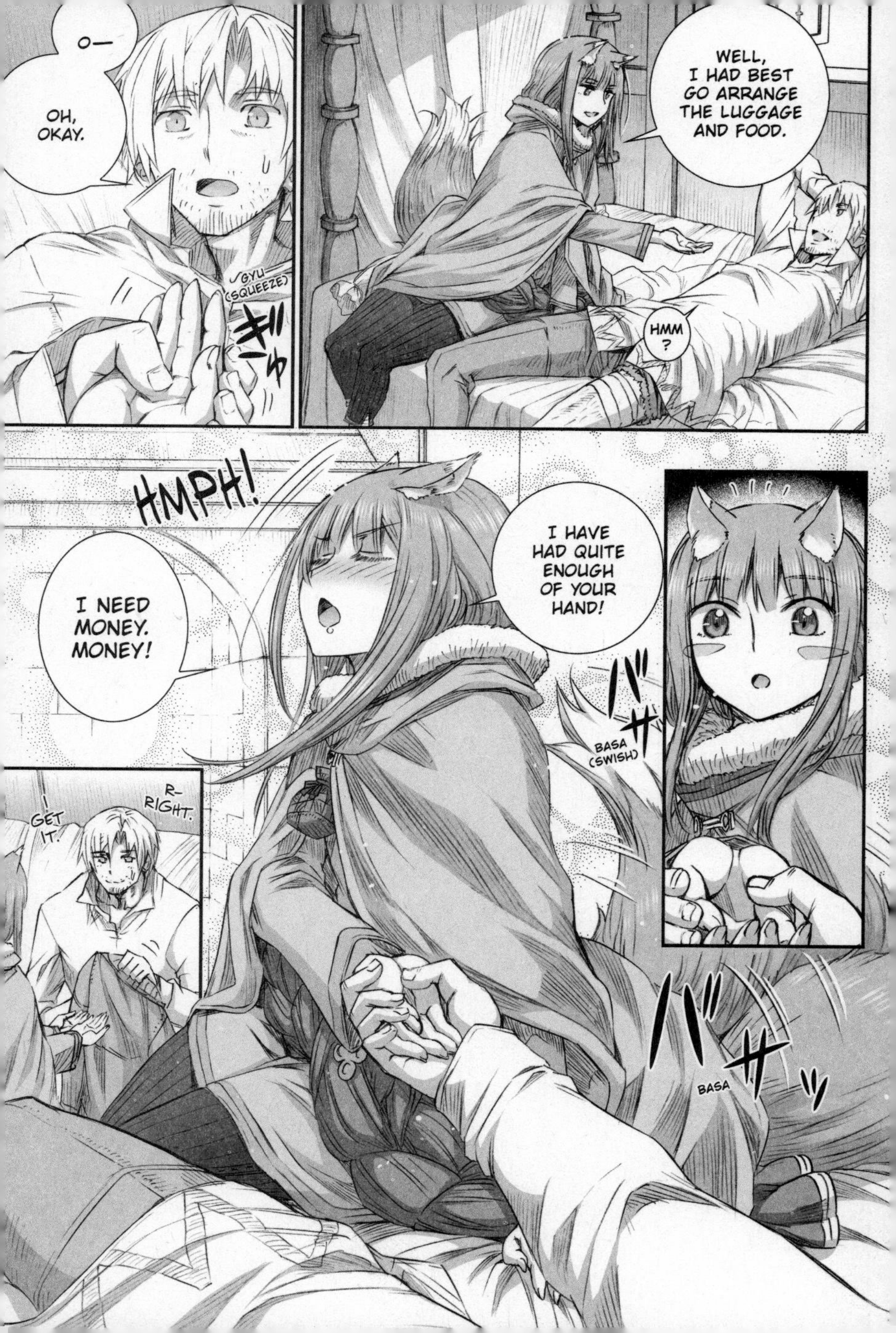
WELL, I HAD BEST GO ARRANGE THE LUGGAGE AND FOOD.
HMM?
O—
OH, OKAY.
GYU (SQUEEZE)
BASA (SWISH)
I HAVE HAD QUITE ENOUGH OF YOUR HAND!
HMPH!
I NEED MONEY. MONEY!
BASA
R-RIGHT.
I GET IT.

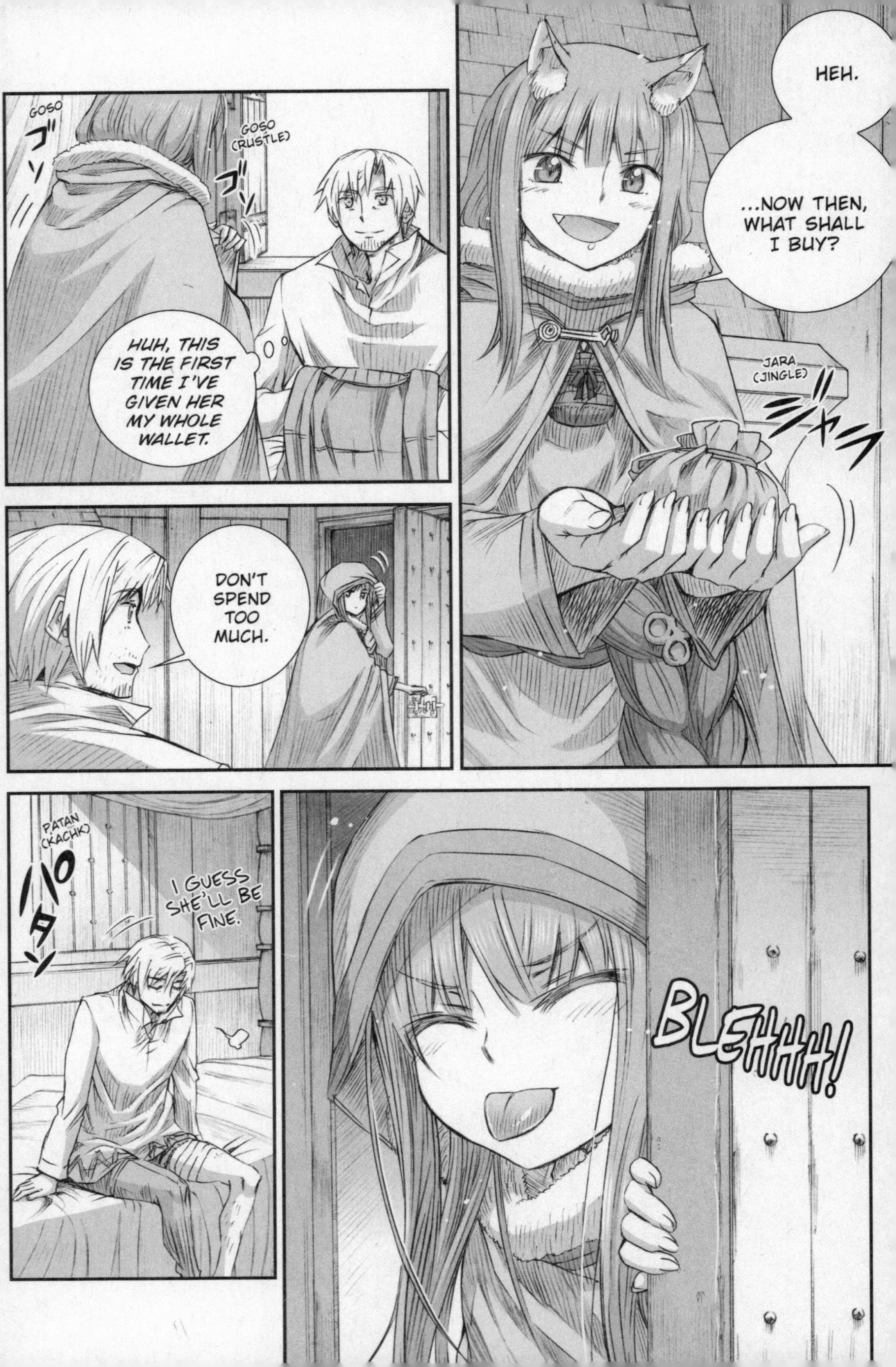
HEH.
...NOW THEN, WHAT SHALL I BUY?
JARA (JINGLE)
ジャラ
GOSO
ゴソ
GOSO (RUSTLE)
ゴソ
HUH, THIS IS THE FIRST TIME I'VE GIVEN HER MY WHOLE WALLET.
DON'T SPEND TOO MUCH.
BLEHHH!
PATAN (KACHK)
パタン
I GUESS SHE'LL BE FINE.

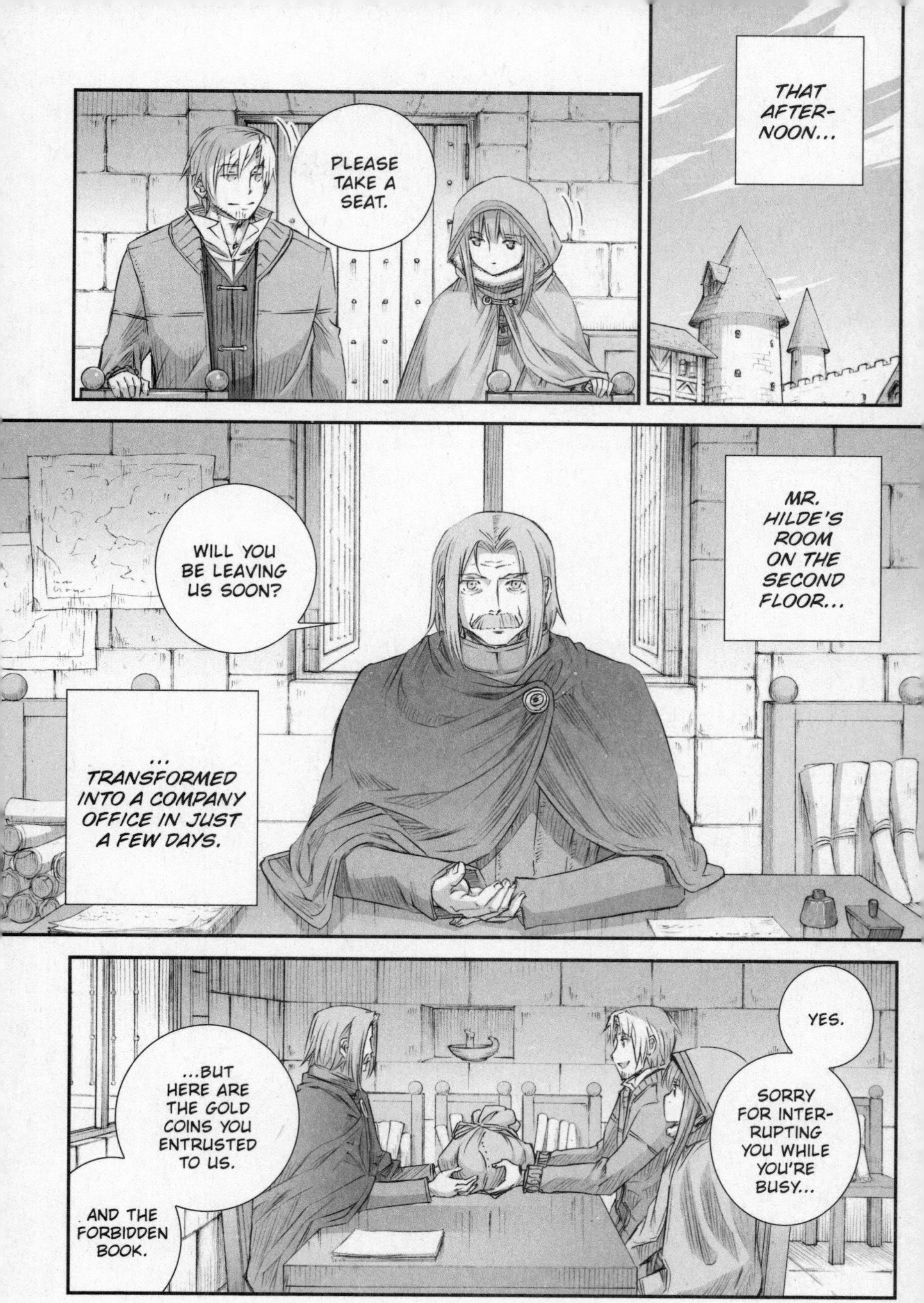

THAT AFTER-NOON...
PLEASE TAKE A SEAT.
MR. HILDE'S ROOM ON THE SECOND FLOOR...
WILL YOU BE LEAVING US SOON?
...TRANSFORMED INTO A COMPANY OFFICE IN JUST A FEW DAYS.
YES.
SORRY FOR INTER-RUPTING YOU WHILE YOU'RE BUSY...
...BUT HERE ARE THE GOLD COINS YOU ENTRUSTED TO US.
AND THE FORBIDDEN BOOK.

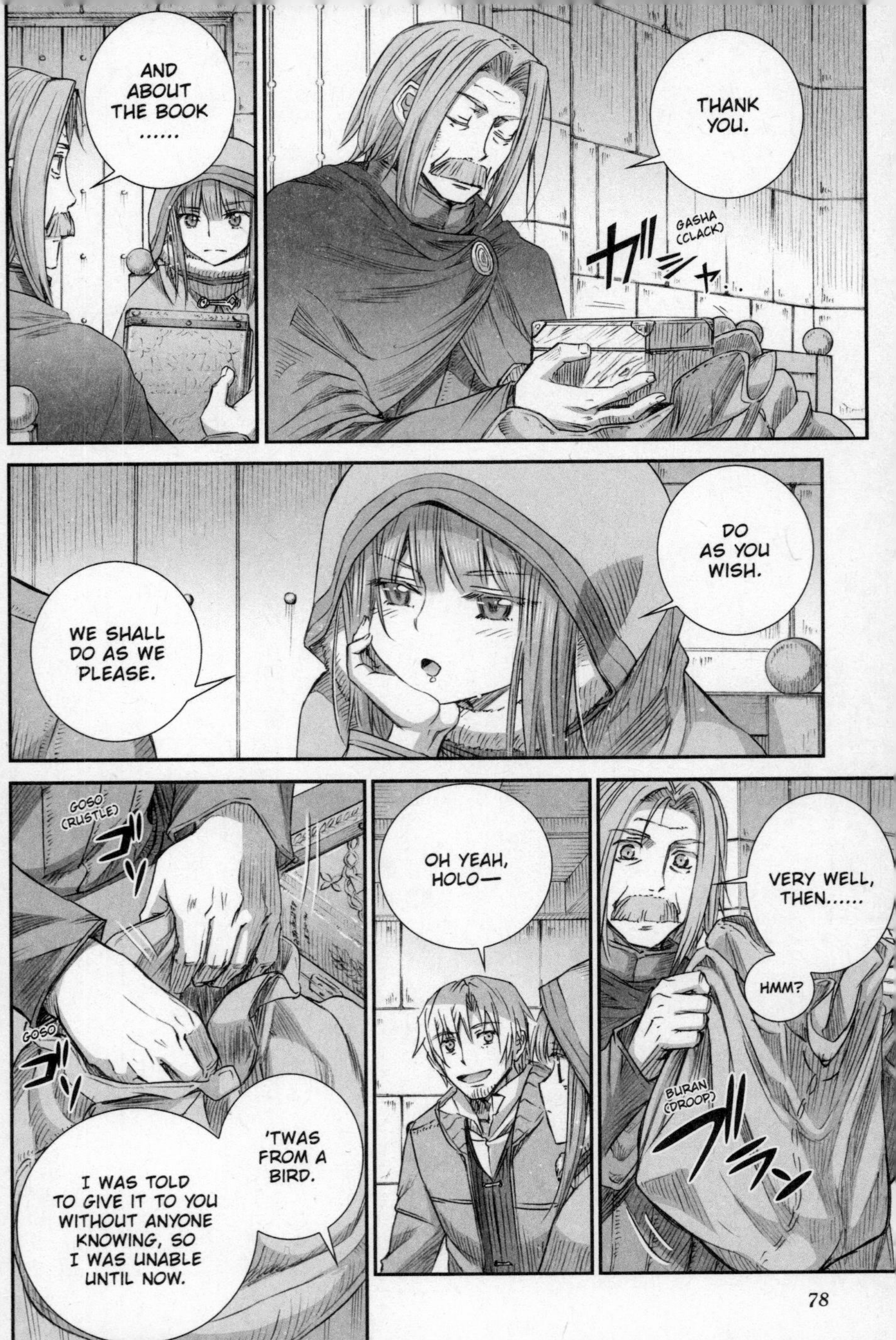
THANK YOU.
GASHA (CLACK)
AND ABOUT THE BOOK ......
DO AS YOU WISH.
WE SHALL DO AS WE PLEASE.
VERY WELL, THEN......
HMM?
BURAN (DROOP)
OH YEAH, HOLO—
GOSO (RUSTLE)
GOSO
'TWAS FROM A BIRD.
I WAS TOLD TO GIVE IT TO YOU WITHOUT ANYONE KNOWING, SO I WAS UNABLE UNTIL NOW.

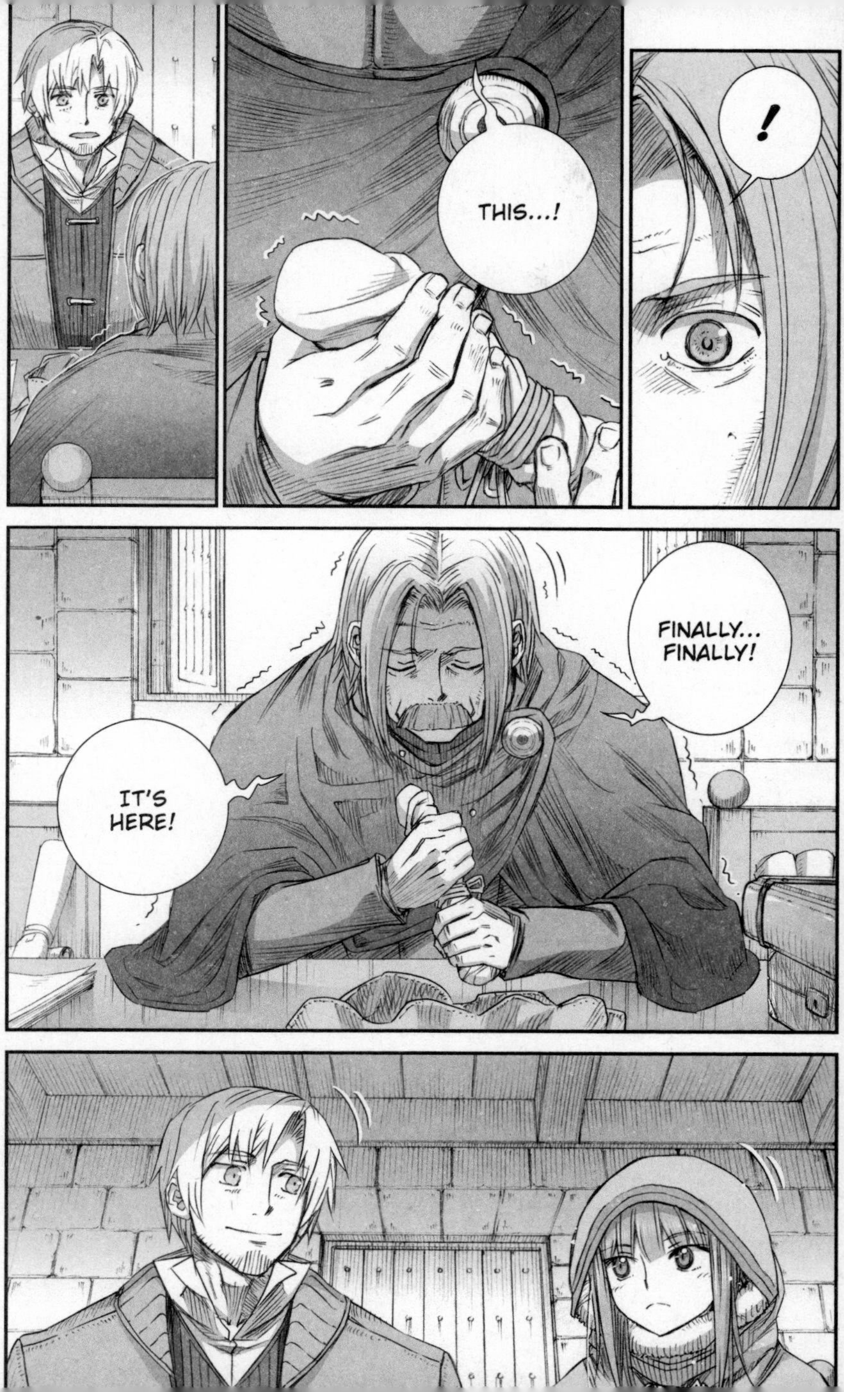
!
THIS...!
FINALLY... FINALLY!
IT'S HERE!

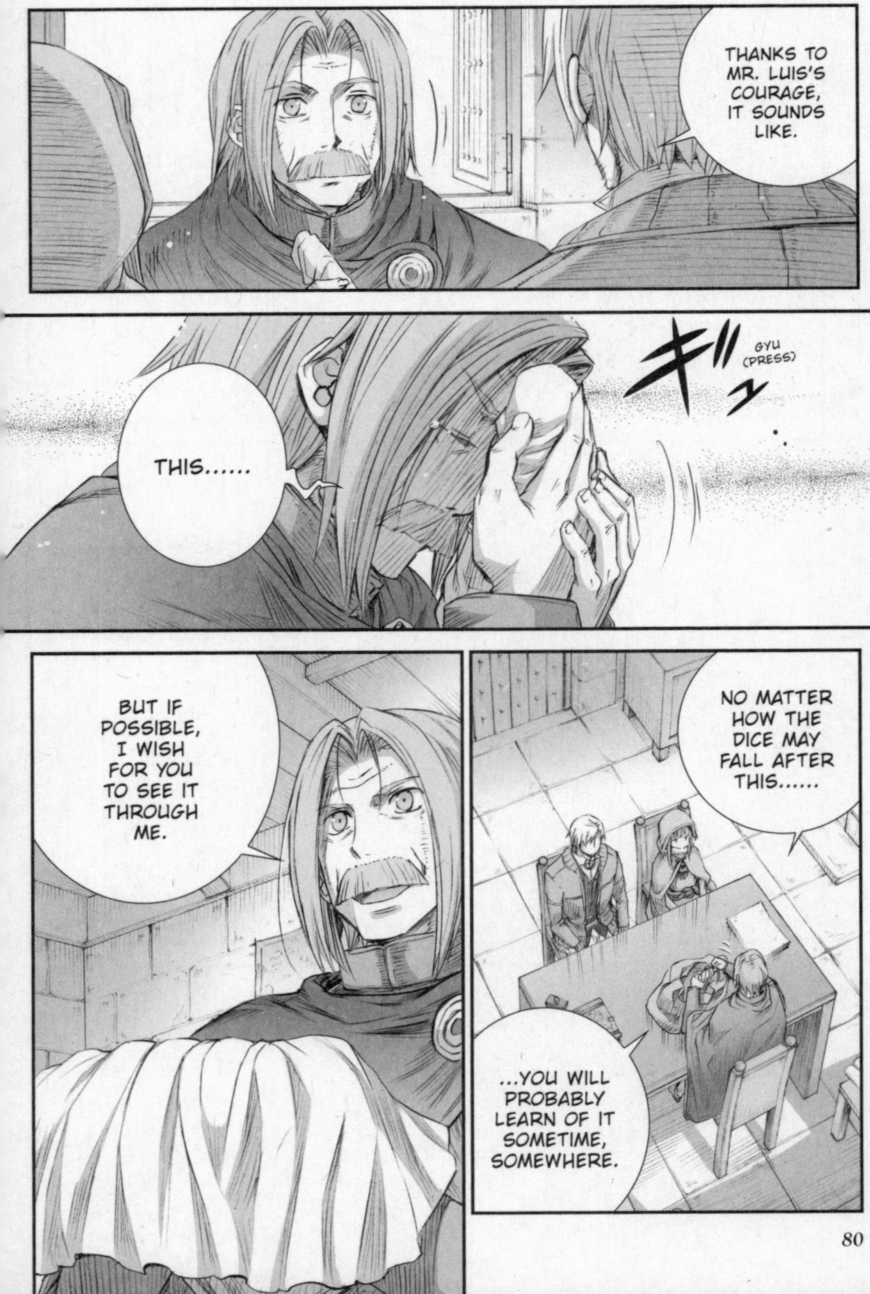
THANKS TO MR. LUIS'S COURAGE, IT SOUNDS LIKE.
ギュ
GYU (PRESS)
THIS......
NO MATTER HOW THE DICE MAY FALL AFTER THIS......
...YOU WILL PROBABLY LEARN OF IT SOMETIME, SOMEWHERE.
BUT IF POSSIBLE, I WISH FOR YOU TO SEE IT THROUGH ME.

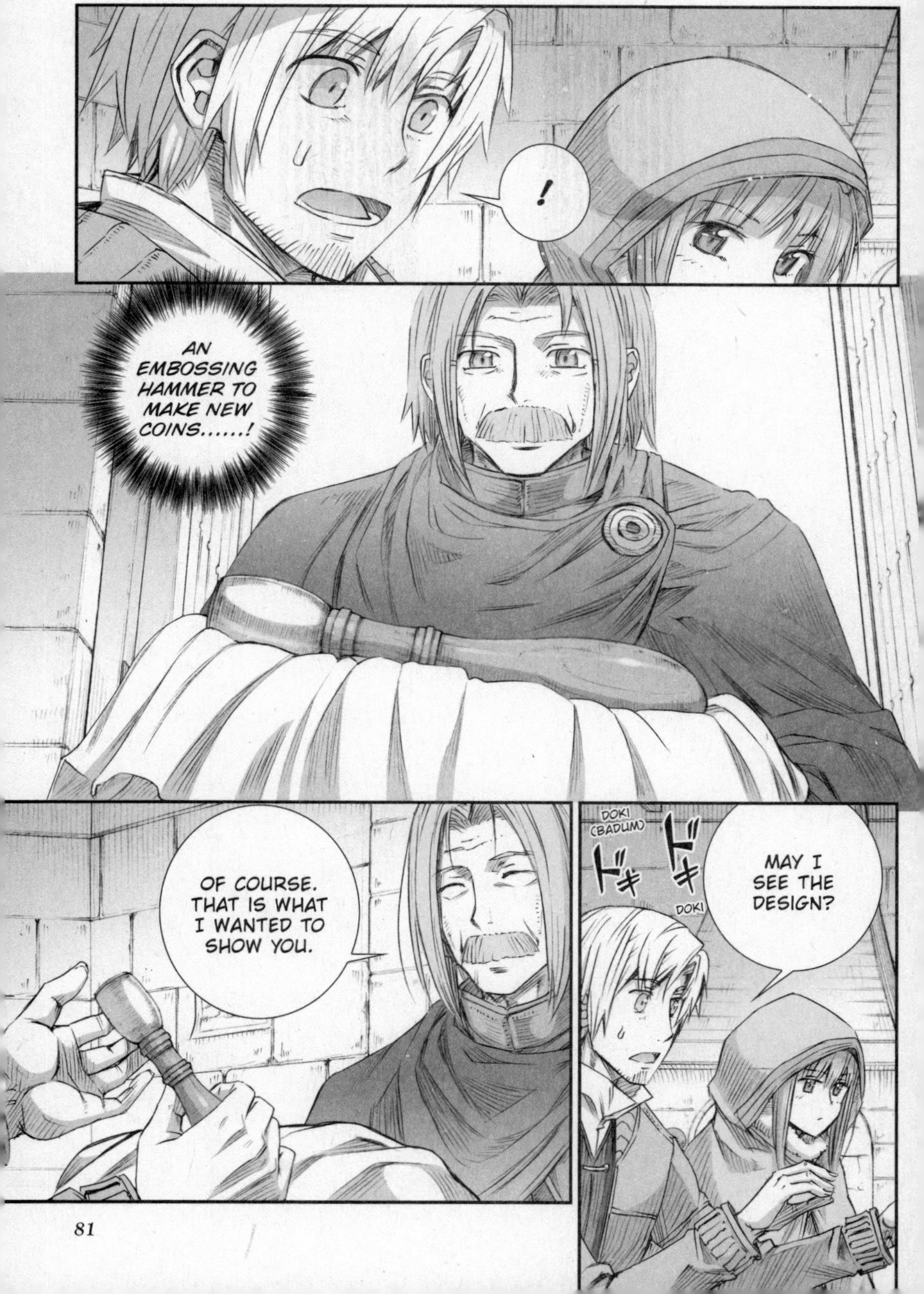
!
AN EMBOSSING HAMMER TO MAKE NEW COINS......!
DOKI (BADUM)
ドキドキ
DOKI
MAY I SEE THE DESIGN?
OF COURSE. THAT IS WHAT I WANTED TO SHOW YOU.

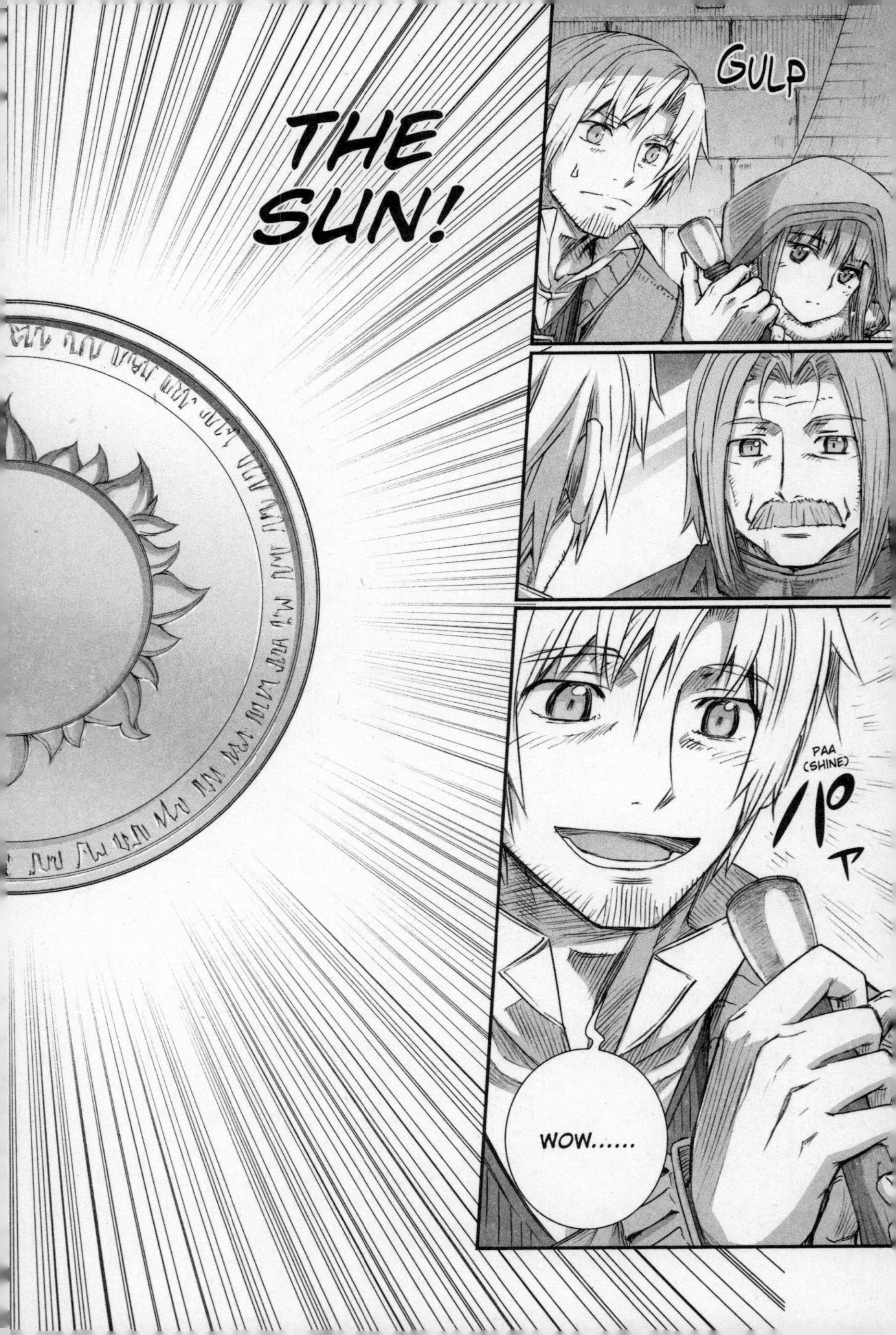
GULP
PAA (SHINE)
WOW......
THE SUN!

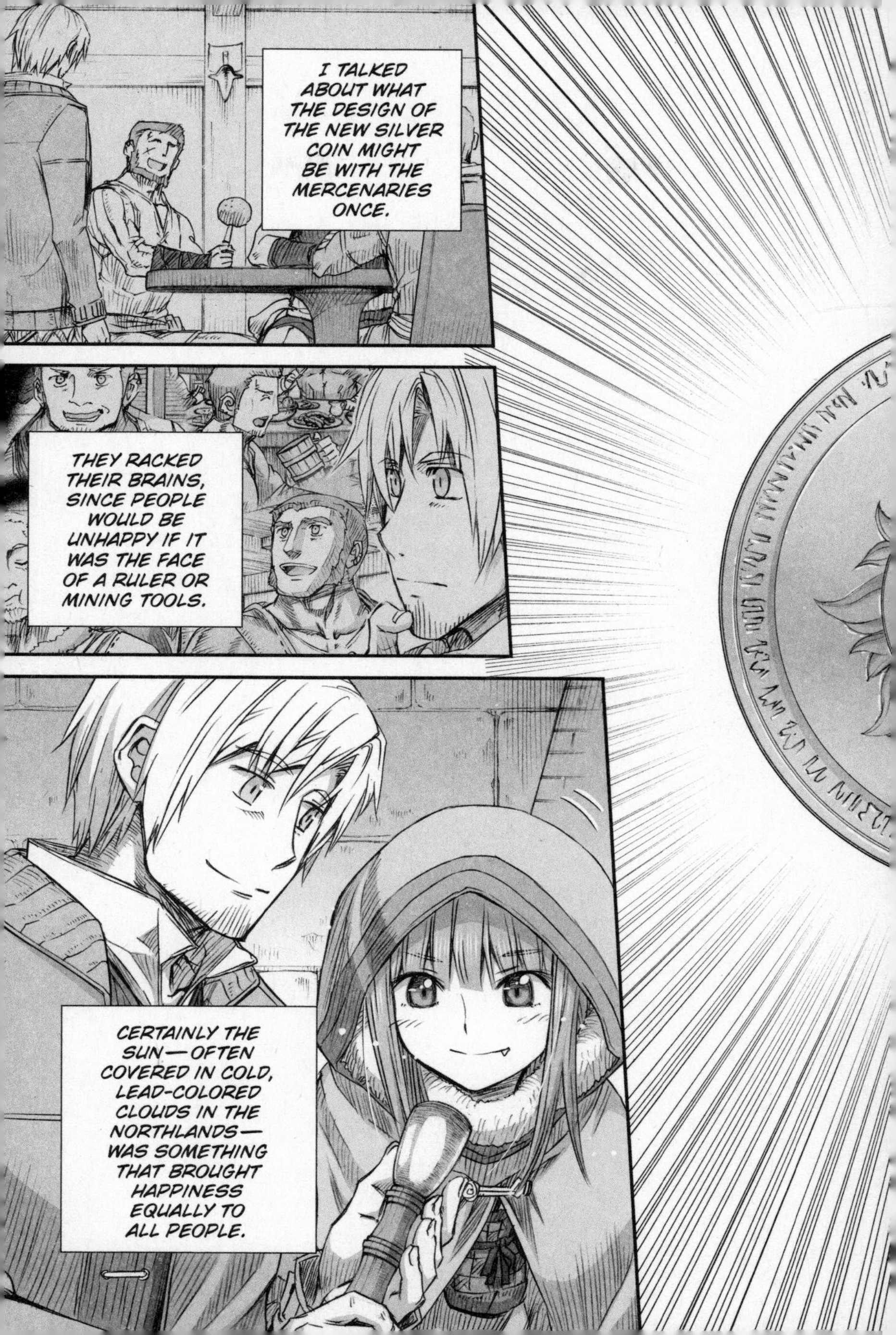
I TALKED ABOUT WHAT THE DESIGN OF THE NEW SILVER COIN MIGHT BE WITH THE MERCENARIES ONCE.
THEY RACKED THEIR BRAINS, SINCE PEOPLE WOULD BE UNHAPPY IF IT WAS THE FACE OF A RULER OR MINING TOOLS.
CERTAINLY THE SUN—OFTEN COVERED IN COLD, LEAD-COLORED CLOUDS IN THE NORTHLANDS—WAS SOMETHING THAT BROUGHT HAPPINESS EQUALLY TO ALL PEOPLE.

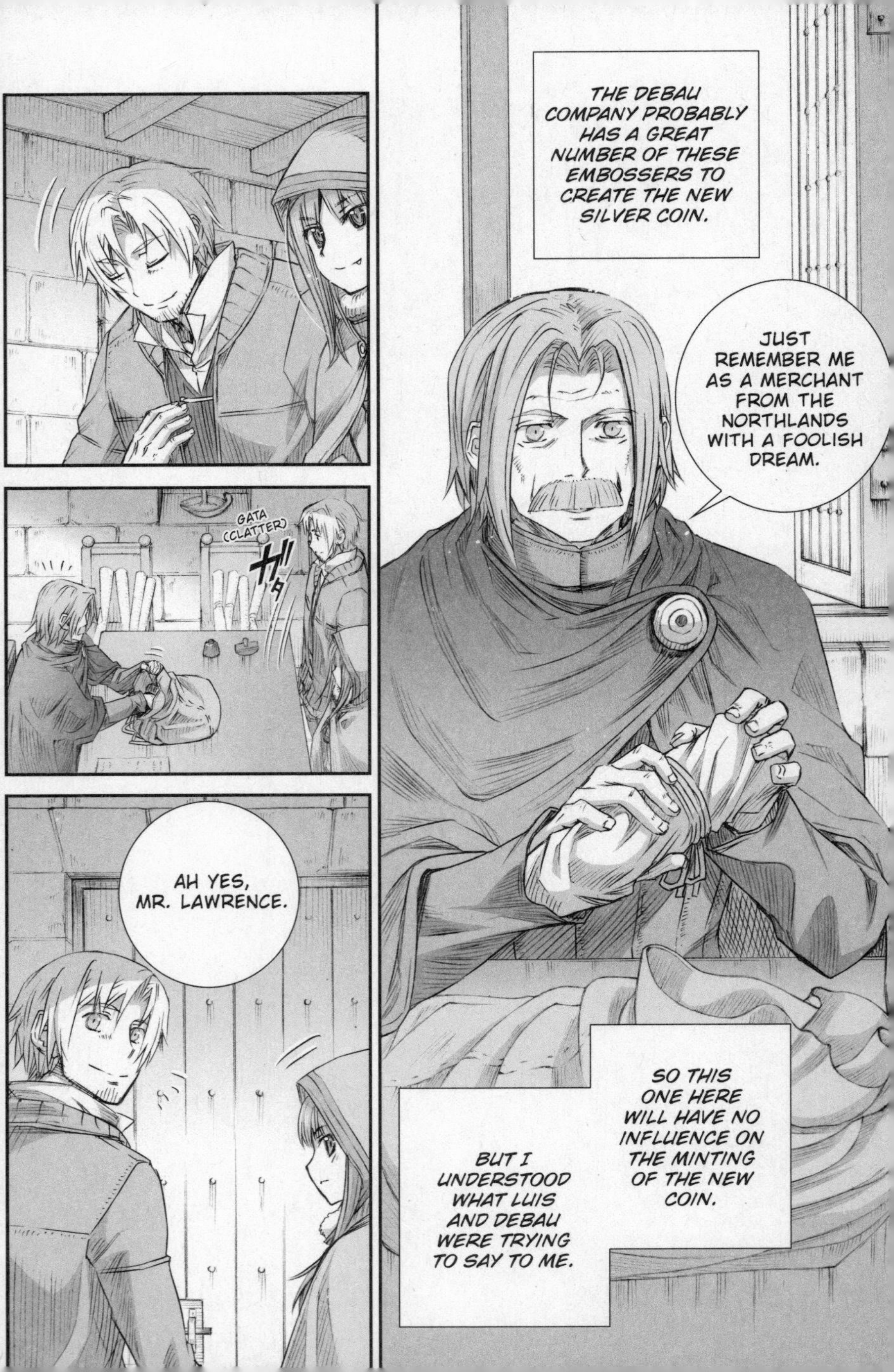
THE DEBAU COMPANY PROBABLY HAS A GREAT NUMBER OF THESE EMBOSSERS TO CREATE THE NEW SILVER COIN.
JUST REMEMBER ME AS A MERCHANT FROM THE NORTHLANDS WITH A FOOLISH DREAM.
SO THIS ONE HERE WILL HAVE NO INFLUENCE ON THE MINTING OF THE NEW COIN.
BUT I UNDERSTOOD WHAT LUIS AND DEBAU WERE TRYING TO SAY TO ME.
GATA (CLATTER)
AH YES, MR. LAWRENCE.

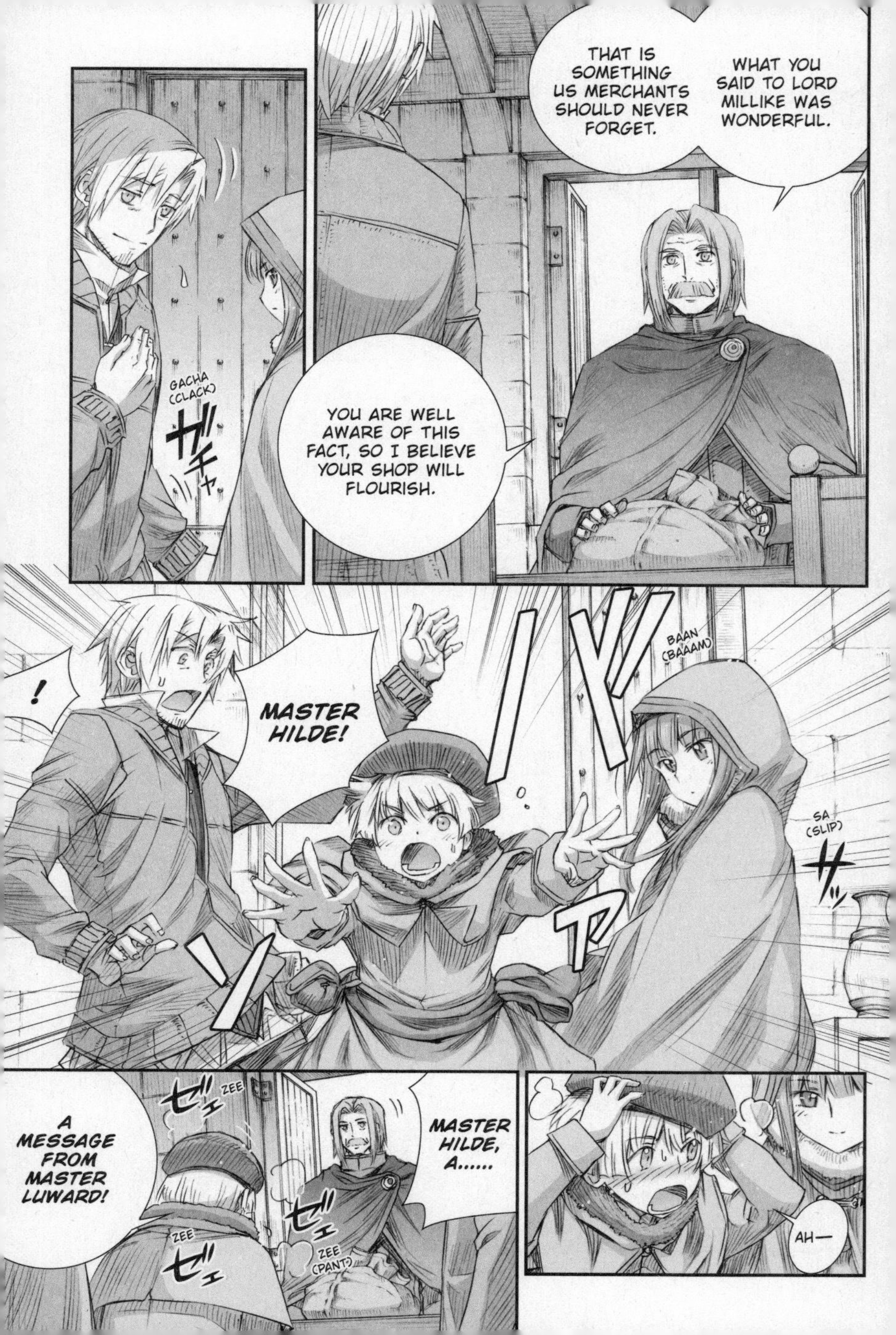
WHAT YOU SAID TO LORD MILLIKE WAS WONDERFUL.
THAT IS SOMETHING US MERCHANTS SHOULD NEVER FORGET.
YOU ARE WELL AWARE OF THIS FACT, SO I BELIEVE YOUR SHOP WILL FLOURISH.
GACHA (CLACK)
BAAN (BAAM)
SA (SLIP)
MASTER HILDE!
!
AH—
MASTER HILDE, A......
ZEE
A MESSAGE FROM MASTER LUWARD!
ZEE
ZEE (PANT)

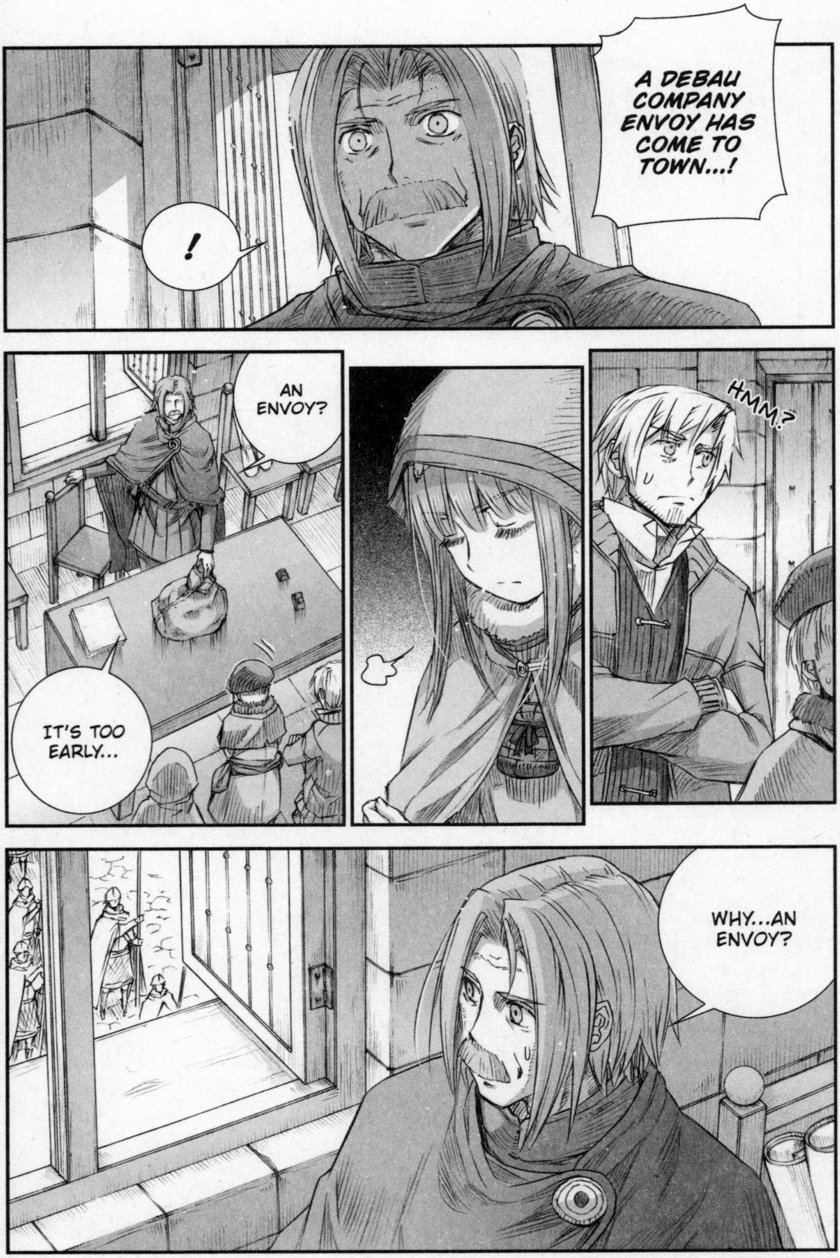
A DEBAU COMPANY ENVOY HAS COME TO TOWN...!
!
HMM?
AN ENVOY?
IT'S TOO EARLY...
WHY...AN ENVOY?

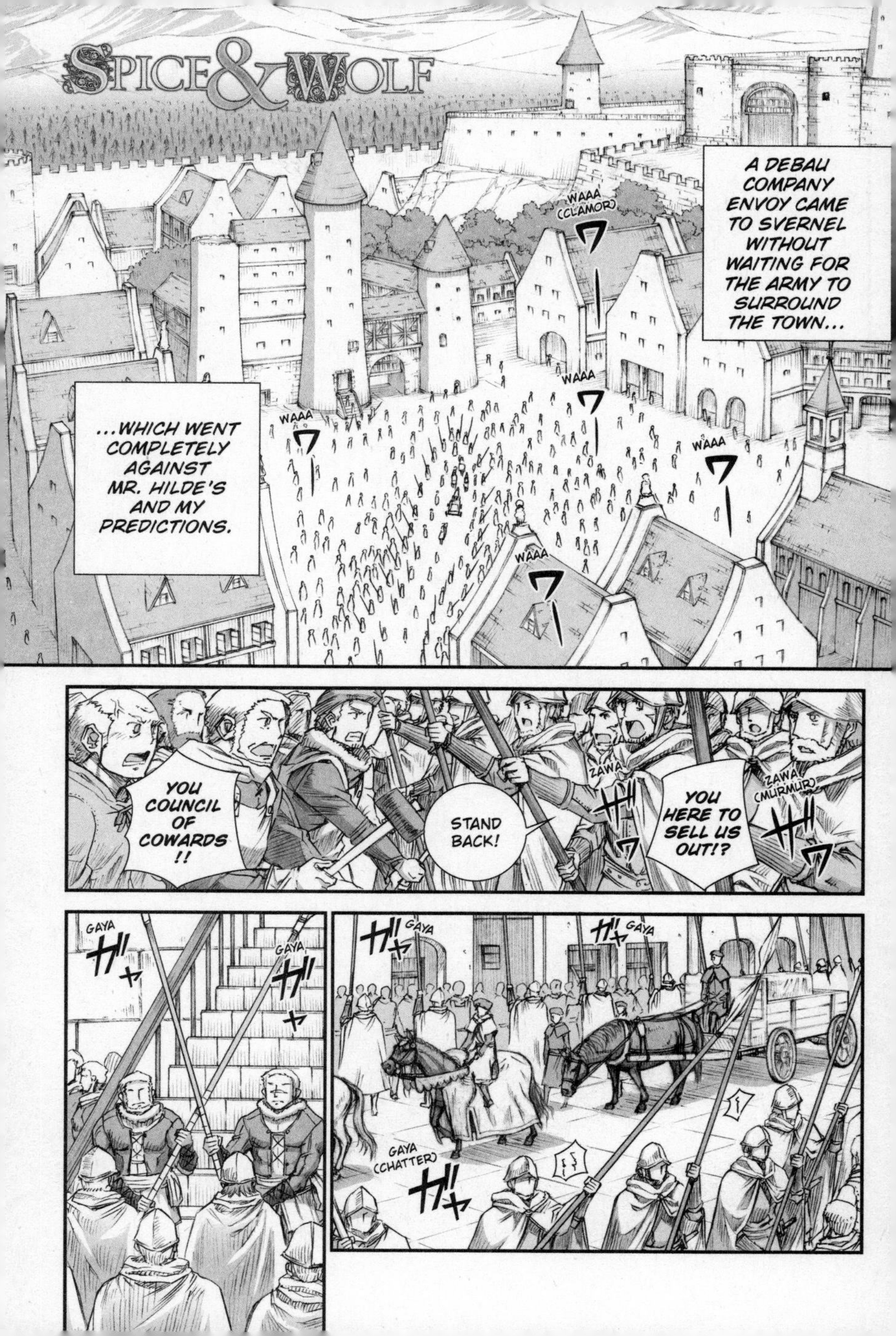
SPICE & WOLF
A DEBAU COMPANY ENVOY CAME TO SVERNEL WITHOUT WAITING FOR THE ARMY TO SURROUND THE TOWN...
WAAA (CLAMOR)
WAAA
WAAA
WAAA
WAAA
...WHICH WENT COMPLETELY AGAINST MR. HILDE'S AND MY PREDICTIONS.
ZAWA (MURMUR)
YOU HERE TO SELL US OUT!?
ZAWA
STAND BACK!
YOU COUNCIL OF COWARDS!!
GAYA
GAYA
GAYA (CHATTER)
GAYA
GAYA

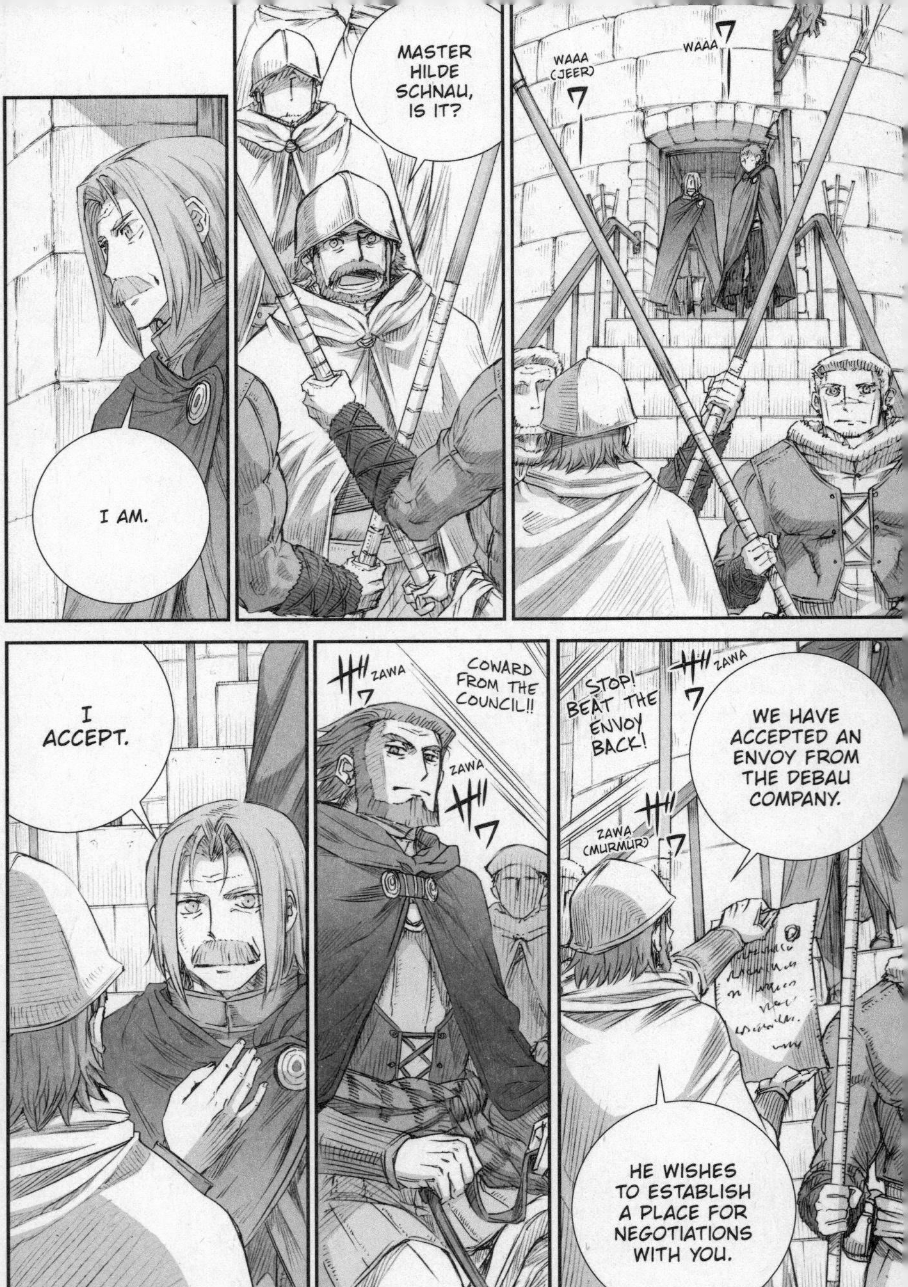
WAAA
WAAA (JEER)
MASTER HILDE SCHNAU, IS IT?
I AM.
ZAWA
WE HAVE ACCEPTED AN ENVOY FROM THE DEBAU COMPANY.
STOP! BEAT THE ENVOY BACK!
ZAWA (MURMUR)
HE WISHES TO ESTABLISH A PLACE FOR NEGOTIATIONS WITH YOU.
COWARD FROM THE COUNCIL!!
ZAWA
ZAWA
I ACCEPT.

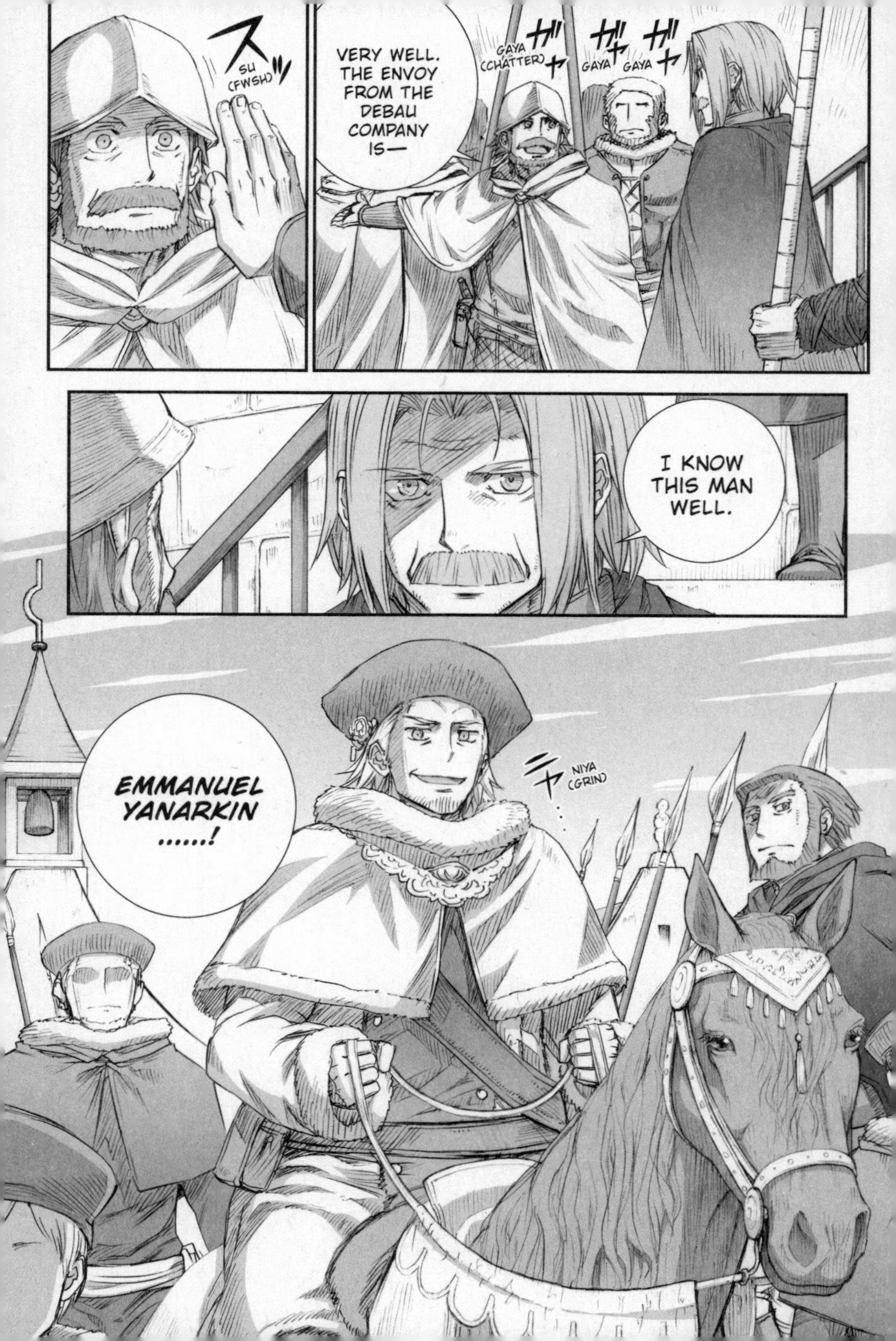
ガヤ GAYA
ガヤ GAYA
ガヤ GAYA (CHATTER)
VERY WELL. THE ENVOY FROM THE DEBAU COMPANY IS—
ス SU (FWSH)
I KNOW THIS MAN WELL.
EMMANUEL YANARKIN ......!
ニヤ NIYA (GRIN)

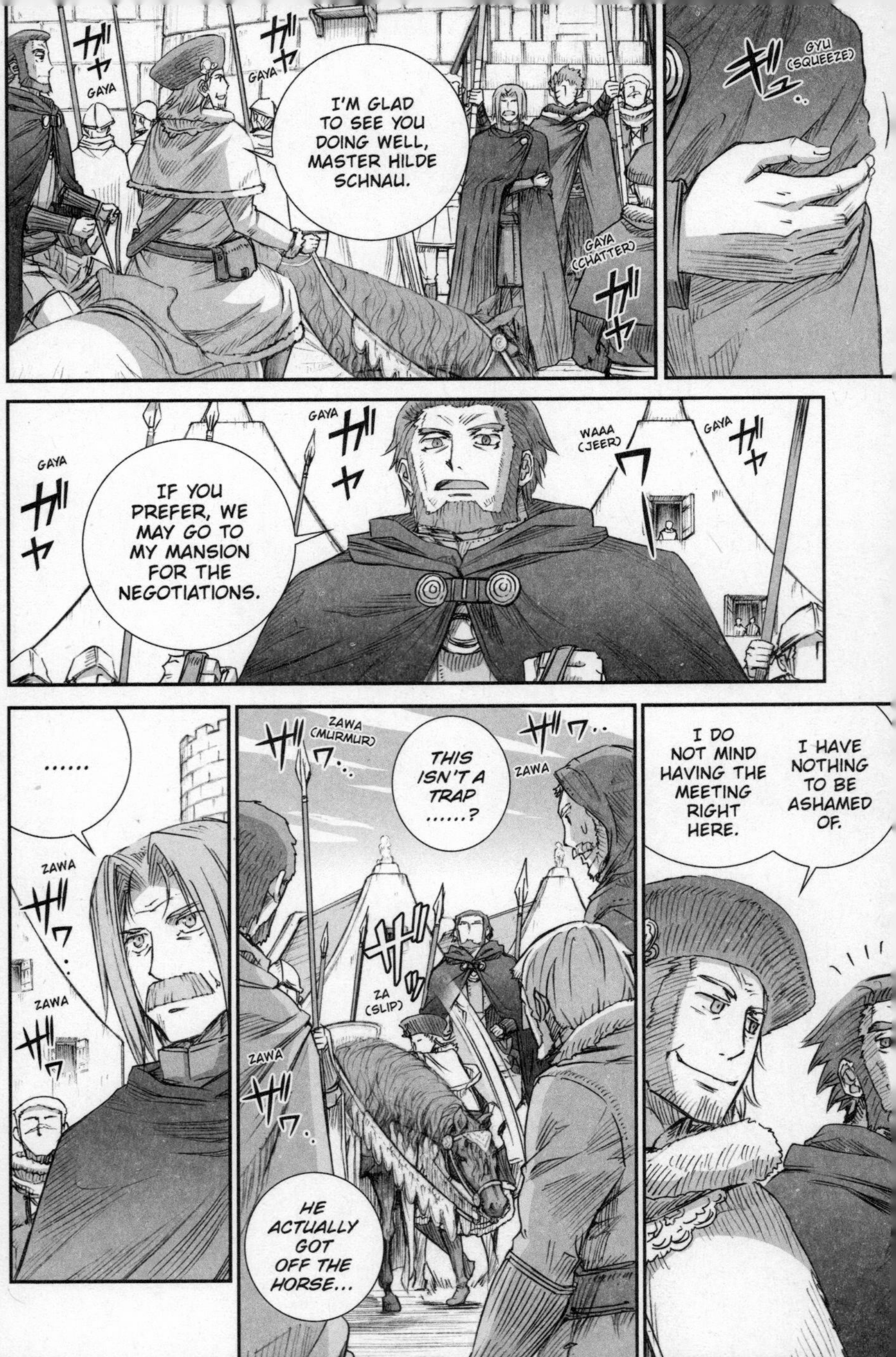

ギュ
GYU (SQUEEZE)
ガヤ
GAYA (CHATTER)
ガヤ
GAYA
I'M GLAD TO SEE YOU DOING WELL, MASTER HILDE SCHNAU.
ガヤ
GAYA
ガヤ
GAYA
ワー
WAAA (JEER)
ガヤ
GAYA
IF YOU PREFER, WE MAY GO TO MY MANSION FOR THE NEGOTIATIONS.
ガヤ
GAYA
I HAVE NOTHING TO BE ASHAMED OF.
I DO NOT MIND HAVING THE MEETING RIGHT HERE.
ザワ..
ZAWA
THIS ISN'T A TRAP ......?
ザワ..
ZAWA (MURMUR)
ザッ
ZA (SLIP)
ザワ..
ZAWA
HE ACTUALLY GOT OFF THE HORSE...
......
ザワ..
ZAWA
ザワ
ZAWA

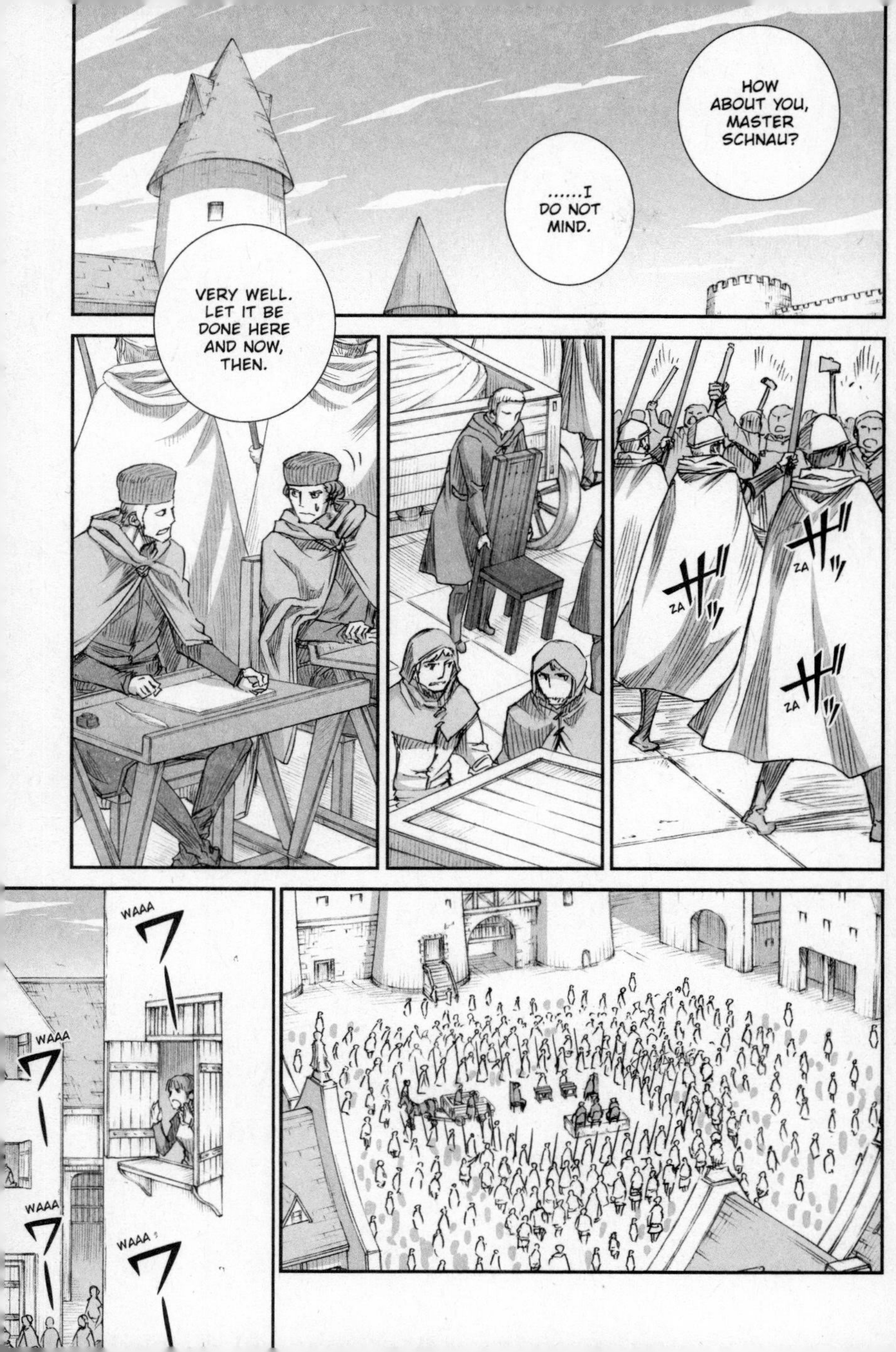
HOW ABOUT YOU, MASTER SCHNAU?
......I DO NOT MIND.
VERY WELL. LET IT BE DONE HERE AND NOW, THEN.
ZA
ZA
ZA
WAAA
WAAA
WAAA
WAAA

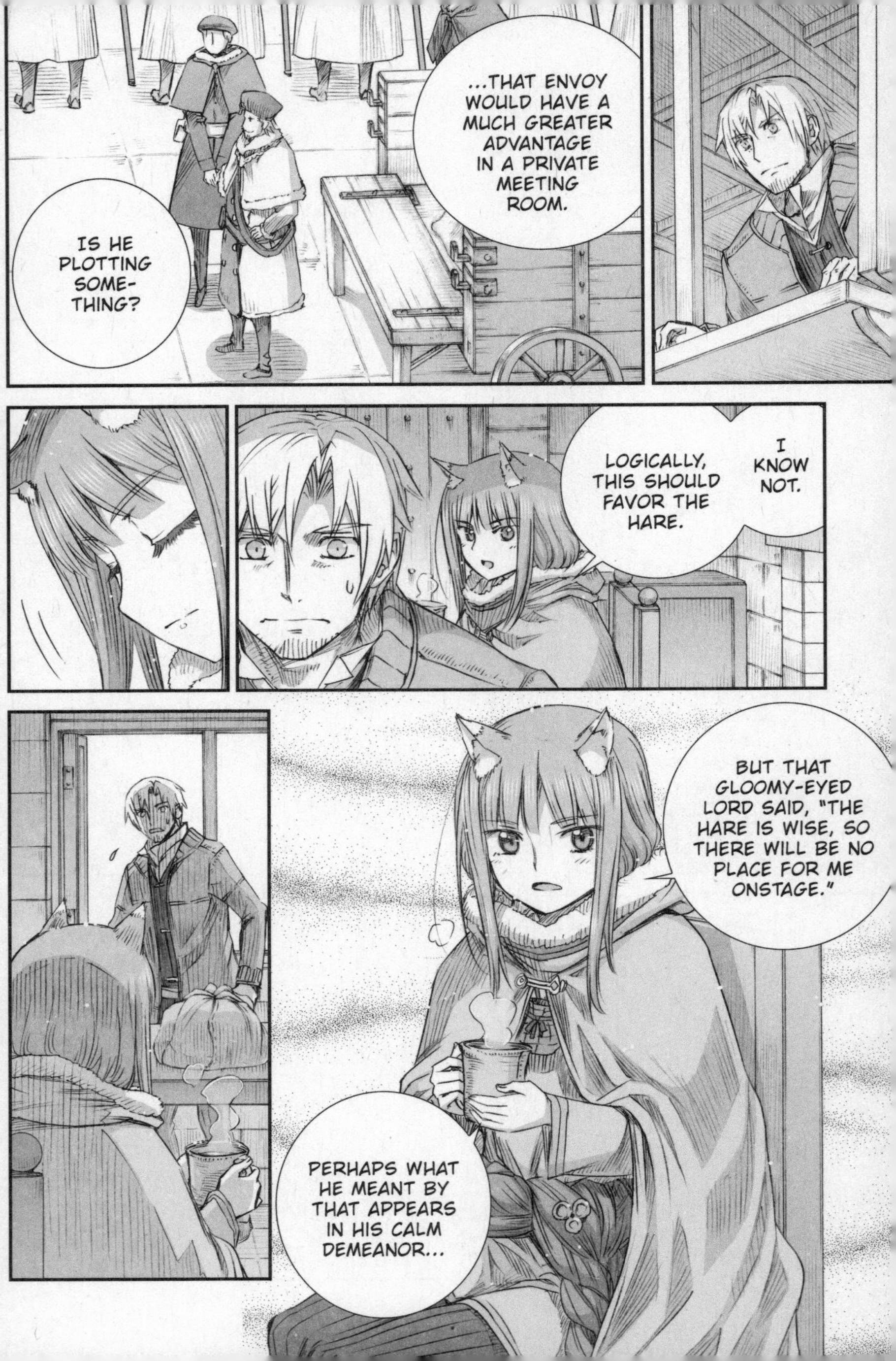
...THAT ENVOY WOULD HAVE A MUCH GREATER ADVANTAGE IN A PRIVATE MEETING ROOM.
IS HE PLOTTING SOME-THING?
I KNOW NOT.
LOGICALLY, THIS SHOULD FAVOR THE HARE.
BUT THAT GLOOMY-EYED LORD SAID, "THE HARE IS WISE, SO THERE WILL BE NO PLACE FOR ME ONSTAGE."
PERHAPS WHAT HE MEANT BY THAT APPEARS IN HIS CALM DEMEANOR...

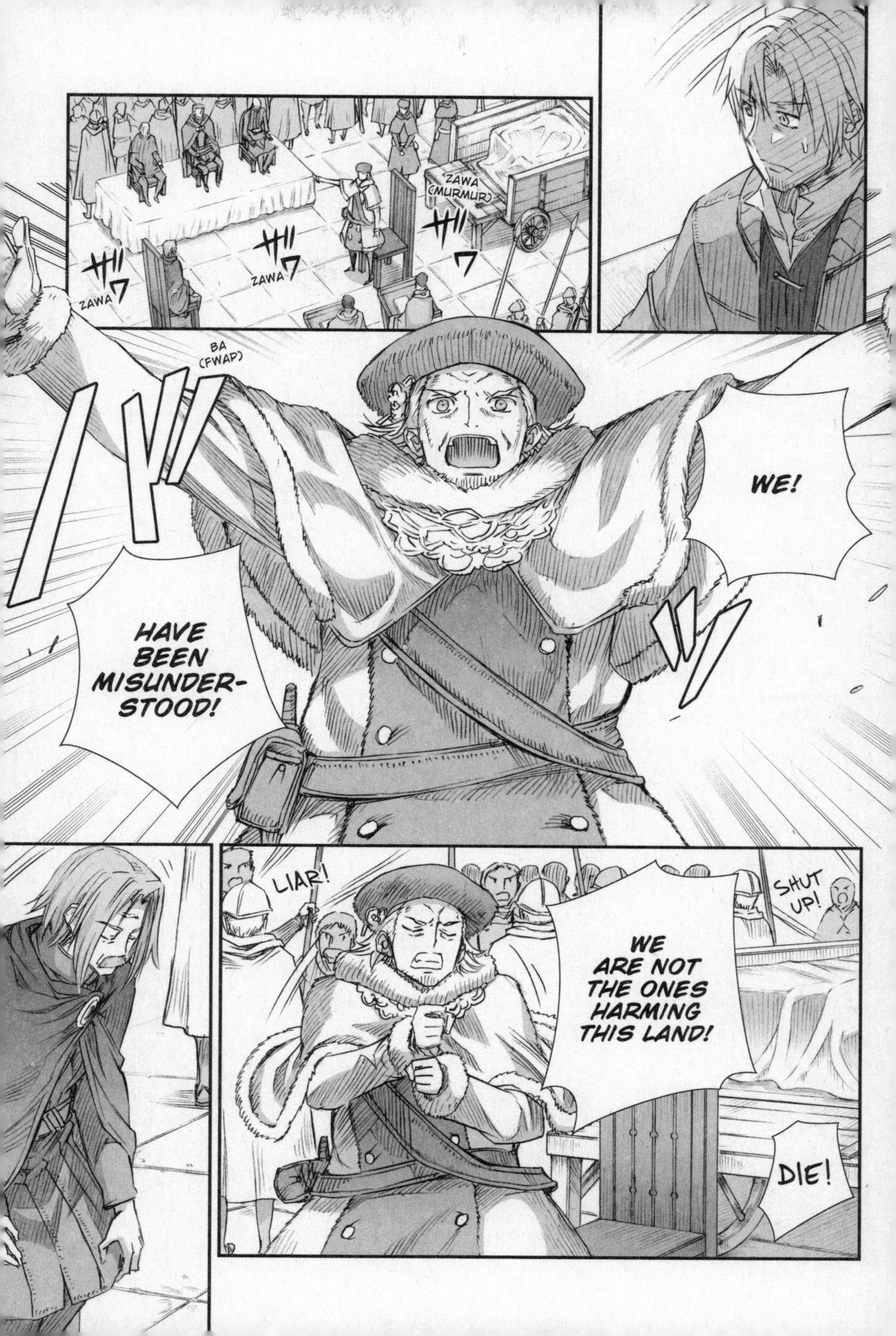ZAWA (MURMUR)
ZAWA
ZAWA
BA (FWAP)
WE!
HAVE BEEN MISUNDER-STOOD!
SHUT UP!
WE ARE NOT THE ONES HARMING THIS LAND!
DIE!
LIAR!

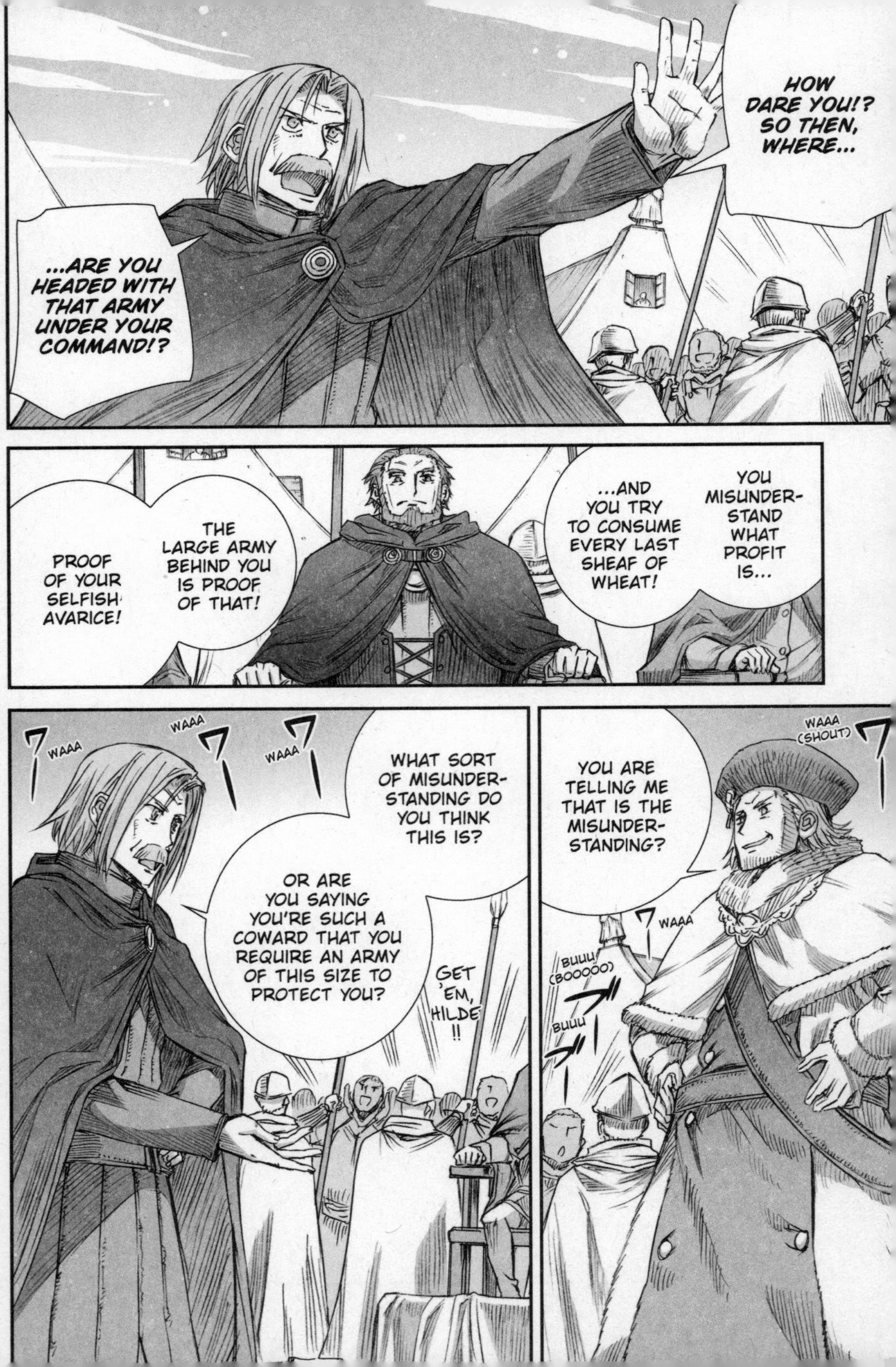
HOW DARE YOU!? SO THEN, WHERE...
...ARE YOU HEADED WITH THAT ARMY UNDER YOUR COMMAND!?
YOU MISUNDERSTAND WHAT PROFIT IS...
...AND YOU TRY TO CONSUME EVERY LAST SHEAF OF WHEAT!
THE LARGE ARMY BEHIND YOU IS PROOF OF THAT!
PROOF OF YOUR SELFISH AVARICE!
WAAA (SHOUT)
YOU ARE TELLING ME THAT IS THE MISUNDERSTANDING?
WAAA
BUUU (BOOOOO)
BUUU
WHAT SORT OF MISUNDERSTANDING DO YOU THINK THIS IS?
WAAA
WAAA
WAAA
OR ARE YOU SAYING YOU'RE SUCH A COWARD THAT YOU REQUIRE AN ARMY OF THIS SIZE TO PROTECT YOU?
GET 'EM, HILDE!!

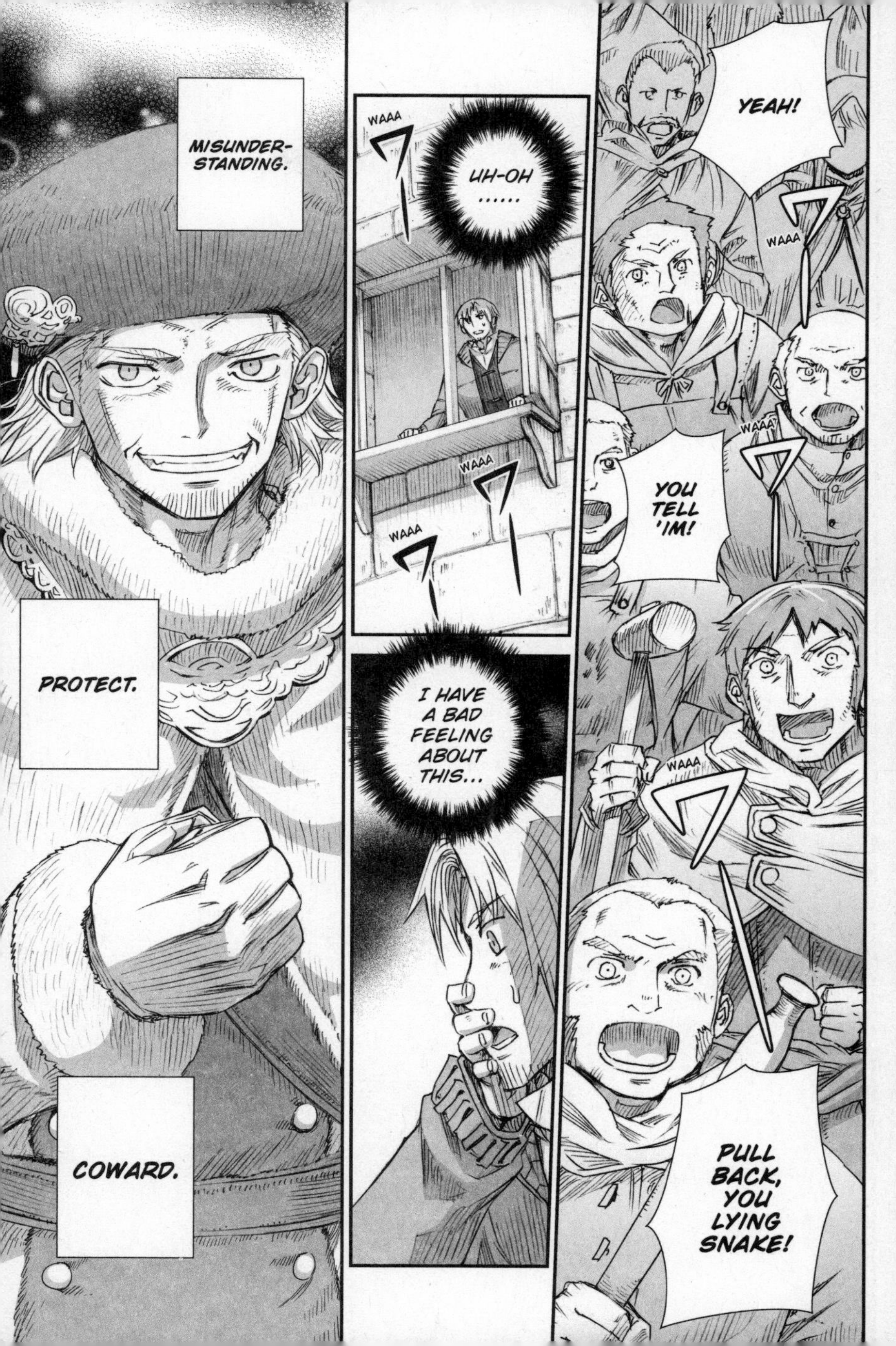
YEAH!
WAAA
WAAA
YOU TELL 'IM!
WAAA
PULL BACK, YOU LYING SNAKE!
WAAA
UH-OH ......
WAAA
WAAA
I HAVE A BAD FEELING ABOUT THIS...
MISUNDER-STANDING.
PROTECT.
COWARD.

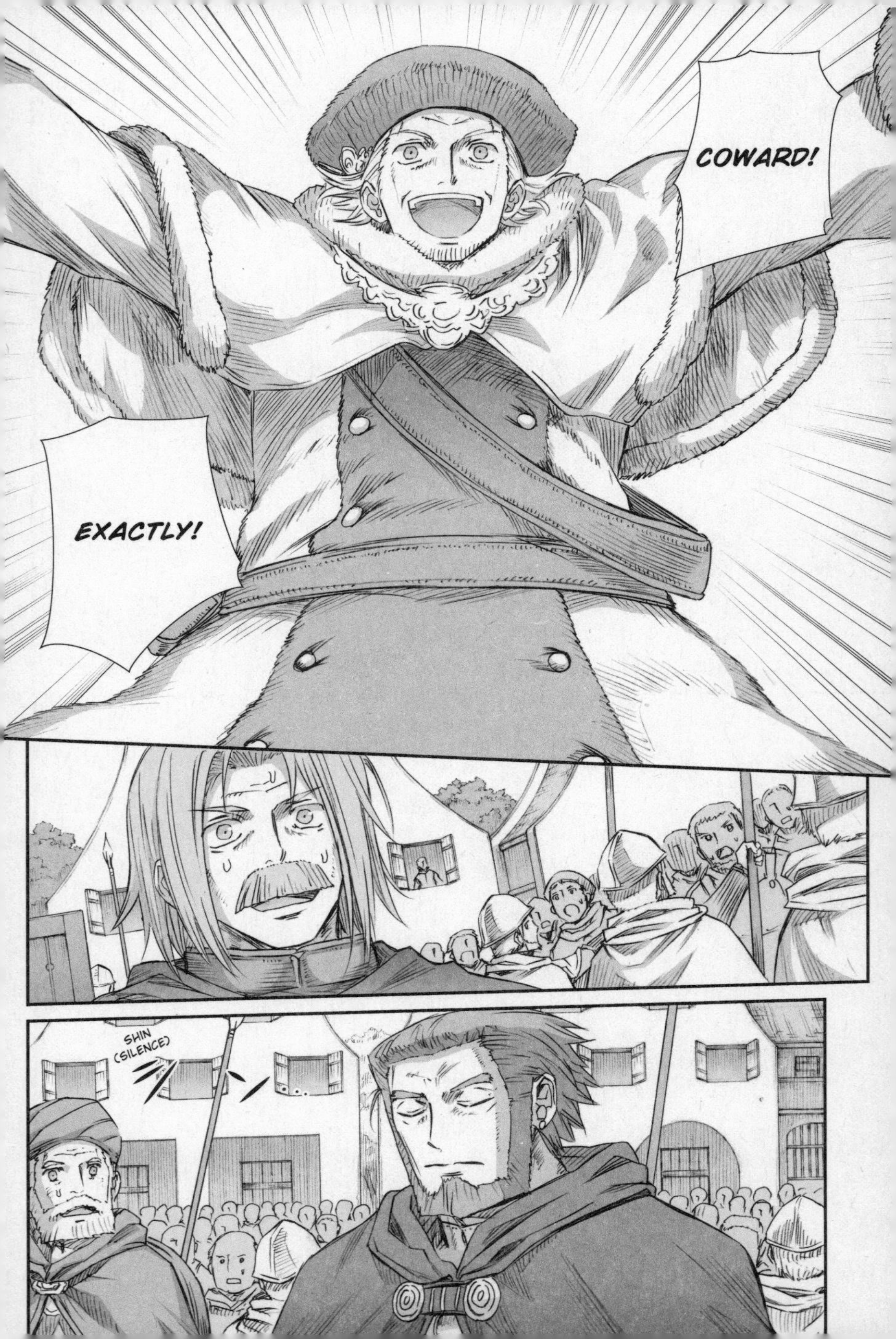
COWARD!
EXACTLY!
SHIN (SILENCE)

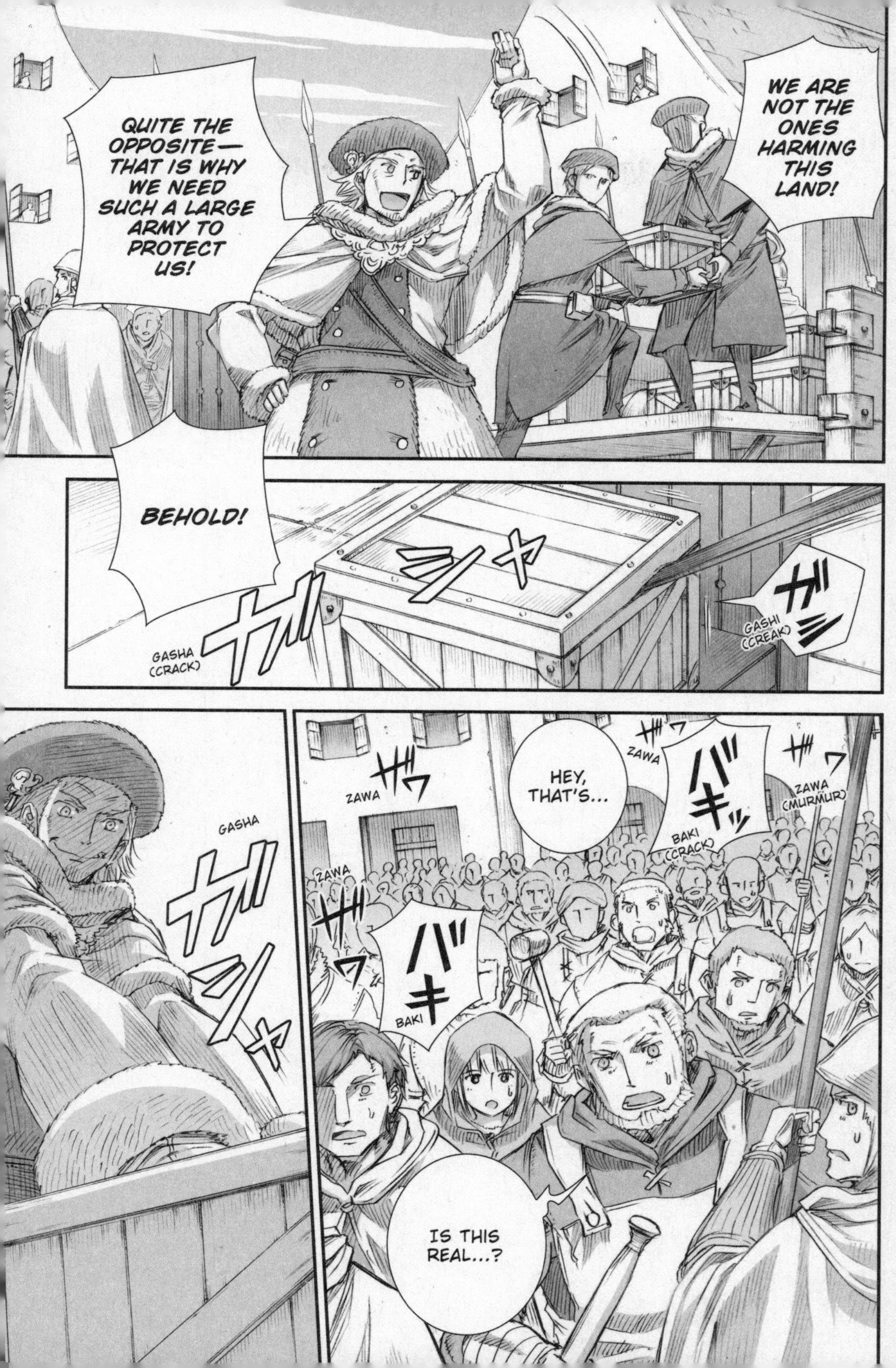
WE ARE NOT THE ONES HARMING THIS LAND!
QUITE THE OPPOSITE—THAT IS WHY WE NEED SUCH A LARGE ARMY TO PROTECT US!
BEHOLD!
GASHI (CREAK)
GASHA (CRACK)
ZAWA (MURMUR)
BAKI (CRACK)
ZAWA
HEY, THAT'S...
ZAWA
ZAWA
BAKI
IS THIS REAL...?
GASHA

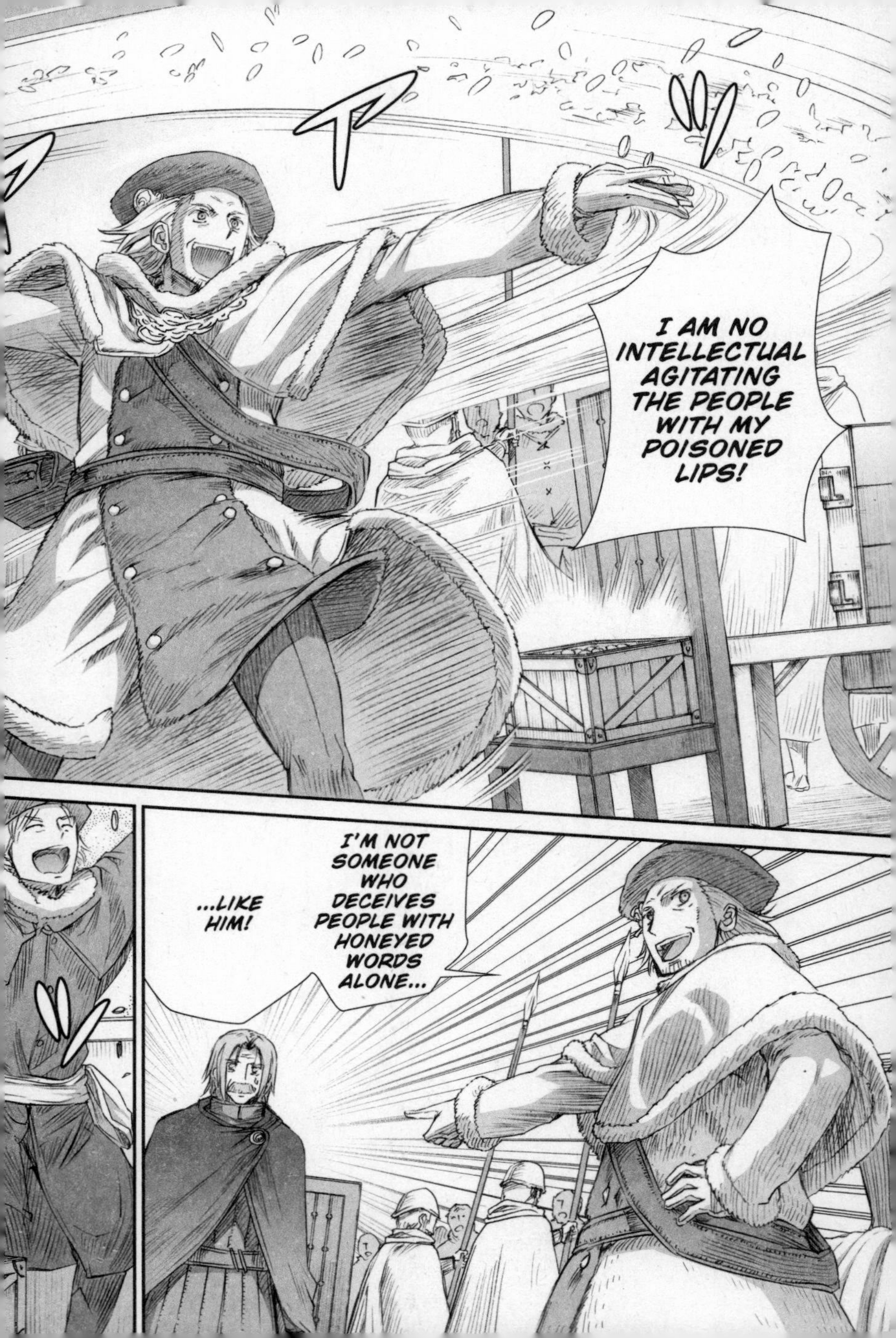
I AM NO INTELLECTUAL AGITATING THE PEOPLE WITH MY POISONED LIPS!
I'M NOT SOMEONE WHO DECEIVES PEOPLE WITH HONEYED WORDS ALONE...
...LIKE HIM!

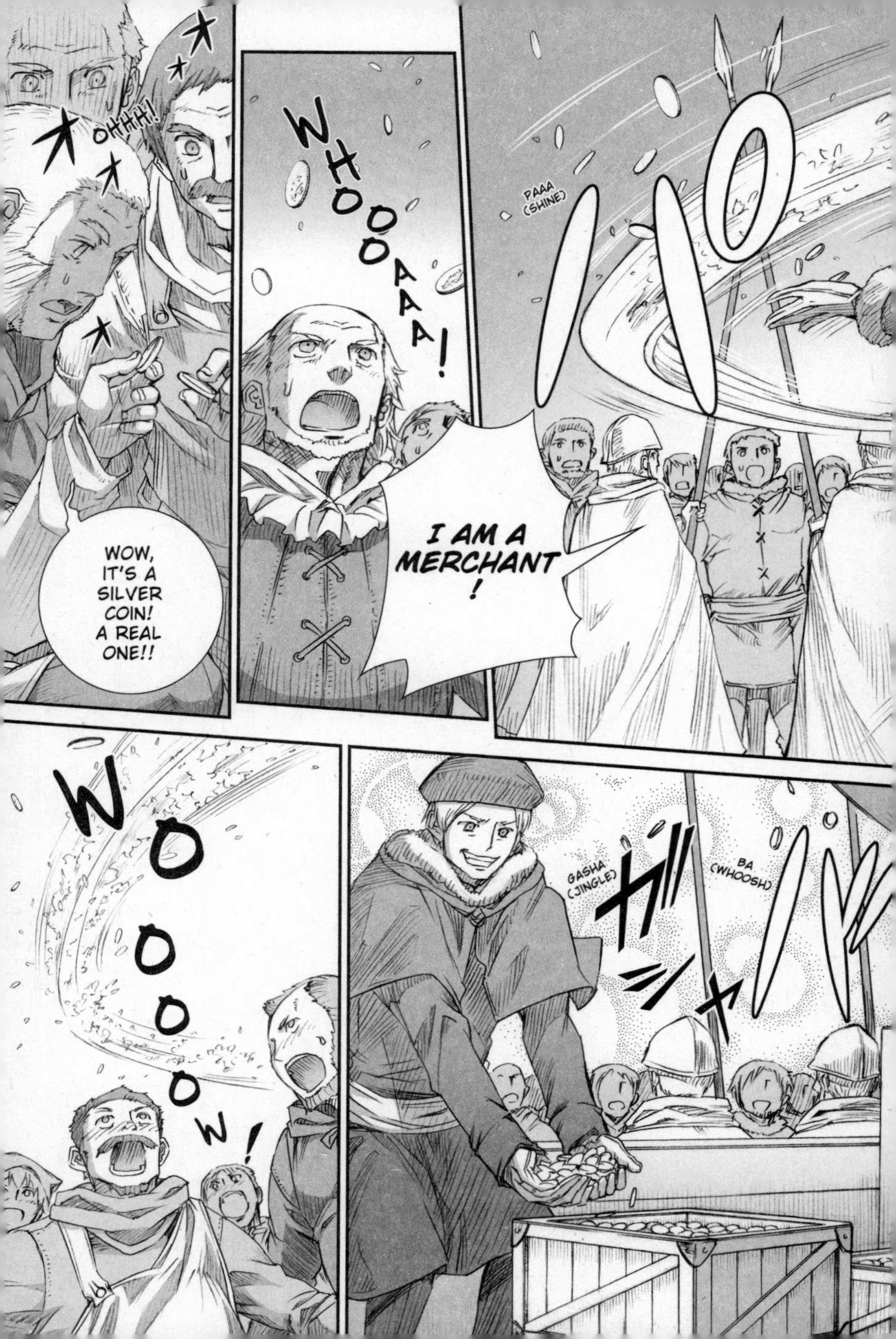
PAAA (SHINE)
I AM A MERCHANT!
WHOOOAAA!
OHHH!
WOW, IT'S A SILVER COIN! A REAL ONE!!
GASHA (JINGLE)
BA (WHOOSH)
WOOOOOW!

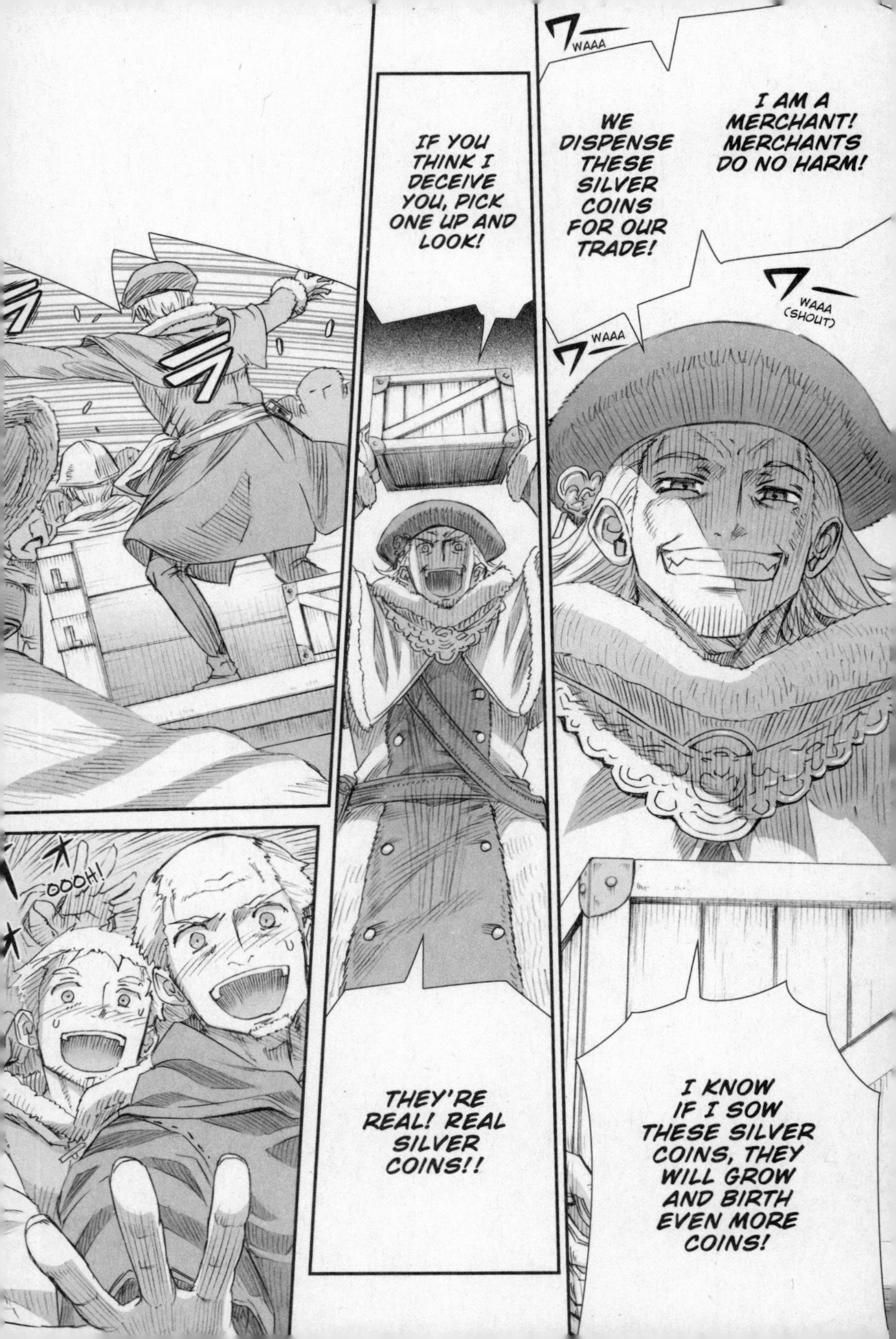
WAAA
I AM A MERCHANT! MERCHANTS DO NO HARM!
WE DISPENSE THESE SILVER COINS FOR OUR TRADE!
WAAA (SHOUT)
WAAA
I KNOW IF I SOW THESE SILVER COINS, THEY WILL GROW AND BIRTH EVEN MORE COINS!
IF YOU THINK I DECEIVE YOU, PICK ONE UP AND LOOK!
THEY'RE REAL! REAL SILVER COINS!!
OOOH!

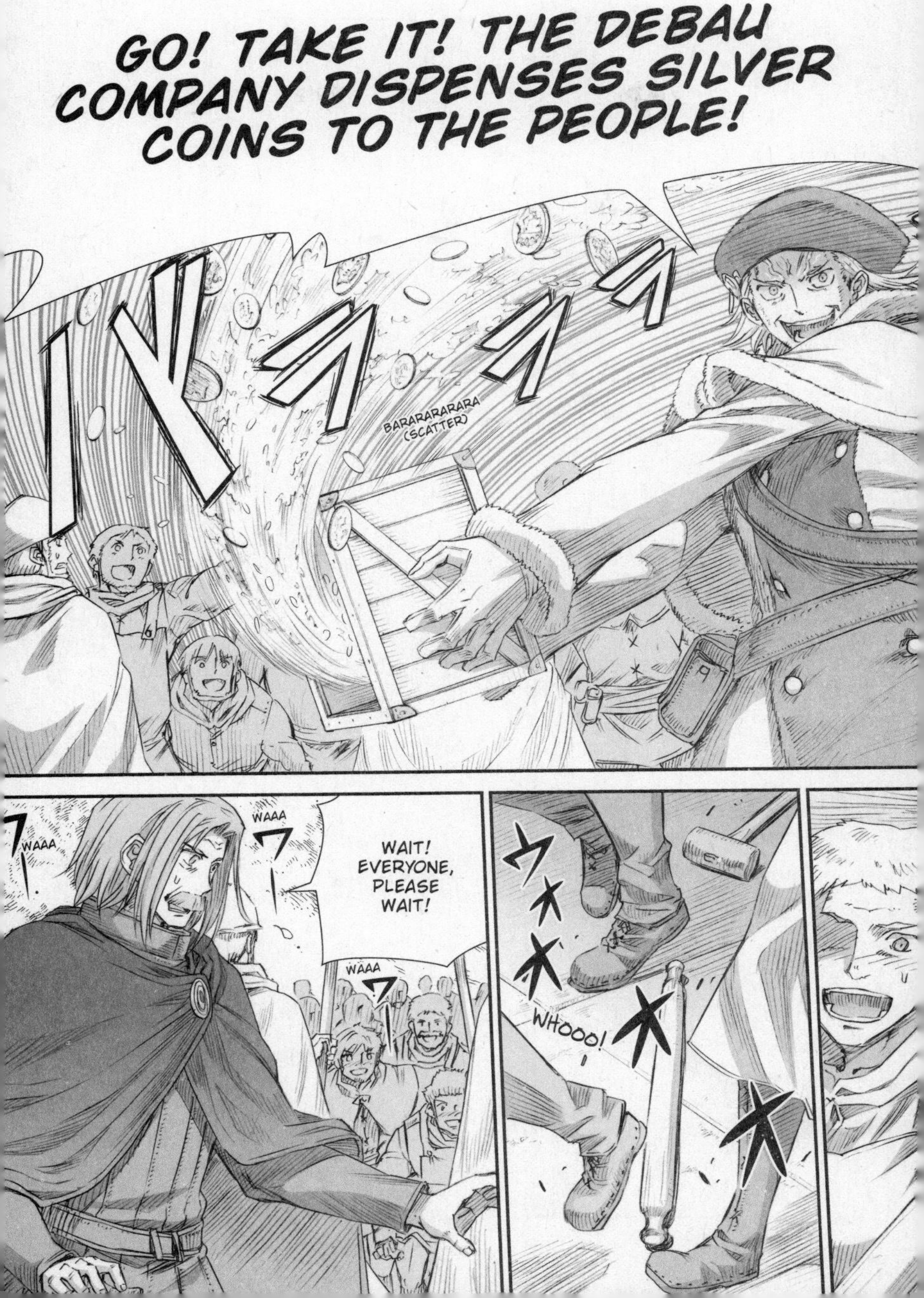
GO! TAKE IT! THE DEBAU COMPANY DISPENSES SILVER COINS TO THE PEOPLE!
BARARARARARA (SCATTER)
WHOOO!
WAAA
WAIT! EVERYONE, PLEASE WAIT!
WAAA
WAAA

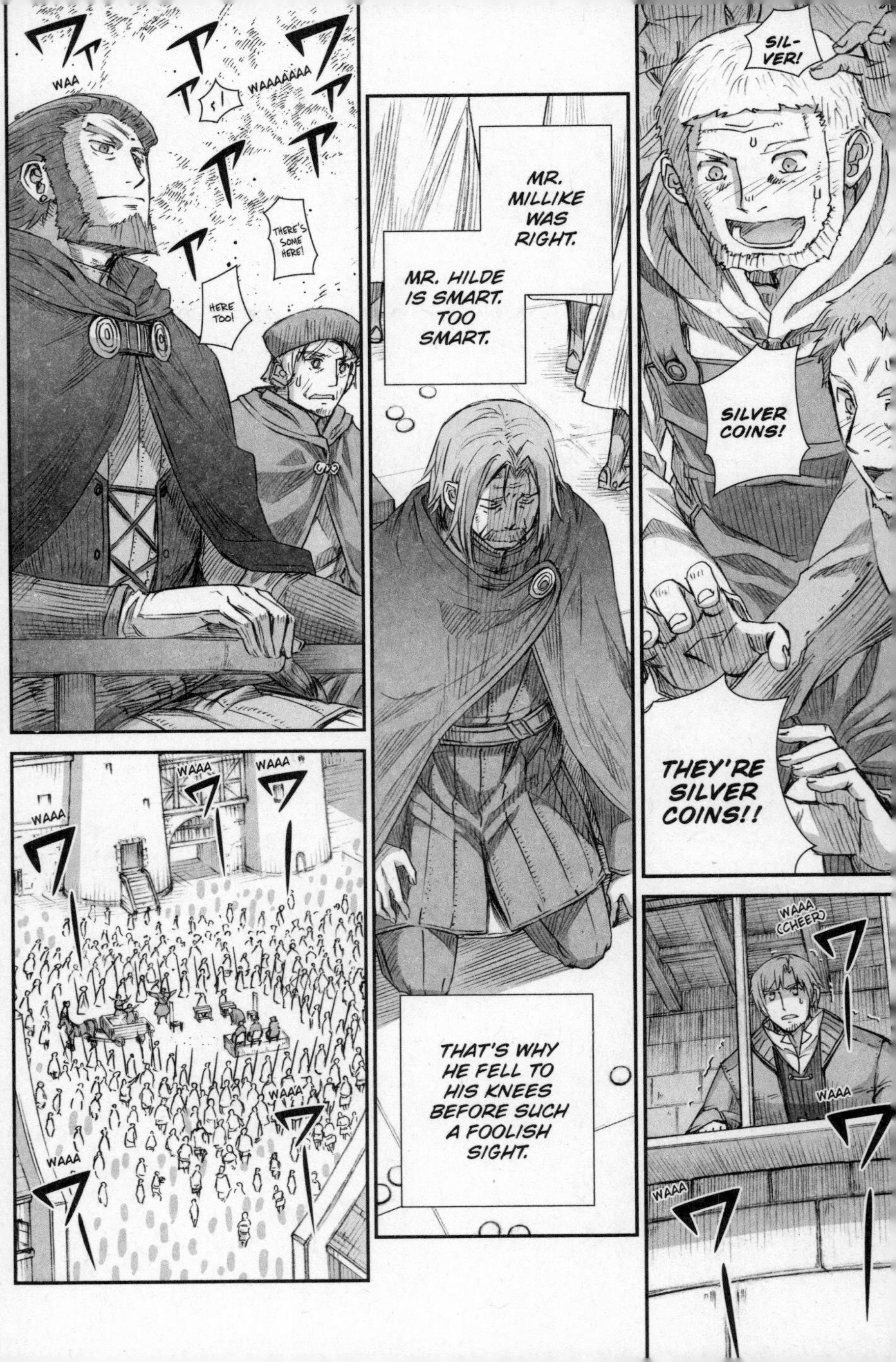
SIL-VER!
SILVER COINS!
THEY'RE SILVER COINS!!
WAAA (CHEER)
WAAA
WAAA
MR. MILLIKE WAS RIGHT.
MR. HILDE IS SMART. TOO SMART.
THAT'S WHY HE FELL TO HIS KNEES BEFORE SUCH A FOOLISH SIGHT.
WAAAAAAA
WAA
THERE'S SOME HERE!
HERE TOO!
WAAA
WAAA
WAAA
WAAA
WAAA

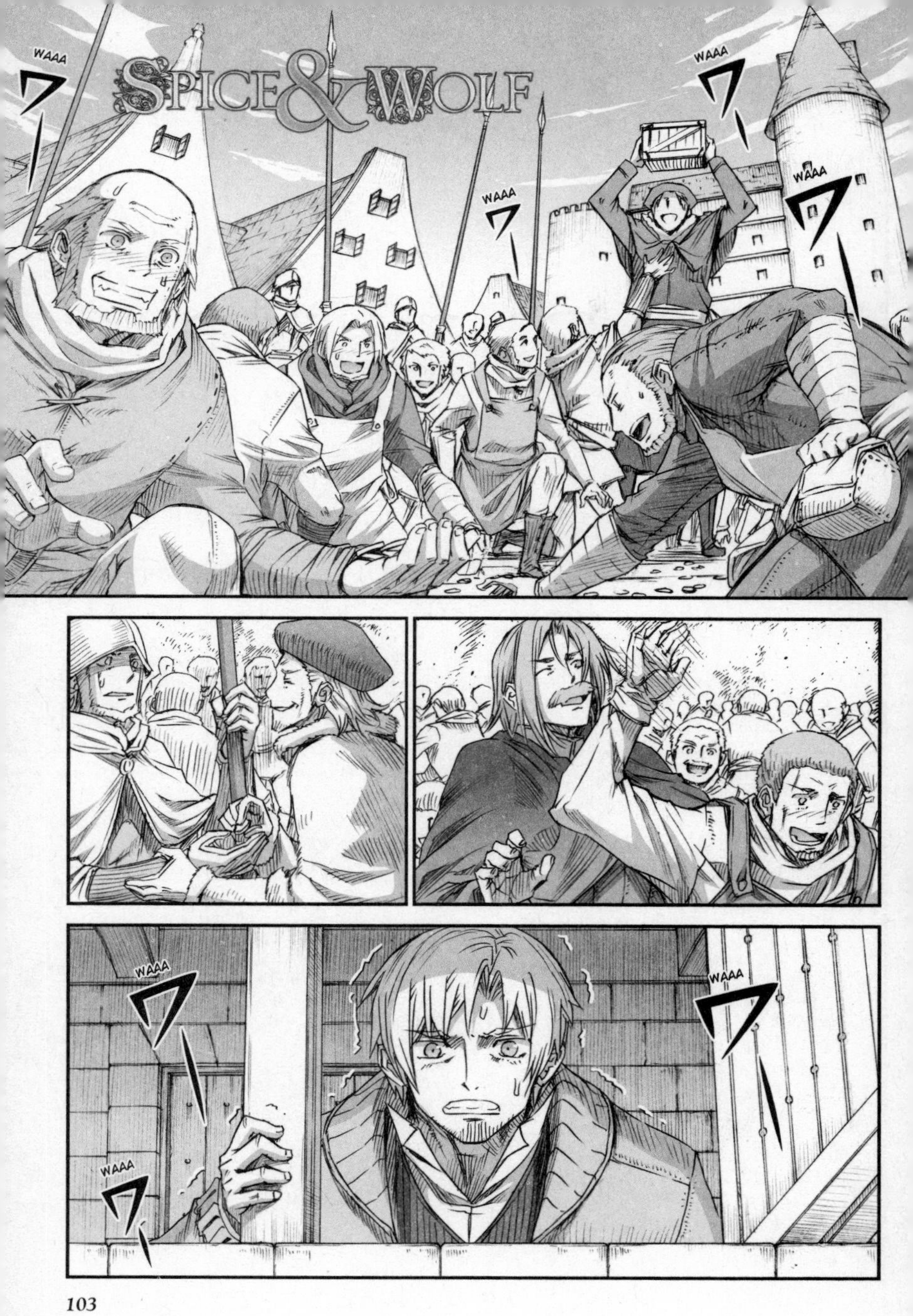

WAAA
WAAA
WAAA
SPICE & WOLF
WAAA
WAAA
WAAA
WAAA

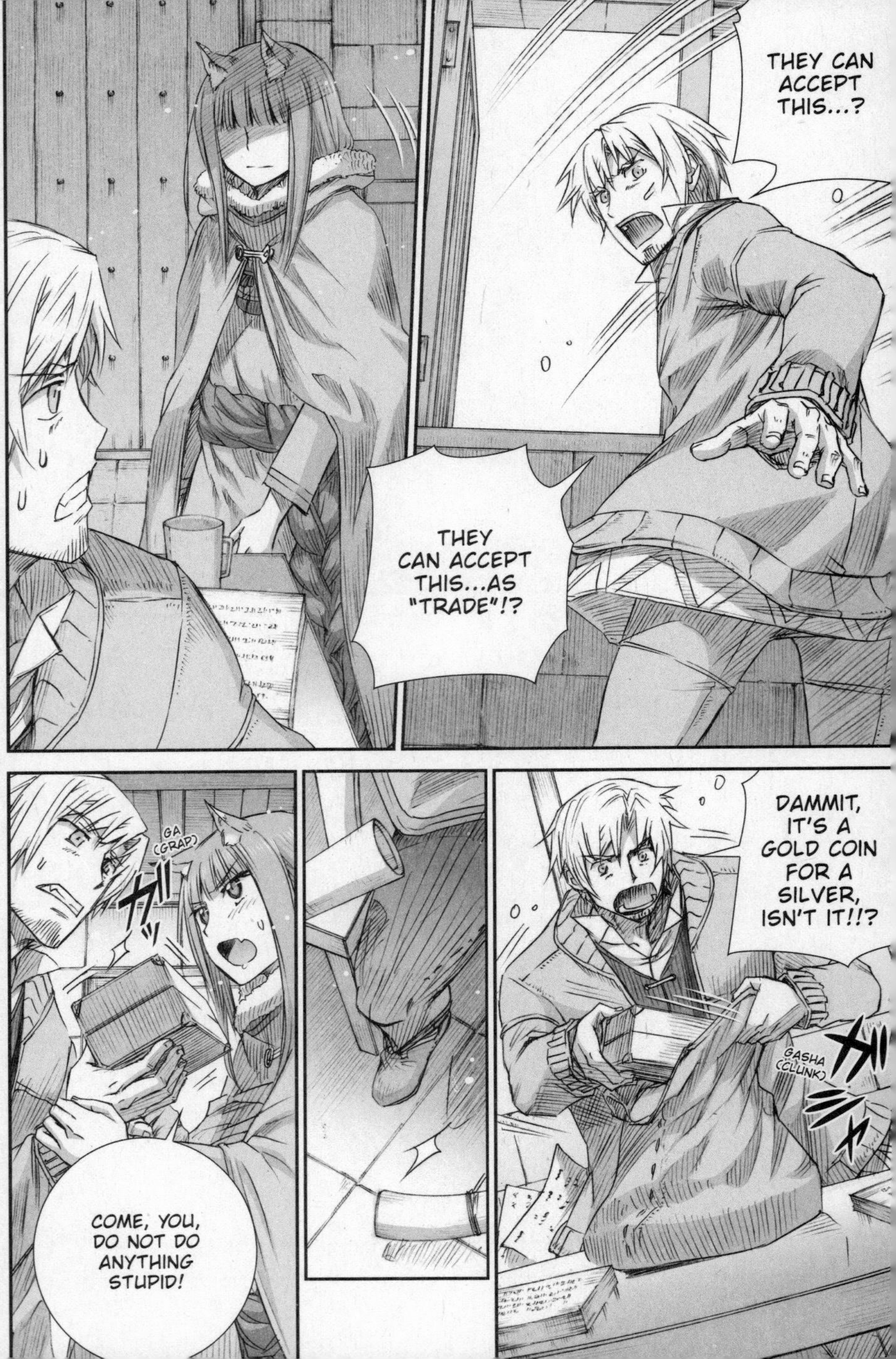
THEY CAN ACCEPT THIS...?
THEY CAN ACCEPT THIS...AS "TRADE"!?
DAMMIT, IT'S A GOLD COIN FOR A SILVER, ISN'T IT!!?
GASHA (CLUNK)
GA (GRAP)
COME, YOU, DO NOT DO ANYTHING STUPID!

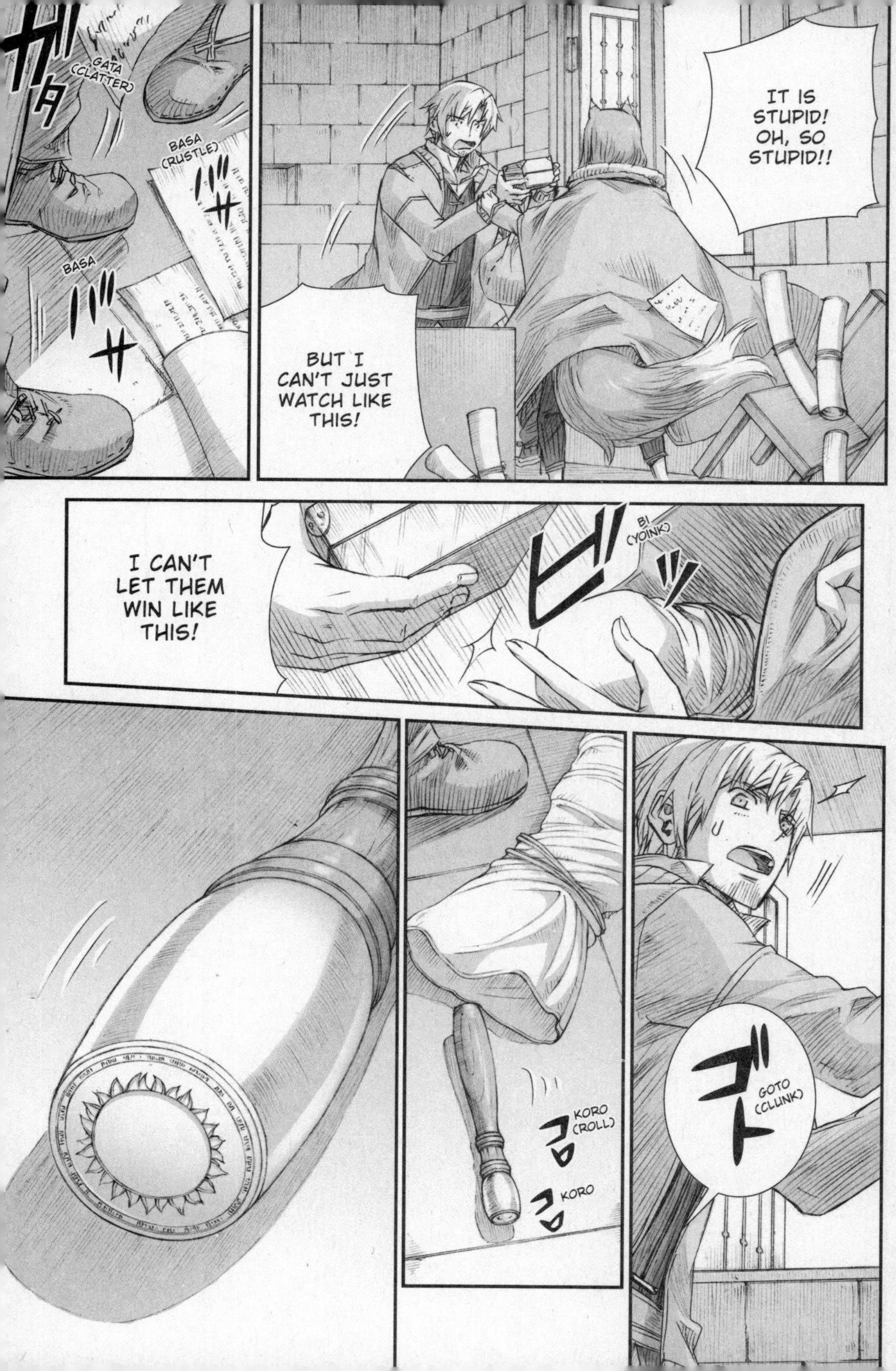
IT IS STUPID! OH, SO STUPID!!
BUT I CAN'T JUST WATCH LIKE THIS!
GATA (CLATTER)
BASA (RUSTLE)
BASA
BI (YOINK)
I CAN'T LET THEM WIN LIKE THIS!
GOTO (CLUNK)
KORO (ROLL)
KORO

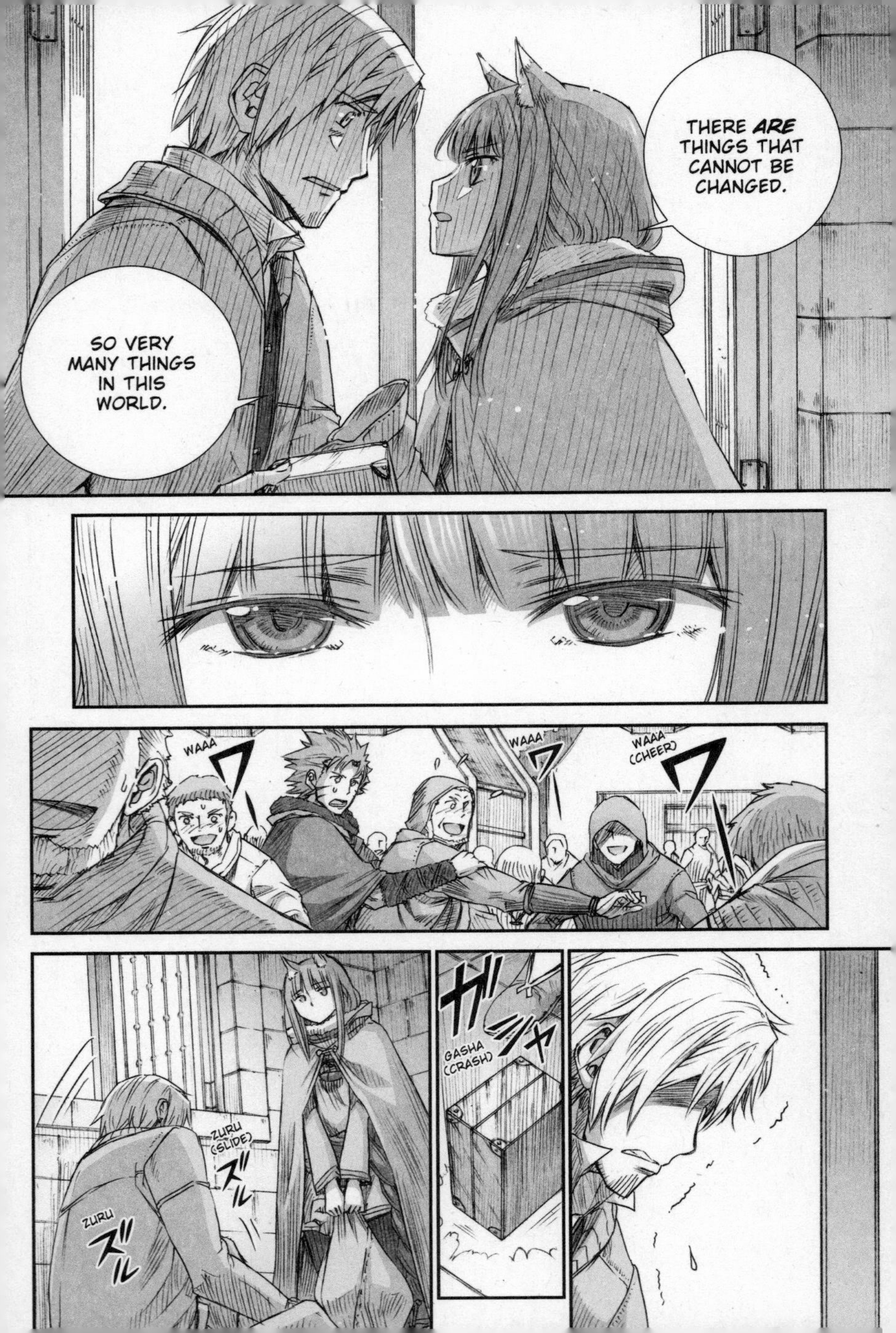
THERE **ARE** THINGS THAT CANNOT BE CHANGED.
SO VERY MANY THINGS IN THIS WORLD.
WAAA (CHEER)
ワ
WAAA
ワ
WAAA
ワ
GASHA (CRASH)
ガシャ
ZURU (SLIDE)
ズル
ZURU
ズル

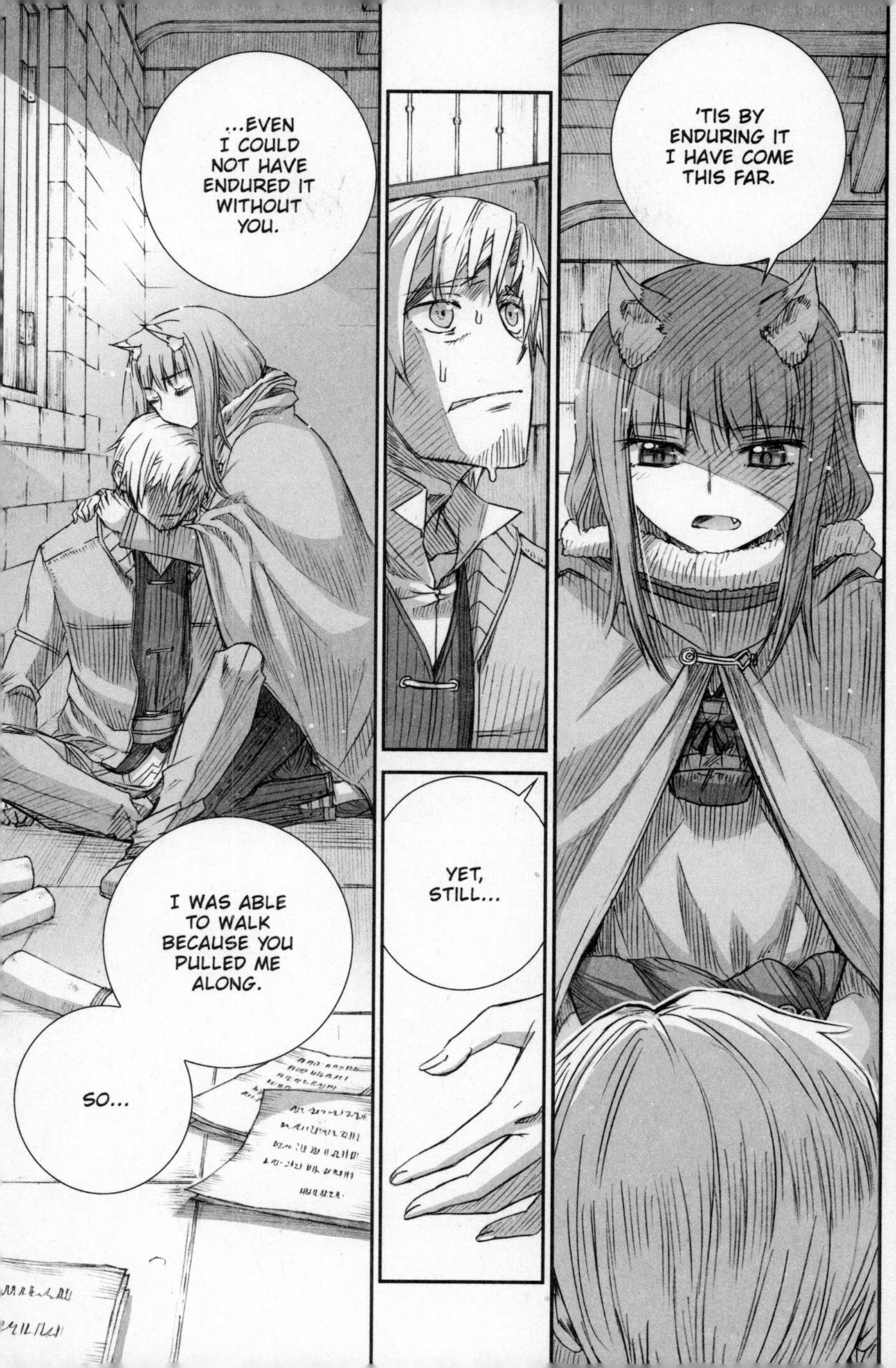
'TIS BY ENDURING IT I HAVE COME THIS FAR.
YET, STILL...
...EVEN I COULD NOT HAVE ENDURED IT WITHOUT YOU.
I WAS ABLE TO WALK BECAUSE YOU PULLED ME ALONG.
SO...

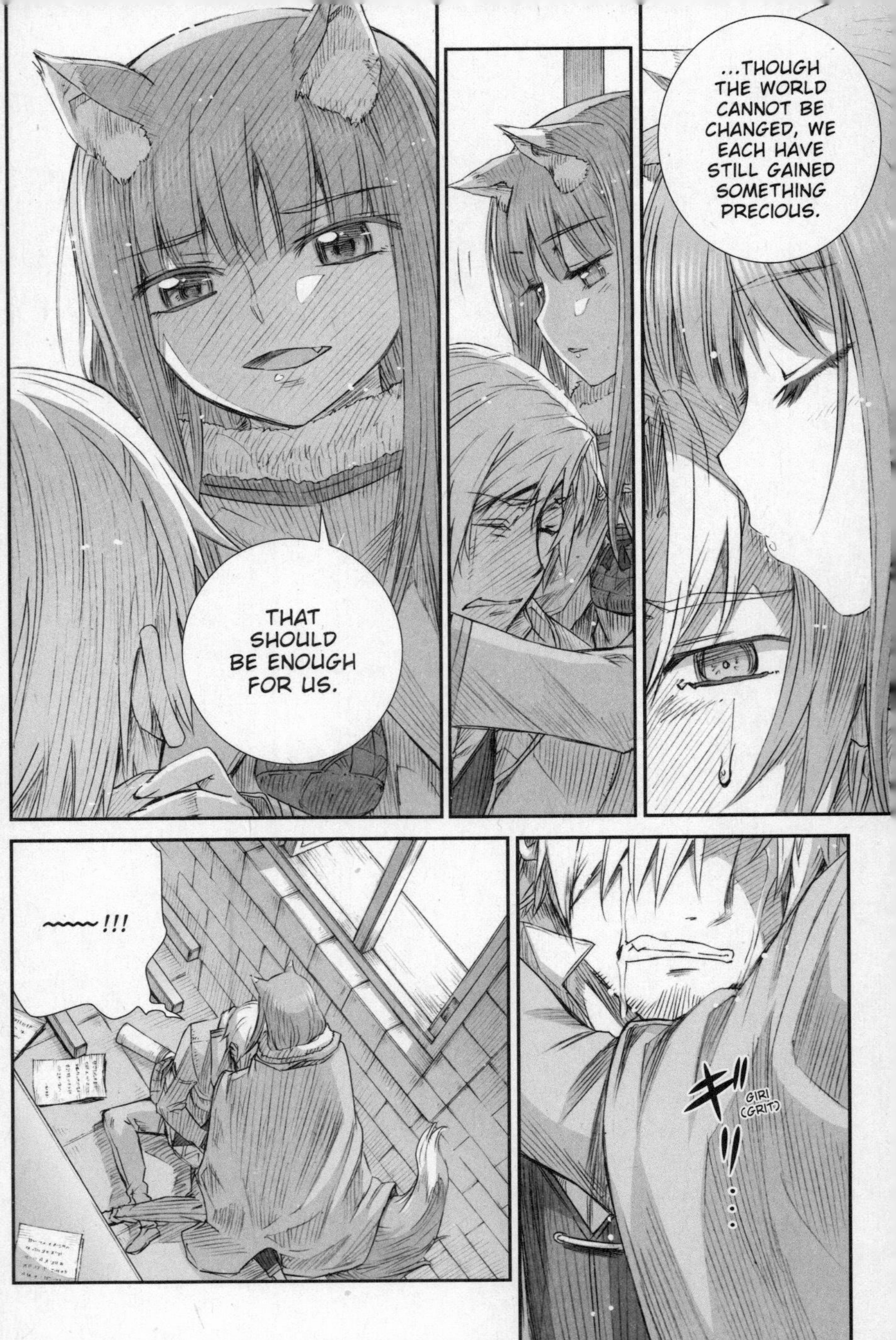
...THOUGH THE WORLD CANNOT BE CHANGED, WE EACH HAVE STILL GAINED SOMETHING PRECIOUS.
THAT SHOULD BE ENOUGH FOR US.
GIRI (GRIT)
~~~!!!
~~~

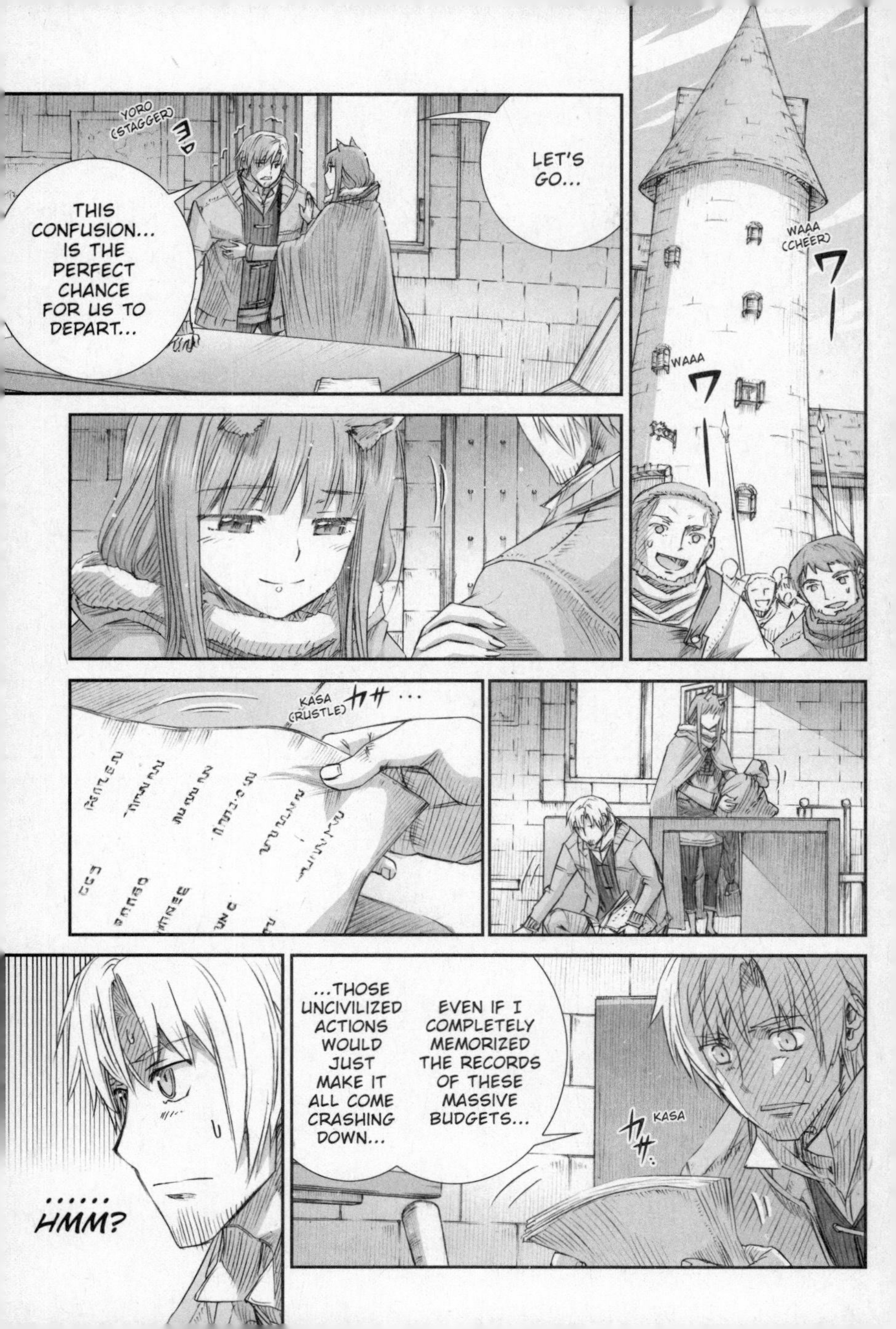
WAAA (CHEER)
WAAA
LET'S GO...
YORO (STAGGER)
THIS CONFUSION... IS THE PERFECT CHANCE FOR US TO DEPART...
KASA (RUSTLE) ...
EVEN IF I COMPLETELY MEMORIZED THE RECORDS OF THESE MASSIVE BUDGETS...
...THOSE UNCIVILIZED ACTIONS WOULD JUST MAKE IT ALL COME CRASHING DOWN...
KASA
......HMM?

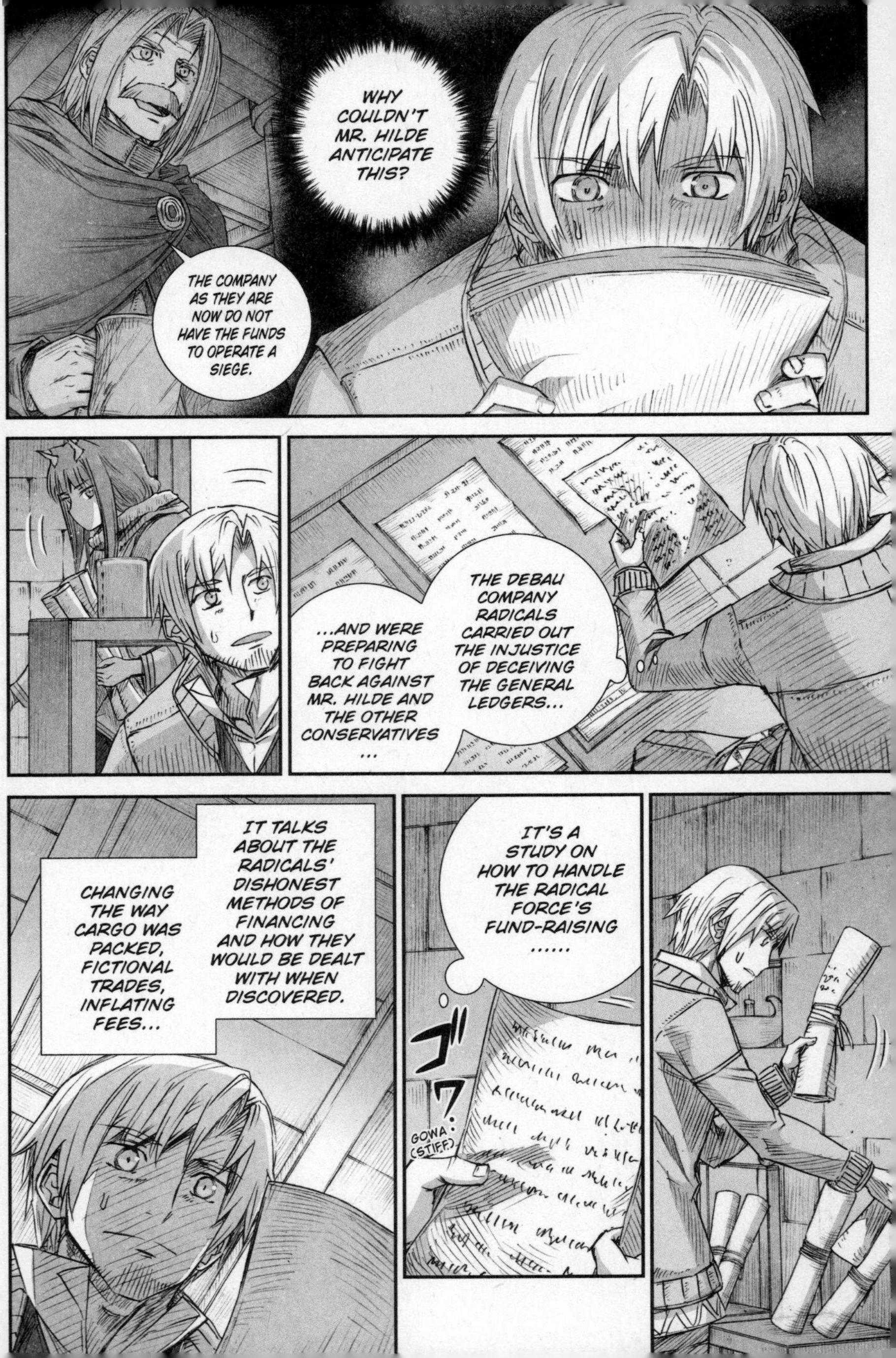
WHY COULDN'T MR. HILDE ANTICIPATE THIS?
THE COMPANY AS THEY ARE NOW DO NOT HAVE THE FUNDS TO OPERATE A SIEGE.
THE DEBAU COMPANY RADICALS CARRIED OUT THE INJUSTICE OF DECEIVING THE GENERAL LEDGERS...
...AND WERE PREPARING TO FIGHT BACK AGAINST MR. HILDE AND THE OTHER CONSERVATIVES...
IT'S A STUDY ON HOW TO HANDLE THE RADICAL FORCE'S FUND-RAISING......
GOWA (STIFF)
IT TALKS ABOUT THE RADICALS' DISHONEST METHODS OF FINANCING AND HOW THEY WOULD BE DEALT WITH WHEN DISCOVERED.
CHANGING THE WAY CARGO WAS PACKED, FICTIONAL TRADES, INFLATING FEES...

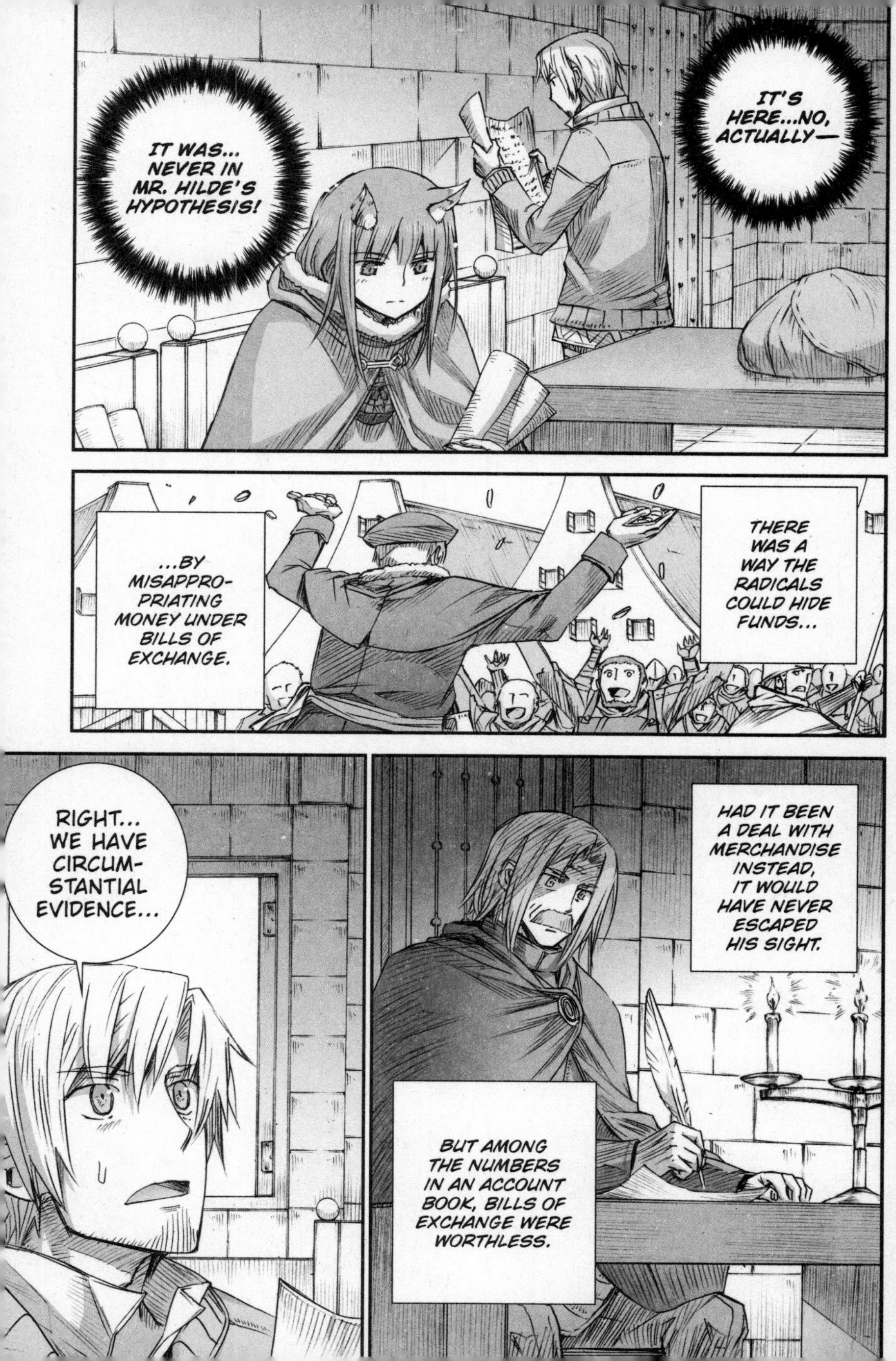
IT'S HERE...NO, ACTUALLY—
IT WAS... NEVER IN MR. HILDE'S HYPOTHESIS!
THERE WAS A WAY THE RADICALS COULD HIDE FUNDS...
...BY MISAPPROPRIATING MONEY UNDER BILLS OF EXCHANGE.
HAD IT BEEN A DEAL WITH MERCHANDISE INSTEAD, IT WOULD HAVE NEVER ESCAPED HIS SIGHT.
BUT AMONG THE NUMBERS IN AN ACCOUNT BOOK, BILLS OF EXCHANGE WERE WORTHLESS.
RIGHT... WE HAVE CIRCUMSTANTIAL EVIDENCE...

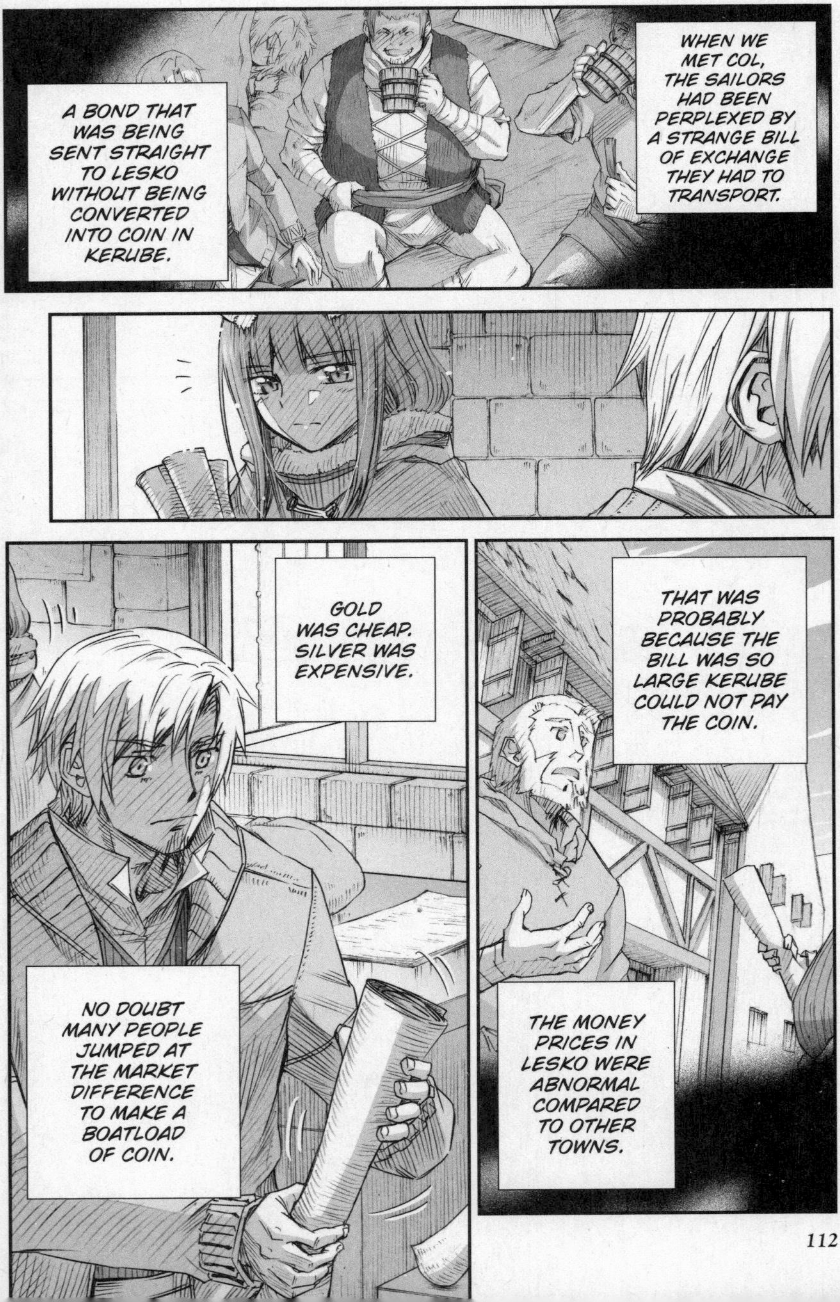
WHEN WE MET COL, THE SAILORS HAD BEEN PERPLEXED BY A STRANGE BILL OF EXCHANGE THEY HAD TO TRANSPORT.
A BOND THAT WAS BEING SENT STRAIGHT TO LESKO WITHOUT BEING CONVERTED INTO COIN IN KERUBE.
THAT WAS PROBABLY BECAUSE THE BILL WAS SO LARGE KERUBE COULD NOT PAY THE COIN.
THE MONEY PRICES IN LESKO WERE ABNORMAL COMPARED TO OTHER TOWNS.
GOLD WAS CHEAP. SILVER WAS EXPENSIVE.
NO DOUBT MANY PEOPLE JUMPED AT THE MARKET DIFFERENCE TO MAKE A BOATLOAD OF COIN.

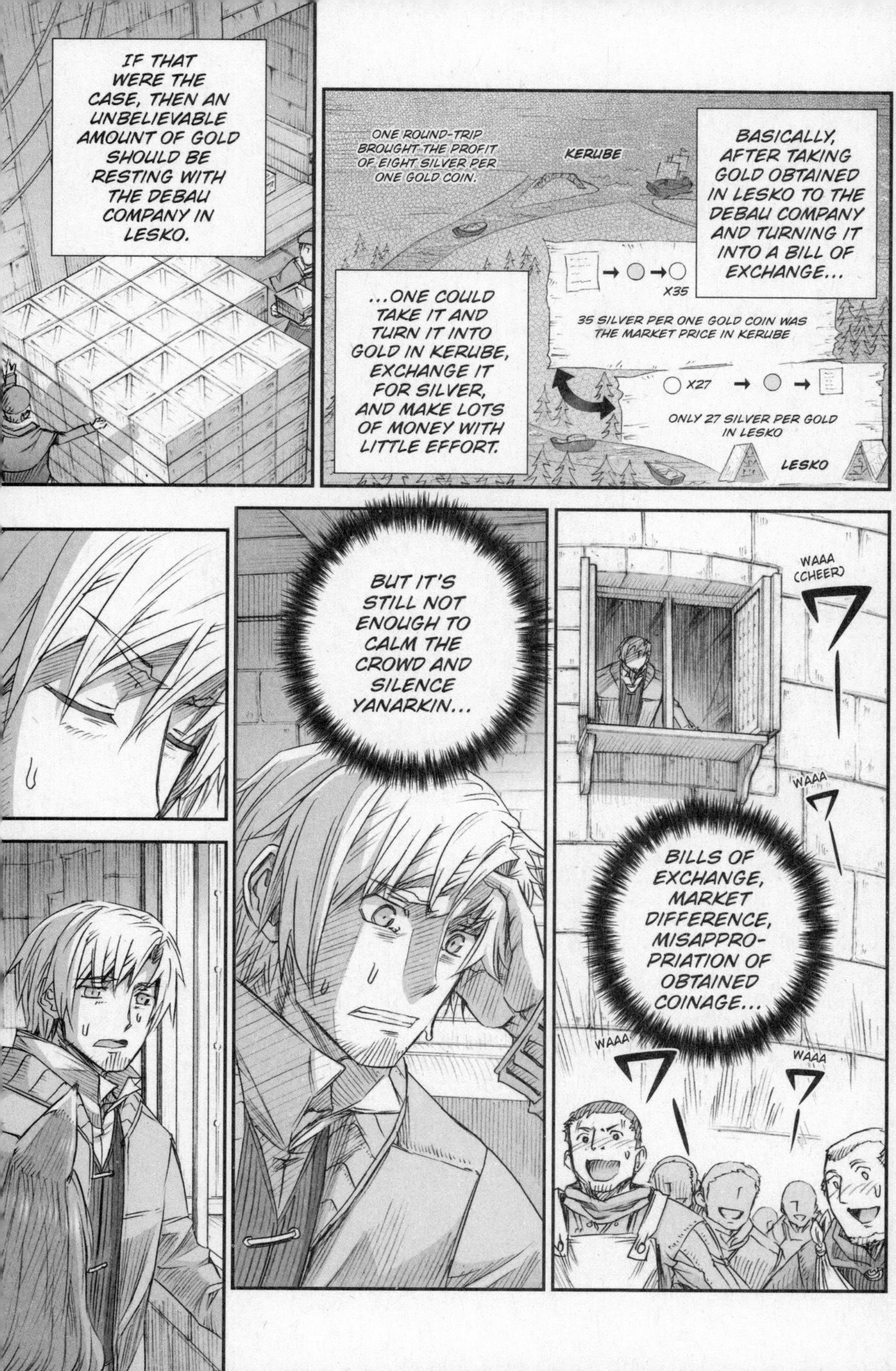
BASICALLY, AFTER TAKING GOLD OBTAINED IN LESKO TO THE DEBAU COMPANY AND TURNING IT INTO A BILL OF EXCHANGE...
KERUBE
ONE ROUND-TRIP BROUGHT THE PROFIT OF EIGHT SILVER PER ONE GOLD COIN.
X35
35 SILVER PER ONE GOLD COIN WAS THE MARKET PRICE IN KERUBE
...ONE COULD TAKE IT AND TURN IT INTO GOLD IN KERUBE, EXCHANGE IT FOR SILVER, AND MAKE LOTS OF MONEY WITH LITTLE EFFORT.
X27
ONLY 27 SILVER PER GOLD IN LESKO
LESKO
IF THAT WERE THE CASE, THEN AN UNBELIEVABLE AMOUNT OF GOLD SHOULD BE RESTING WITH THE DEBAU COMPANY IN LESKO.
WAAA (CHEER)
WAAA
BILLS OF EXCHANGE, MARKET DIFFERENCE, MISAPPRO-PRIATION OF OBTAINED COINAGE...
WAAA
WAAA
BUT IT'S STILL NOT ENOUGH TO CALM THE CROWD AND SILENCE YANARKIN...

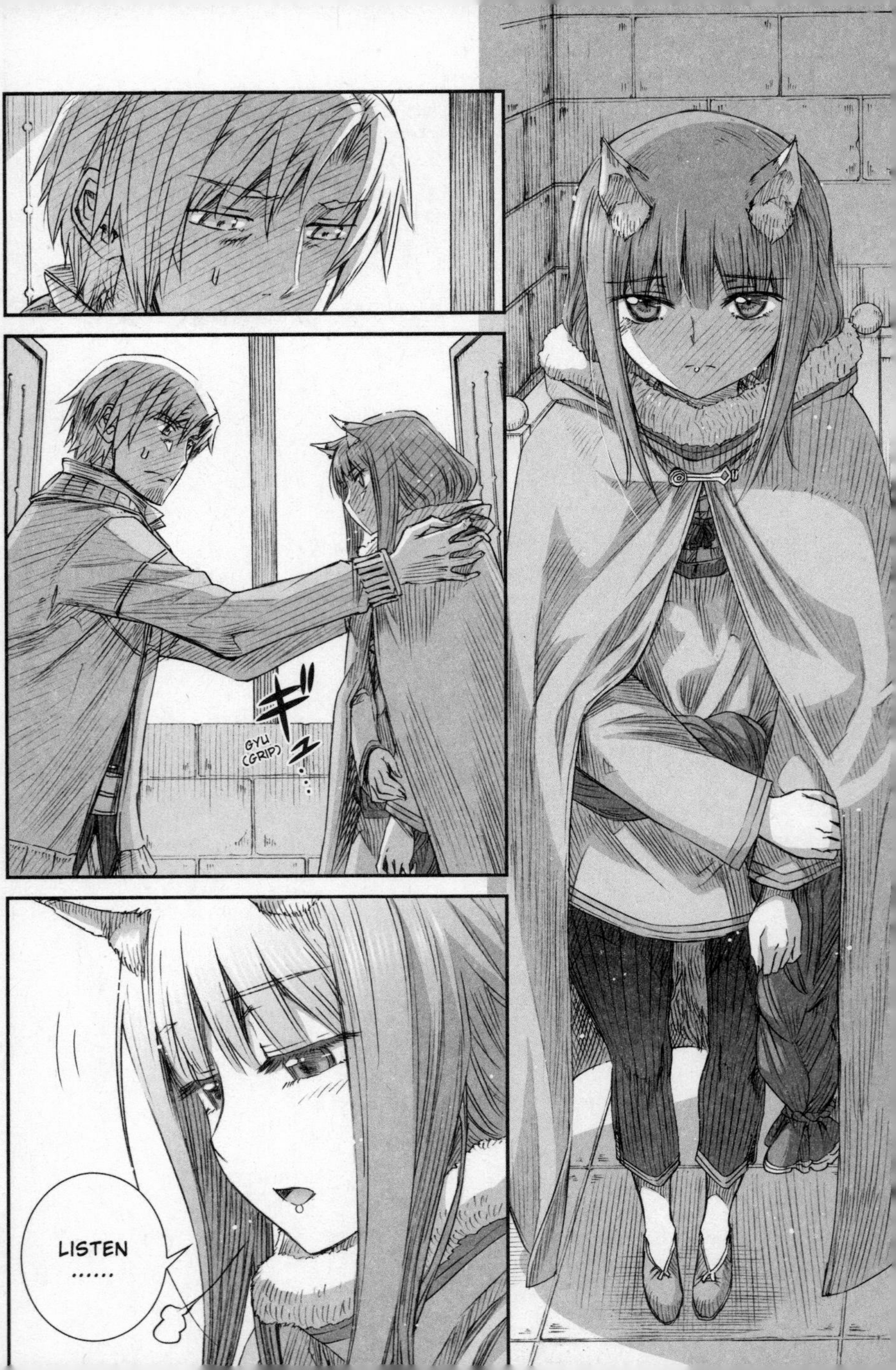
ギュ
GYU (GRIP)
LISTEN ......

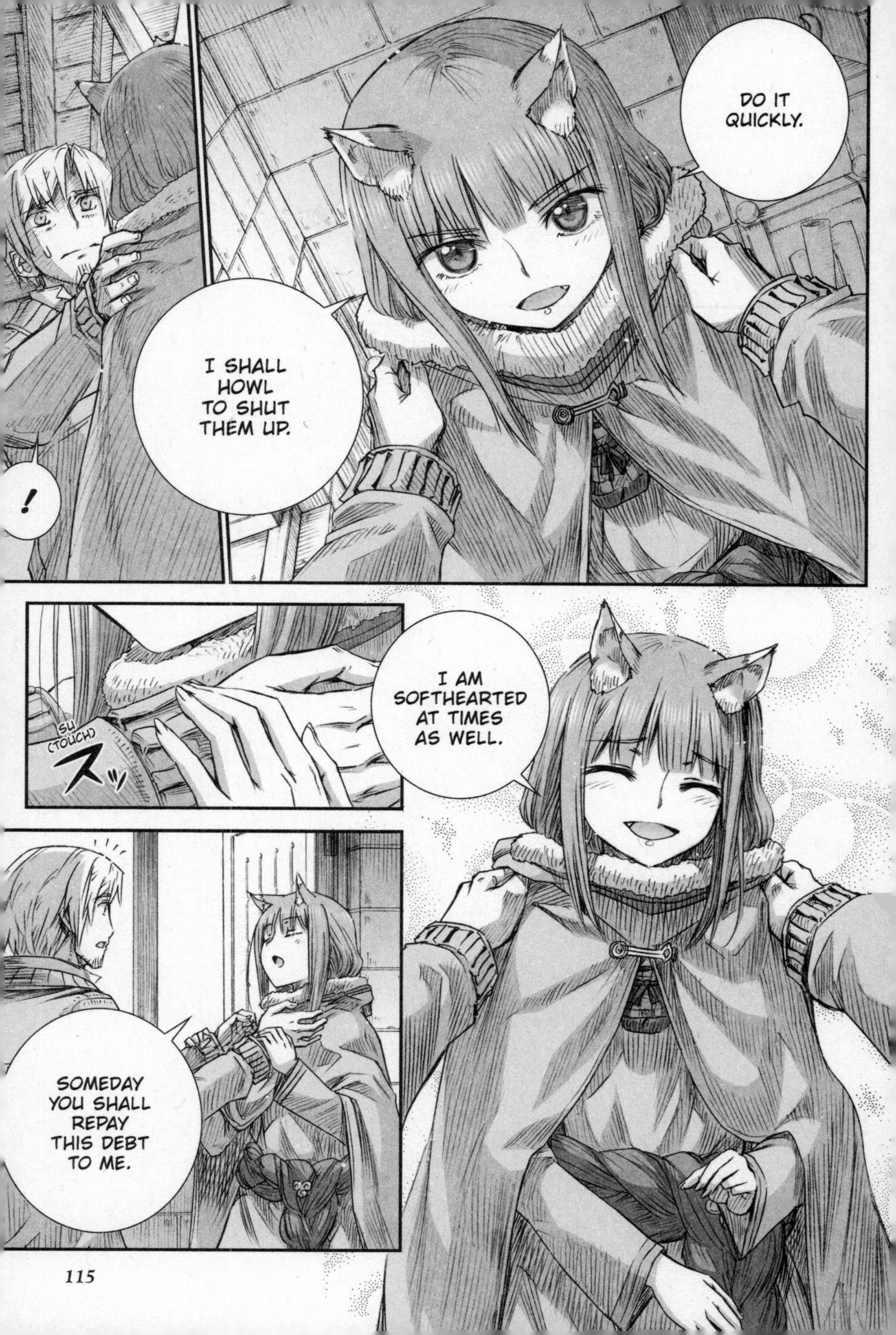
DO IT QUICKLY.
I SHALL HOWL TO SHUT THEM UP.
!
I AM SOFTHEARTED AT TIMES AS WELL.
SU (TOUCH)
スッ
SOMEDAY YOU SHALL REPAY THIS DEBT TO ME.

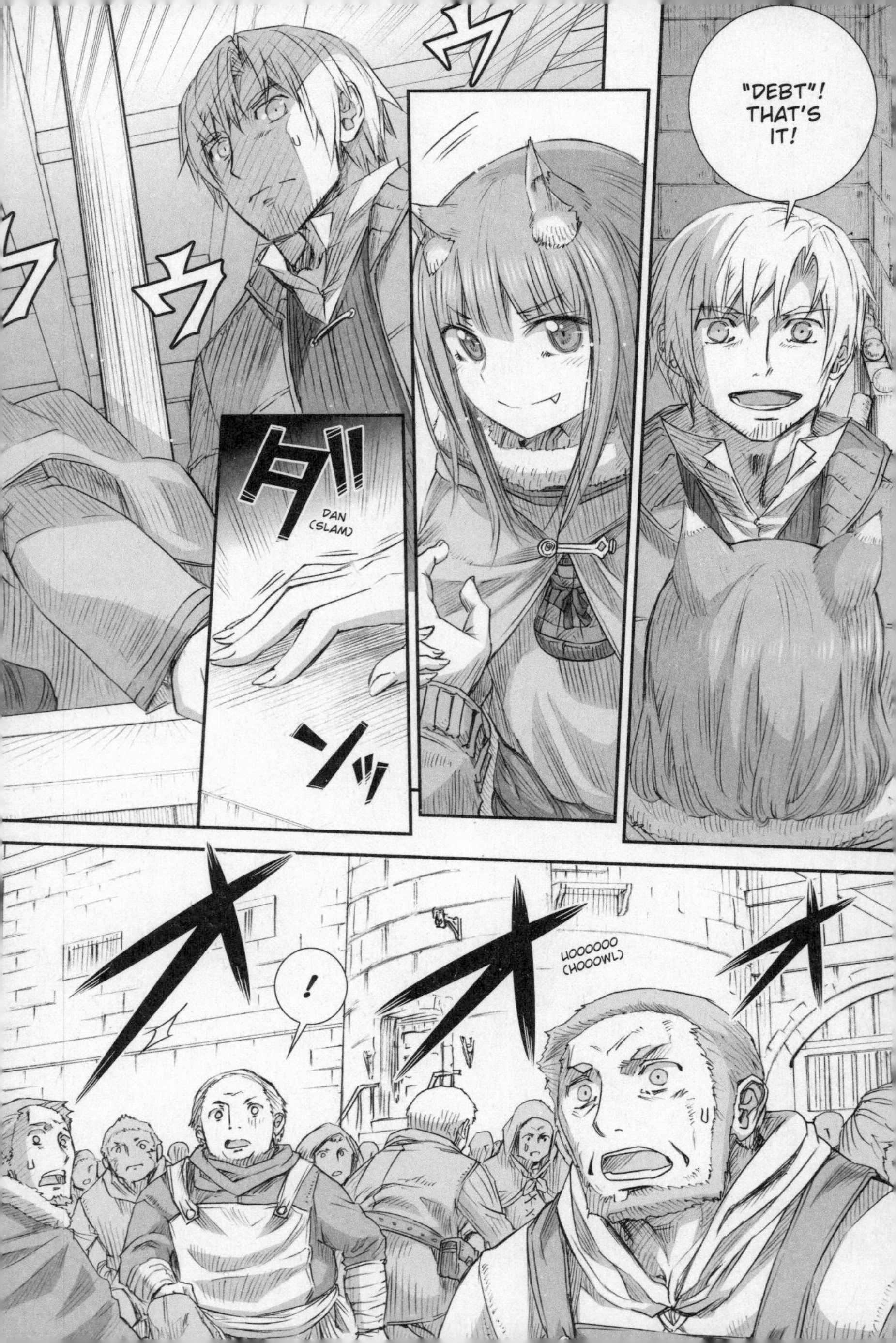
"DEBT"! THAT'S IT!
DAN (SLAM)
HOOOOOO (HOOOWL)
!

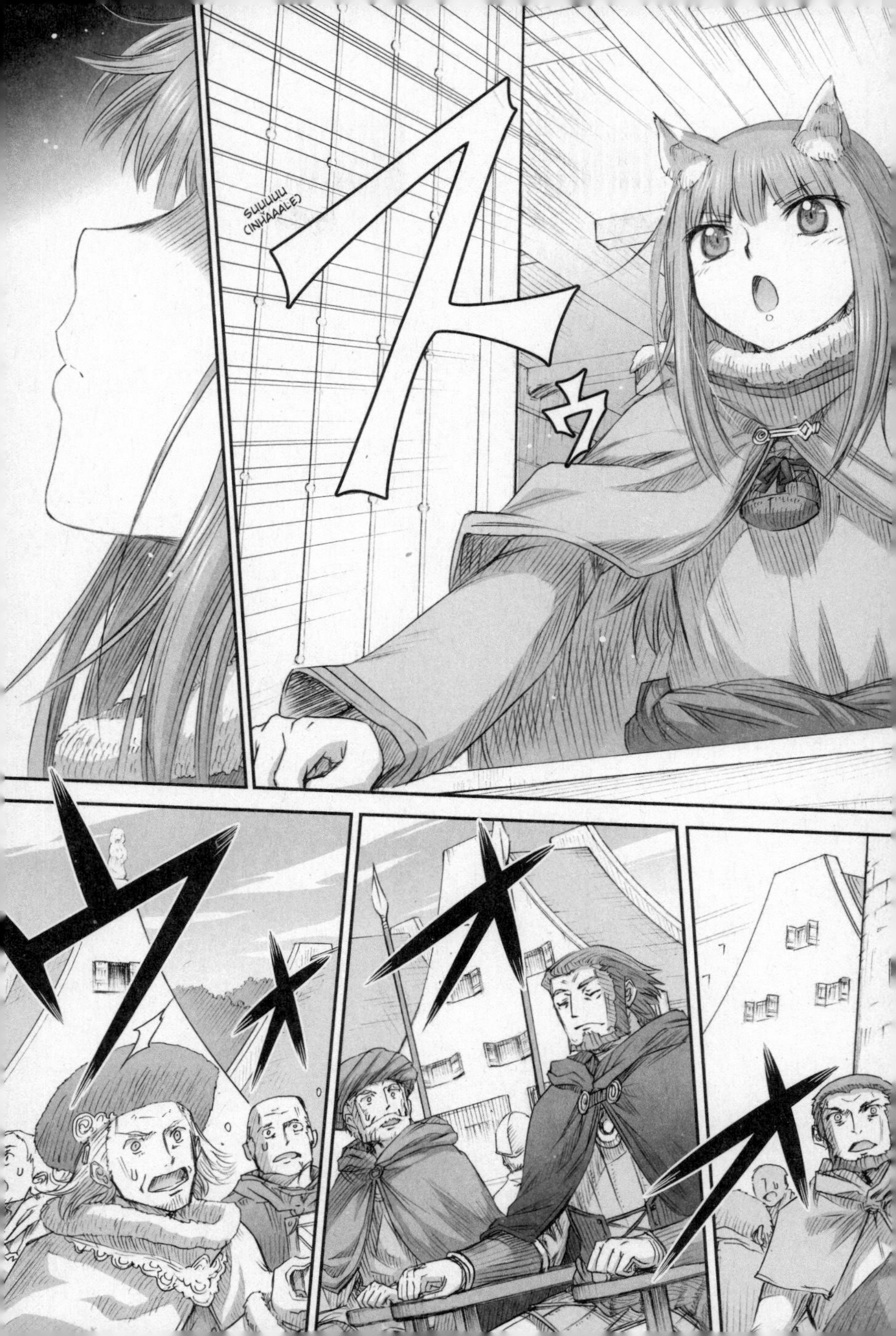
スゥ
SUUUUU (INHAAALE)

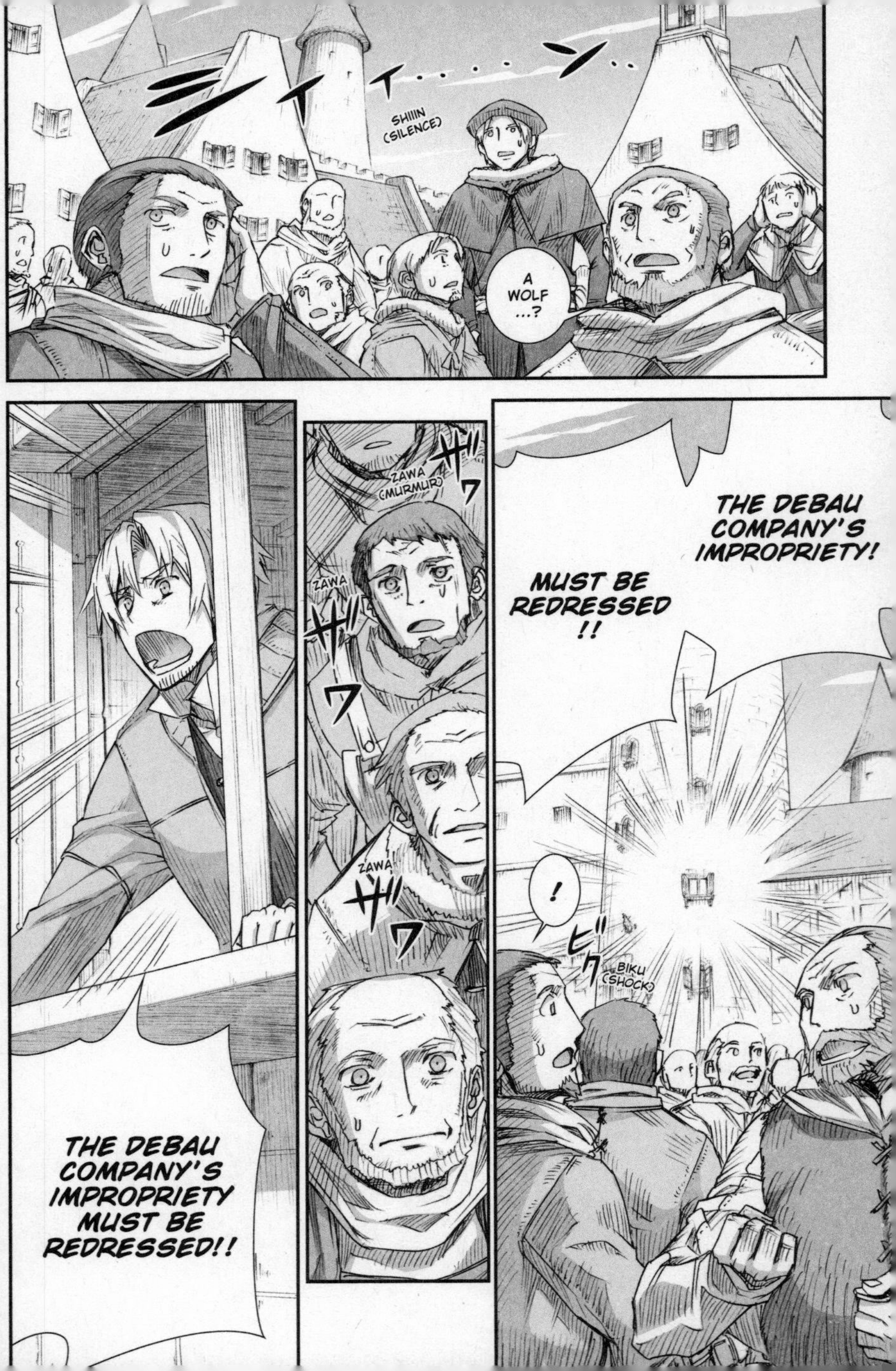
SHIIIN (SILENCE)
A WOLF ...?
THE DEBAU COMPANY'S IMPROPRIETY!
MUST BE REDRESSED !!
!
BIKU (SHOCK)
ZAWA (MURMUR)
ZAWA
ZAWA
THE DEBAU COMPANY'S IMPROPRIETY MUST BE REDRESSED!!

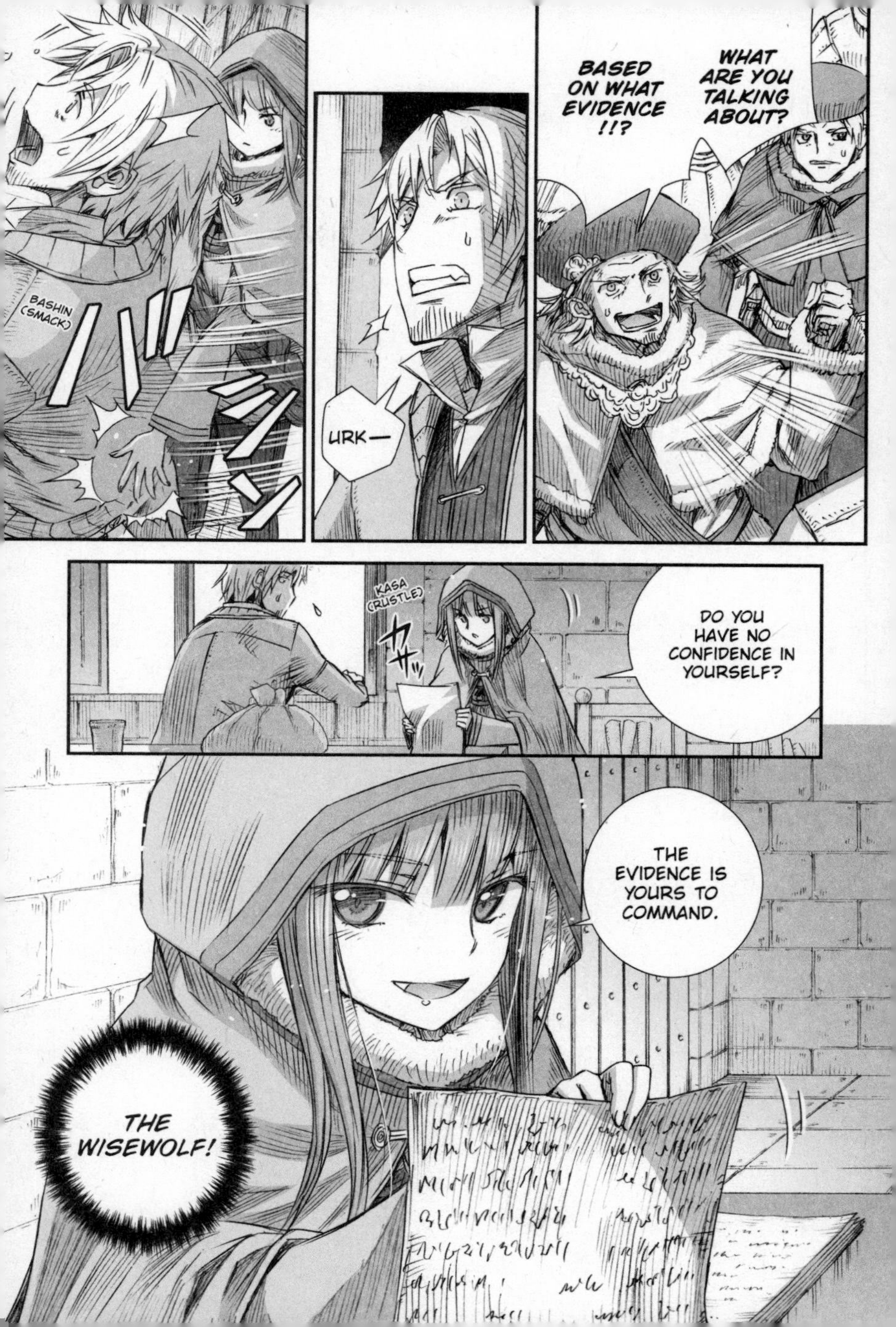
WHAT ARE YOU TALKING ABOUT?
BASED ON WHAT EVIDENCE !!?
URK—
BASHIN (SMACK)
DO YOU HAVE NO CONFIDENCE IN YOURSELF?
KASA (RUSTLE)
THE EVIDENCE IS YOURS TO COMMAND.
THE WISEWOLF!

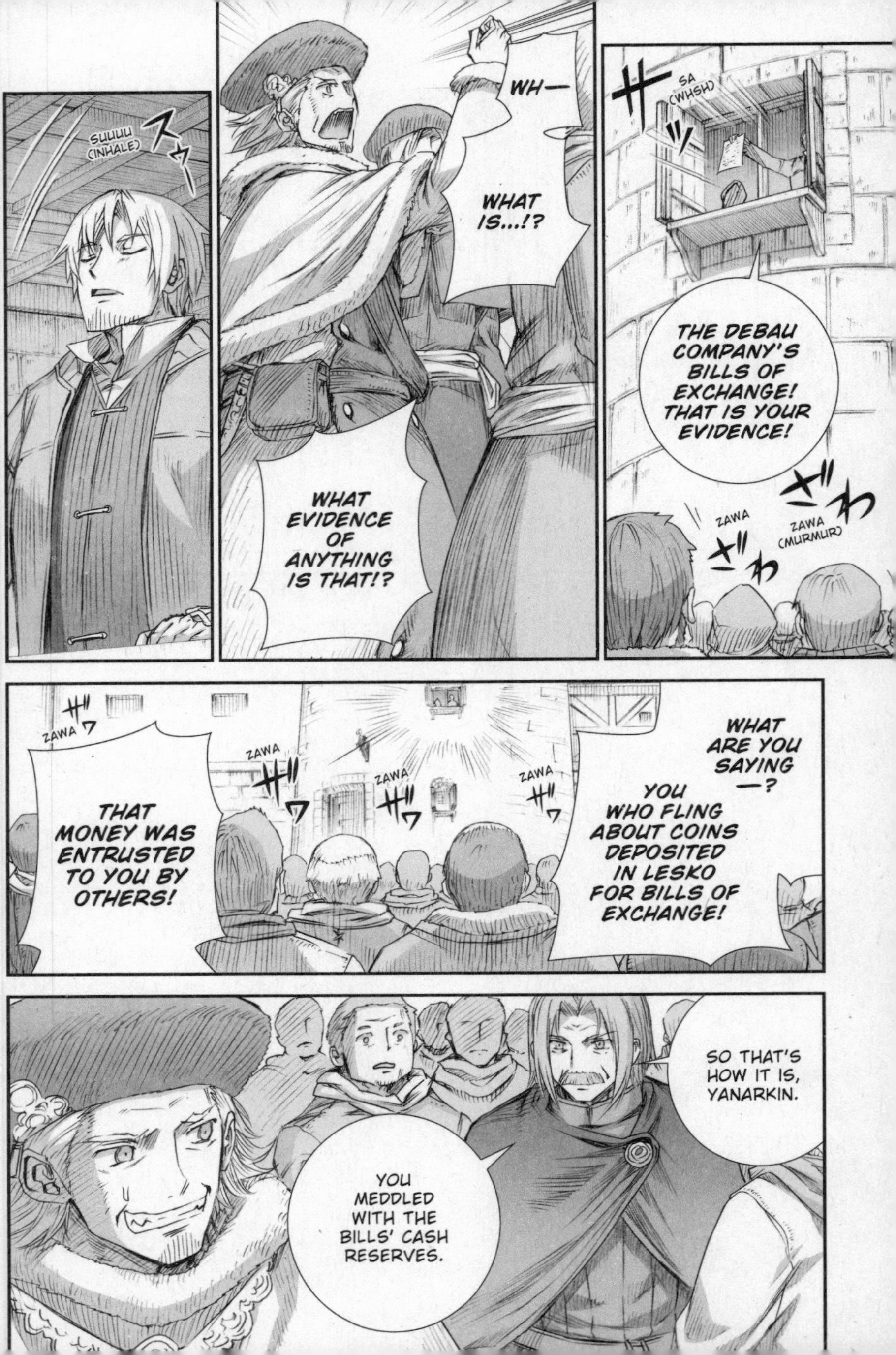
SA (WHSH)
THE DEBAU COMPANY'S BILLS OF EXCHANGE! THAT IS YOUR EVIDENCE!
ZAWA
ZAWA (MURMUR)
WH—
WHAT IS...!?
WHAT EVIDENCE OF ANYTHING IS THAT!?
SUUUU (INHALE)
WHAT ARE YOU SAYING—?
YOU WHO FLING ABOUT COINS DEPOSITED IN LESKO FOR BILLS OF EXCHANGE!
ZAWA
ZAWA
ZAWA
ZAWA
THAT MONEY WAS ENTRUSTED TO YOU BY OTHERS!
SO THAT'S HOW IT IS, YANARKIN.
YOU MEDDLED WITH THE BILLS' CASH RESERVES.

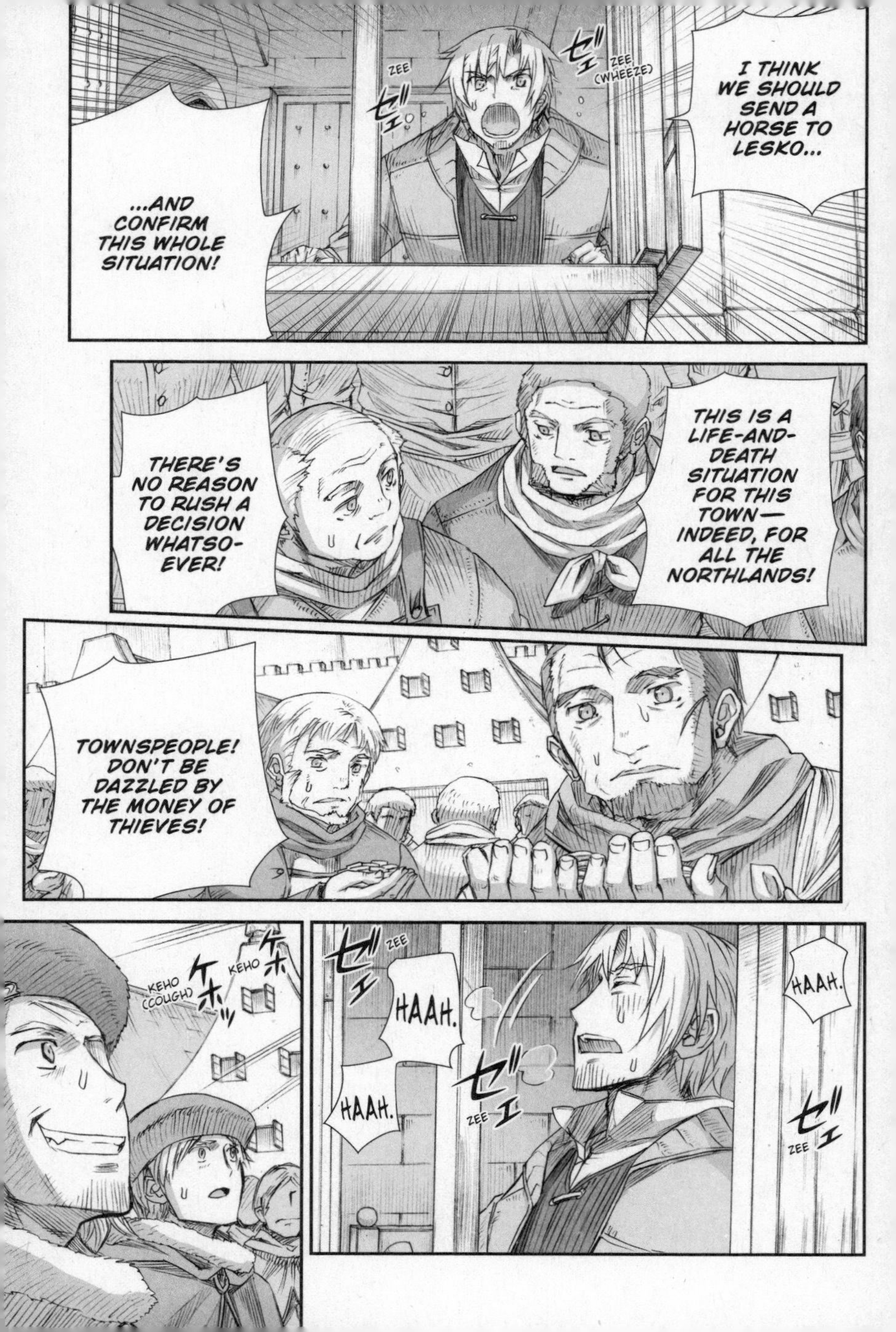
I THINK WE SHOULD SEND A HORSE TO LESKO...
ゼェ
ZEE, (WHEEZE)
ZEE
ゼェ
...AND CONFIRM THIS WHOLE SITUATION!
THIS IS A LIFE-AND-DEATH SITUATION FOR THIS TOWN—INDEED, FOR ALL THE NORTHLANDS!
THERE'S NO REASON TO RUSH A DECISION WHATSO-EVER!
TOWNSPEOPLE! DON'T BE DAZZLED BY THE MONEY OF THIEVES!
HAAH.
ゼェ
ZEE
ゼェ
ZEE
HAAH.
ゼェ
ZEE
HAAH.
ケホ
KEHO
ケホッ
KEHO (COUGH)

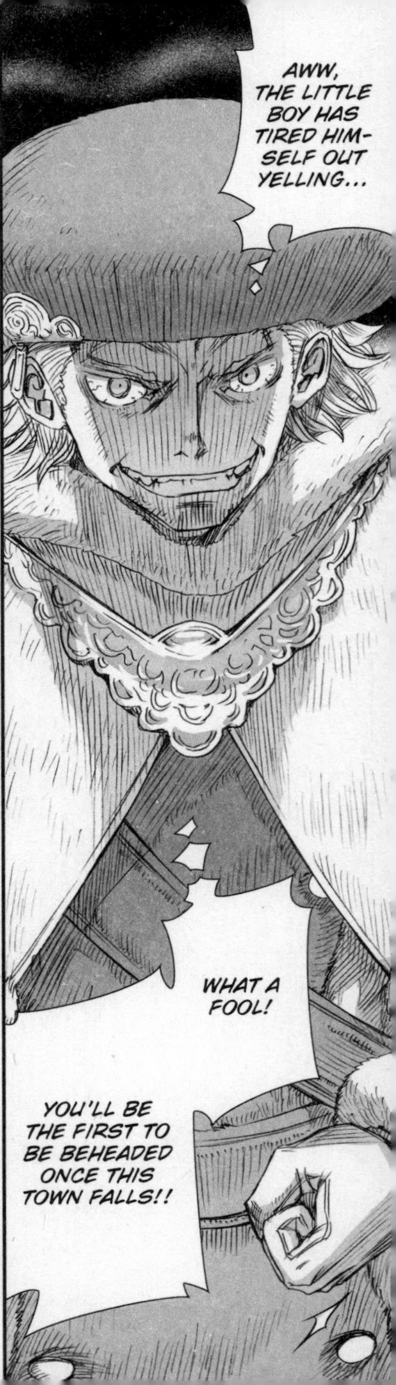
AWW, THE LITTLE BOY HAS TIRED HIMSELF OUT YELLING...
WHAT A FOOL!
YOU'LL BE THE FIRST TO BE BEHEADED ONCE THIS TOWN FALLS!!

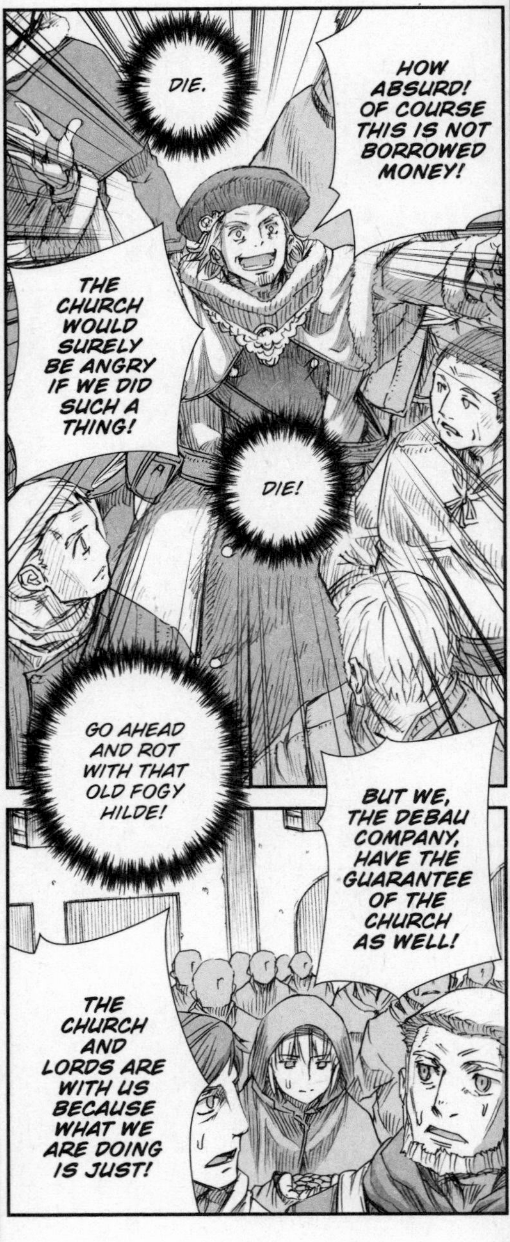
HOW ABSURD! OF COURSE THIS IS NOT BORROWED MONEY!
DIE.
THE CHURCH WOULD SURELY BE ANGRY IF WE DID SUCH A THING!
DIE!
GO AHEAD AND ROT WITH THAT OLD FOGY HILDE!
BUT WE, THE DEBAU COMPANY, HAVE THE GUARANTEE OF THE CHURCH AS WELL!
THE CHURCH AND LORDS ARE WITH US BECAUSE WHAT WE ARE DOING IS JUST!

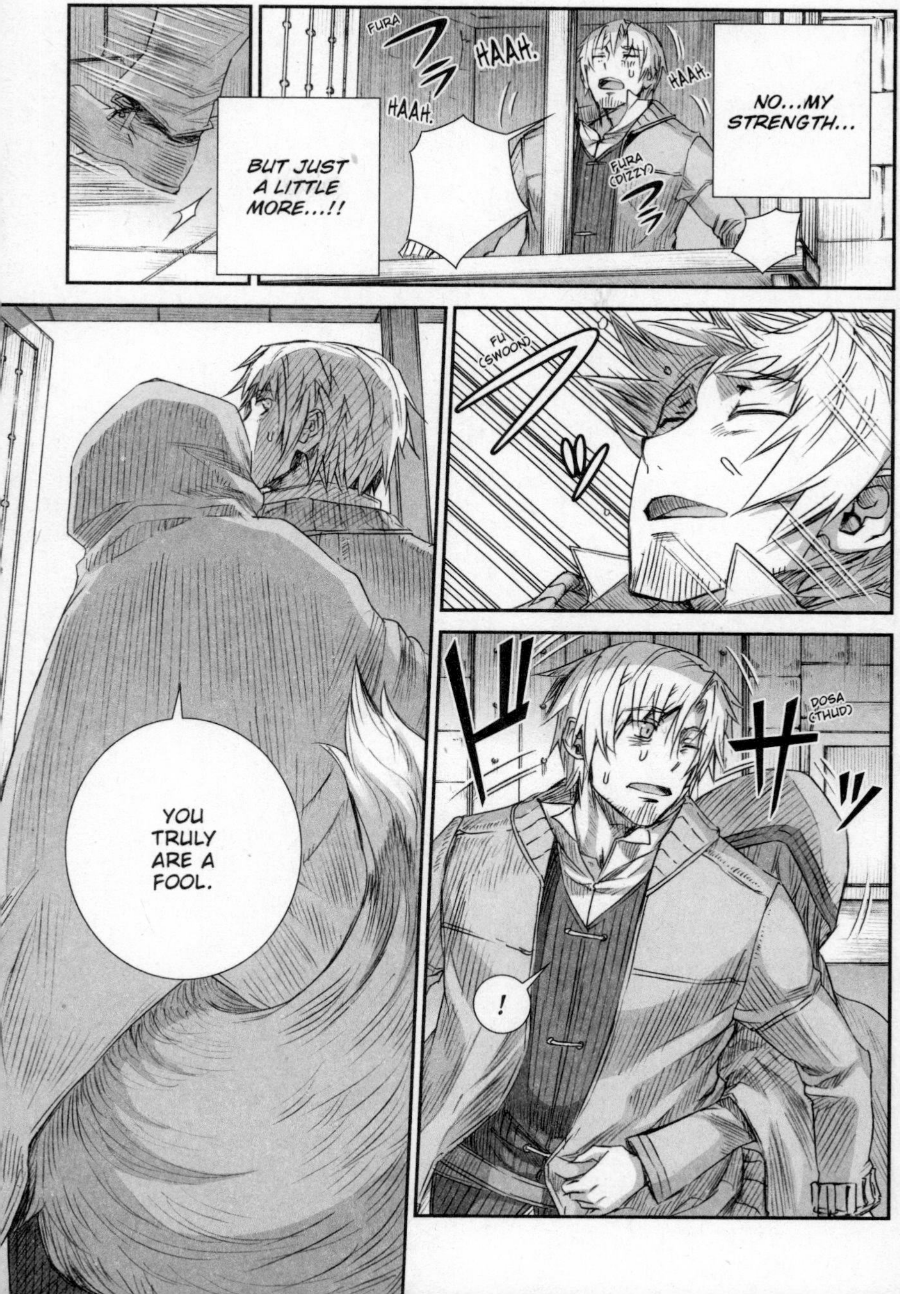
NO...MY STRENGTH...
HAAH.
HAAH.
HAAH.
FURA
FURA (DIZZY)
BUT JUST A LITTLE MORE...!!
FU (SWOON)
DOSA (THUD)
!
YOU TRULY ARE A FOOL.

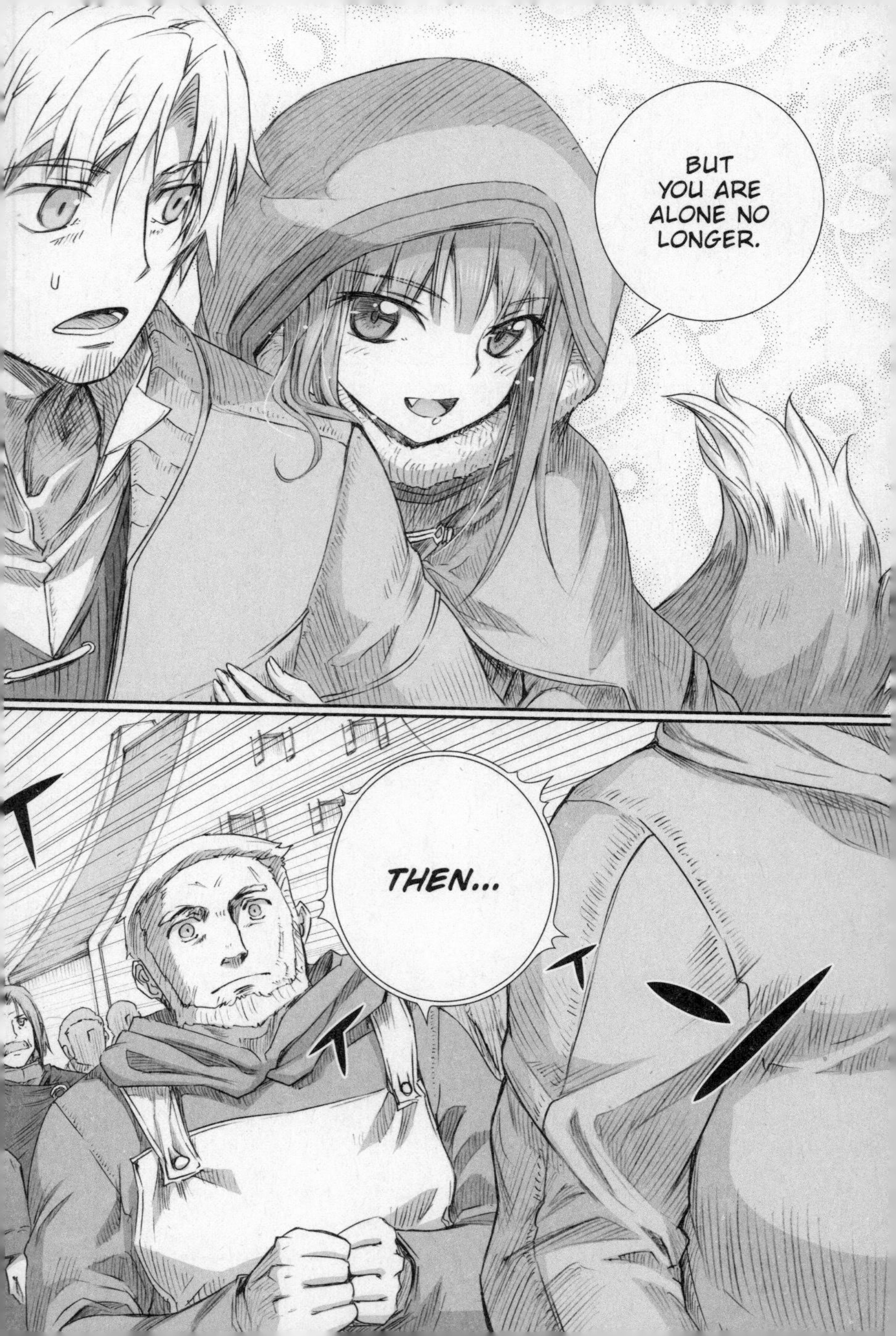
BUT YOU ARE ALONE NO LONGER.
THEN...

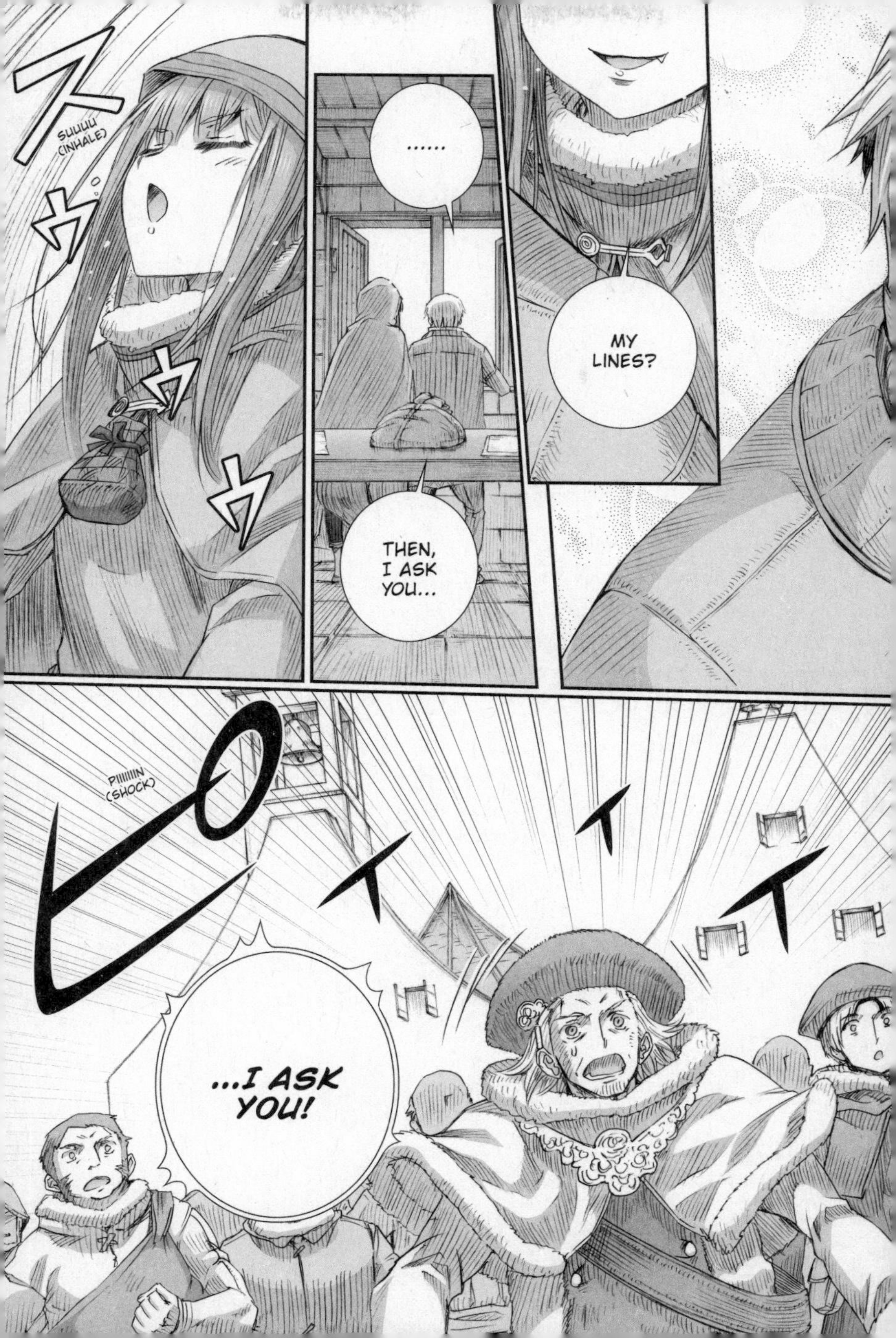

MY LINES?
......
THEN, I ASK YOU...
SUUUUU (INHALE)
PIIIIIIN (SHOCK)
...I ASK YOU!

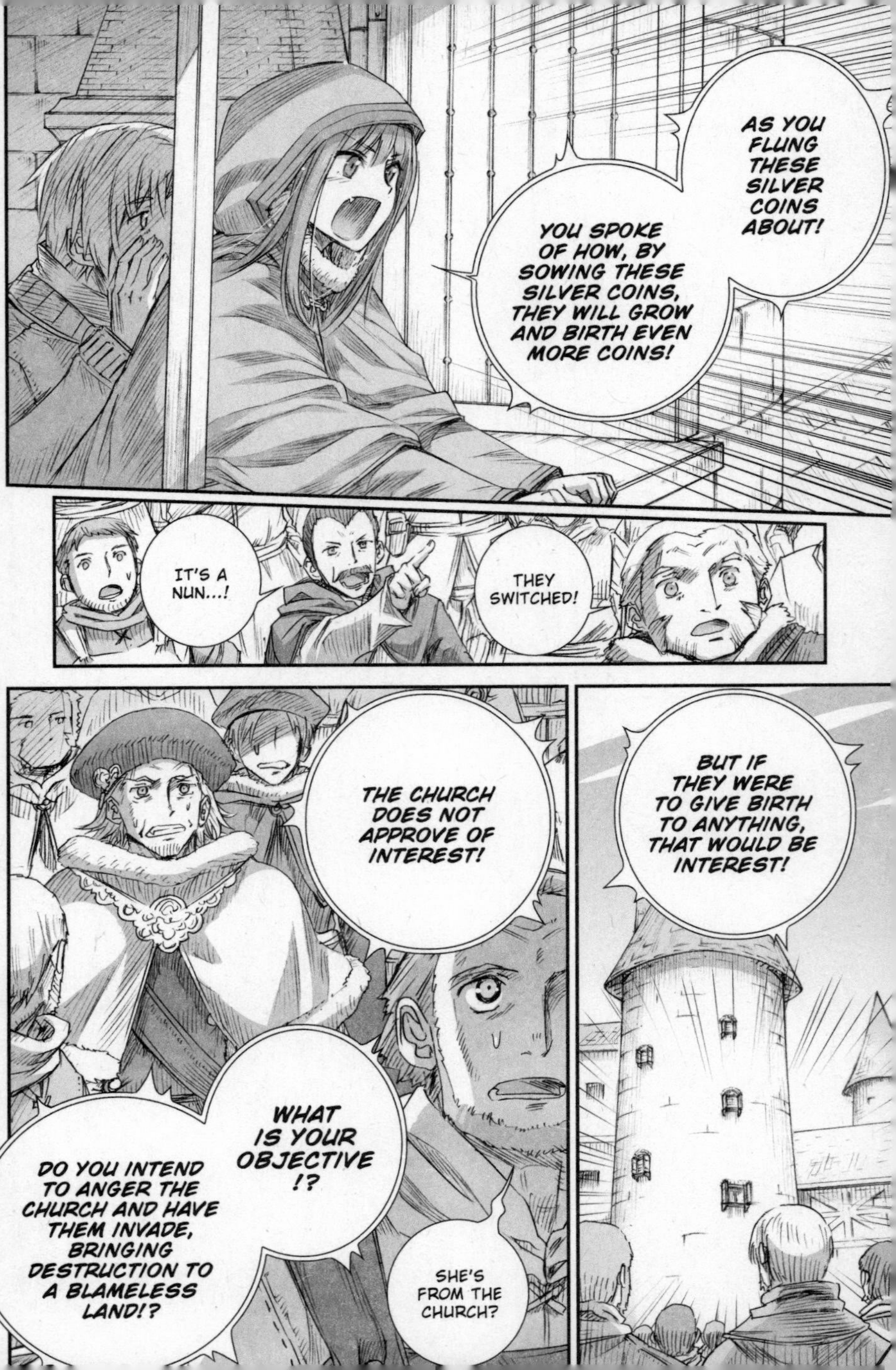
AS YOU FLUNG THESE SILVER COINS ABOUT!
YOU SPOKE OF HOW, BY SOWING THESE SILVER COINS, THEY WILL GROW AND BIRTH EVEN MORE COINS!
THEY SWITCHED!
IT'S A NUN...!
BUT IF THEY WERE TO GIVE BIRTH TO ANYTHING, THAT WOULD BE INTEREST!
THE CHURCH DOES NOT APPROVE OF INTEREST!
WHAT IS YOUR OBJECTIVE!?
DO YOU INTEND TO ANGER THE CHURCH AND HAVE THEM INVADE, BRINGING DESTRUCTION TO A BLAMELESS LAND!?
SHE'S FROM THE CHURCH?

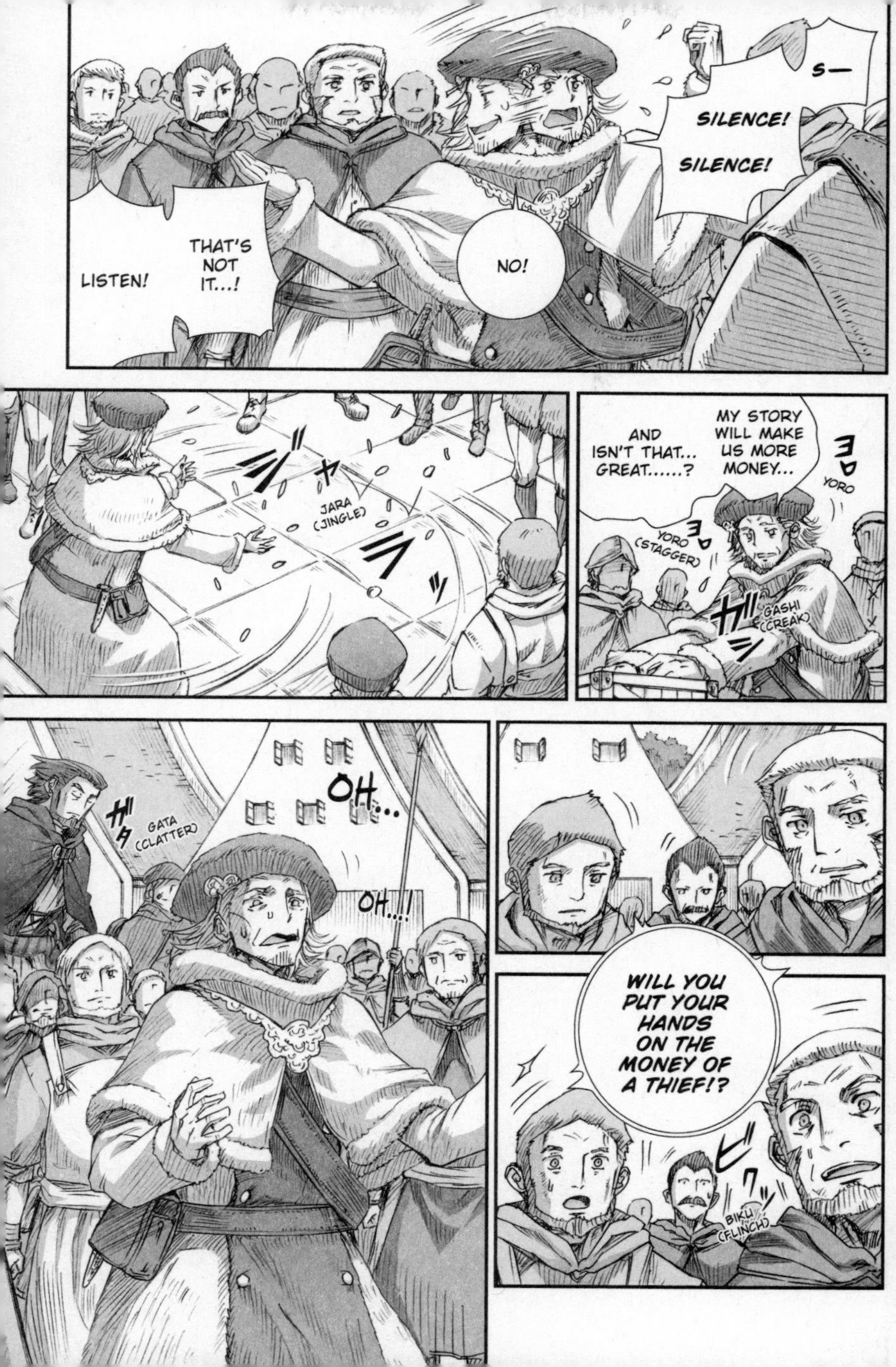
S—
SILENCE!
SILENCE!
NO!
THAT'S NOT IT...!
LISTEN!
MY STORY WILL MAKE US MORE MONEY...
AND ISN'T THAT... GREAT......?
YORO
YORO (STAGGER)
GASHI (CREAK)
JARA (JINGLE)
WILL YOU PUT YOUR HANDS ON THE MONEY OF A THIEF!?
BIKU (FLINCH)
OH...
OH...!
GATA (CLATTER)

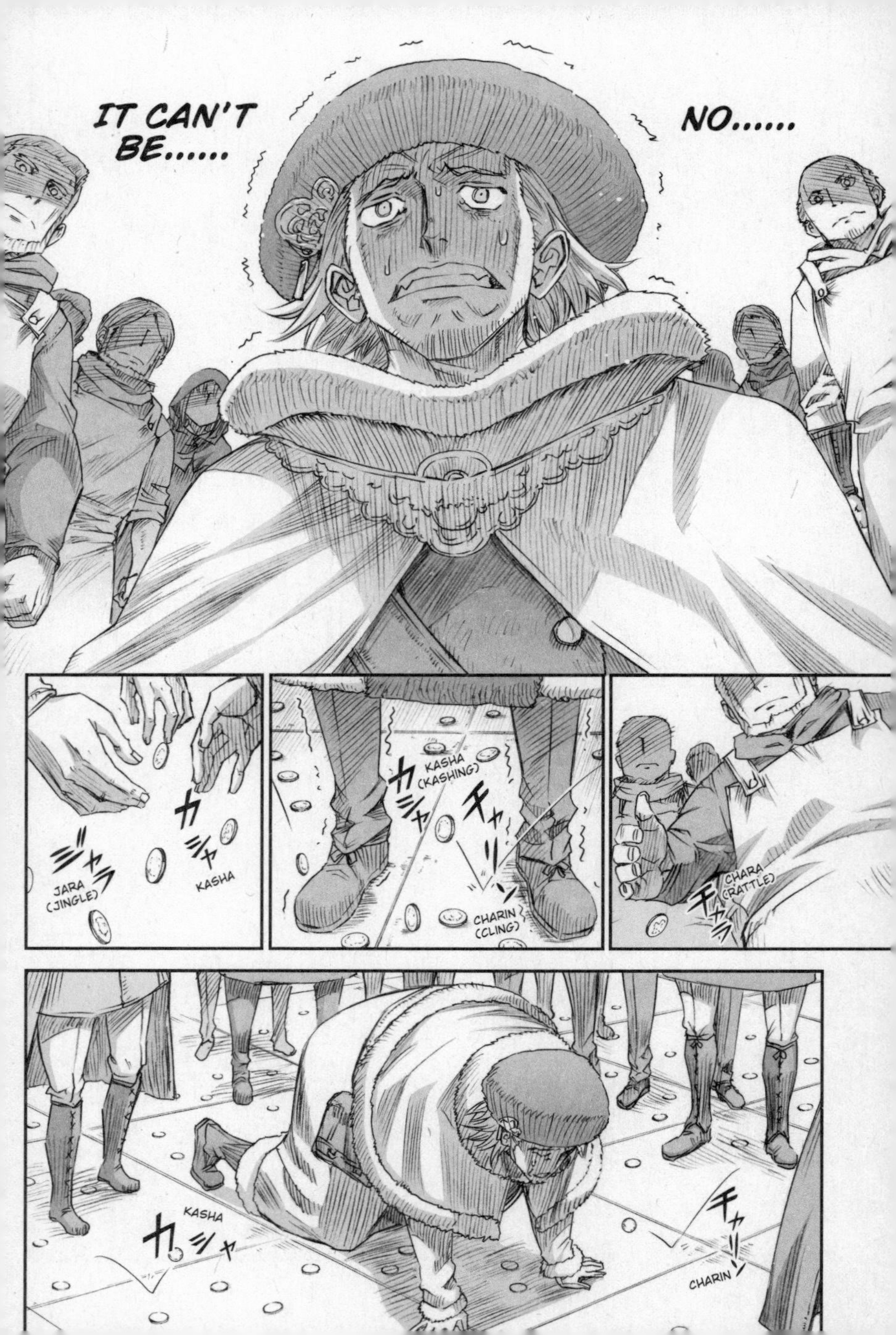
NO......
IT CAN'T BE......
チャラ
CHARA (RATTLE)
カシャ
KASHA (KASHING)
チャリン
CHARIN (CLING)
カシャ
KASHA
ジャラ
JARA (JINGLE)
チャリーン
CHARIN
カシャ
KASHA

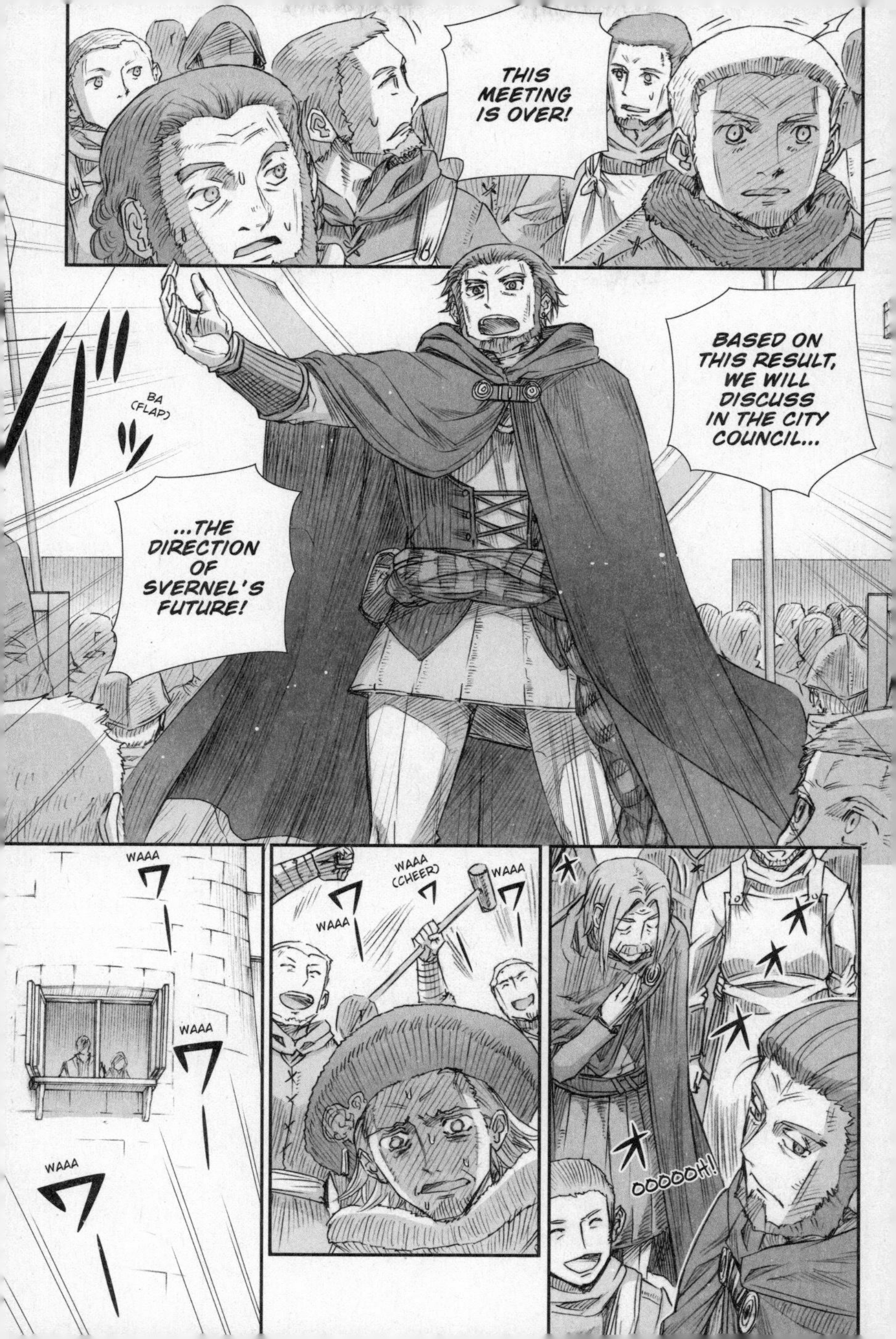
THIS MEETING IS OVER!
BASED ON THIS RESULT, WE WILL DISCUSS IN THE CITY COUNCIL...
...THE DIRECTION OF SVERNEL'S FUTURE!
BA (FLAP)
OOOOOH!
WAAA
WAAA (CHEER)
WAAA
WAAA
WAAA
WAAA

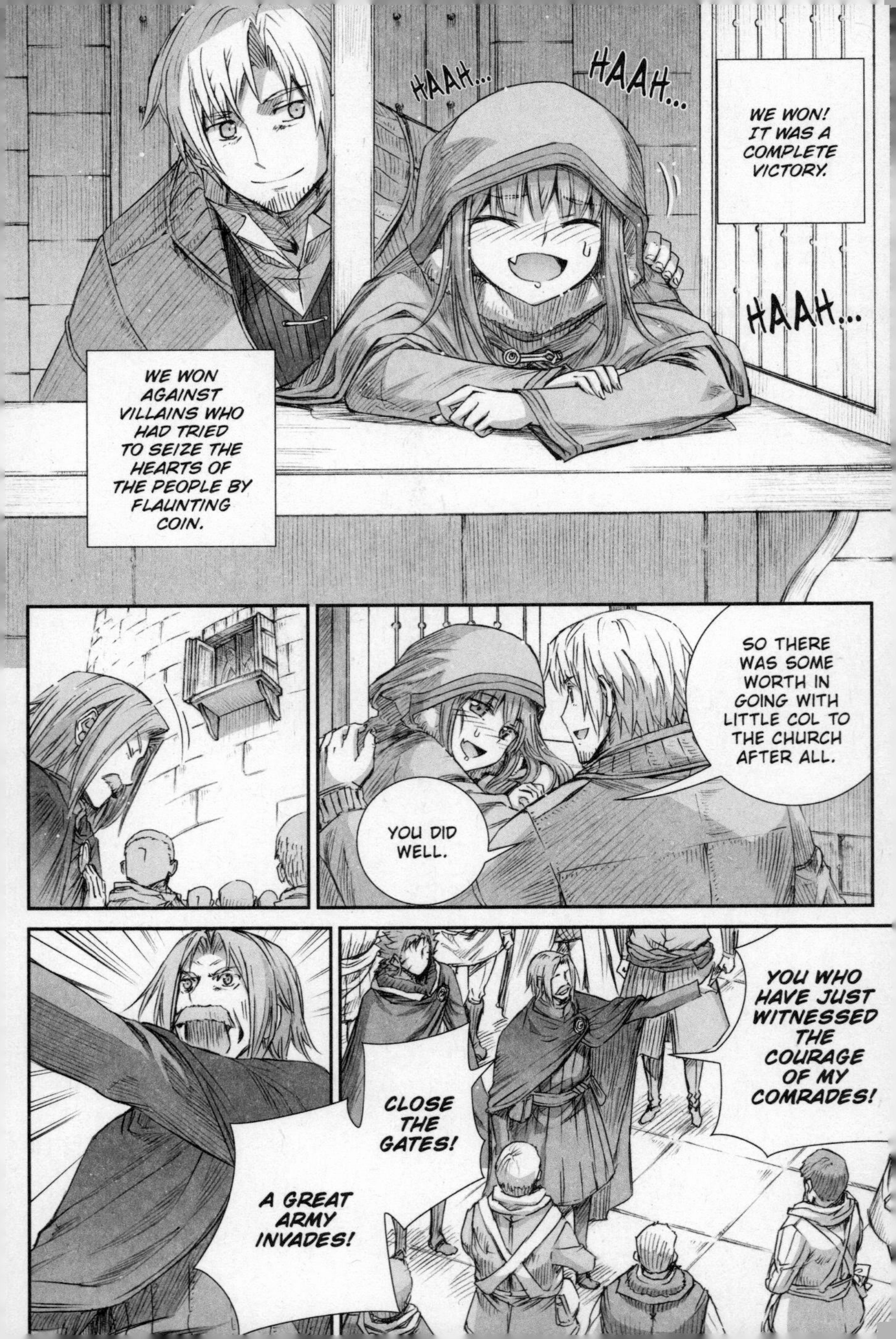
WE WON! IT WAS A COMPLETE VICTORY.
HAAH...
HAAH...
HAAH...
WE WON AGAINST VILLAINS WHO HAD TRIED TO SEIZE THE HEARTS OF THE PEOPLE BY FLAUNTING COIN.
SO THERE WAS SOME WORTH IN GOING WITH LITTLE COL TO THE CHURCH AFTER ALL.
YOU DID WELL.
YOU WHO HAVE JUST WITNESSED THE COURAGE OF MY COMRADES!
CLOSE THE GATES!
A GREAT ARMY INVADES!

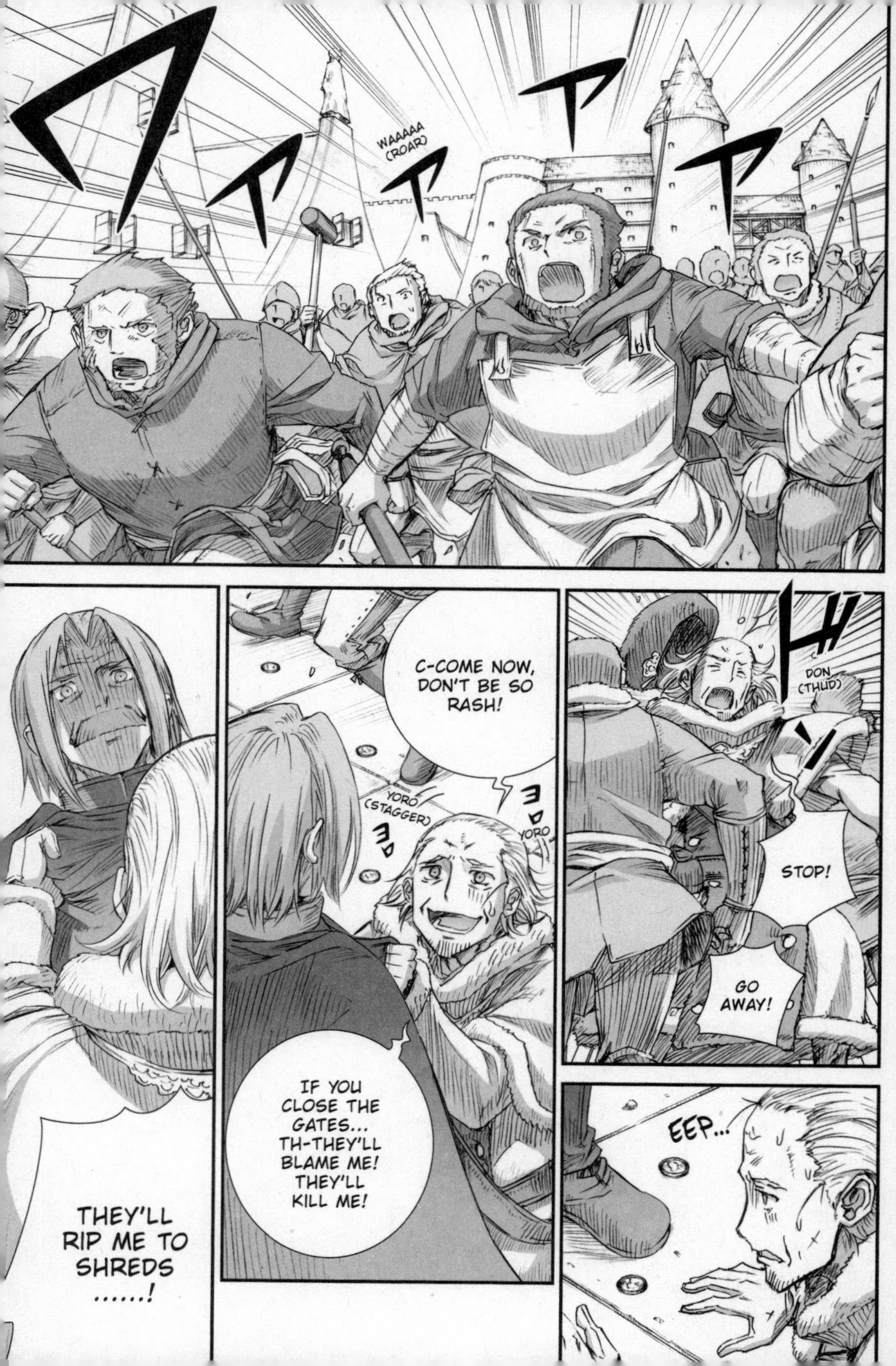
WAAAAA (ROAR)
DON (THUD)
STOP!
GO AWAY!
EEP...
C-COME NOW, DON'T BE SO RASH!
YORO (STAGGER)
YORO
IF YOU CLOSE THE GATES... TH-THEY'LL BLAME ME! THEY'LL KILL ME!
THEY'LL RIP ME TO SHREDS ......!

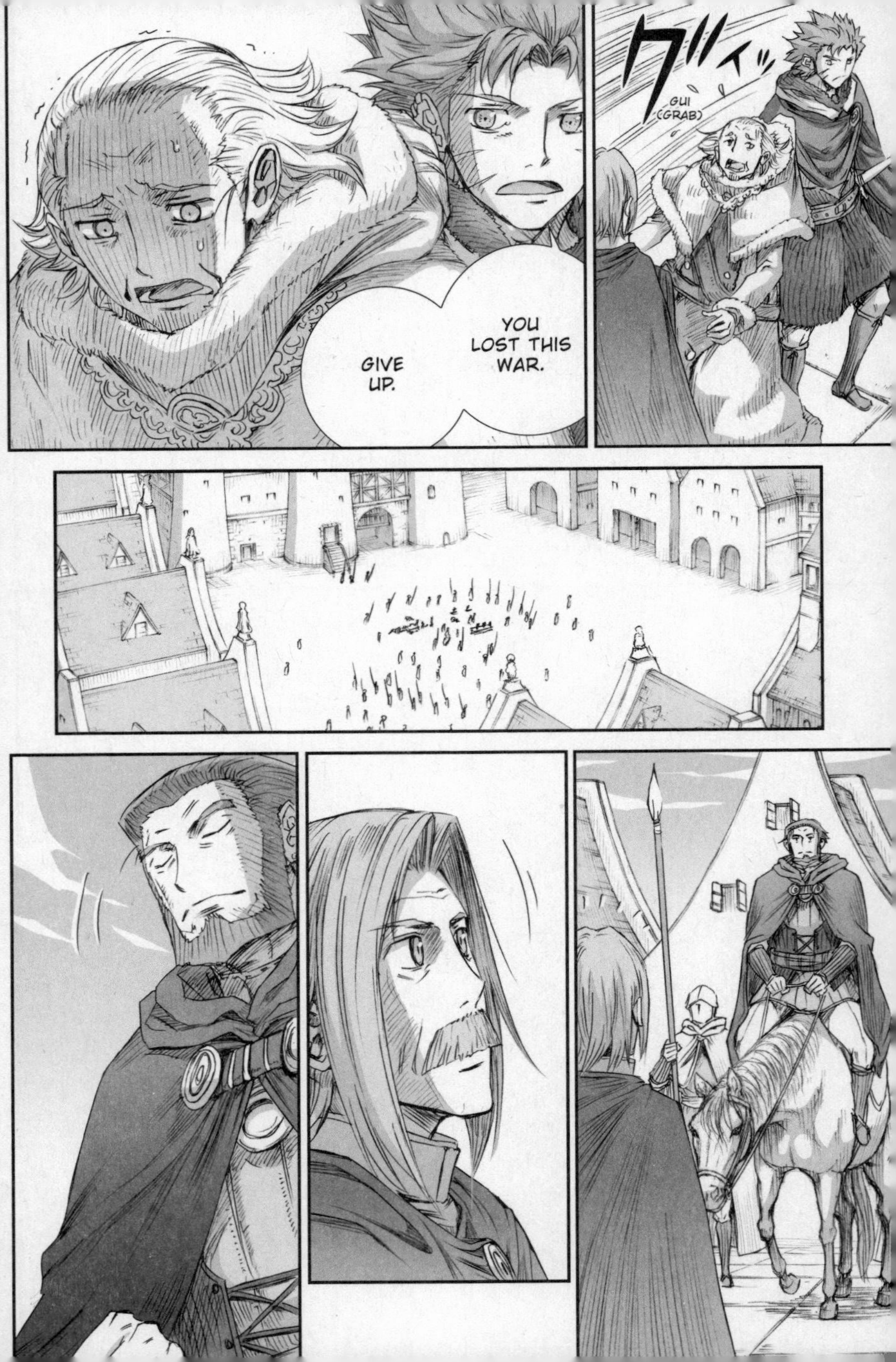
グイッ
GUI (GRAB)
YOU LOST THIS WAR.
GIVE UP.

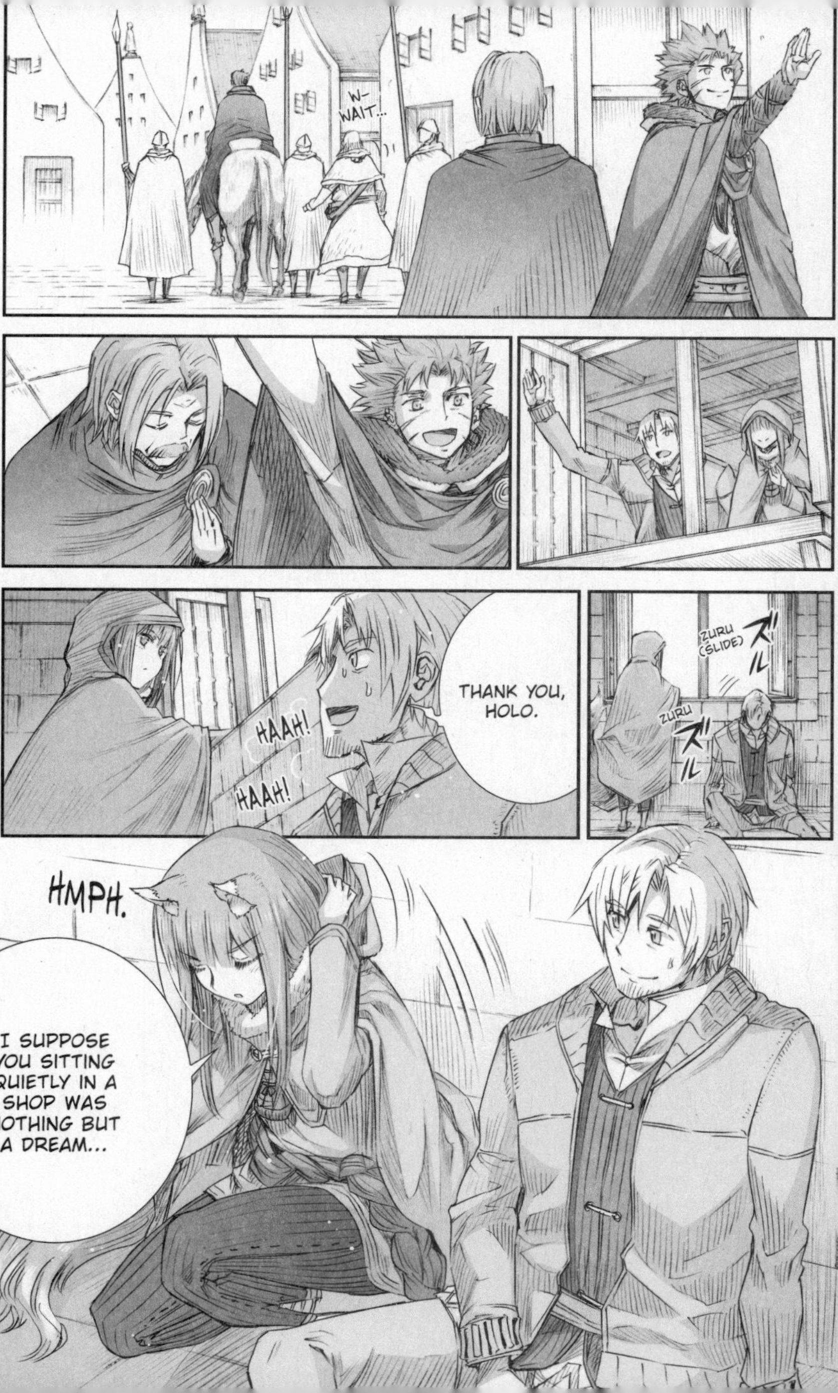
W-WAIT...
ZURU (SLIDE)
ズル
ZURU
ズル
THANK YOU, HOLO.
HAAH!
HAAH!
HMPH.
I SUPPOSE YOU SITTING QUIETLY IN A SHOP WAS NOTHING BUT A DREAM...

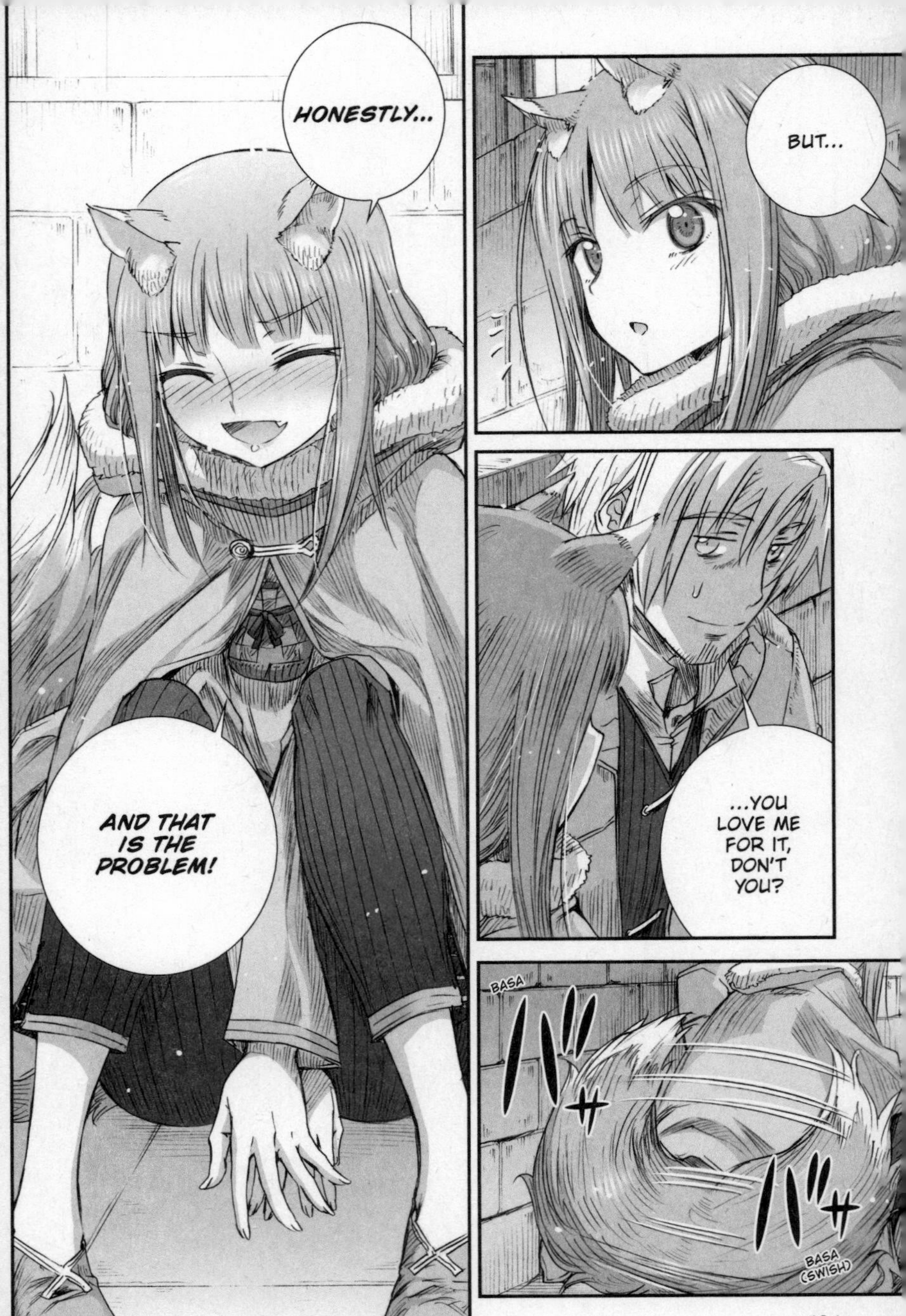
BUT...
...YOU LOVE ME FOR IT, DON'T YOU?
BASA
BASA (SWISH)
HONESTLY...
AND THAT IS THE PROBLEM!

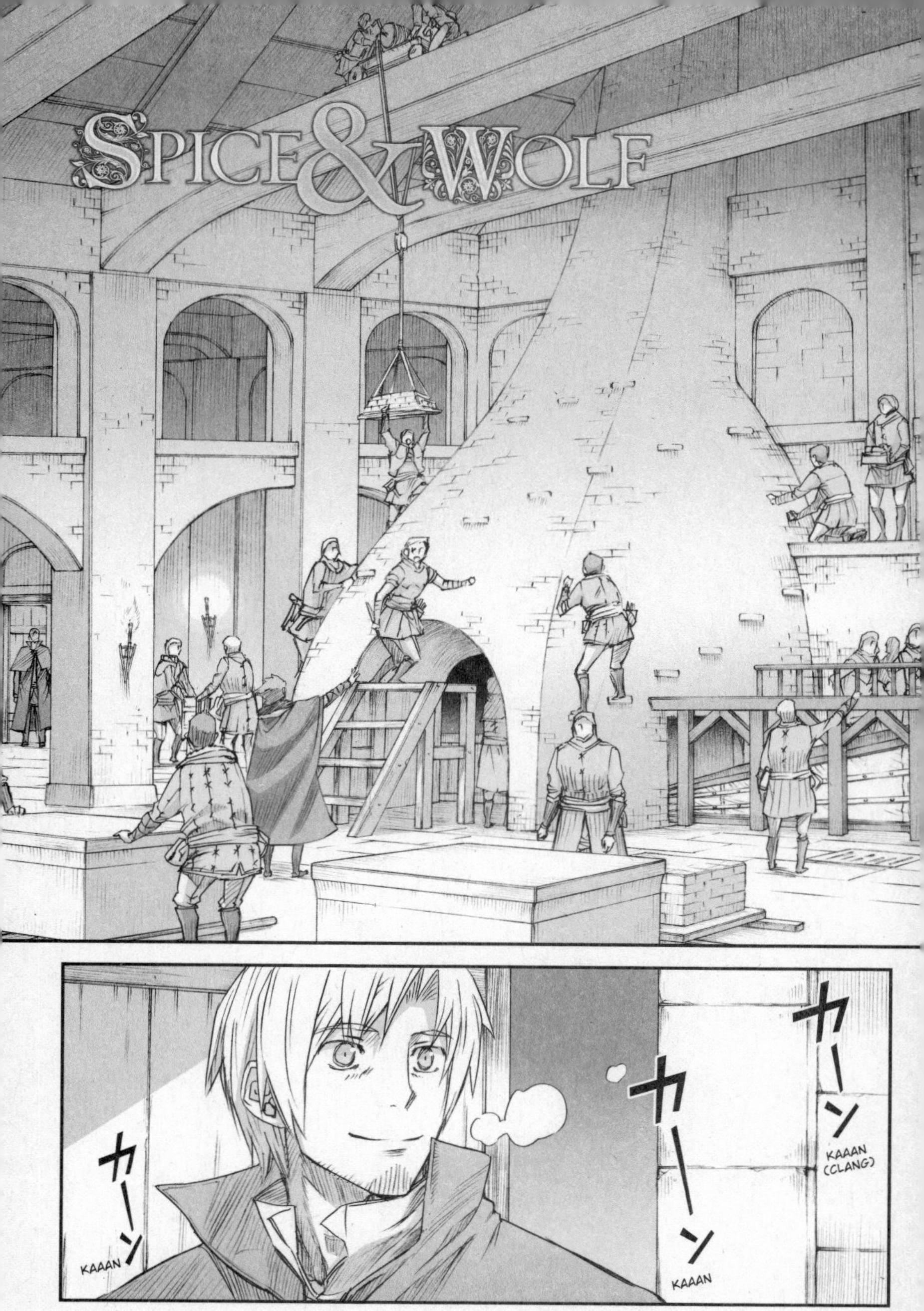
SPICE & WOLF
カーン
KAAAN (CLANG)
カーン
KAAAN
カーン
KAAAN

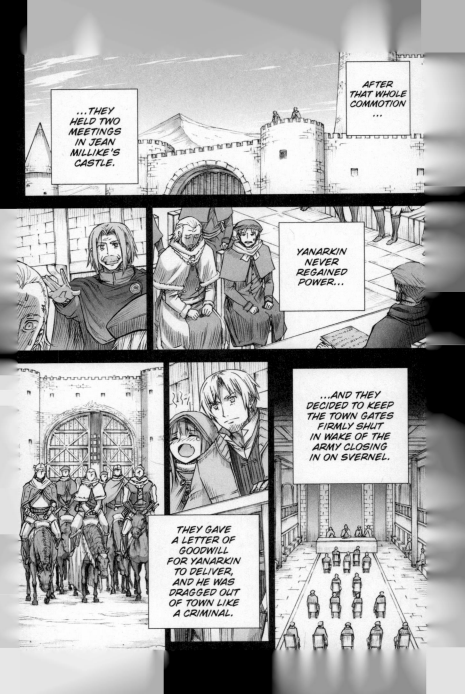

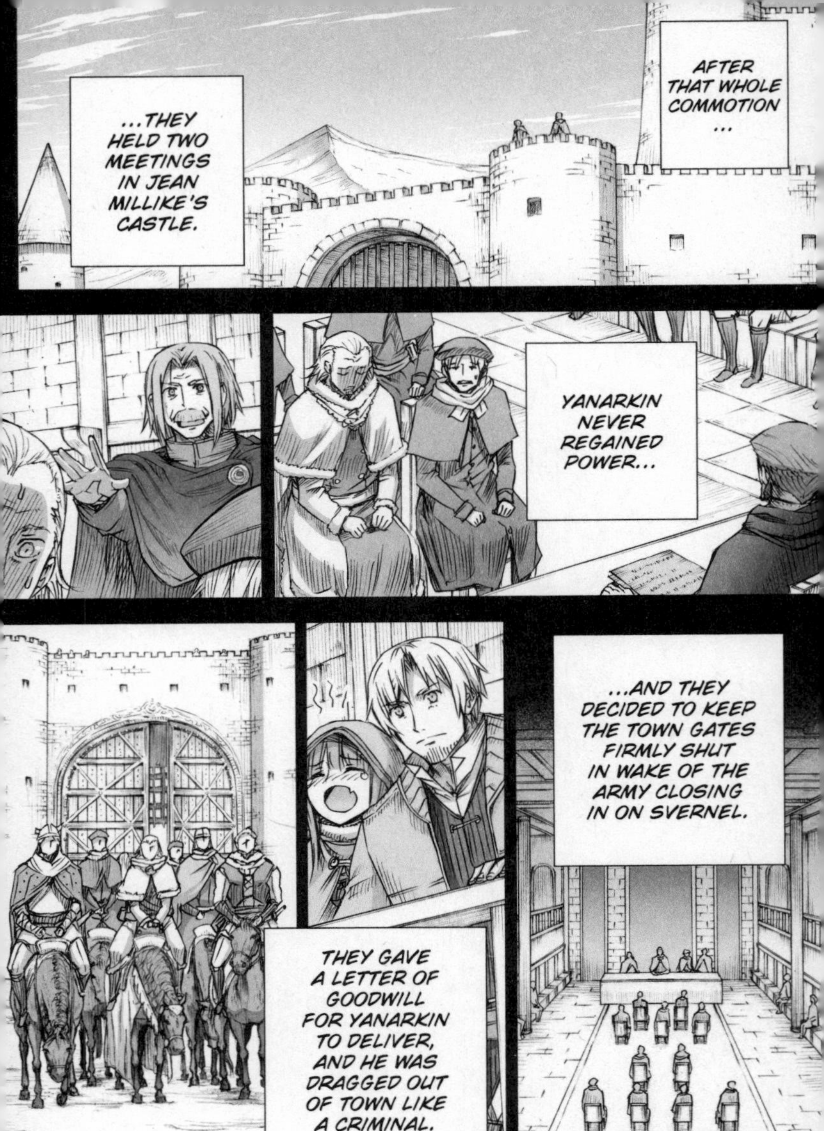
AFTER THAT WHOLE COMMOTION ...
...THEY HELD TWO MEETINGS IN JEAN MILLIKE'S CASTLE.
YANARKIN NEVER REGAINED POWER...
...AND THEY DECIDED TO KEEP THE TOWN GATES FIRMLY SHUT IN WAKE OF THE ARMY CLOSING IN ON SVERNEL.
THEY GAVE A LETTER OF GOODWILL FOR YANARKIN TO DELIVER, AND HE WAS DRAGGED OUT OF TOWN LIKE A CRIMINAL.

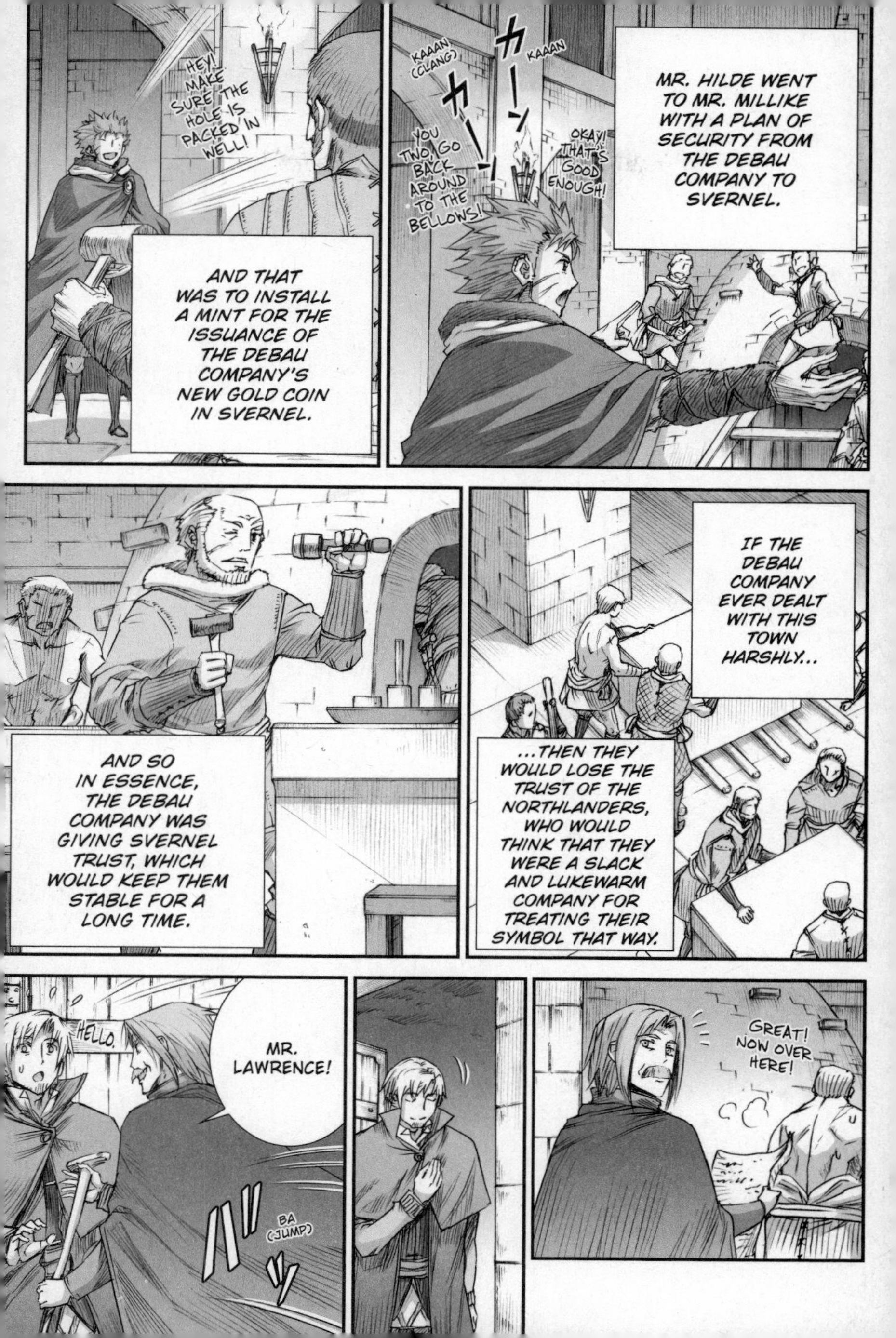
MR. HILDE WENT TO MR. MILLIKE WITH A PLAN OF SECURITY FROM THE DEBAU COMPANY TO SVERNEL.
KAAAN
KAAAN (CLANG)
OKAY! THAT'S GOOD ENOUGH!
YOU TWO, GO BACK AROUND TO THE BELLOWS!
HEY! MAKE SURE THE HOLE IS PACKED IN WELL!
AND THAT WAS TO INSTALL A MINT FOR THE ISSUANCE OF THE DEBAU COMPANY'S NEW GOLD COIN IN SVERNEL.
IF THE DEBAU COMPANY EVER DEALT WITH THIS TOWN HARSHLY...
...THEN THEY WOULD LOSE THE TRUST OF THE NORTHLANDERS, WHO WOULD THINK THAT THEY WERE A SLACK AND LUKEWARM COMPANY FOR TREATING THEIR SYMBOL THAT WAY.
AND SO IN ESSENCE, THE DEBAU COMPANY WAS GIVING SVERNEL TRUST, WHICH WOULD KEEP THEM STABLE FOR A LONG TIME.
GREAT! NOW OVER HERE!
MR. LAWRENCE!
HELLO.
BA (JUMP)

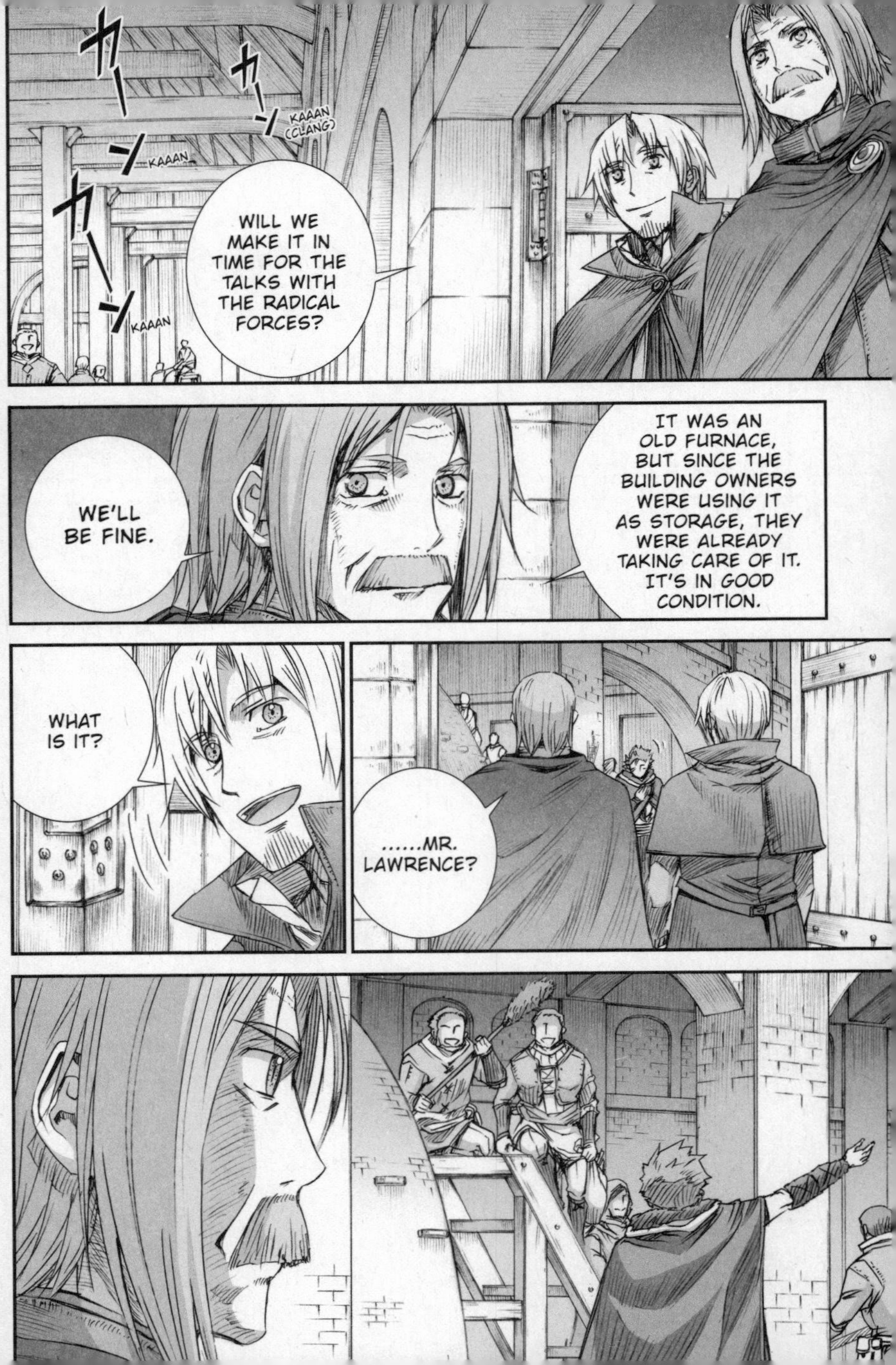

KAAAN (CLANG)
WILL WE MAKE IT IN TIME FOR THE TALKS WITH THE RADICAL FORCES?
KAAAN
KAAAN
IT WAS AN OLD FURNACE, BUT SINCE THE BUILDING OWNERS WERE USING IT AS STORAGE, THEY WERE ALREADY TAKING CARE OF IT. IT'S IN GOOD CONDITION.
WE'LL BE FINE.
......MR. LAWRENCE?
WHAT IS IT?

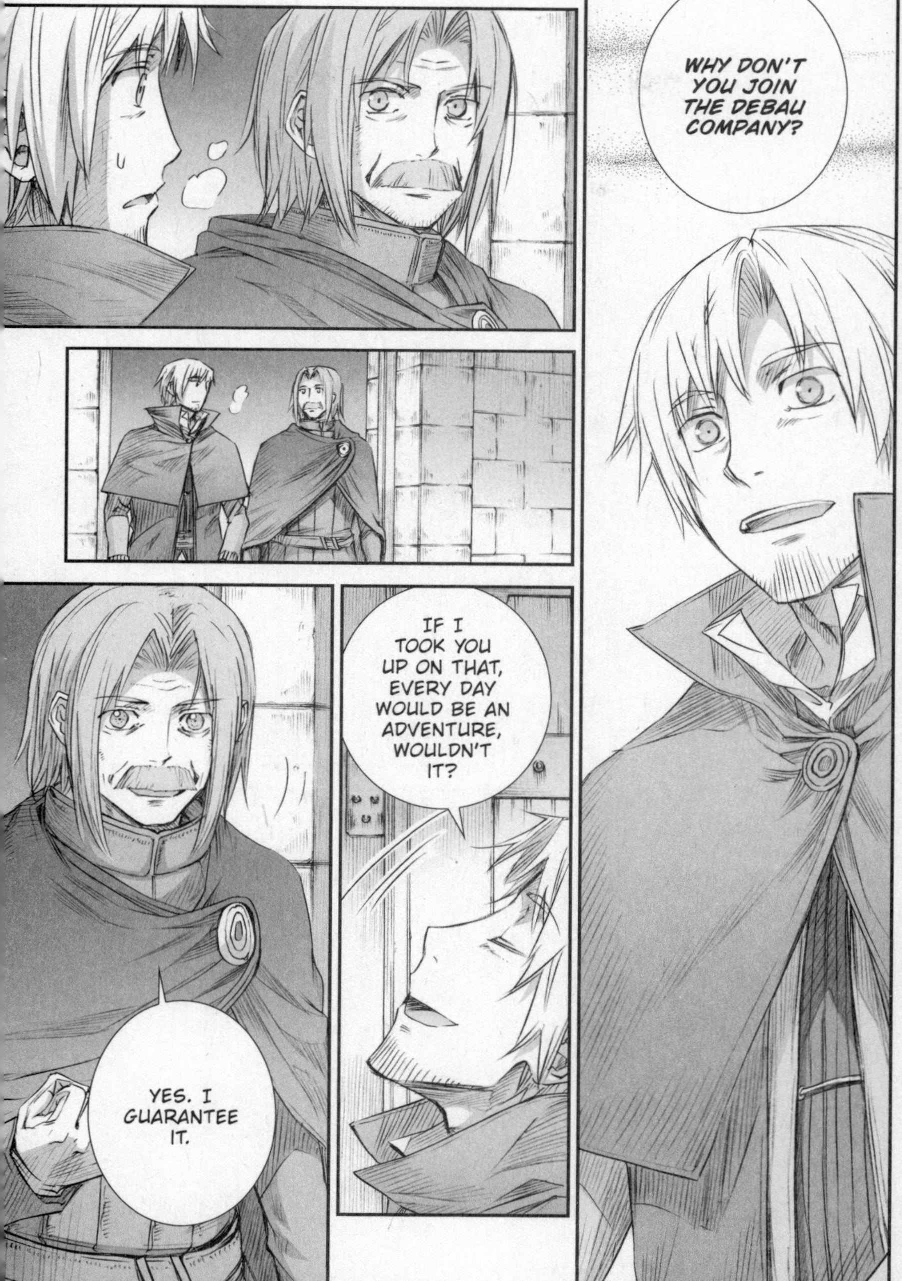
WHY DON'T YOU JOIN THE DEBAU COMPANY?
IF I TOOK YOU UP ON THAT, EVERY DAY WOULD BE AN ADVENTURE, WOULDN'T IT?
YES. I GUARANTEE IT.

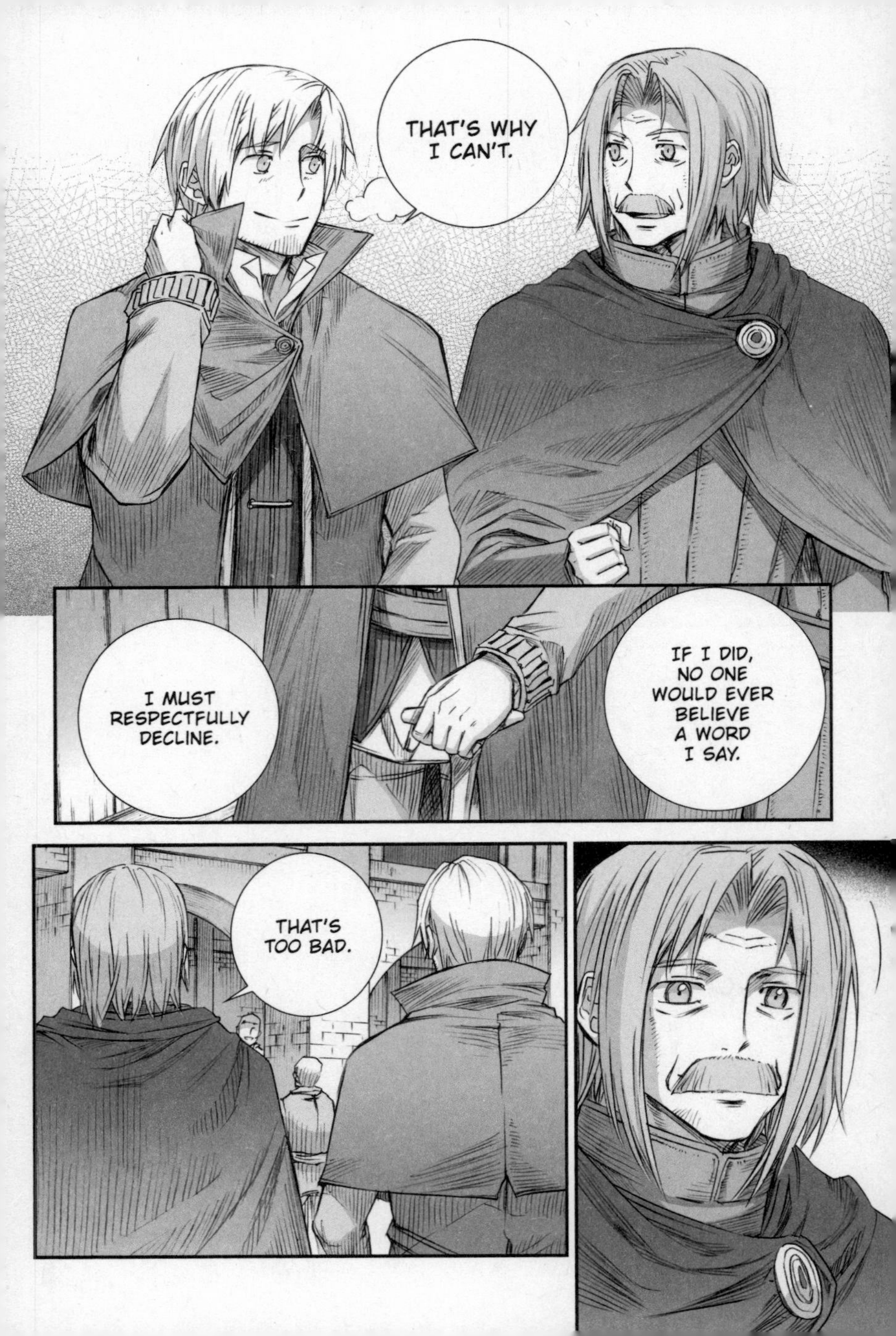
THAT'S WHY I CAN'T.
IF I DID, NO ONE WOULD EVER BELIEVE A WORD I SAY.
I MUST RESPECTFULLY DECLINE.
THAT'S TOO BAD.

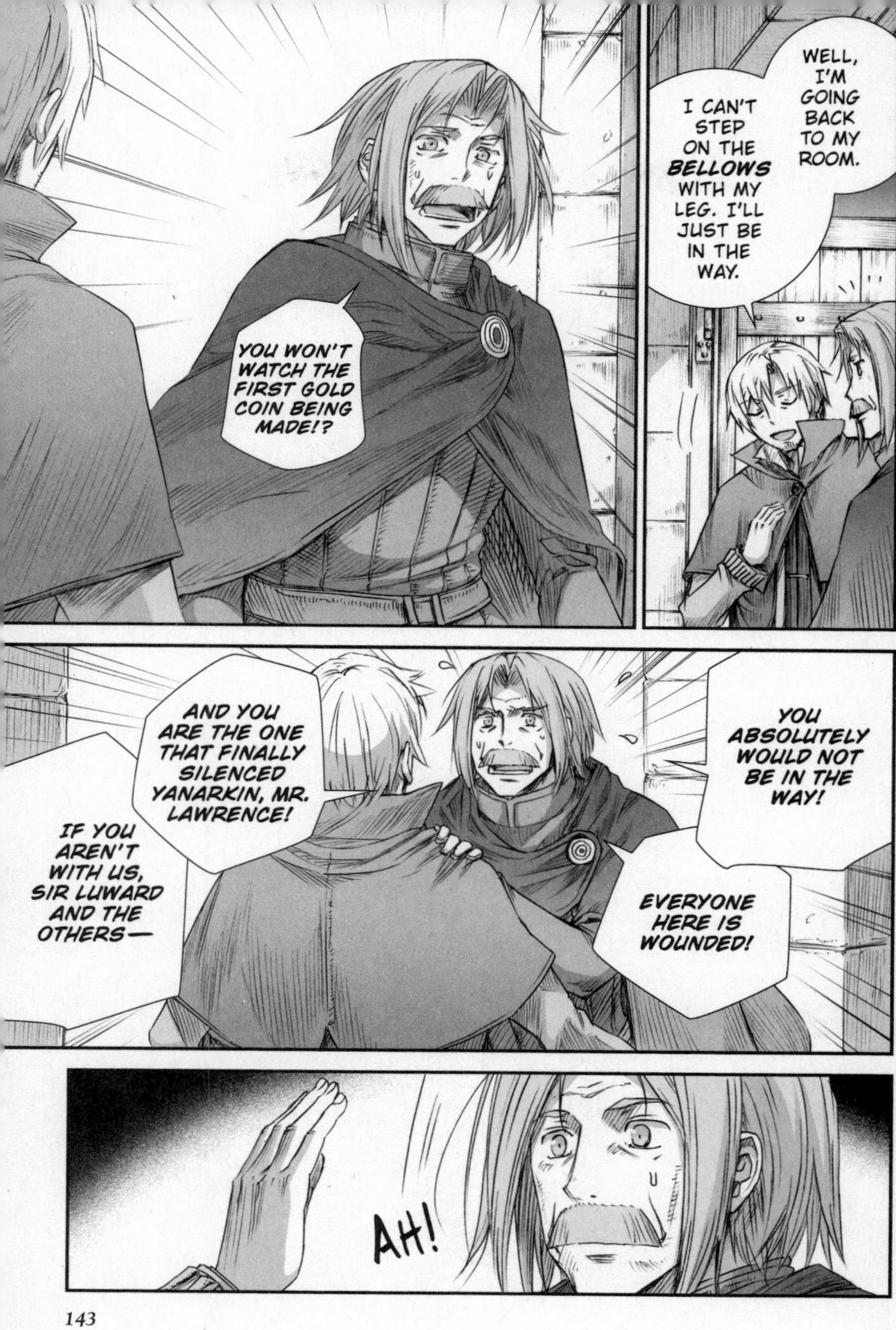
WELL, I'M GOING BACK TO MY ROOM.
I CAN'T STEP ON THE BELLOWS WITH MY LEG. I'LL JUST BE IN THE WAY.
YOU WON'T WATCH THE FIRST GOLD COIN BEING MADE!?
YOU ABSOLUTELY WOULD NOT BE IN THE WAY!
AND YOU ARE THE ONE THAT FINALLY SILENCED YANARKIN, MR. LAWRENCE!
EVERYONE HERE IS WOUNDED!
IF YOU AREN'T WITH US, SIR LUWARD AND THE OTHERS—
AH!

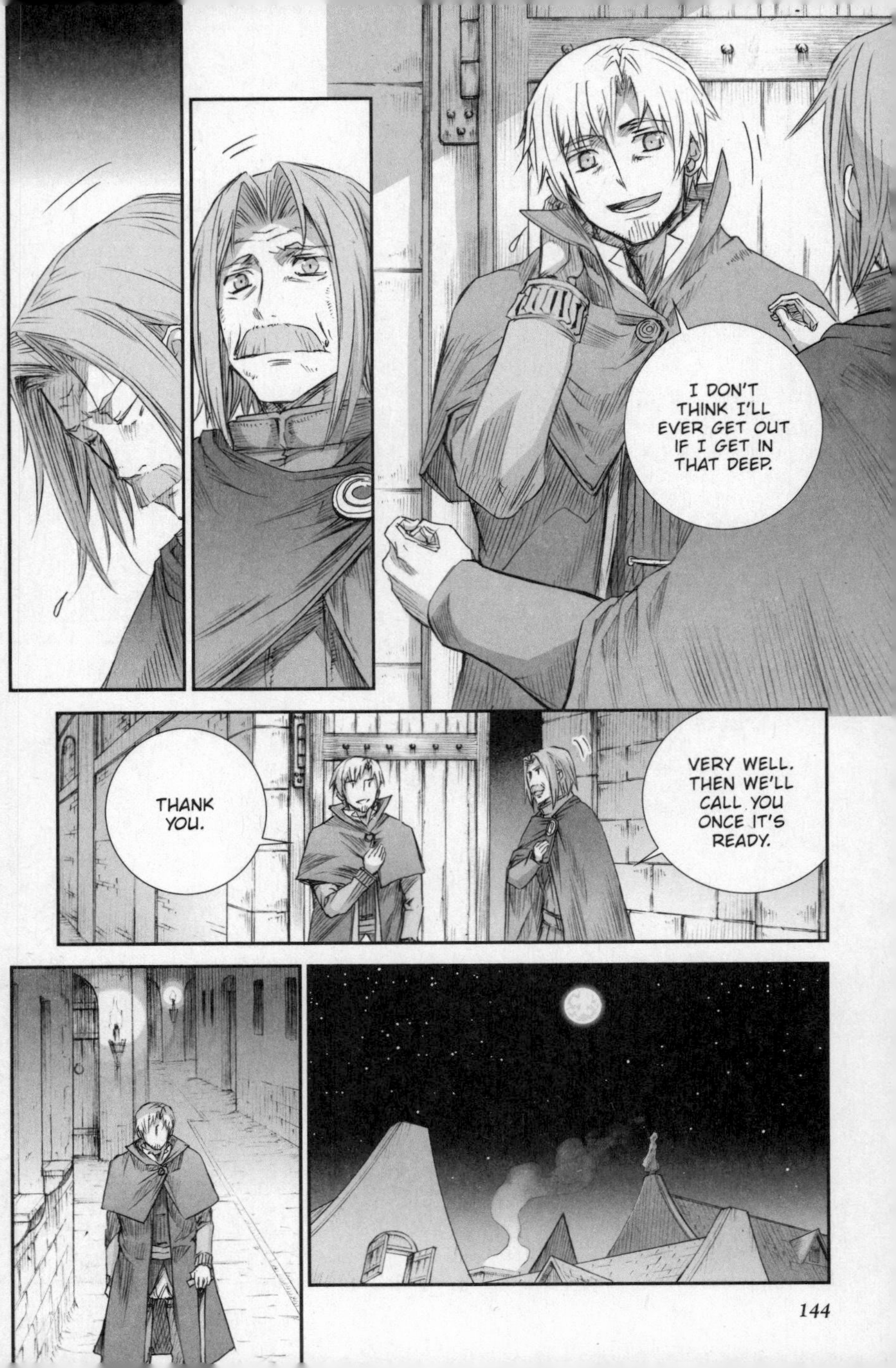
I DON'T THINK I'LL EVER GET OUT IF I GET IN THAT DEEP.
VERY WELL. THEN WE'LL CALL YOU ONCE IT'S READY.
THANK YOU.

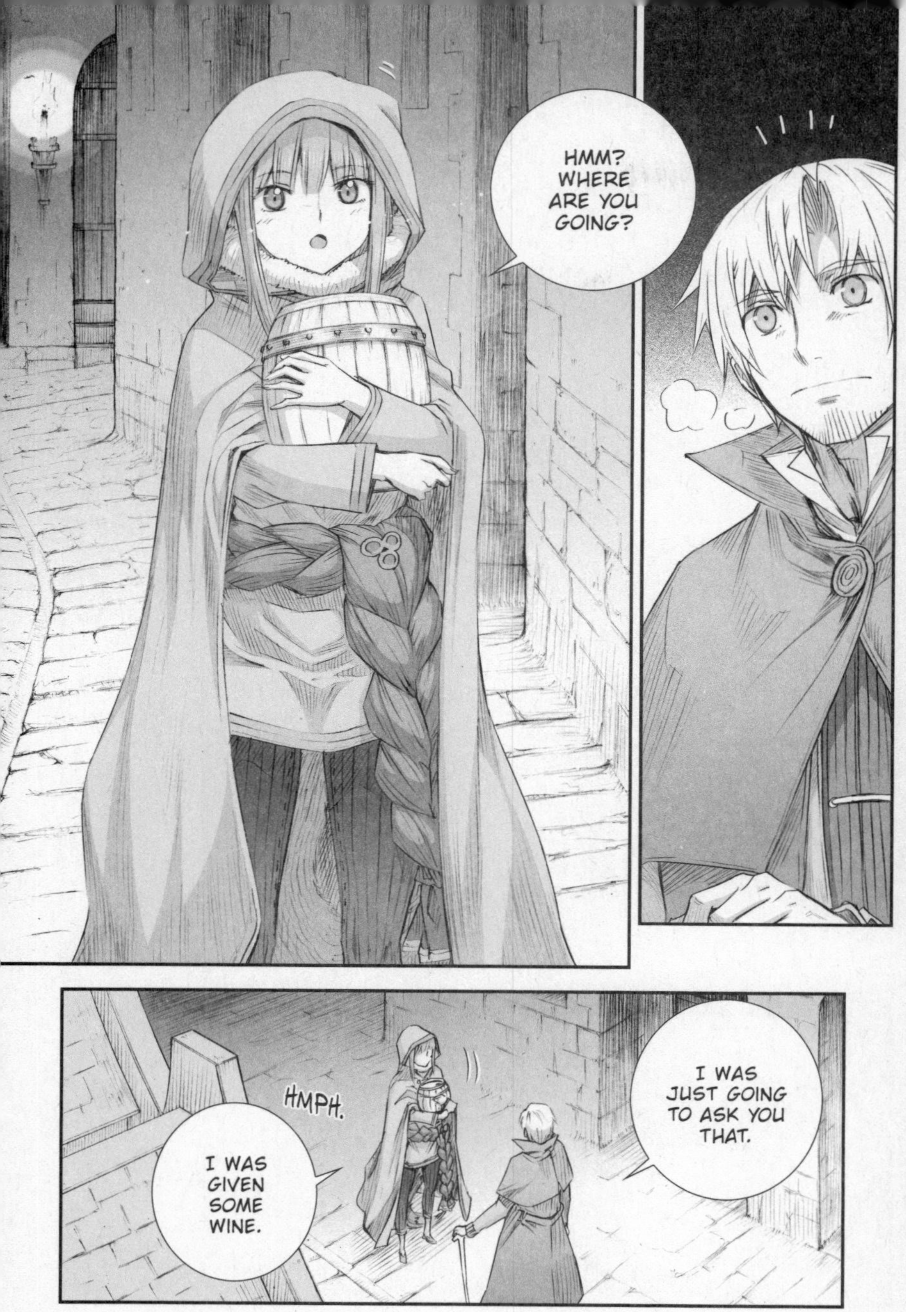
HMM? WHERE ARE YOU GOING?
I WAS JUST GOING TO ASK YOU THAT.
HMPH.
I WAS GIVEN SOME WINE.

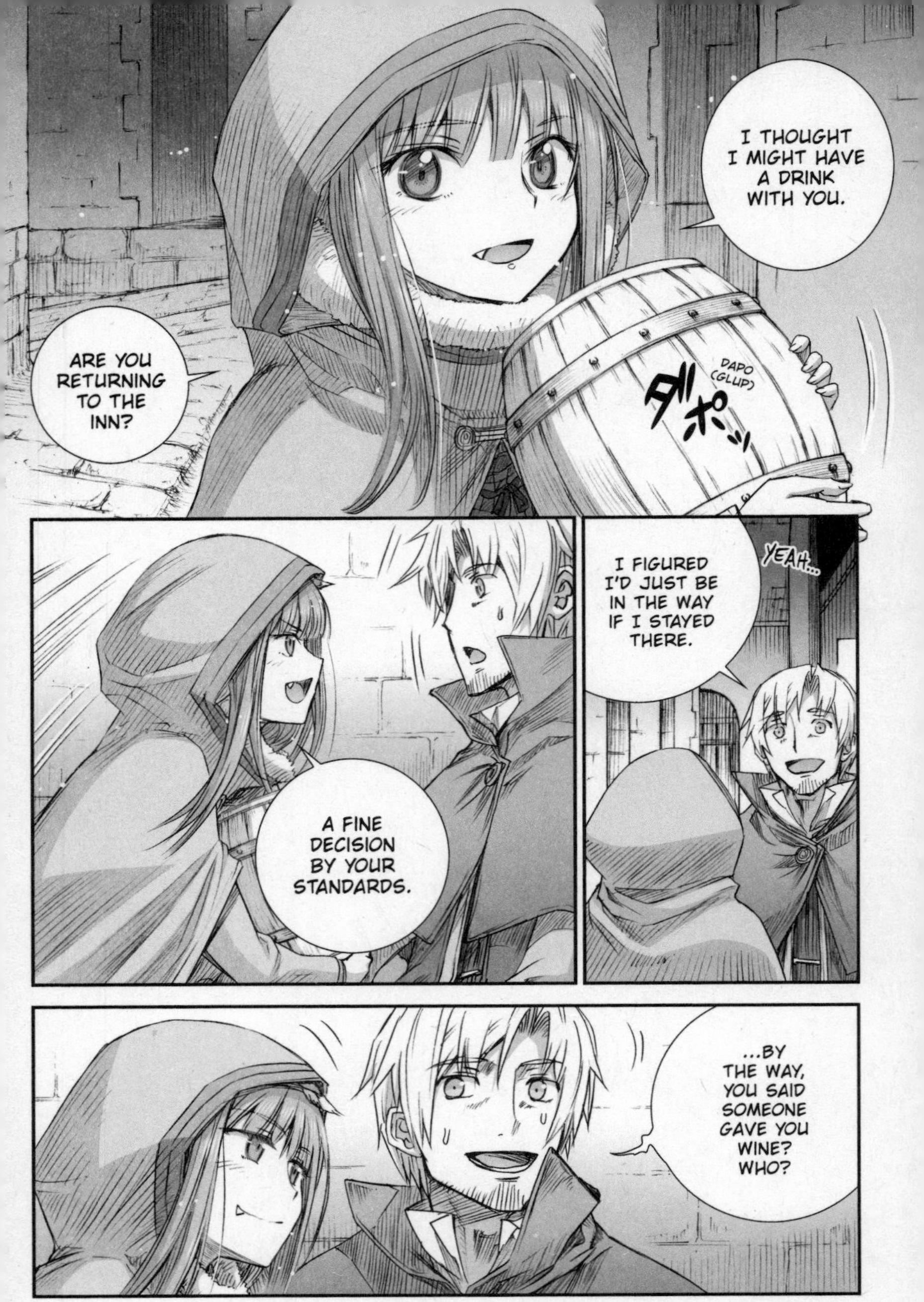
I THOUGHT I MIGHT HAVE A DRINK WITH YOU.
ダポッ
DAPO (GLUP)
ARE YOU RETURNING TO THE INN?
YEAH...
I FIGURED I'D JUST BE IN THE WAY IF I STAYED THERE.
A FINE DECISION BY YOUR STANDARDS.
...BY THE WAY, YOU SAID SOMEONE GAVE YOU WINE? WHO?

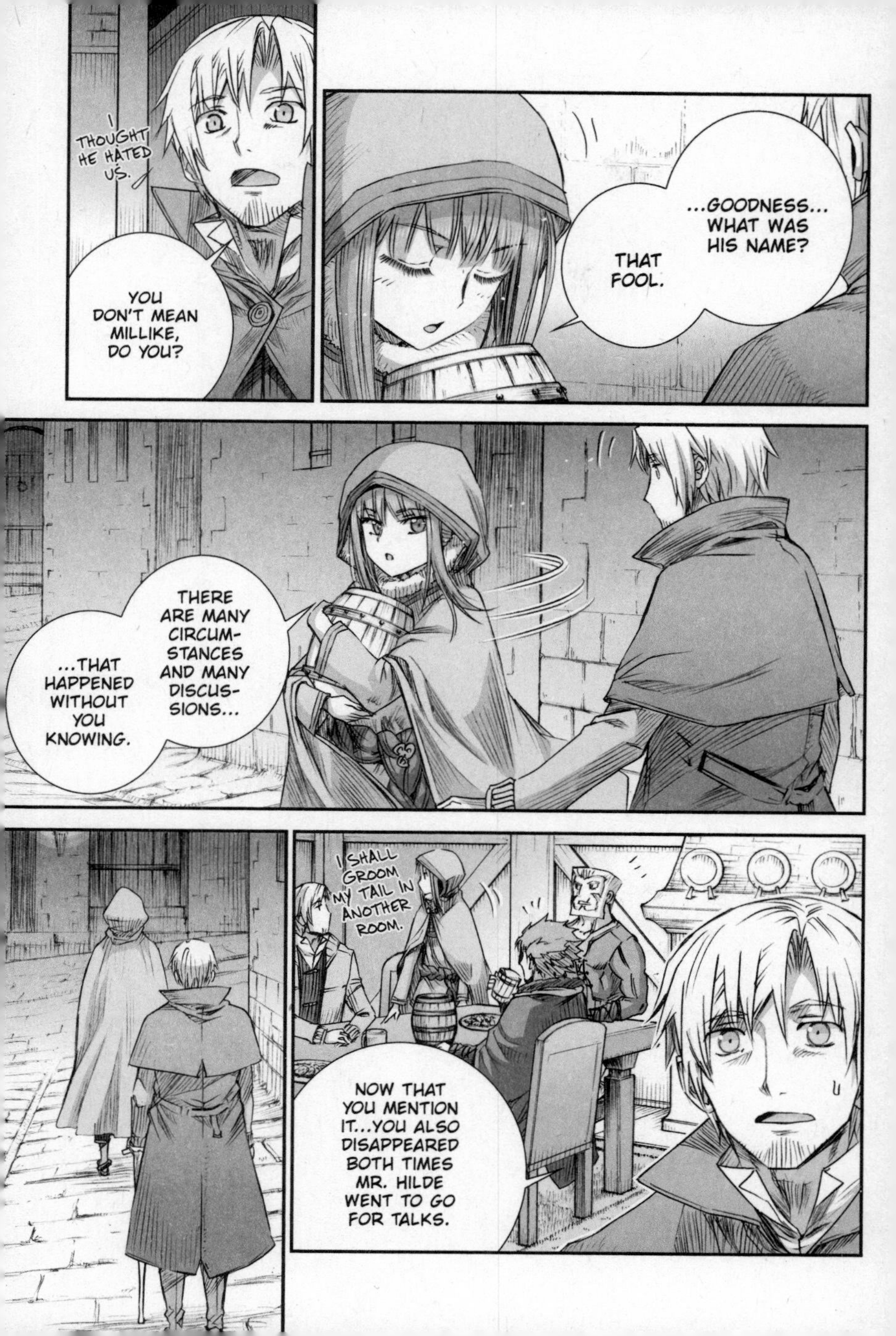
...GOODNESS... WHAT WAS HIS NAME?
THAT FOOL.
YOU DON'T MEAN MILLIKE, DO YOU?
I THOUGHT HE HATED US.
THERE ARE MANY CIRCUM-STANCES AND MANY DISCUS-SIONS...
...THAT HAPPENED WITHOUT YOU KNOWING.
I SHALL GROOM MY TAIL IN ANOTHER ROOM.
NOW THAT YOU MENTION IT...YOU ALSO DISAPPEARED BOTH TIMES MR. HILDE WENT TO GO FOR TALKS.

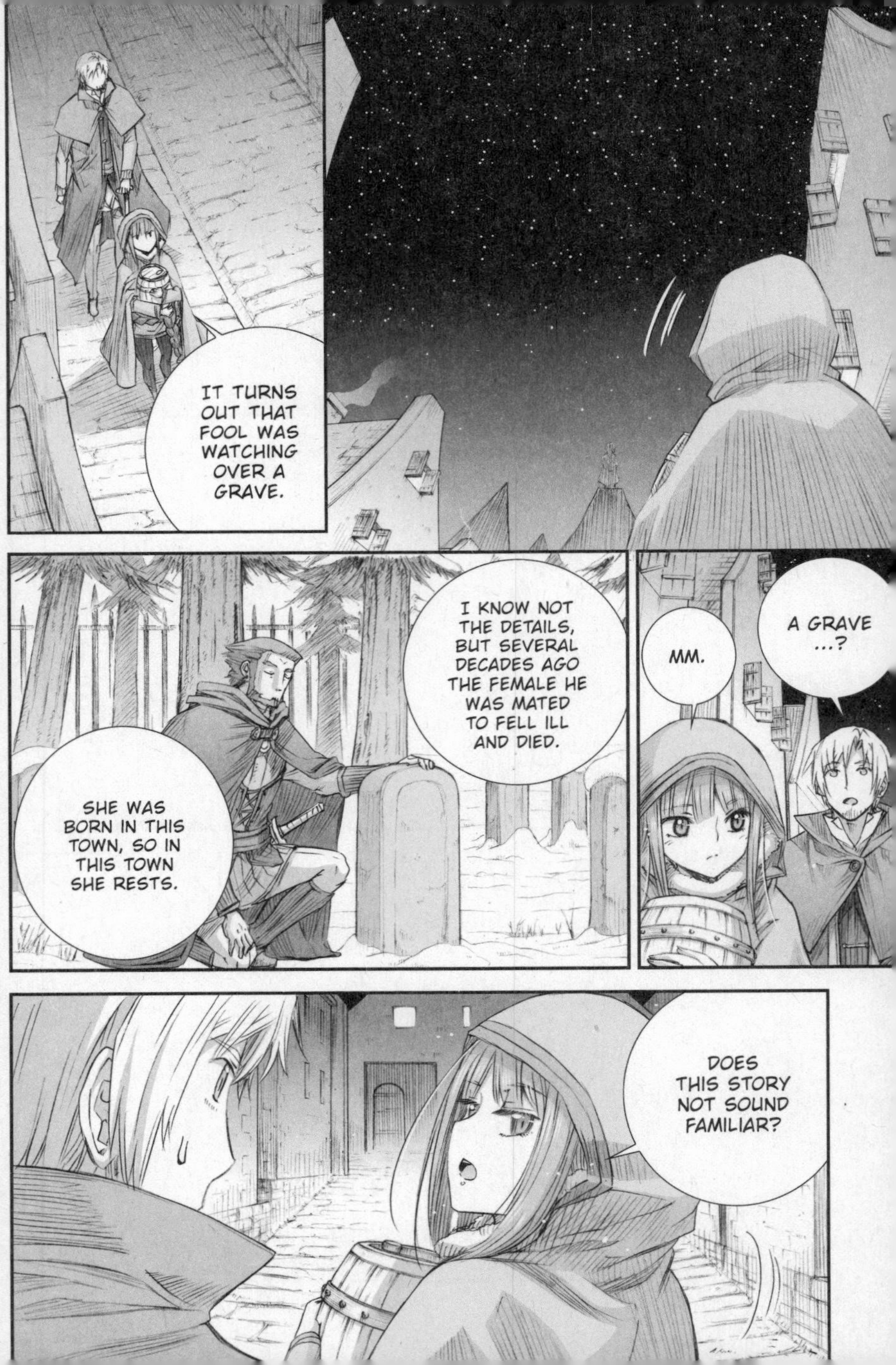
IT TURNS OUT THAT FOOL WAS WATCHING OVER A GRAVE.
A GRAVE ...?
MM.
I KNOW NOT THE DETAILS, BUT SEVERAL DECADES AGO THE FEMALE HE WAS MATED TO FELL ILL AND DIED.
SHE WAS BORN IN THIS TOWN, SO IN THIS TOWN SHE RESTS.
DOES THIS STORY NOT SOUND FAMILIAR?

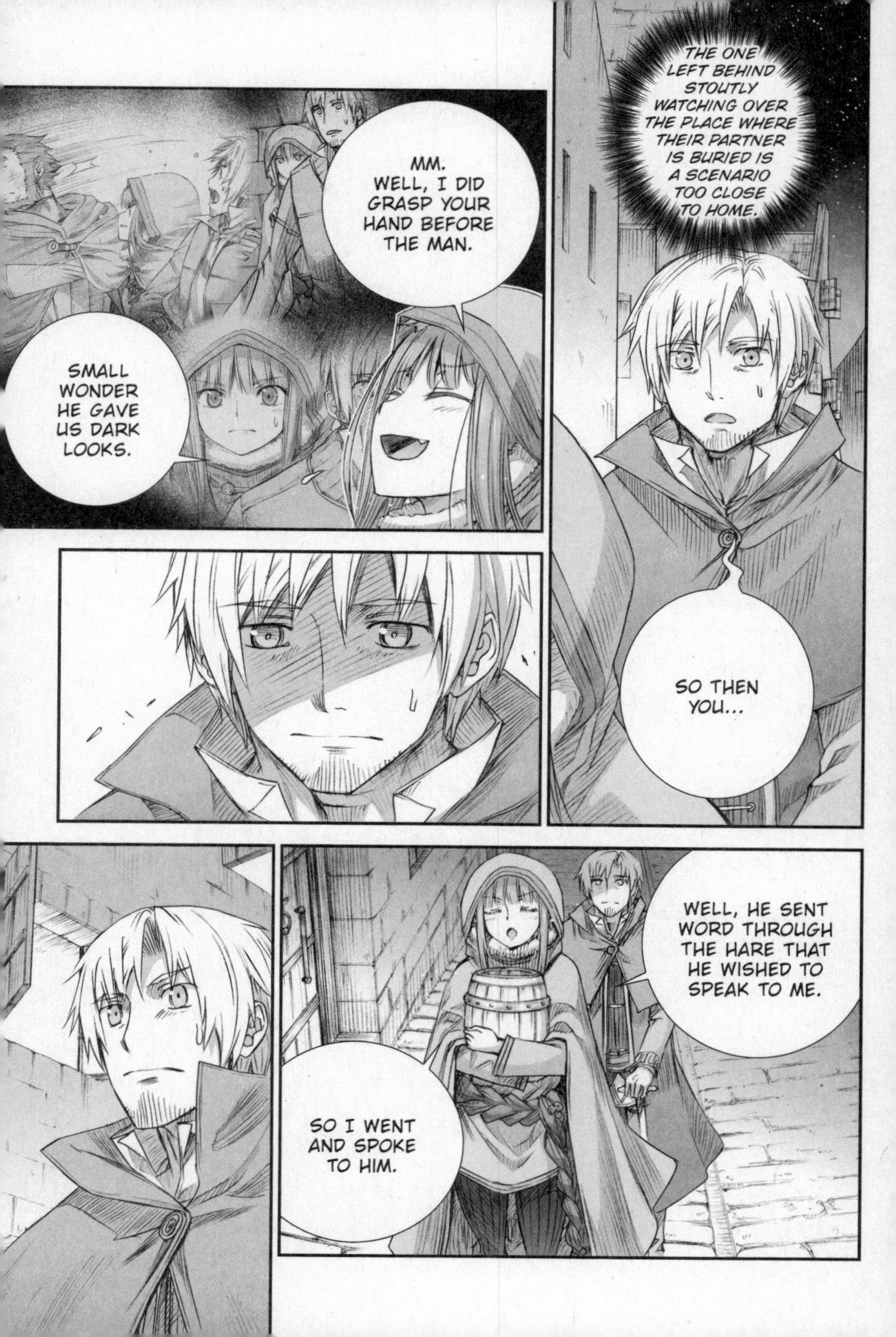
THE ONE LEFT BEHIND STOUTLY WATCHING OVER THE PLACE WHERE THEIR PARTNER IS BURIED IS A SCENARIO TOO CLOSE TO HOME.
SO THEN YOU...
MM. WELL, I DID GRASP YOUR HAND BEFORE THE MAN.
SMALL WONDER HE GAVE US DARK LOOKS.
WELL, HE SENT WORD THROUGH THE HARE THAT HE WISHED TO SPEAK TO ME.
SO I WENT AND SPOKE TO HIM.

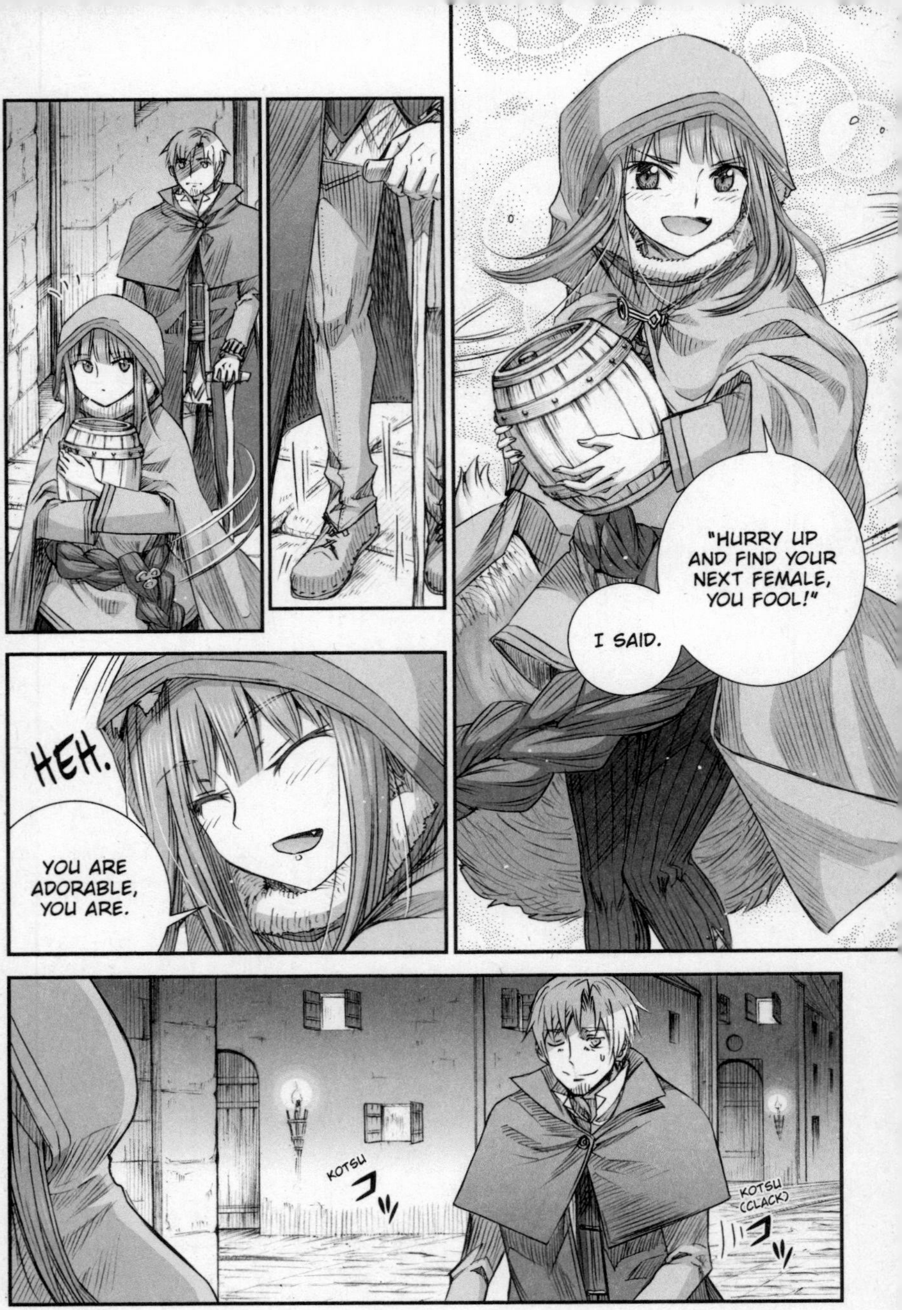

"HURRY UP AND FIND YOUR NEXT FEMALE, YOU FOOL!"
I SAID.
HEH.
YOU ARE ADORABLE, YOU ARE.
KOTSU (CLACK)
KOTSU

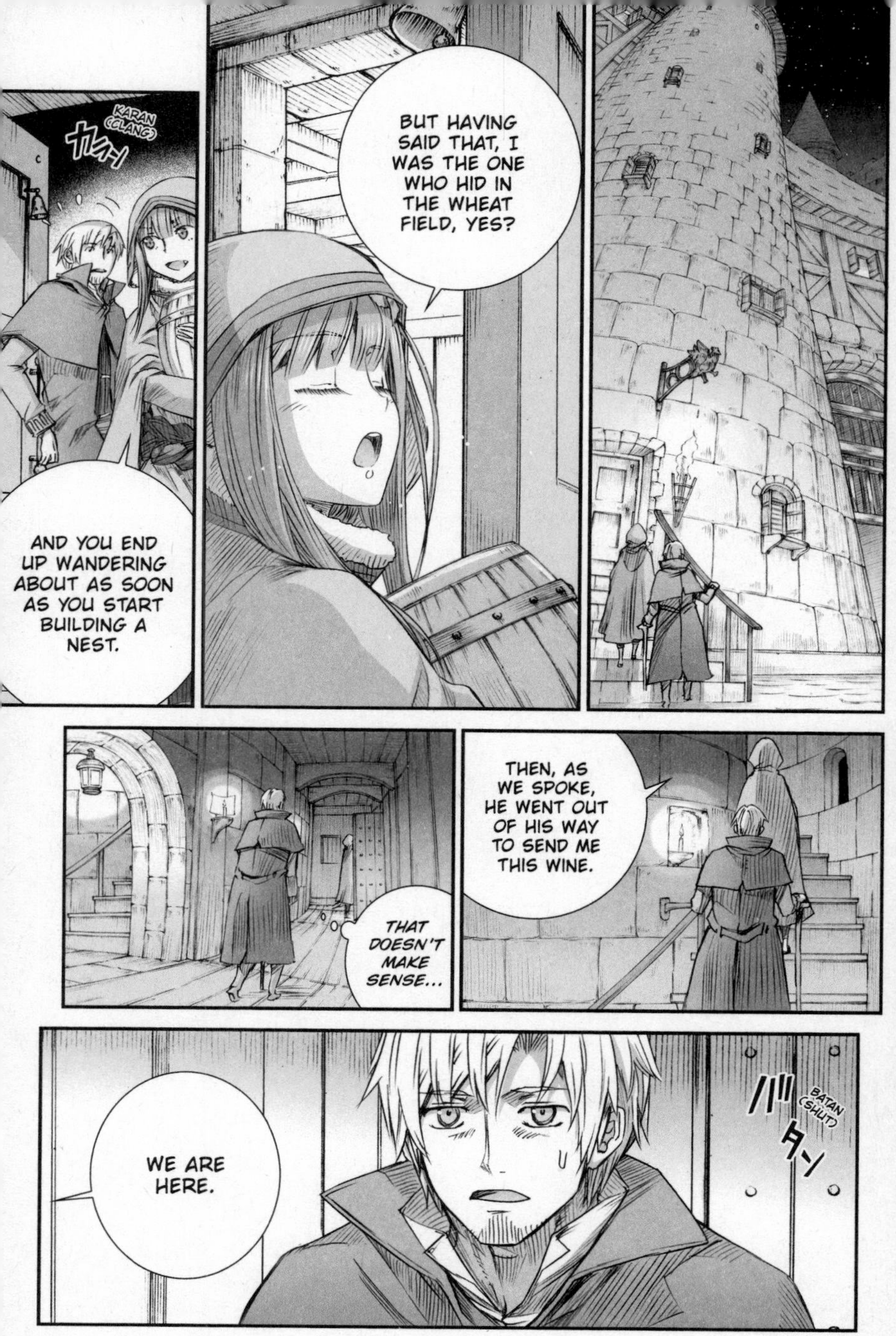
BUT HAVING SAID THAT, I WAS THE ONE WHO HID IN THE WHEAT FIELD, YES?
KARAN (CLANG)
AND YOU END UP WANDERING ABOUT AS SOON AS YOU START BUILDING A NEST.
THEN, AS WE SPOKE, HE WENT OUT OF HIS WAY TO SEND ME THIS WINE.
THAT DOESN'T MAKE SENSE...
BATAN (SHUT)
WE ARE HERE.

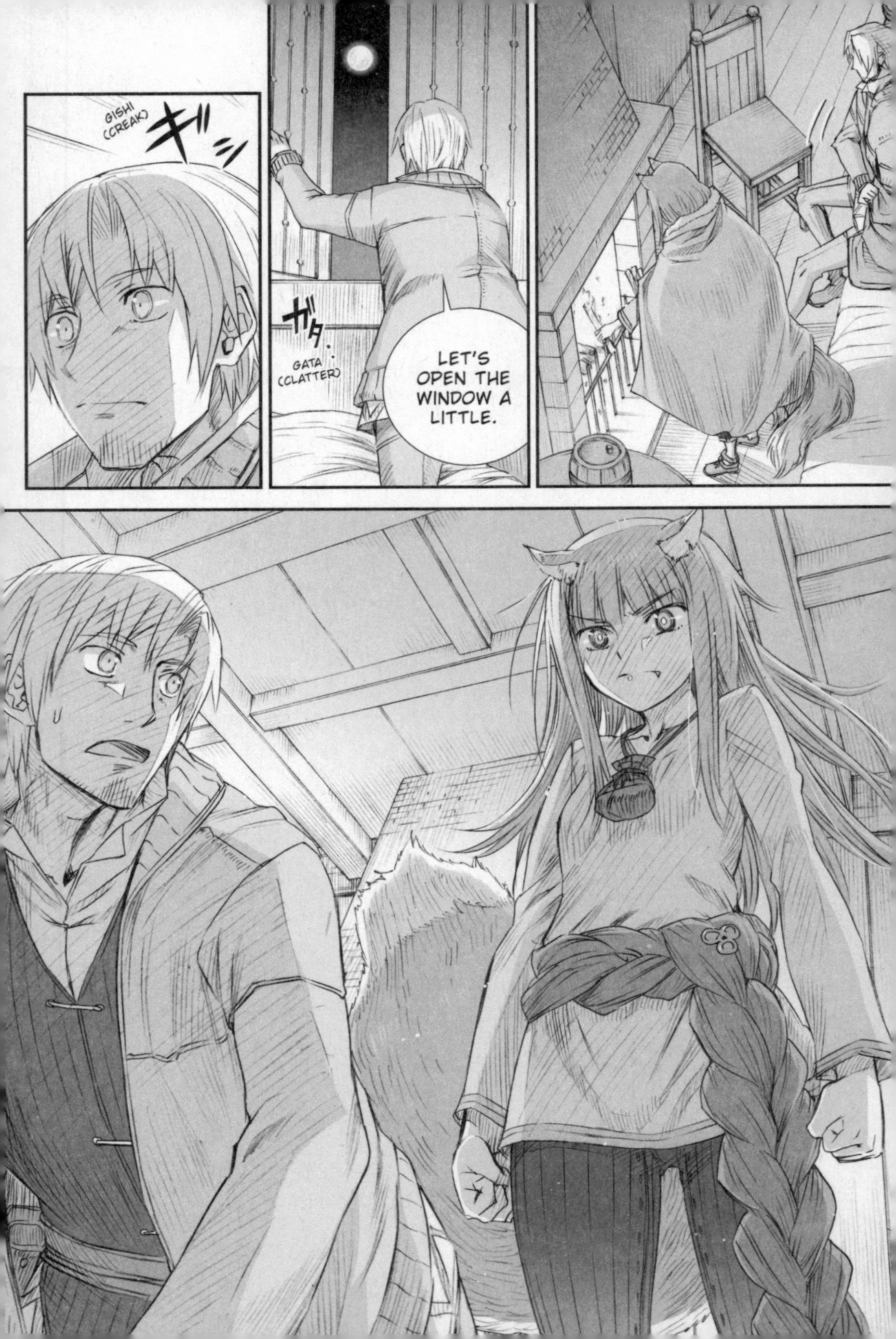
LET'S OPEN THE WINDOW A LITTLE.
ガタ
GATA (CLATTER)
ギシ
GISHI (CREAK)

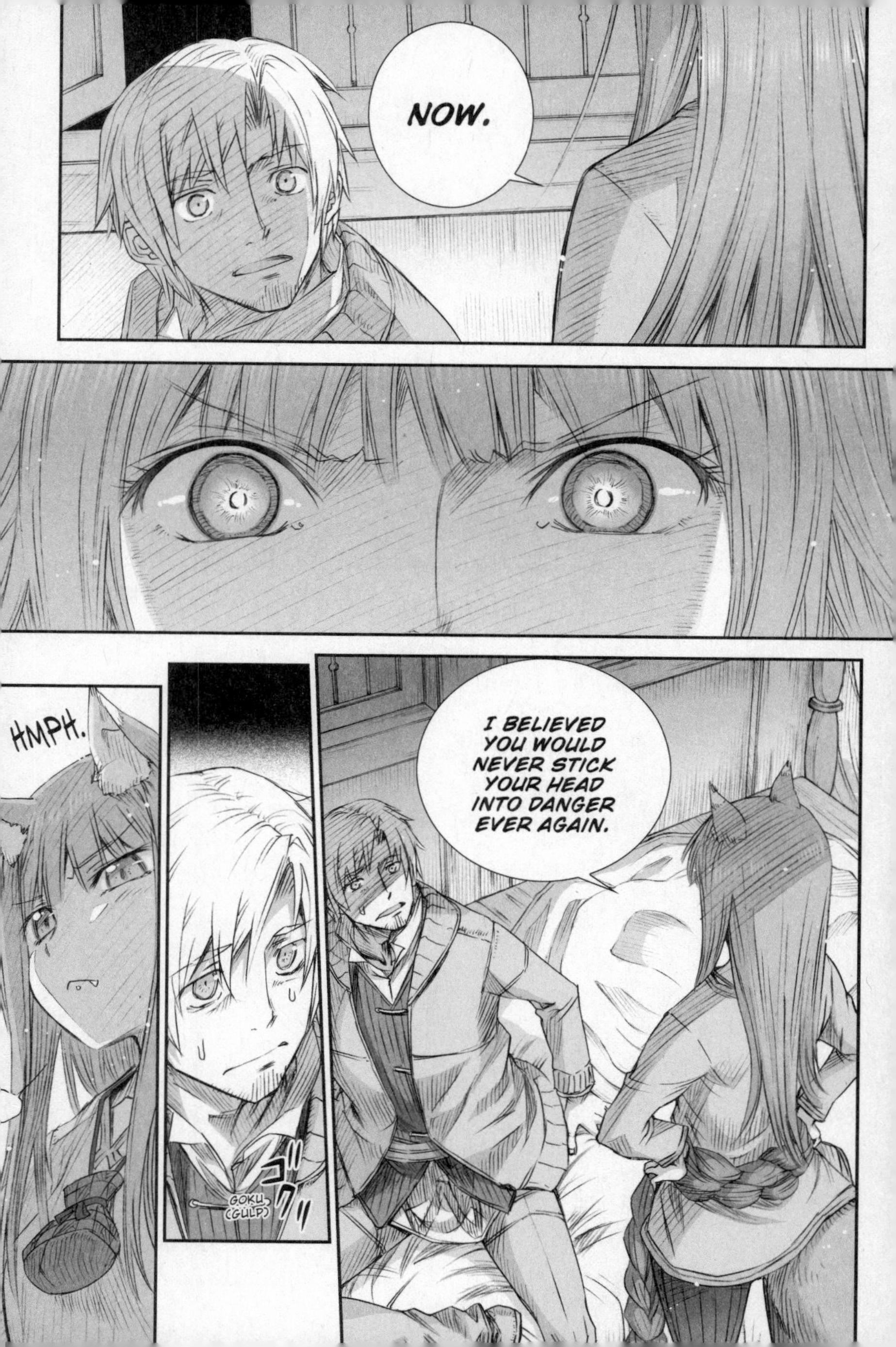
NOW.
I BELIEVED YOU WOULD NEVER STICK YOUR HEAD INTO DANGER EVER AGAIN.
GOKU (GULP)
HMPH.

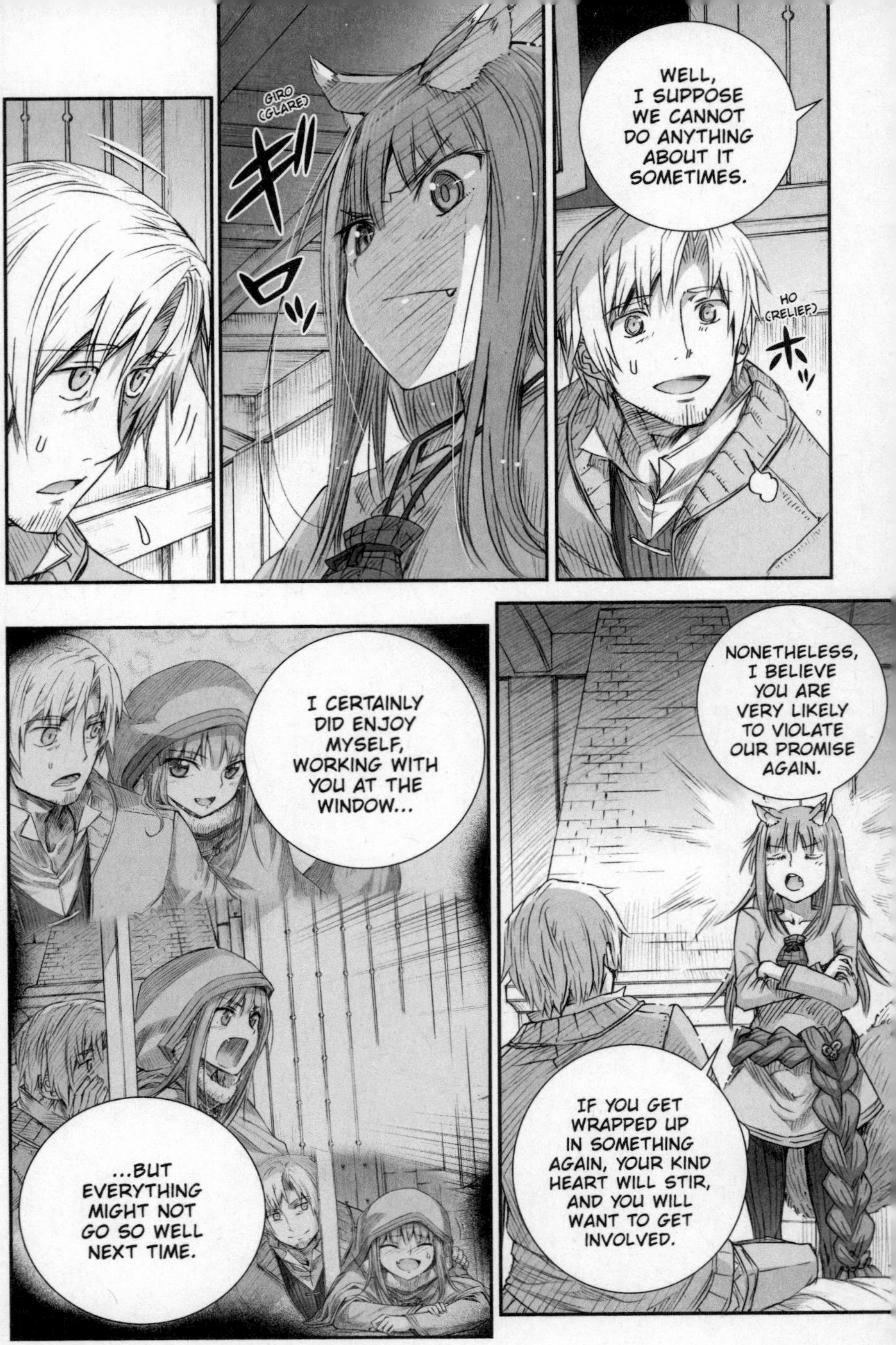
WELL, I SUPPOSE WE CANNOT DO ANYTHING ABOUT IT SOMETIMES.
HO (RELIEF)
GIRO (GLARE)
NONETHELESS, I BELIEVE YOU ARE VERY LIKELY TO VIOLATE OUR PROMISE AGAIN.
IF YOU GET WRAPPED UP IN SOMETHING AGAIN, YOUR KIND HEART WILL STIR, AND YOU WILL WANT TO GET INVOLVED.
I CERTAINLY DID ENJOY MYSELF, WORKING WITH YOU AT THE WINDOW...
...BUT EVERYTHING MIGHT NOT GO SO WELL NEXT TIME.

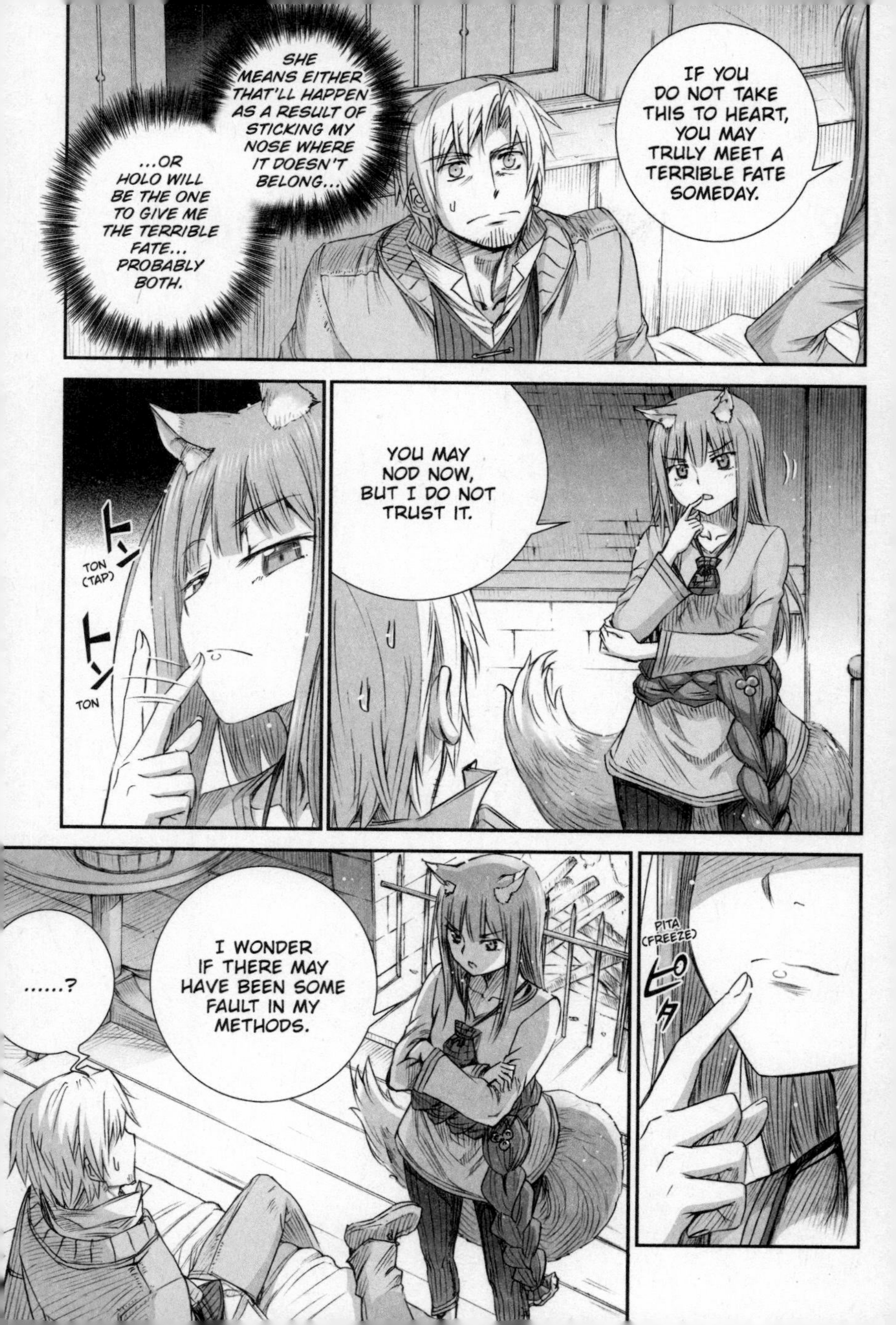
IF YOU DO NOT TAKE THIS TO HEART, YOU MAY TRULY MEET A TERRIBLE FATE SOMEDAY.
SHE MEANS EITHER THAT'LL HAPPEN AS A RESULT OF STICKING MY NOSE WHERE IT DOESN'T BELONG...
...OR HOLO WILL BE THE ONE TO GIVE ME THE TERRIBLE FATE... PROBABLY BOTH.
YOU MAY NOD NOW, BUT I DO NOT TRUST IT.
トン
TON (TAP)
トン
TON
ピタ
PITA (FREEZE)
I WONDER IF THERE MAY HAVE BEEN SOME FAULT IN MY METHODS.
......?

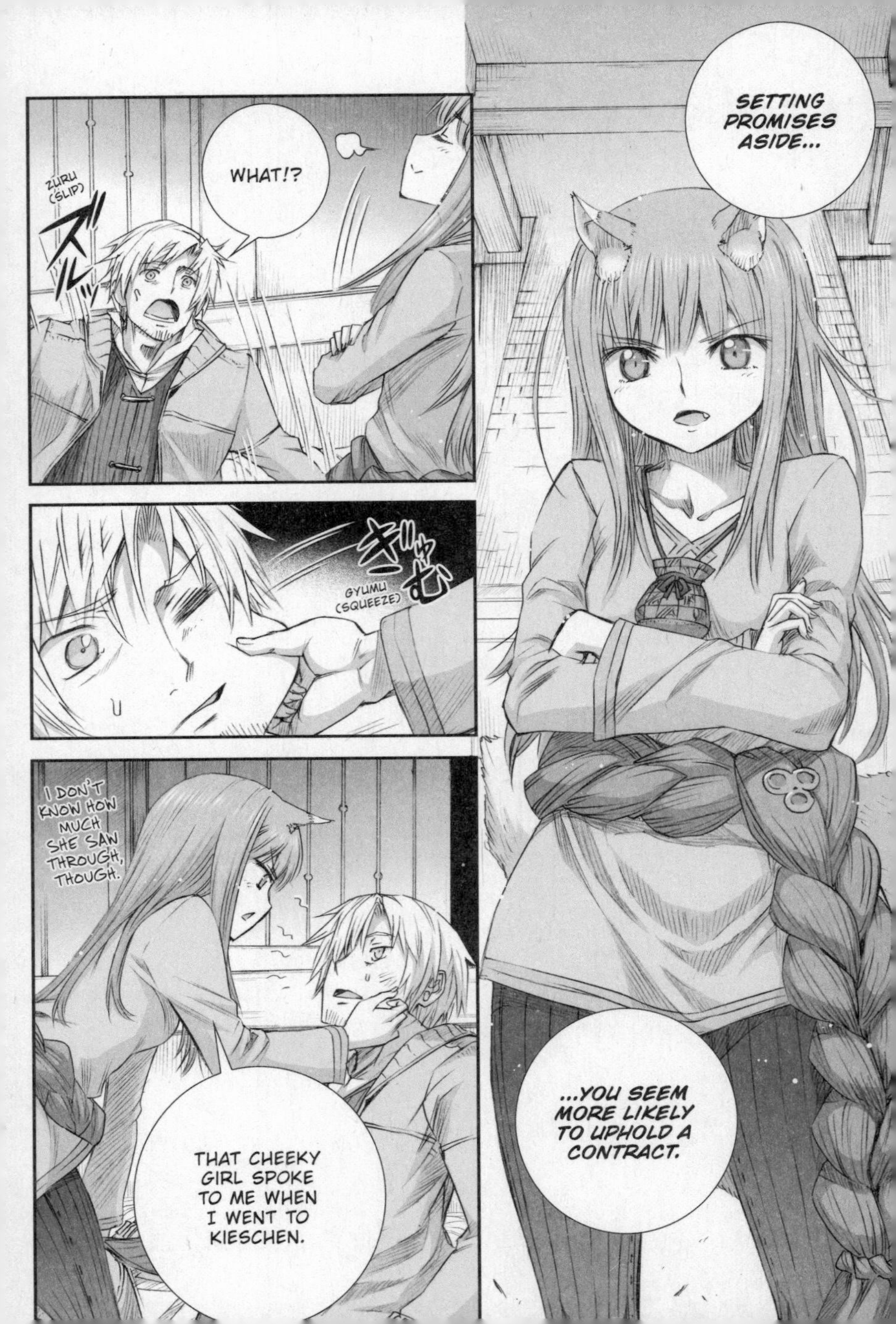
SETTING PROMISES ASIDE...
...YOU SEEM MORE LIKELY TO UPHOLD A CONTRACT.
WHAT!?
ZURU (SLIP)
GYUMU (SQUEEZE)
I DON'T KNOW HOW MUCH SHE SAW THROUGH, THOUGH.
THAT CHEEKY GIRL SPOKE TO ME WHEN I WENT TO KIESCHEN.

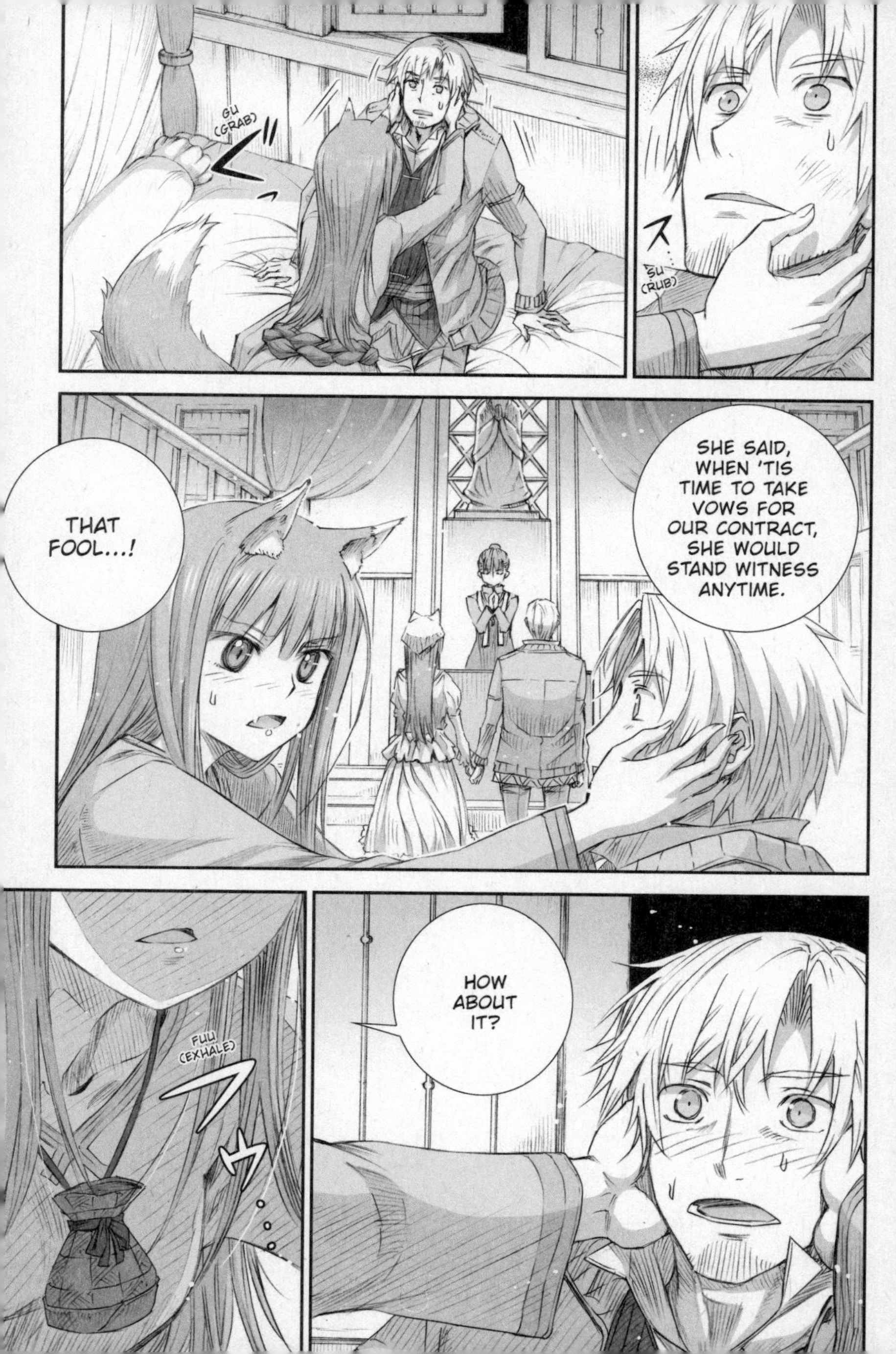
SU (RUB)
GU (GRAB)
SHE SAID, WHEN 'TIS TIME TO TAKE VOWS FOR OUR CONTRACT, SHE WOULD STAND WITNESS ANYTIME.
THAT FOOL...!
HOW ABOUT IT?
FUU (EXHALE)

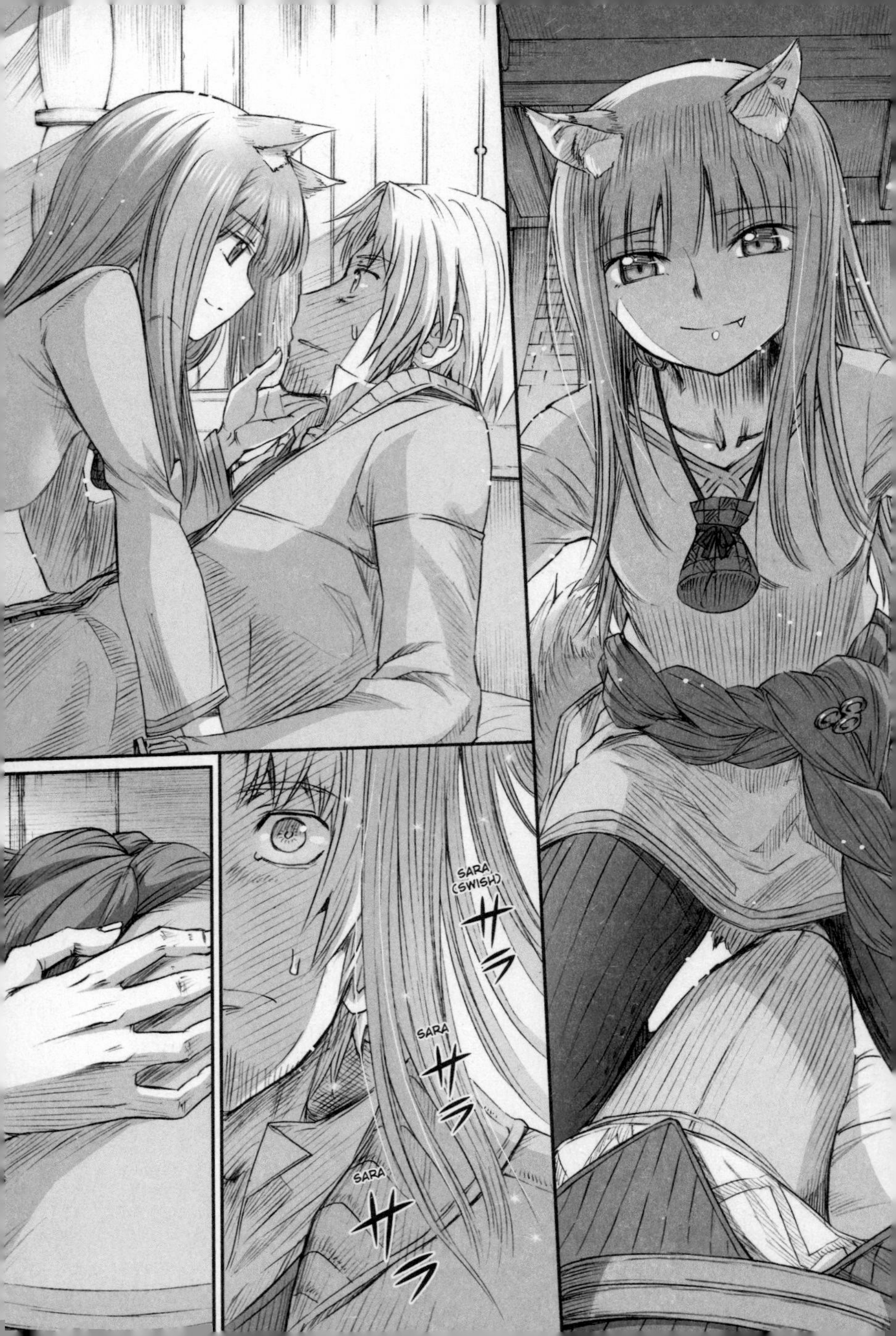
SARA (SWISH)
サラ
SARA
サラ
SARA
サラ

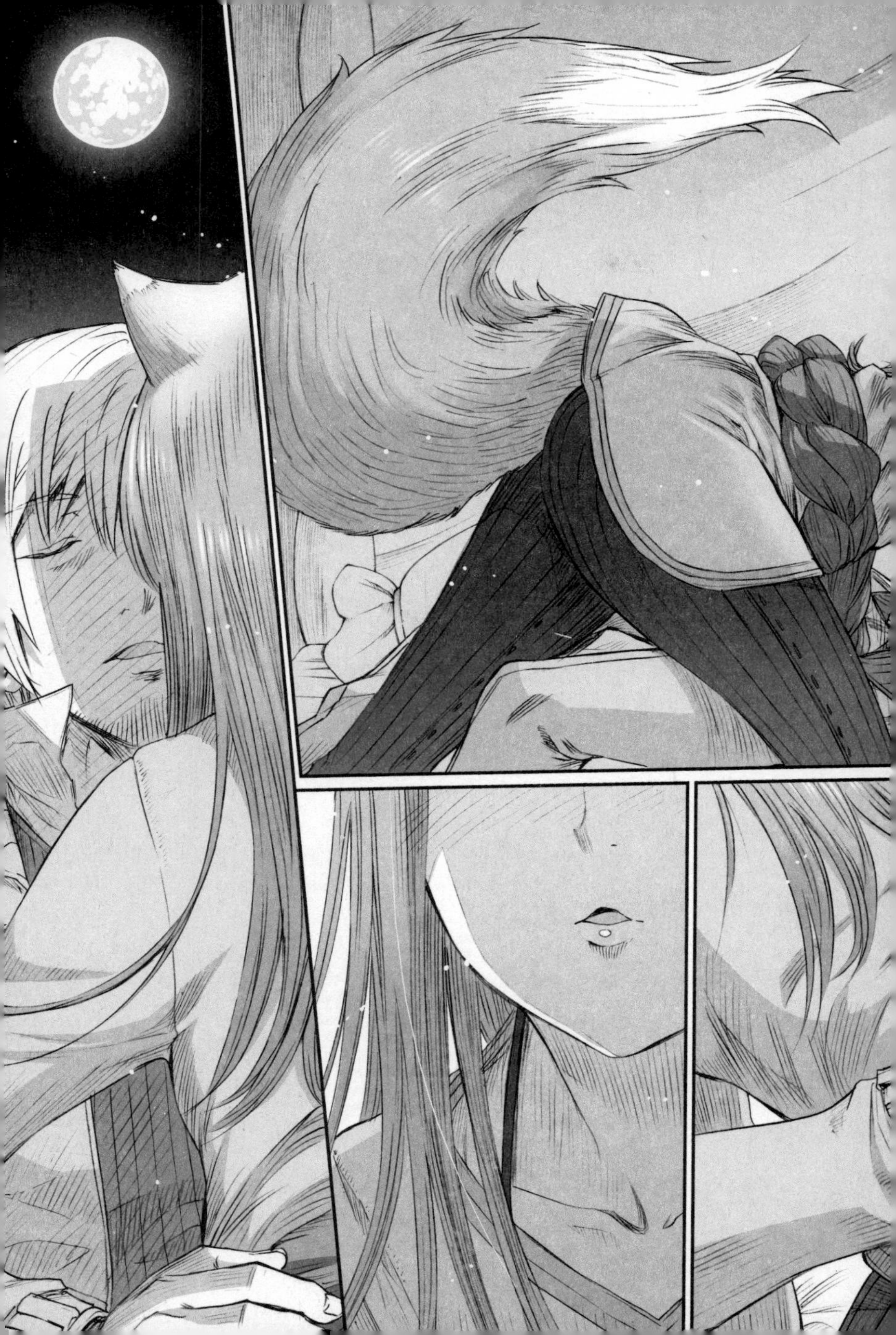

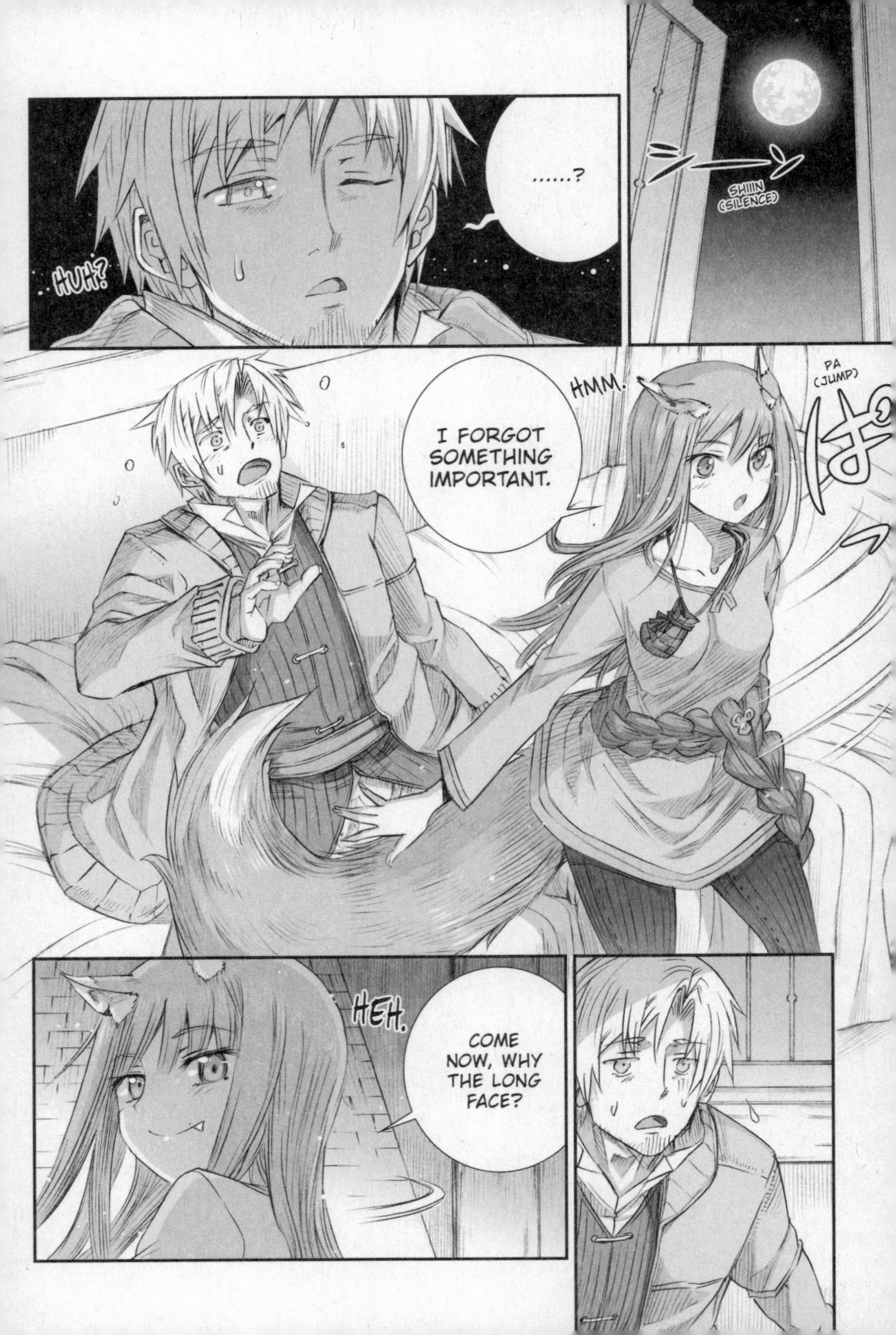
SHIIIN (SILENCE)
......?
HUH?
PA (JUMP)
HMM.
I FORGOT SOMETHING IMPORTANT.
HEH.
COME NOW, WHY THE LONG FACE?

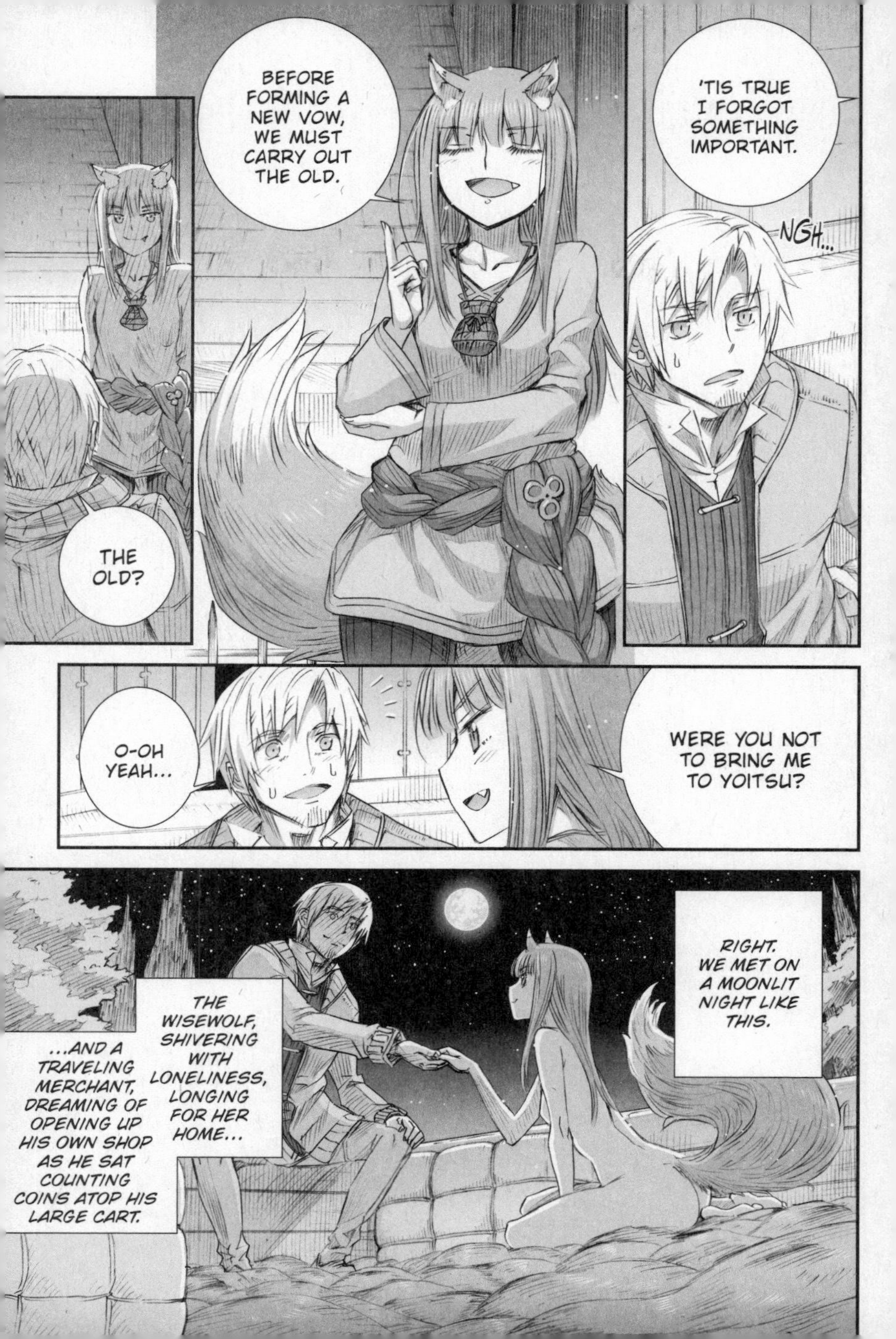
'TIS TRUE I FORGOT SOMETHING IMPORTANT.
NGH...
BEFORE FORMING A NEW VOW, WE MUST CARRY OUT THE OLD.
THE OLD?
WERE YOU NOT TO BRING ME TO YOITSU?
O-OH YEAH...
RIGHT. WE MET ON A MOONLIT NIGHT LIKE THIS.
THE WISEWOLF, SHIVERING WITH LONELINESS, LONGING FOR HER HOME...
...AND A TRAVELING MERCHANT, DREAMING OF OPENING UP HIS OWN SHOP AS HE SAT COUNTING COINS ATOP HIS LARGE CART.

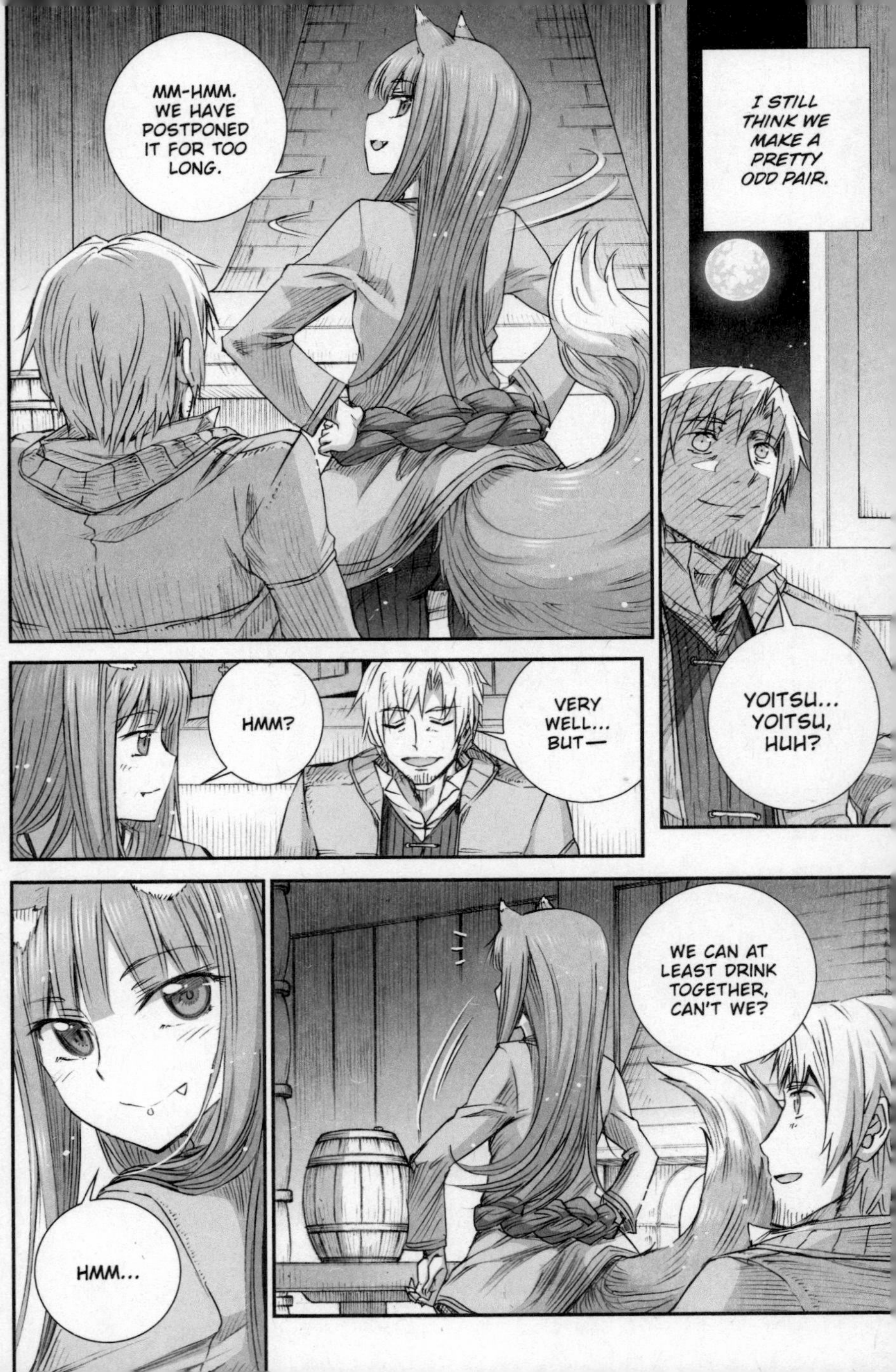
I STILL THINK WE MAKE A PRETTY ODD PAIR.
YOITSU... YOITSU, HUH?
MM-HMM. WE HAVE POSTPONED IT FOR TOO LONG.
VERY WELL... BUT—
HMM?
WE CAN AT LEAST DRINK TOGETHER, CAN'T WE?
HMM...

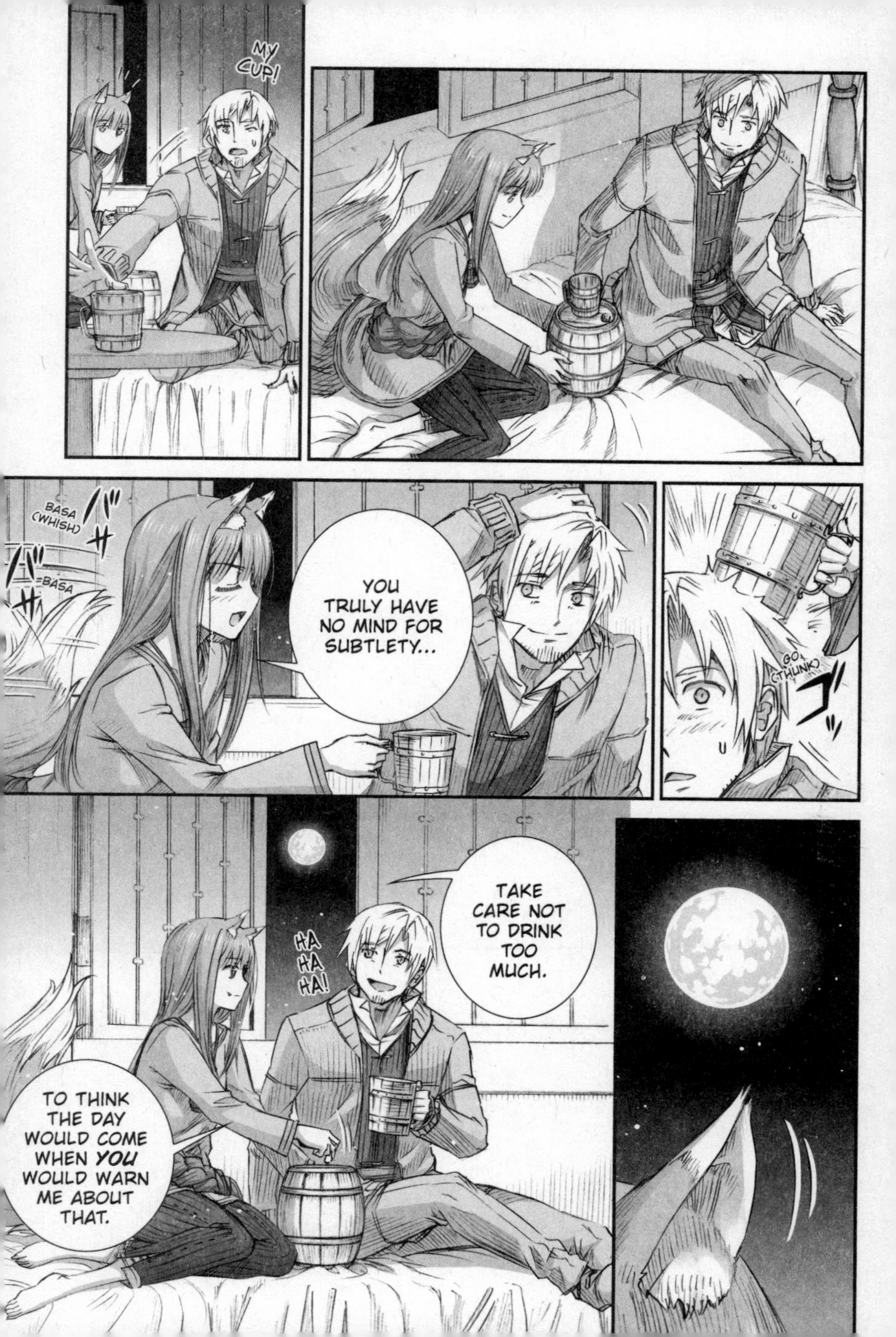
MY CUP!
GO (THUNK)
BASA (WHISH)
BASA
YOU TRULY HAVE NO MIND FOR SUBTLETY...
TAKE CARE NOT TO DRINK TOO MUCH.
HA HA HA!
TO THINK THE DAY WOULD COME WHEN *YOU* WOULD WARN ME ABOUT THAT.

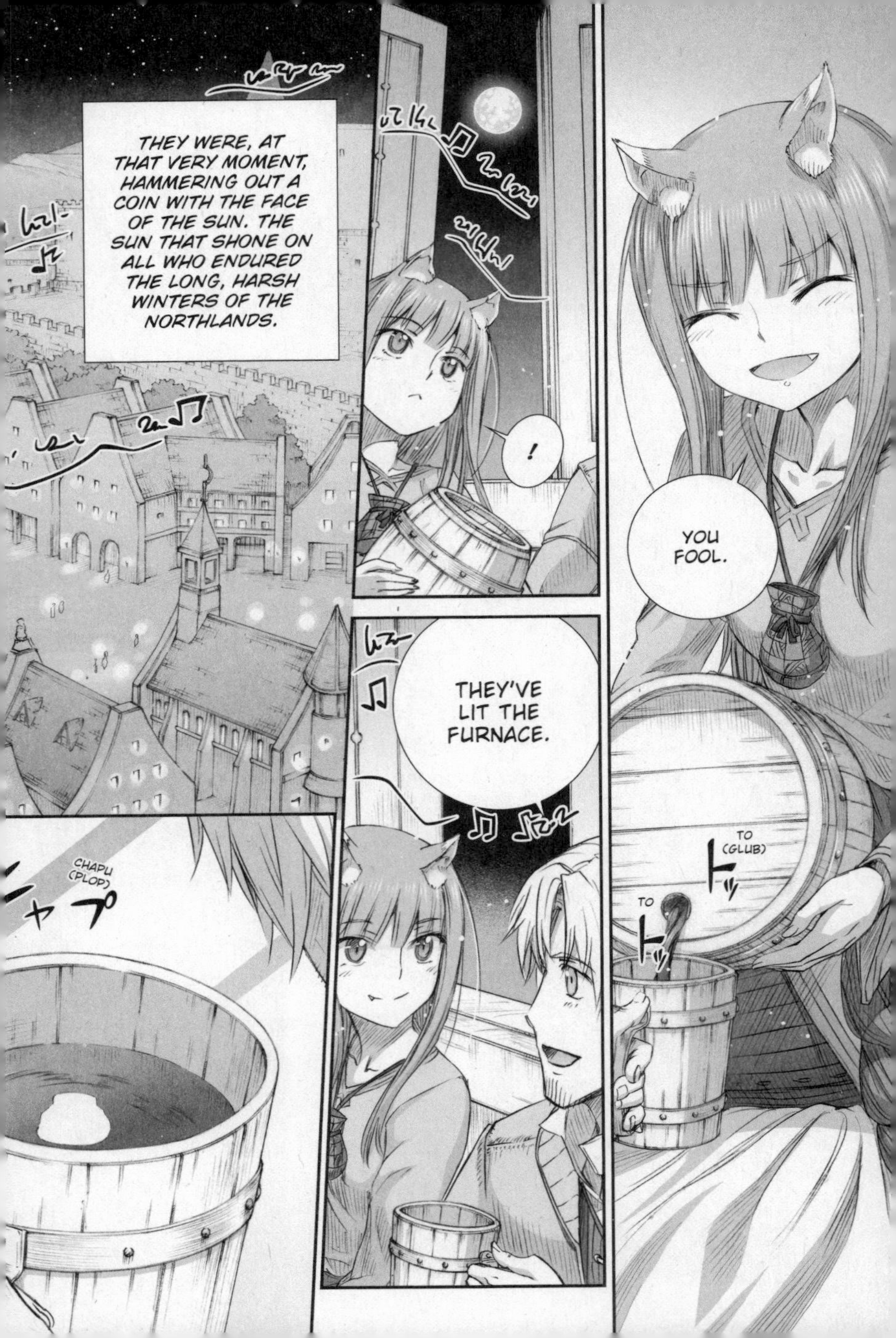
YOU FOOL.
TO (GLUB)
TO
!
THEY WERE, AT THAT VERY MOMENT, HAMMERING OUT A COIN WITH THE FACE OF THE SUN. THE SUN THAT SHONE ON ALL WHO ENDURED THE LONG, HARSH WINTERS OF THE NORTHLANDS.
THEY'VE LIT THE FURNACE.
CHAPU (PLOP)

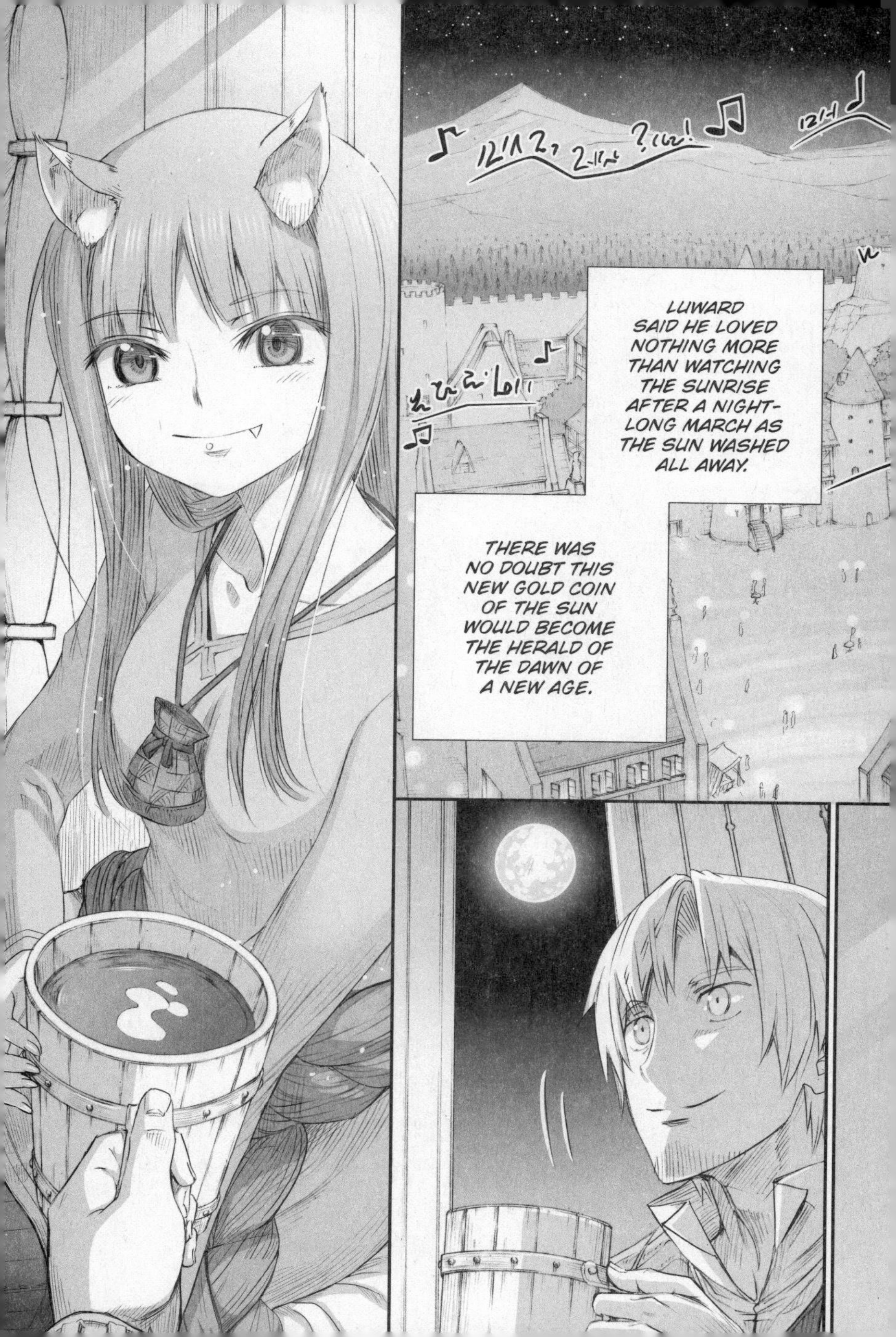
LUWARD SAID HE LOVED NOTHING MORE THAN WATCHING THE SUNRISE AFTER A NIGHT-LONG MARCH AS THE SUN WASHED ALL AWAY.
THERE WAS NO DOUBT THIS NEW GOLD COIN OF THE SUN WOULD BECOME THE HERALD OF THE DAWN OF A NEW AGE.

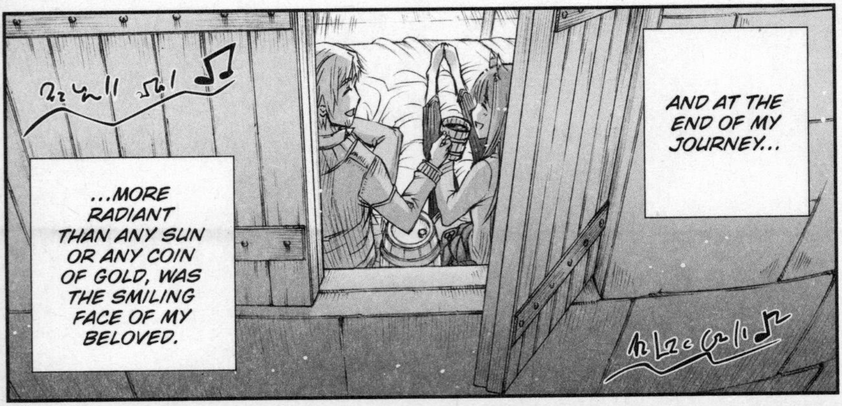
AND AT THE END OF MY JOURNEY...
...MORE RADIANT THAN ANY SUN OR ANY COIN OF GOLD, WAS THE SMILING FACE OF MY BELOVED.
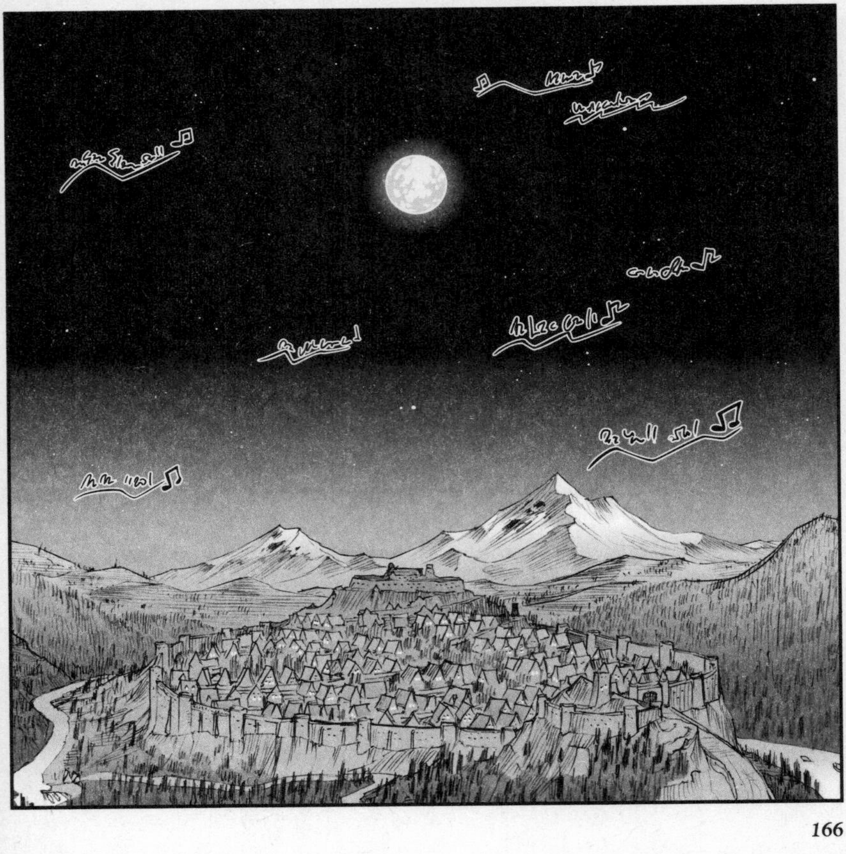

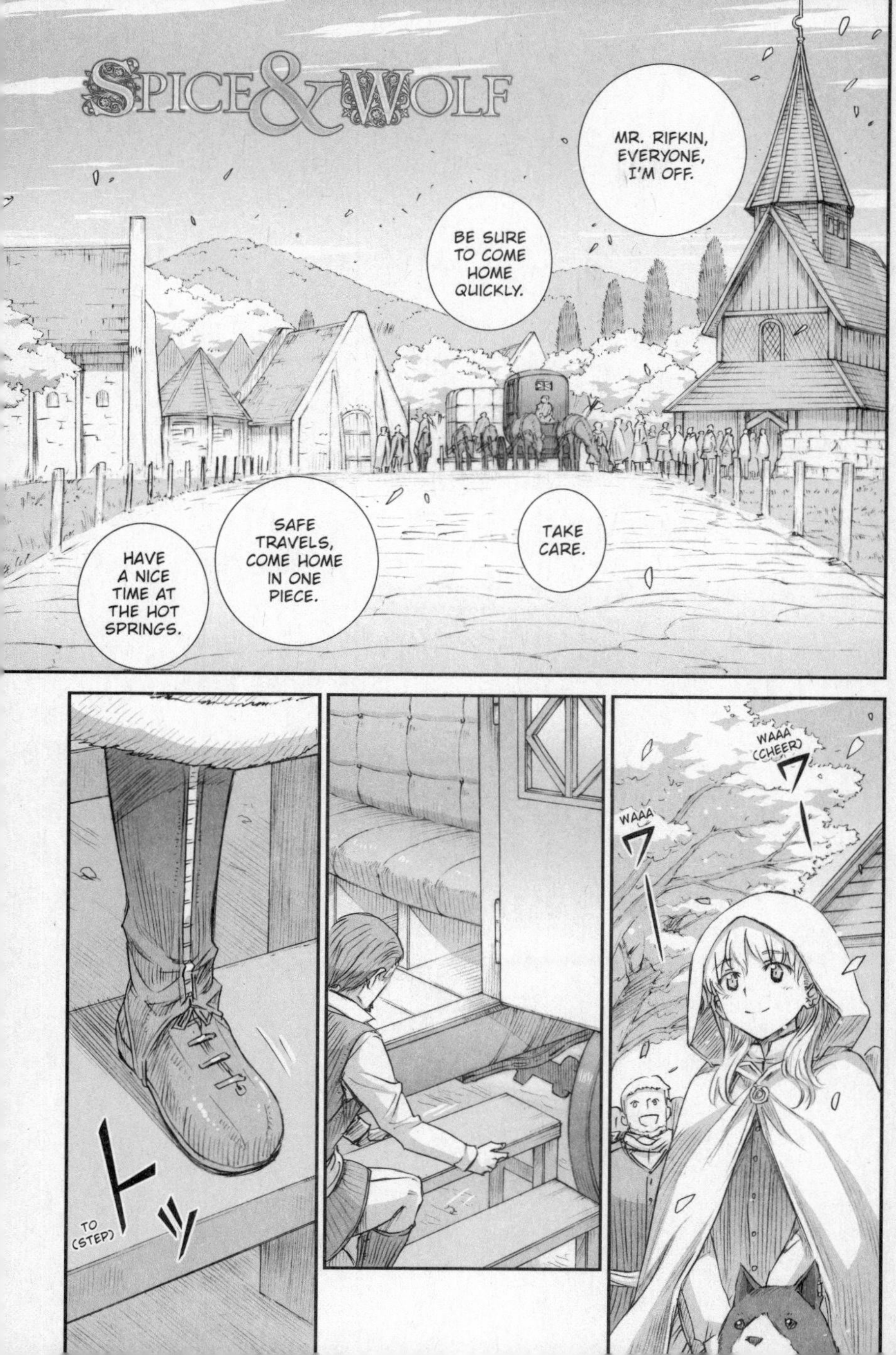
SPICE & WOLF
MR. RIFKIN, EVERYONE, I'M OFF.
BE SURE TO COME HOME QUICKLY.
TAKE CARE.
SAFE TRAVELS, COME HOME IN ONE PIECE.
HAVE A NICE TIME AT THE HOT SPRINGS.
WAAA (CHEER)
WAAA
TO (STEP)

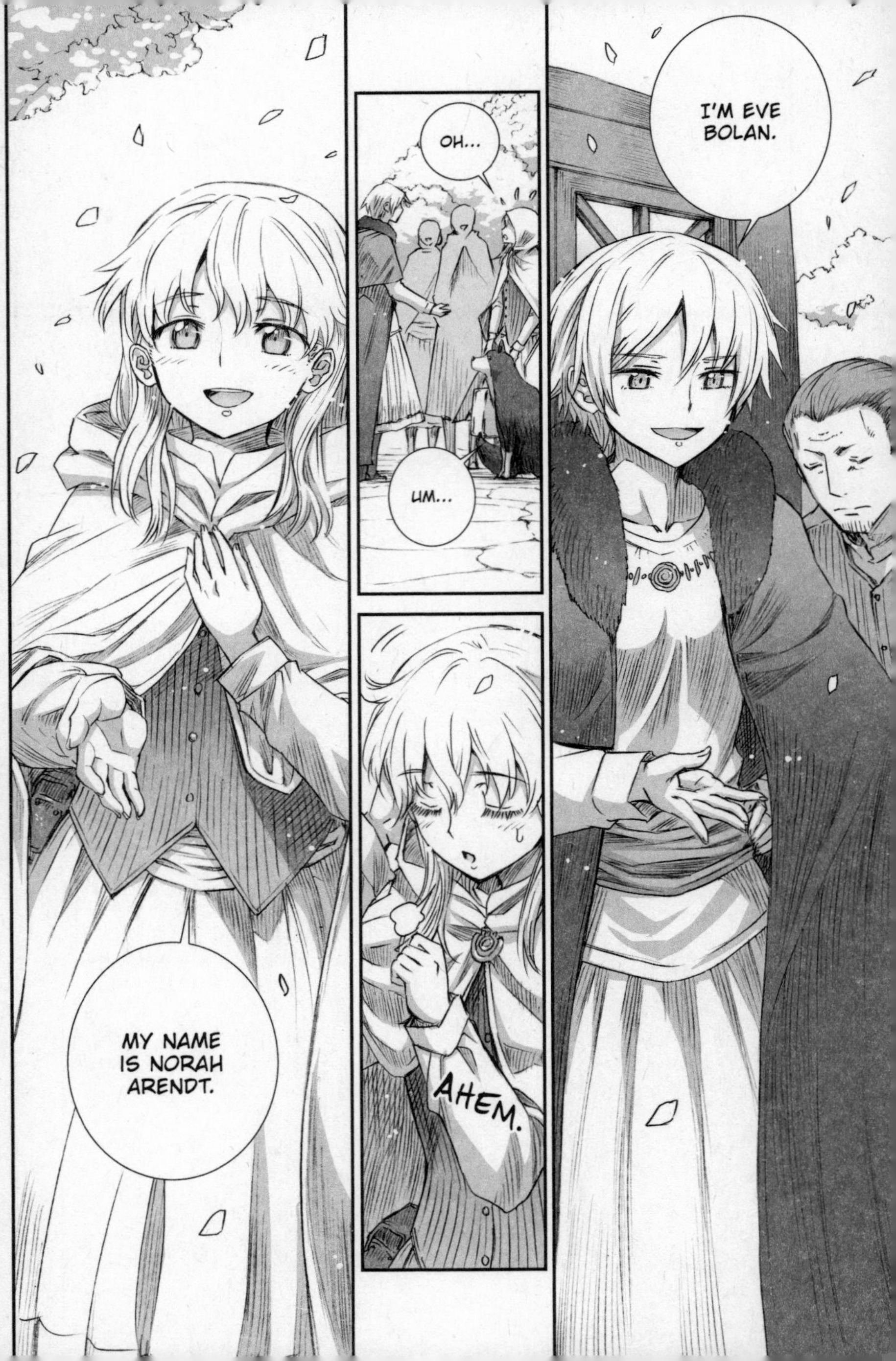
I'M EVE BOLAN.
OH...
UM...
AHEM.
MY NAME IS NORAH ARENDT.

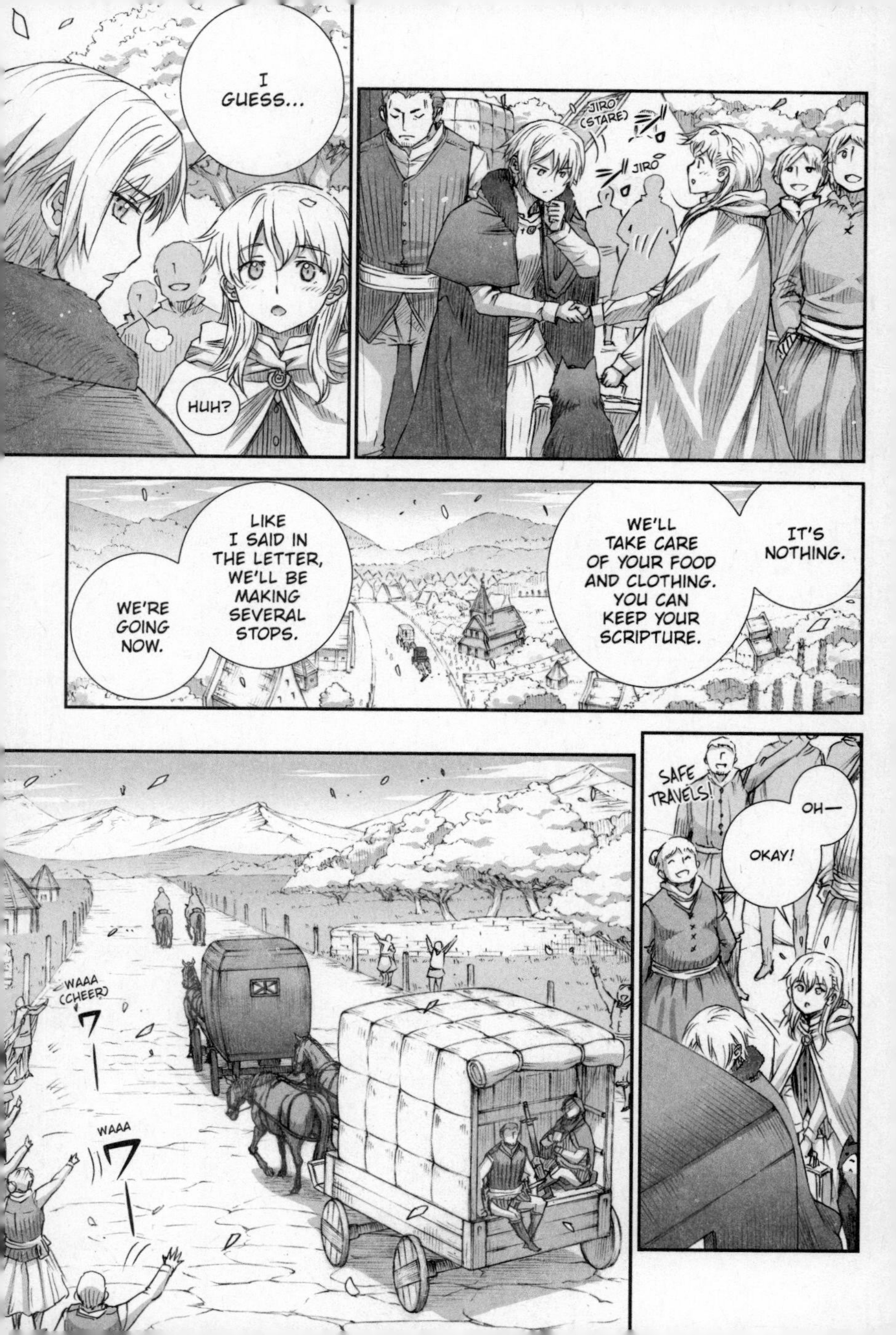

JIRO (STARE)
JIRO
I GUESS...
HUH?
IT'S NOTHING.
WE'LL TAKE CARE OF YOUR FOOD AND CLOTHING. YOU CAN KEEP YOUR SCRIPTURE.
LIKE I SAID IN THE LETTER, WE'LL BE MAKING SEVERAL STOPS.
WE'RE GOING NOW.
SAFE TRAVELS!
OH—
OKAY!
WAAA (CHEER)
WAAA

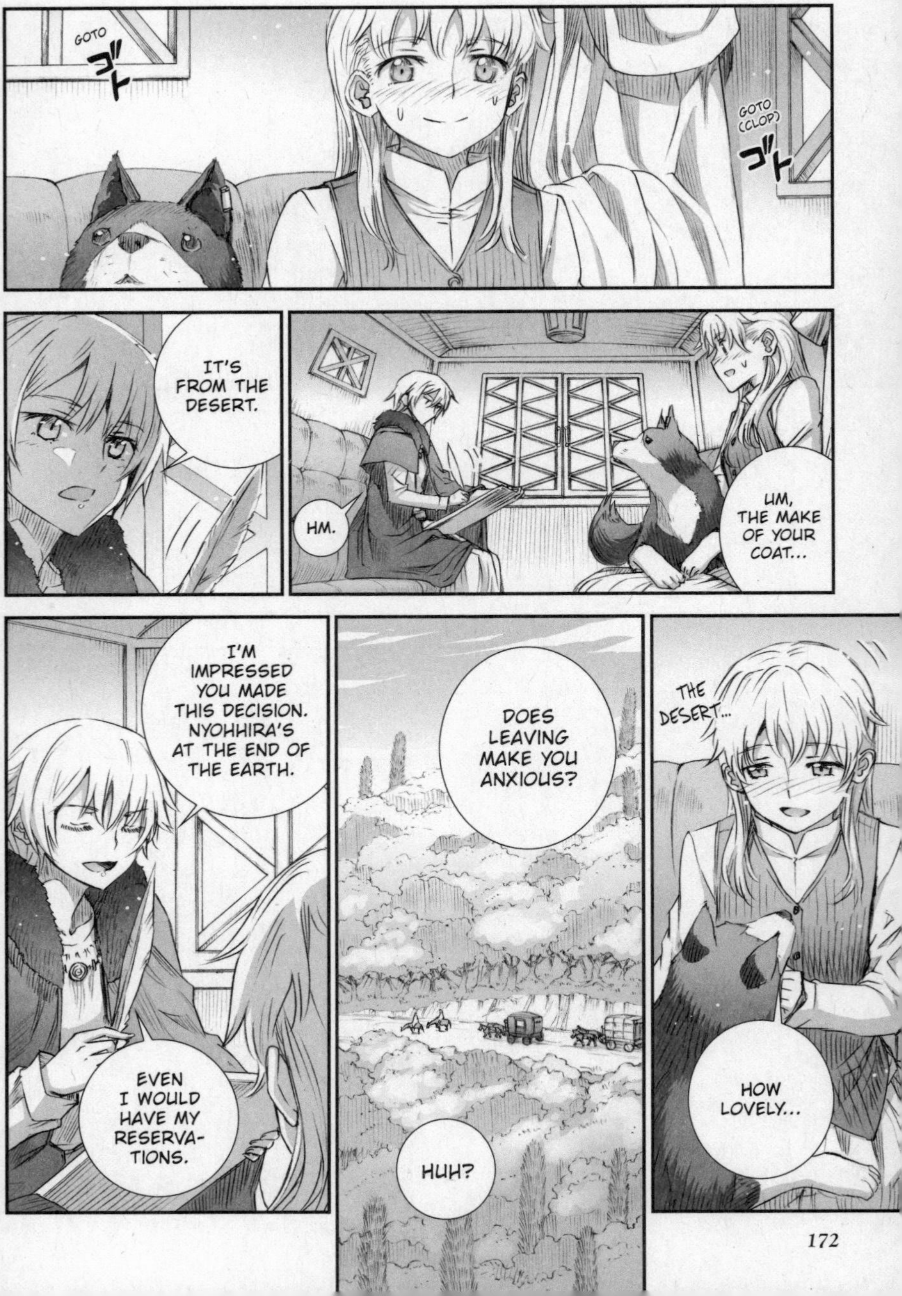
GOTO (CLOP)
ゴト
GOTO
ゴト
UM, THE MAKE OF YOUR COAT...
HM.
IT'S FROM THE DESERT.
THE DESERT...
HOW LOVELY...
DOES LEAVING MAKE YOU ANXIOUS?
HUH?
I'M IMPRESSED YOU MADE THIS DECISION. NYOHHIRA'S AT THE END OF THE EARTH.
EVEN I WOULD HAVE MY RESERVATIONS.

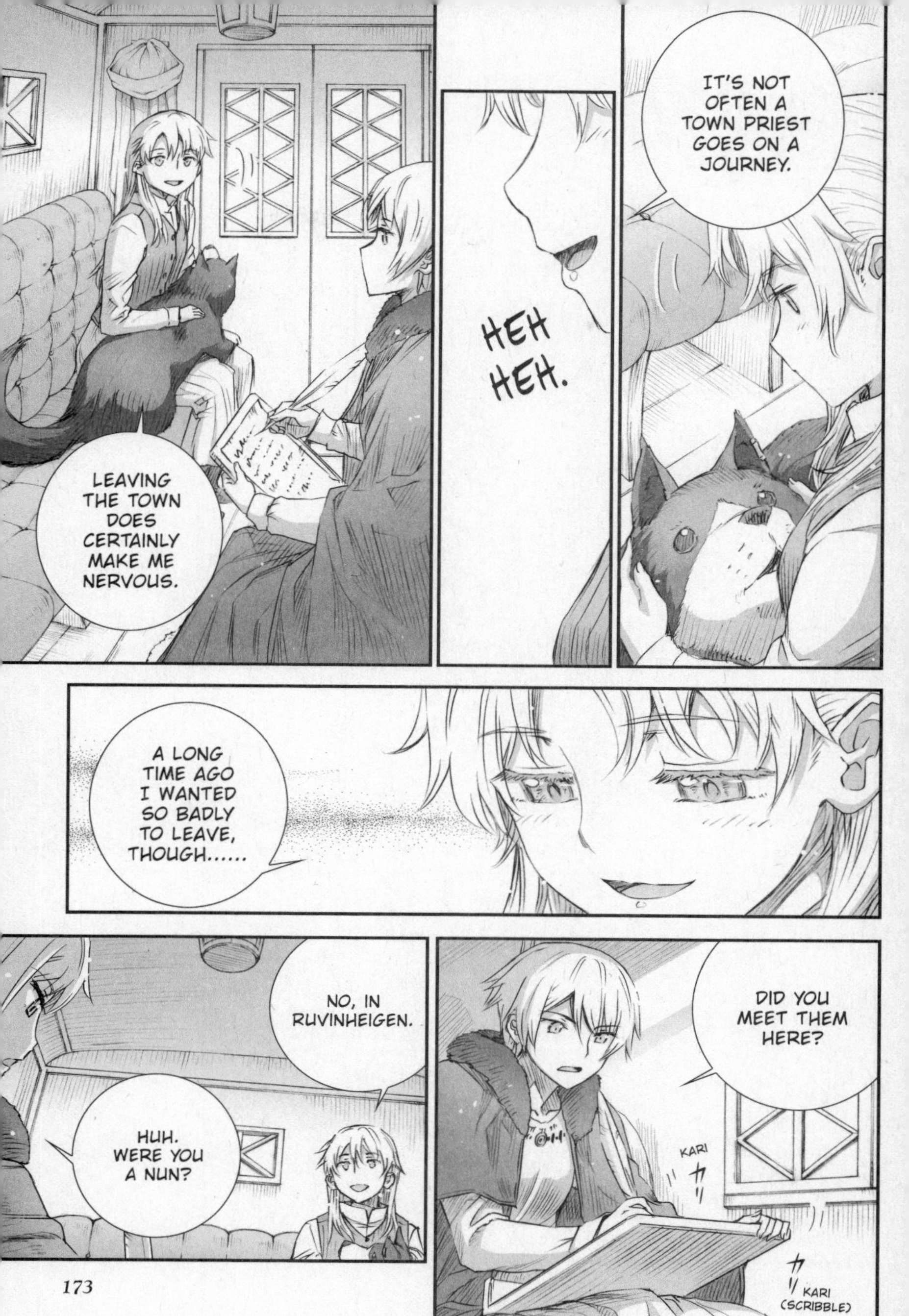
IT'S NOT OFTEN A TOWN PRIEST GOES ON A JOURNEY.
HEH HEH.
LEAVING THE TOWN DOES CERTAINLY MAKE ME NERVOUS.
A LONG TIME AGO I WANTED SO BADLY TO LEAVE, THOUGH......
DID YOU MEET THEM HERE?
KARI
カリ
カリ
KARI (SCRIBBLE)
NO, IN RUVINHEIGEN.
HUH. WERE YOU A NUN?

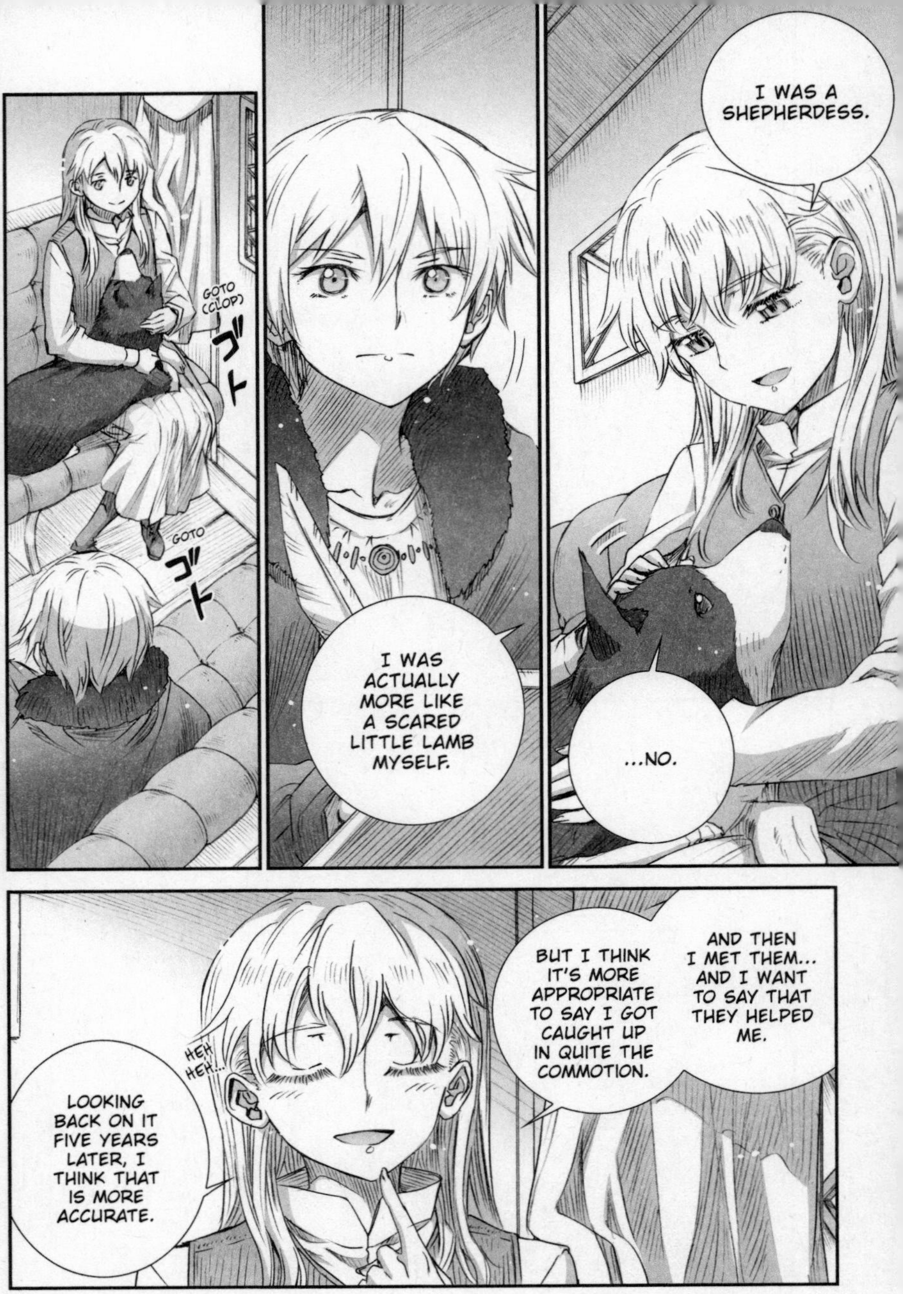
I WAS A SHEPHERDESS.
...NO.
I WAS ACTUALLY MORE LIKE A SCARED LITTLE LAMB MYSELF.
GOTO (CLOP)
ゴト
GOTO
ゴト
AND THEN I MET THEM... AND I WANT TO SAY THAT THEY HELPED ME.
BUT I THINK IT'S MORE APPROPRIATE TO SAY I GOT CAUGHT UP IN QUITE THE COMMOTION.
HEH HEH...
LOOKING BACK ON IT FIVE YEARS LATER, I THINK THAT IS MORE ACCURATE.

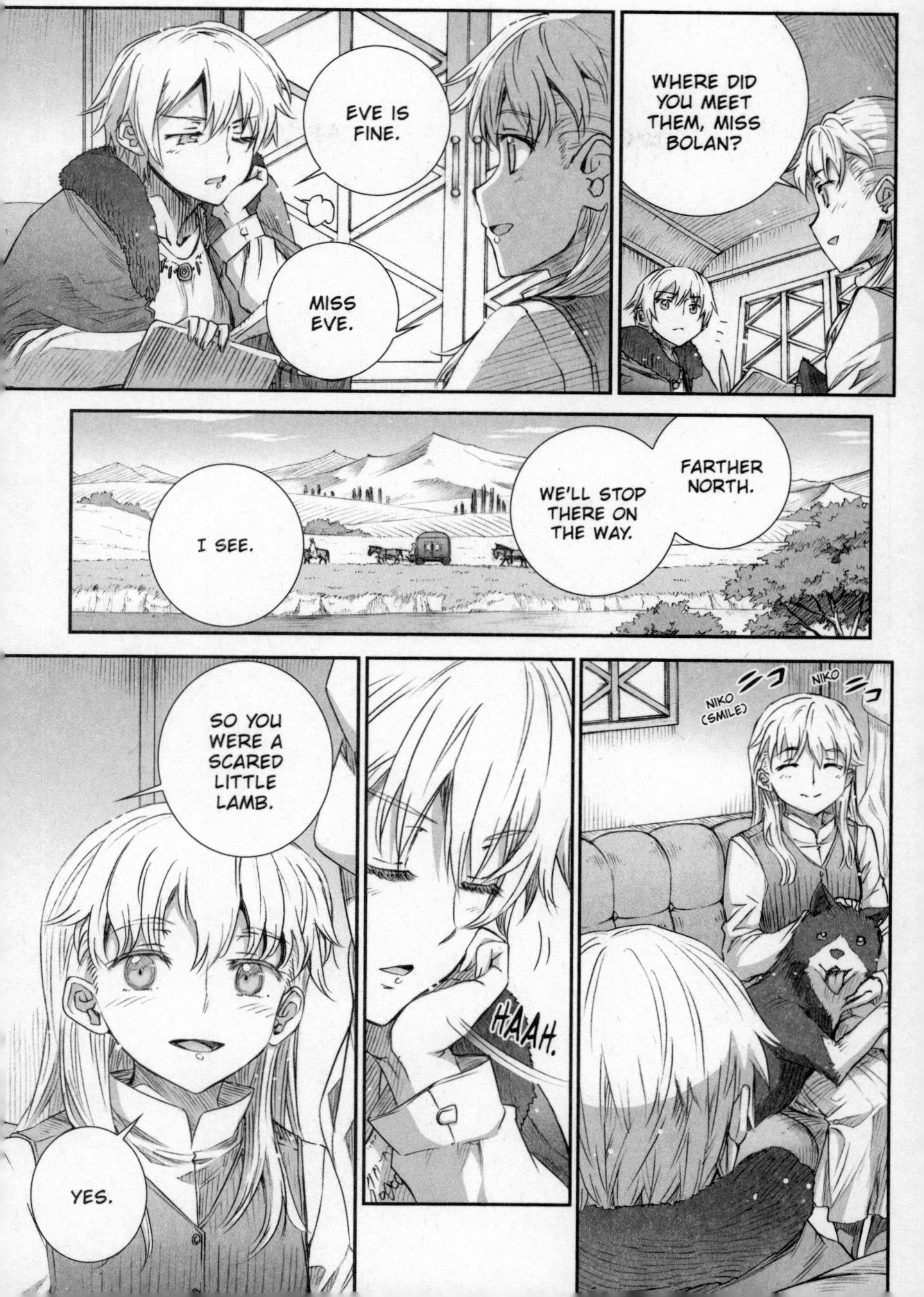
WHERE DID YOU MEET THEM, MISS BOLAN?
EVE IS FINE.
MISS EVE.
FARTHER NORTH.
WE'LL STOP THERE ON THE WAY.
I SEE.
ニコ
NIKO
ニコ
NIKO (SMILE)
HAAH.
SO YOU WERE A SCARED LITTLE LAMB.
YES.

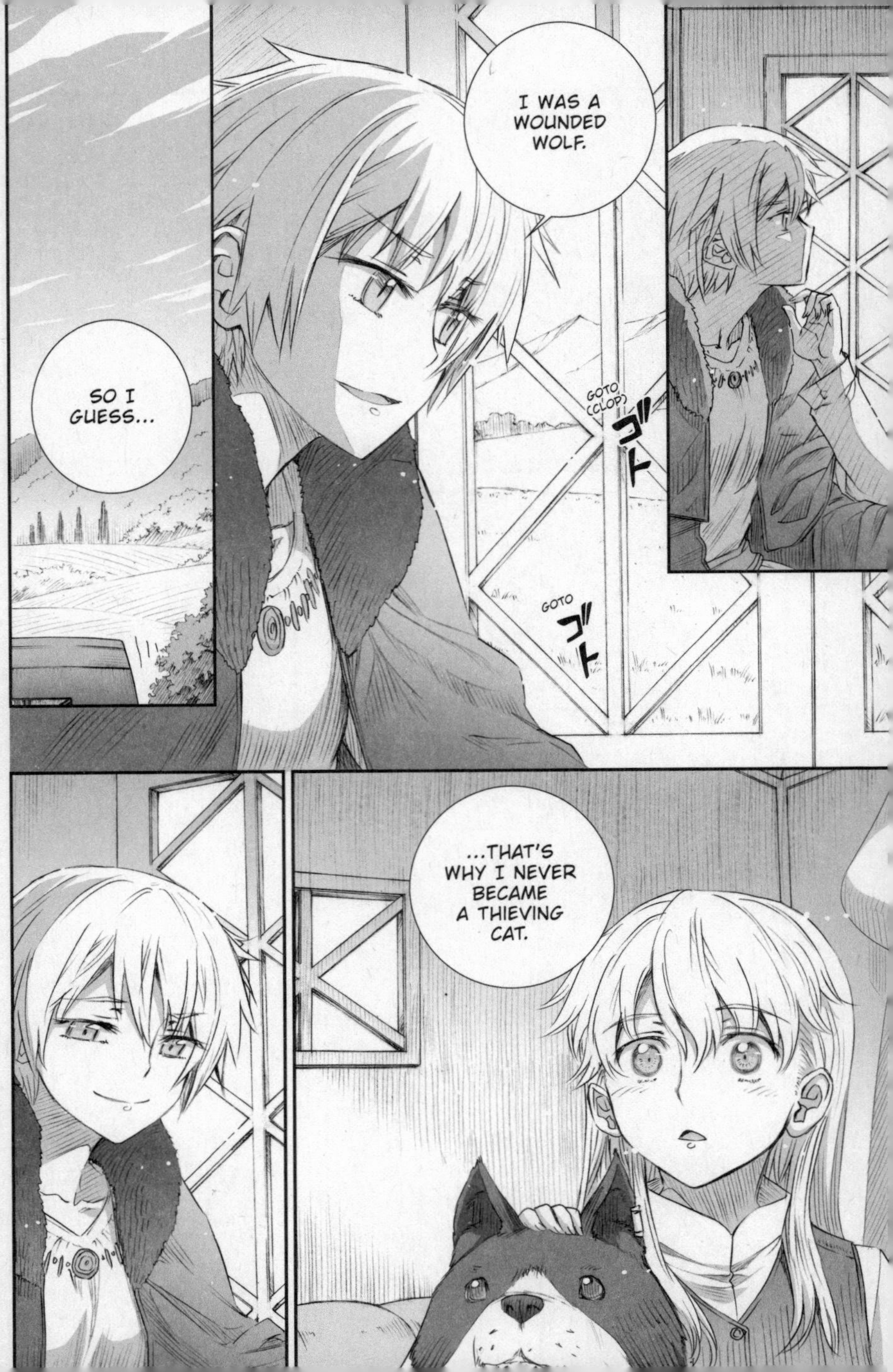
I WAS A WOUNDED WOLF.
GOTO (CLOP)
ゴト
GOTO
ゴト
SO I GUESS...
...THAT'S WHY I NEVER BECAME A THIEVING CAT.

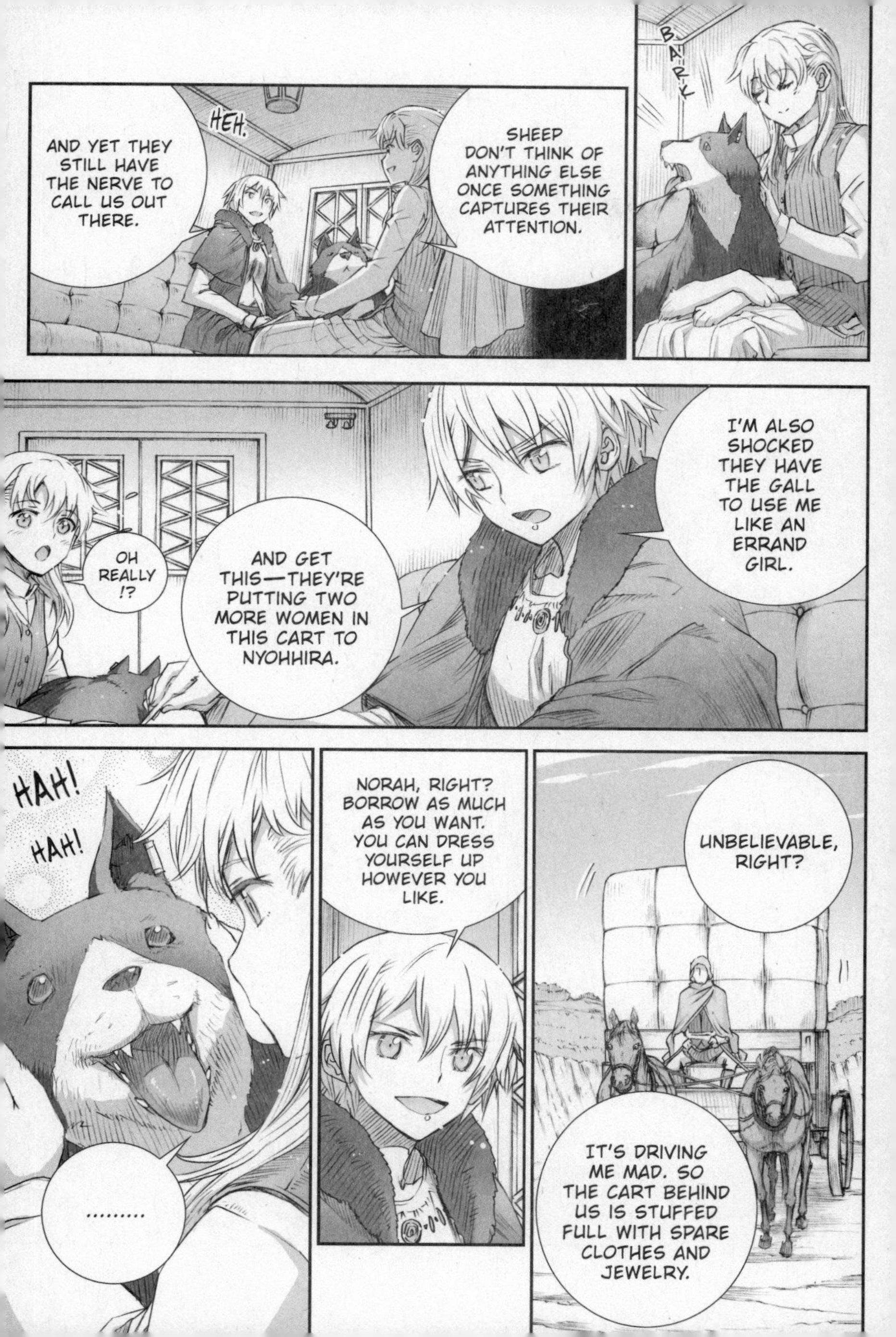
BARK
SHEEP DON'T THINK OF ANYTHING ELSE ONCE SOMETHING CAPTURES THEIR ATTENTION.
HEH.
AND YET THEY STILL HAVE THE NERVE TO CALL US OUT THERE.
I'M ALSO SHOCKED THEY HAVE THE GALL TO USE ME LIKE AN ERRAND GIRL.
AND GET THIS—THEY'RE PUTTING TWO MORE WOMEN IN THIS CART TO NYOHHIRA.
OH REALLY !?
UNBELIEVABLE, RIGHT?
IT'S DRIVING ME MAD. SO THE CART BEHIND US IS STUFFED FULL WITH SPARE CLOTHES AND JEWELRY.
NORAH, RIGHT? BORROW AS MUCH AS YOU WANT. YOU CAN DRESS YOURSELF UP HOWEVER YOU LIKE.
HAH!
HAH!
....

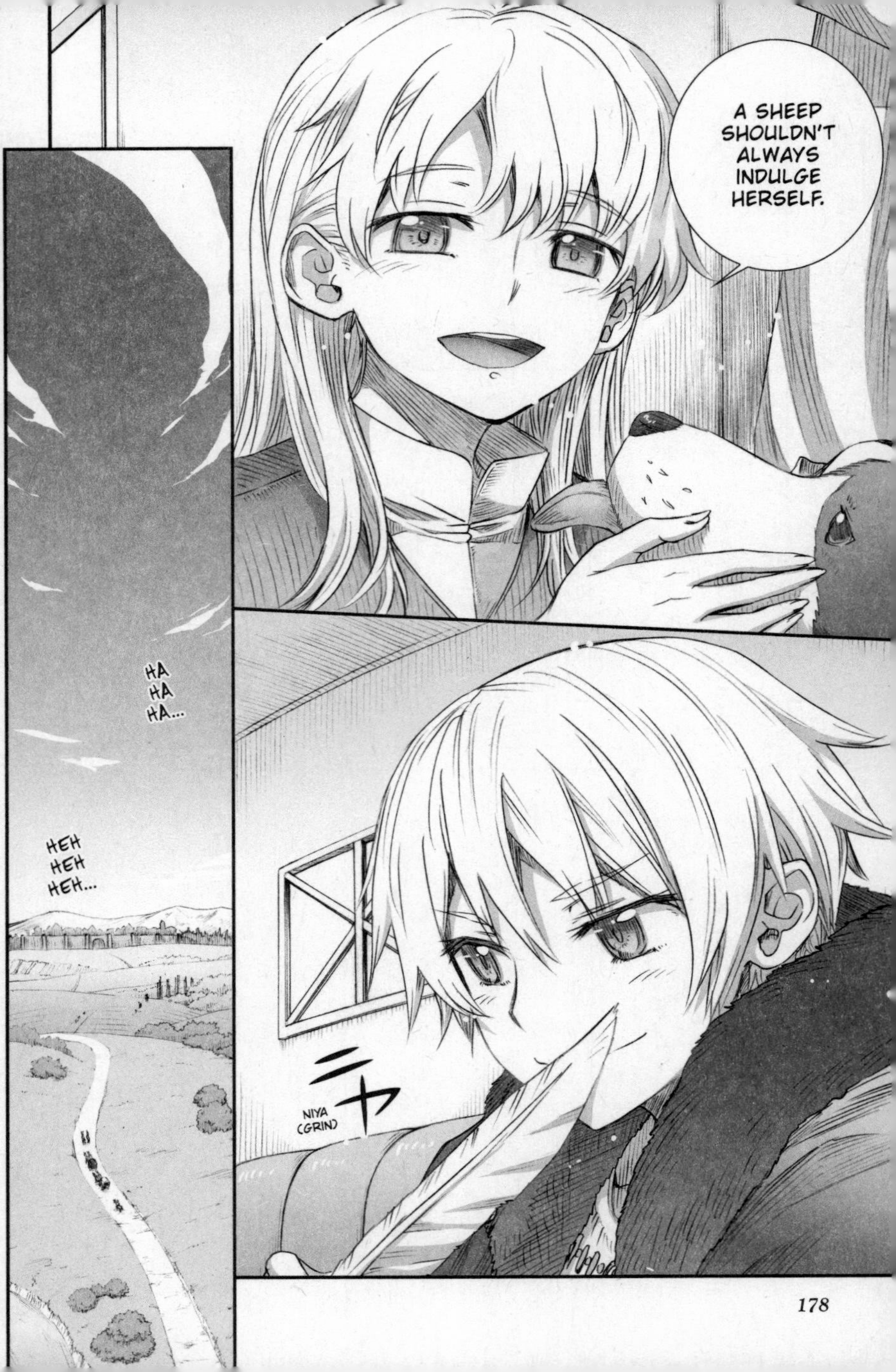
A SHEEP SHOULDN'T ALWAYS INDULGE HERSELF.
ニヤ
NIYA (GRIN)
HA HA HA...
HEH HEH HEH...

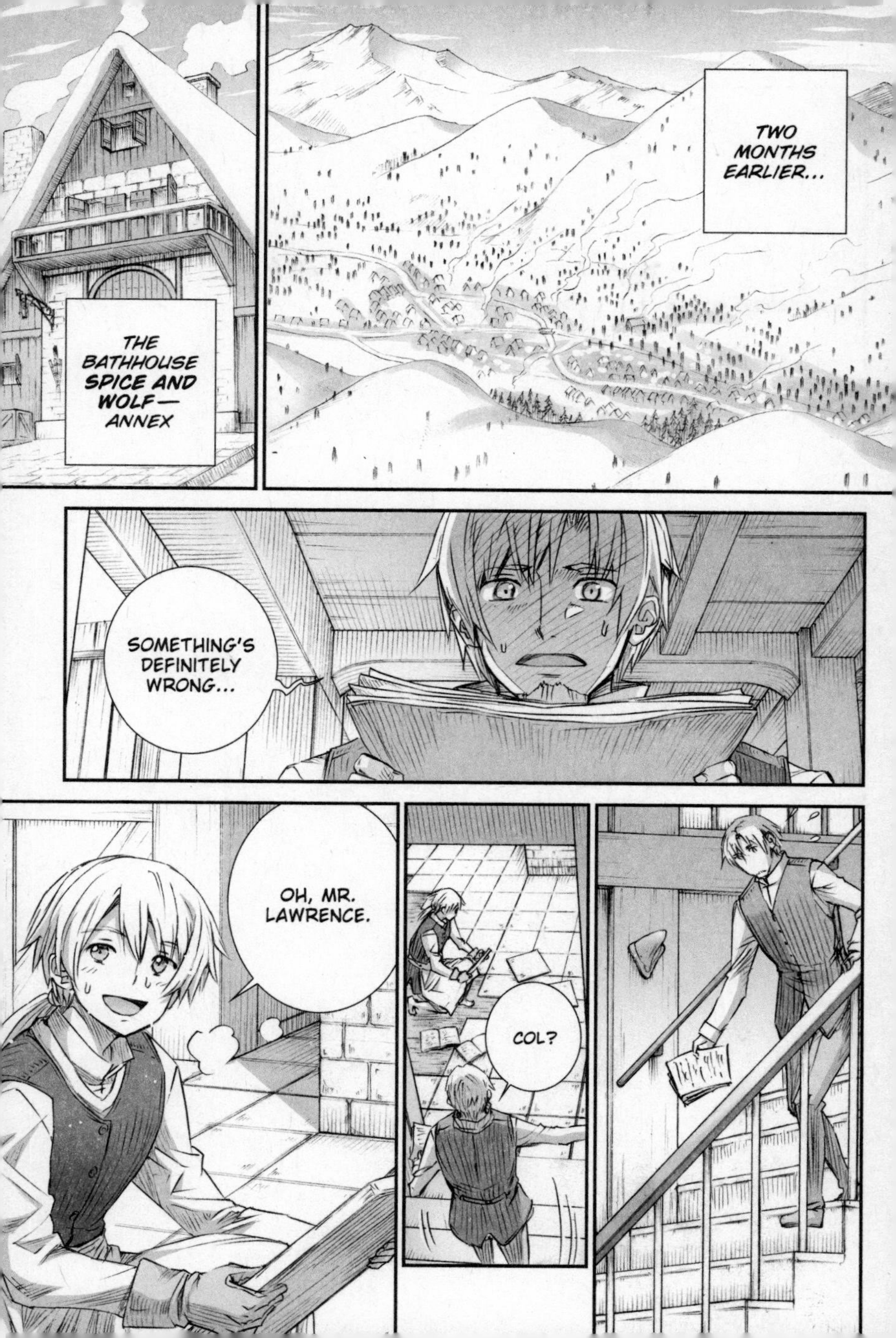
TWO MONTHS EARLIER...
THE BATHHOUSE SPICE AND WOLF—ANNEX
SOMETHING'S DEFINITELY WRONG...
COL?
OH, MR. LAWRENCE.

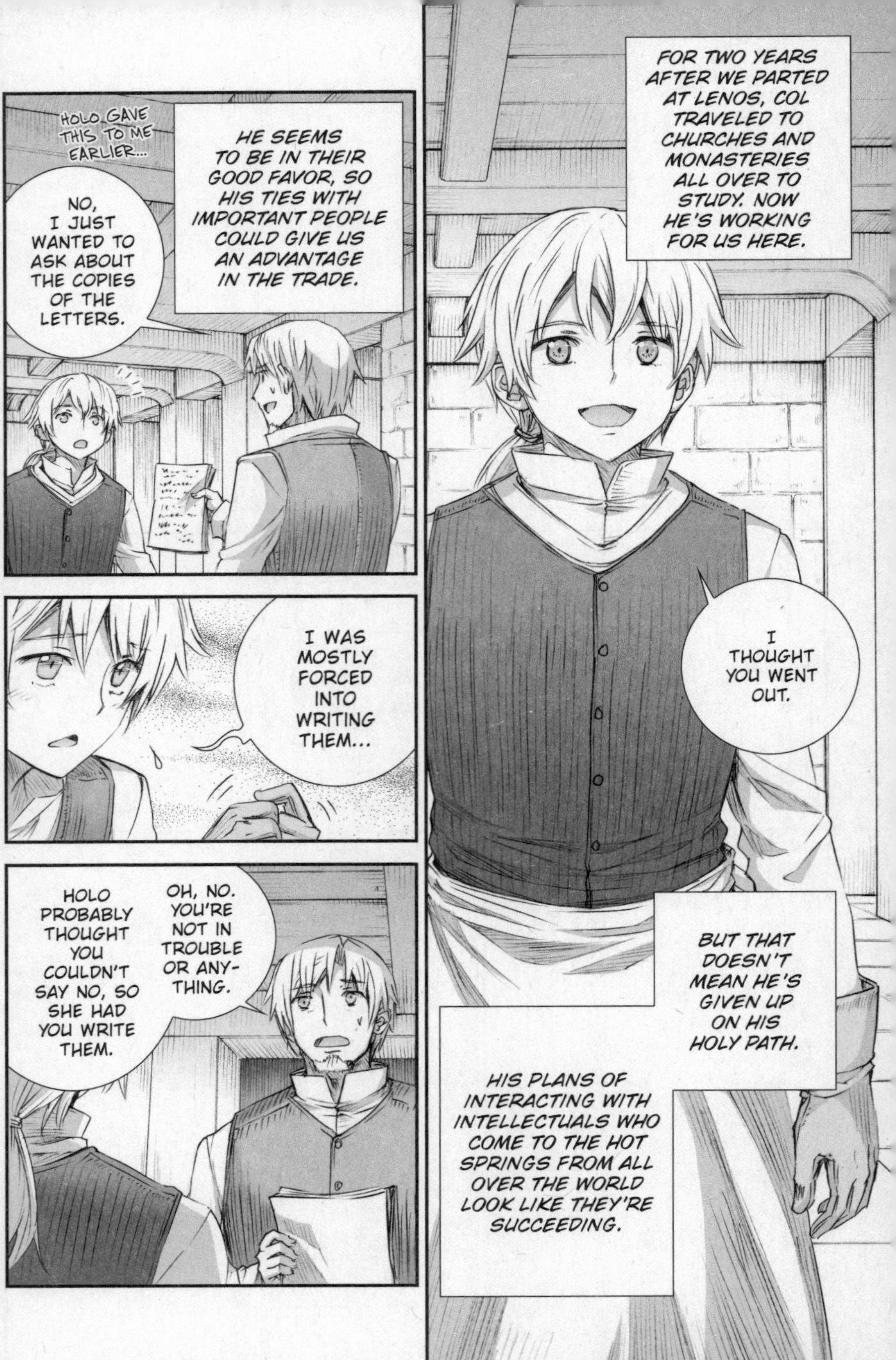
FOR TWO YEARS AFTER WE PARTED AT LENOS, COL TRAVELED TO CHURCHES AND MONASTERIES ALL OVER TO STUDY. NOW HE'S WORKING FOR US HERE.
I THOUGHT YOU WENT OUT.
BUT THAT DOESN'T MEAN HE'S GIVEN UP ON HIS HOLY PATH.
HIS PLANS OF INTERACTING WITH INTELLECTUALS WHO COME TO THE HOT SPRINGS FROM ALL OVER THE WORLD LOOK LIKE THEY'RE SUCCEEDING.
HE SEEMS TO BE IN THEIR GOOD FAVOR, SO HIS TIES WITH IMPORTANT PEOPLE COULD GIVE US AN ADVANTAGE IN THE TRADE.
HOLO GAVE THIS TO ME EARLIER...
NO, I JUST WANTED TO ASK ABOUT THE COPIES OF THE LETTERS.
I WAS MOSTLY FORCED INTO WRITING THEM...
OH, NO. YOU'RE NOT IN TROUBLE OR ANY-THING.
HOLO PROBABLY THOUGHT YOU COULDN'T SAY NO, SO SHE HAD YOU WRITE THEM.

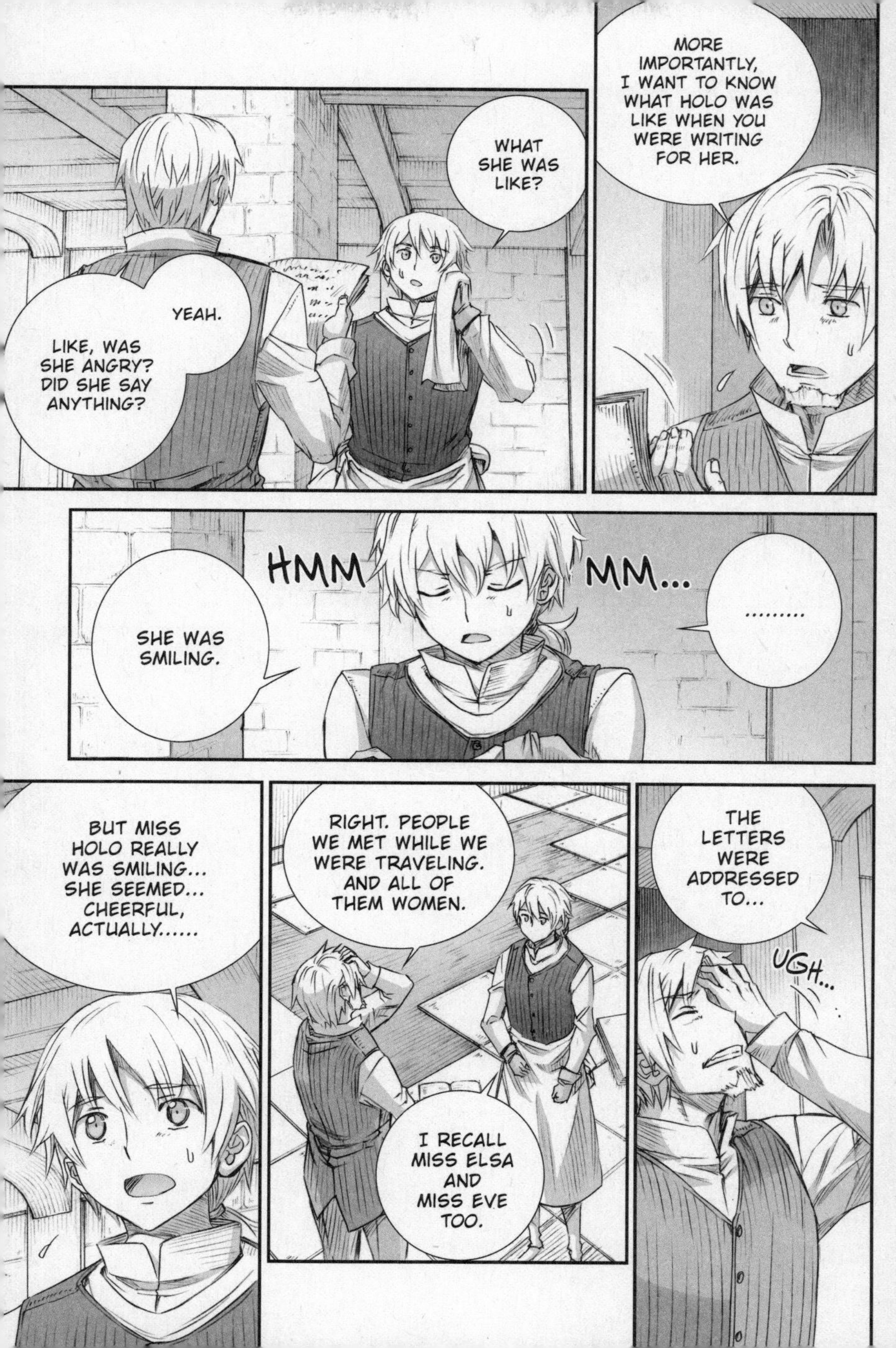
MORE IMPORTANTLY, I WANT TO KNOW WHAT HOLO WAS LIKE WHEN YOU WERE WRITING FOR HER.
WHAT SHE WAS LIKE?
YEAH.
LIKE, WAS SHE ANGRY? DID SHE SAY ANYTHING?
....
HMM MM...
SHE WAS SMILING.
THE LETTERS WERE ADDRESSED TO...
UGH...
RIGHT. PEOPLE WE MET WHILE WE WERE TRAVELING. AND ALL OF THEM WOMEN.
I RECALL MISS ELSA AND MISS EVE TOO.
BUT MISS HOLO REALLY WAS SMILING... SHE SEEMED... CHEERFUL, ACTUALLY......

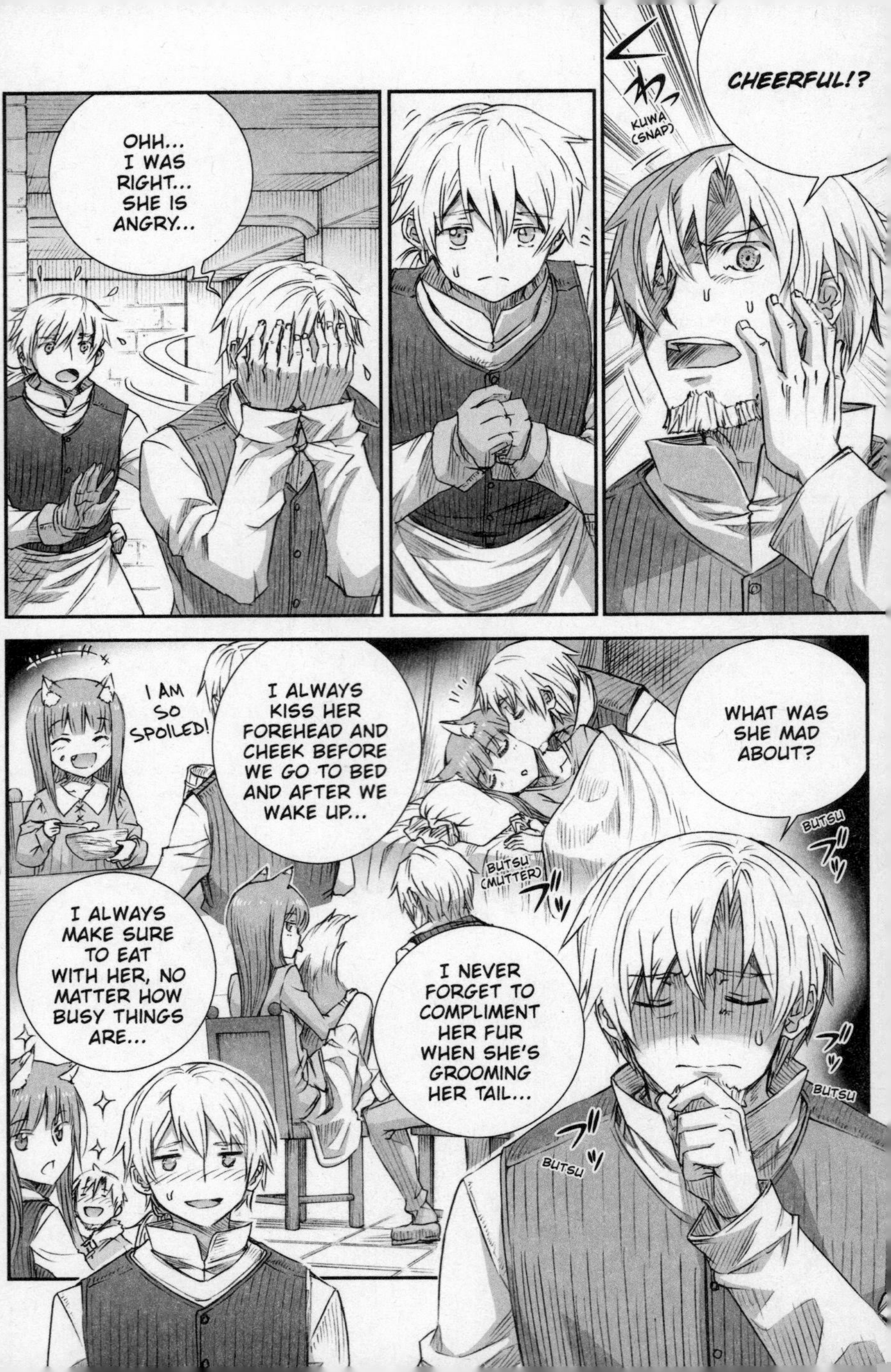
KUWA (SNAP)
CHEERFUL!?
OHH... I WAS RIGHT... SHE IS ANGRY...
WHAT WAS SHE MAD ABOUT?
BUTSU
I ALWAYS KISS HER FOREHEAD AND CHEEK BEFORE WE GO TO BED AND AFTER WE WAKE UP...
I AM SO SPOILED!
BUTSU (MUTTER)
BUTSU
I NEVER FORGET TO COMPLIMENT HER FUR WHEN SHE'S GROOMING HER TAIL...
BUTSU
I ALWAYS MAKE SURE TO EAT WITH HER, NO MATTER HOW BUSY THINGS ARE...

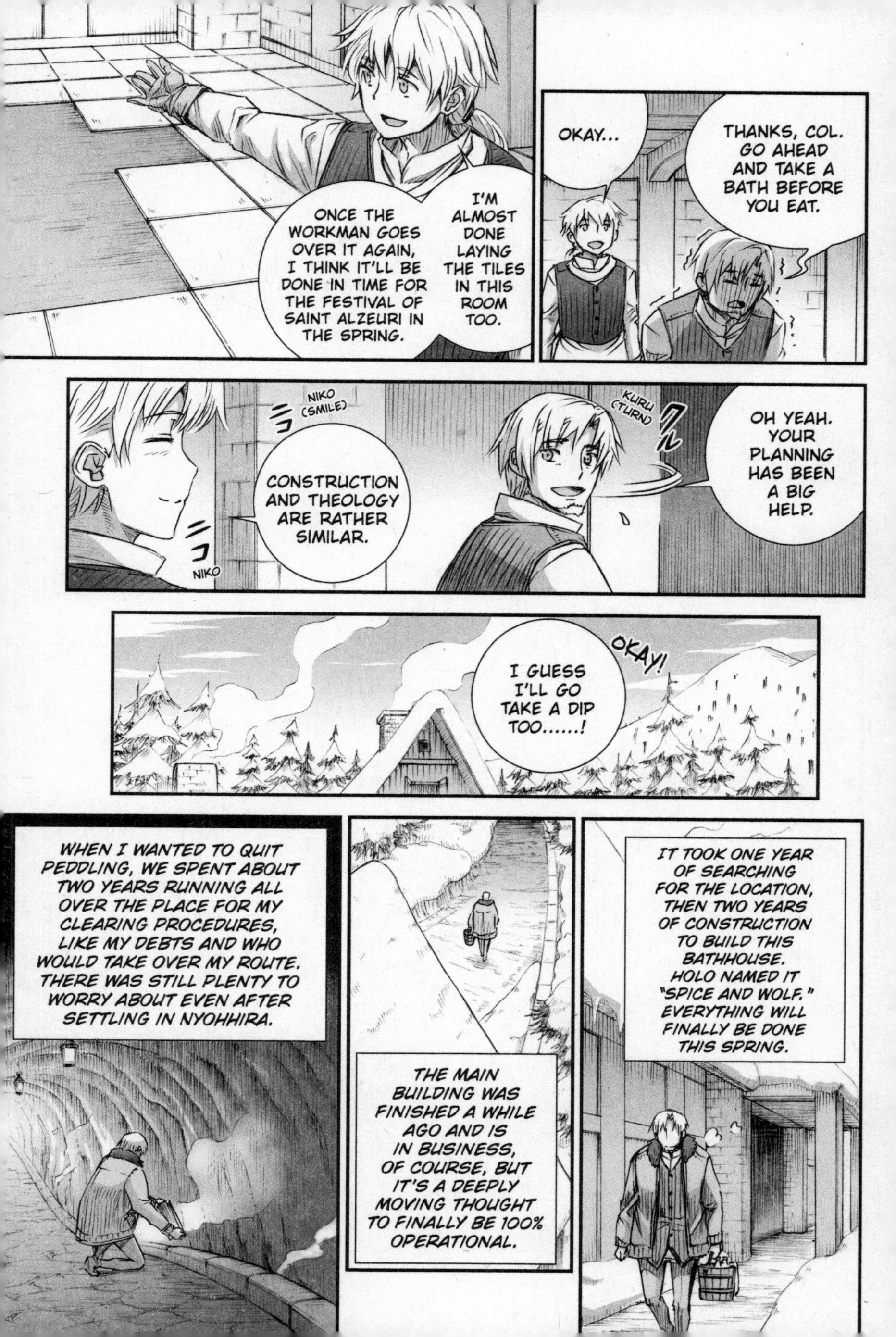
I'M ALMOST DONE LAYING THE TILES IN THIS ROOM TOO.
ONCE THE WORKMAN GOES OVER IT AGAIN, I THINK IT'LL BE DONE IN TIME FOR THE FESTIVAL OF SAINT ALZEURI IN THE SPRING.
THANKS, COL. GO AHEAD AND TAKE A BATH BEFORE YOU EAT.
OKAY...
OH YEAH. YOUR PLANNING HAS BEEN A BIG HELP.
KURU (TURN)
CONSTRUCTION AND THEOLOGY ARE RATHER SIMILAR.
NIKO (SMILE)
NIKO
OKAY!
I GUESS I'LL GO TAKE A DIP TOO......!
WHEN I WANTED TO QUIT PEDDLING, WE SPENT ABOUT TWO YEARS RUNNING ALL OVER THE PLACE FOR MY CLEARING PROCEDURES, LIKE MY DEBTS AND WHO WOULD TAKE OVER MY ROUTE. THERE WAS STILL PLENTY TO WORRY ABOUT EVEN AFTER SETTLING IN NYOHHIRA.
IT TOOK ONE YEAR OF SEARCHING FOR THE LOCATION, THEN TWO YEARS OF CONSTRUCTION TO BUILD THIS BATHHOUSE. HOLO NAMED IT "SPICE AND WOLF." EVERYTHING WILL FINALLY BE DONE THIS SPRING.
THE MAIN BUILDING WAS FINISHED A WHILE AGO AND IS IN BUSINESS, OF COURSE, BUT IT'S A DEEPLY MOVING THOUGHT TO FINALLY BE 100% OPERATIONAL.

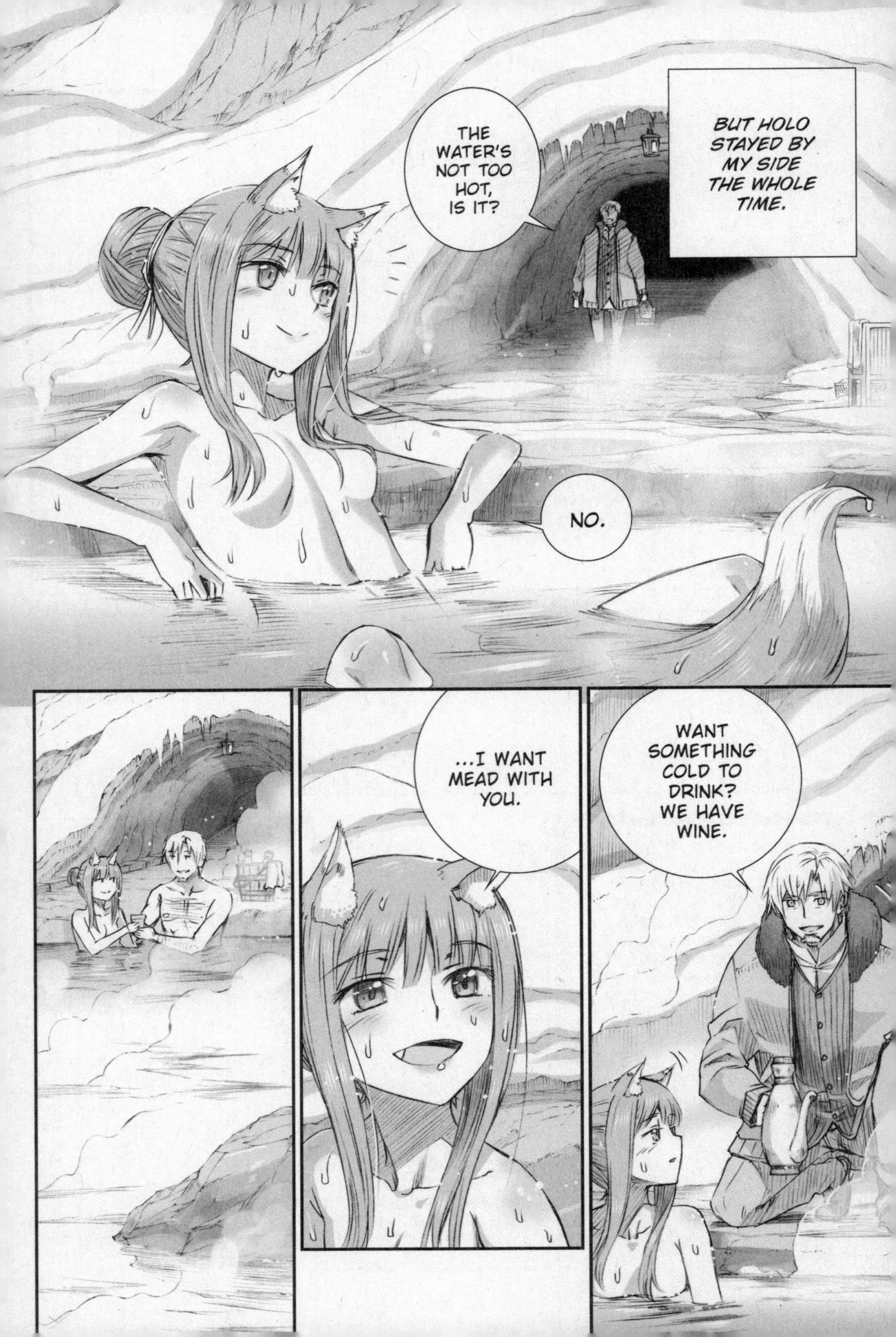
BUT HOLO STAYED BY MY SIDE THE WHOLE TIME.
THE WATER'S NOT TOO HOT, IS IT?
NO.
WANT SOMETHING COLD TO DRINK? WE HAVE WINE.
...I WANT MEAD WITH YOU.

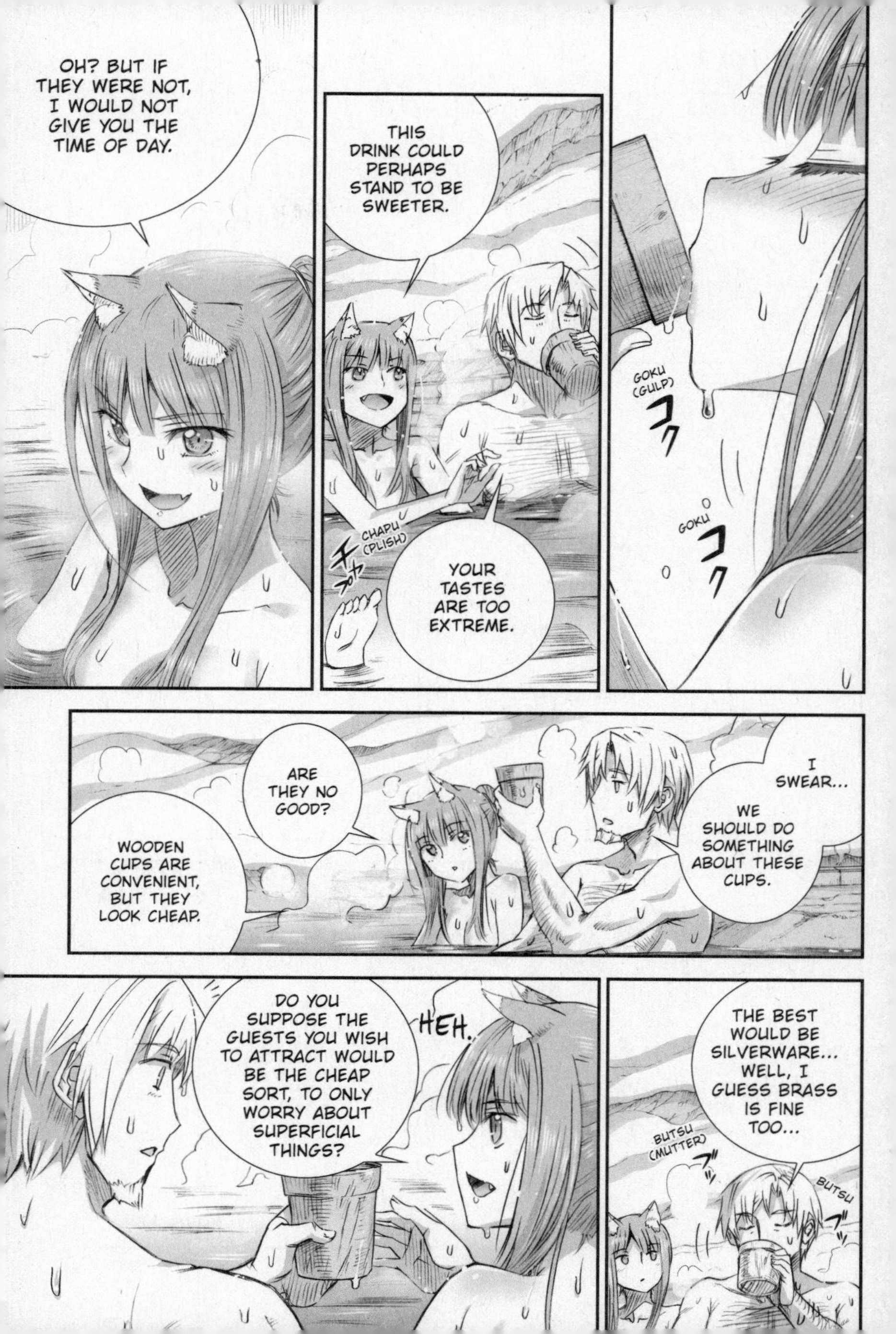
GOKU (GULP)
GOKU
THIS DRINK COULD PERHAPS STAND TO BE SWEETER.
CHAPU (PLISH)
YOUR TASTES ARE TOO EXTREME.
OH? BUT IF THEY WERE NOT, I WOULD NOT GIVE YOU THE TIME OF DAY.
I SWEAR...
WE SHOULD DO SOMETHING ABOUT THESE CUPS.
ARE THEY NO GOOD?
WOODEN CUPS ARE CONVENIENT, BUT THEY LOOK CHEAP.
THE BEST WOULD BE SILVERWARE... WELL, I GUESS BRASS IS FINE TOO...
BUTSU (MUTTER)
BUTSU
HEH.
DO YOU SUPPOSE THE GUESTS YOU WISH TO ATTRACT WOULD BE THE CHEAP SORT, TO ONLY WORRY ABOUT SUPERFICIAL THINGS?

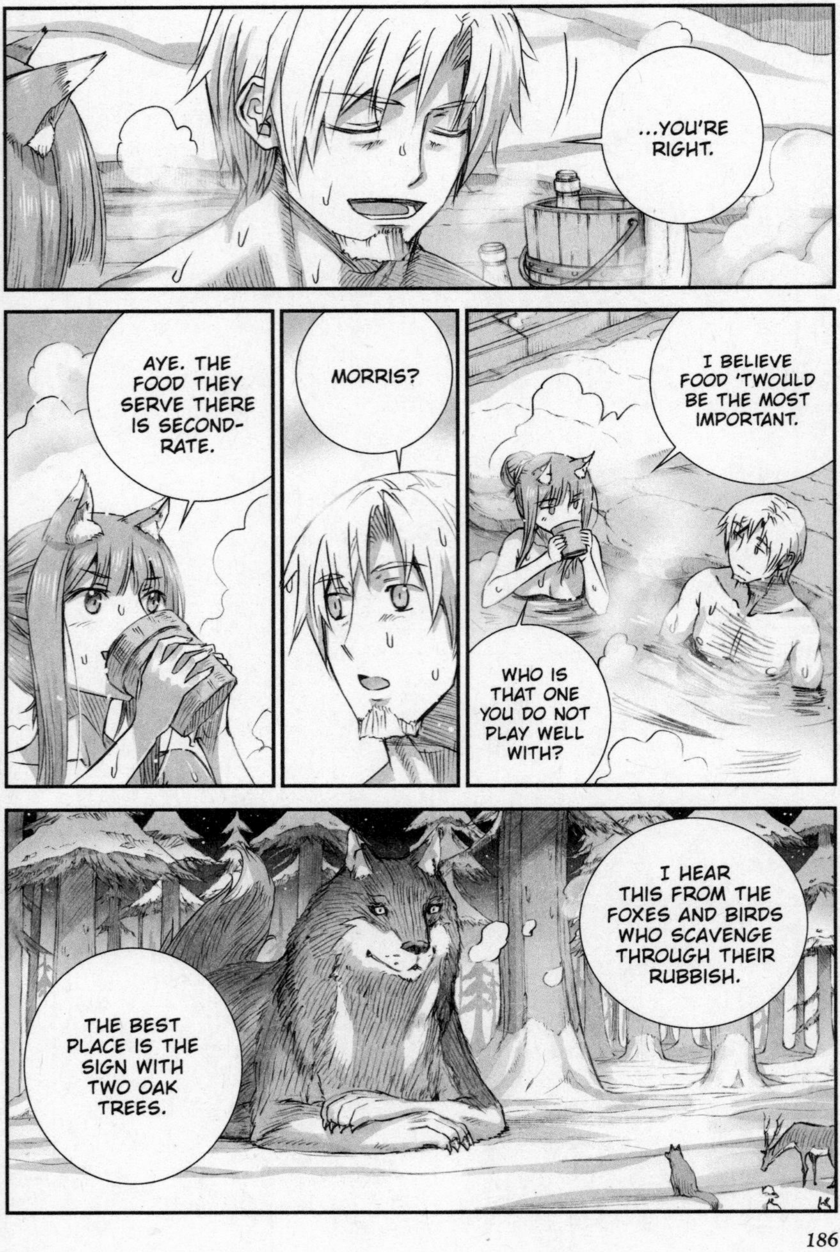
...YOU'RE RIGHT.
I BELIEVE FOOD 'TWOULD BE THE MOST IMPORTANT.
WHO IS THAT ONE YOU DO NOT PLAY WELL WITH?
MORRIS?
AYE. THE FOOD THEY SERVE THERE IS SECOND-RATE.
I HEAR THIS FROM THE FOXES AND BIRDS WHO SCAVENGE THROUGH THEIR RUBBISH.
THE BEST PLACE IS THE SIGN WITH TWO OAK TREES.

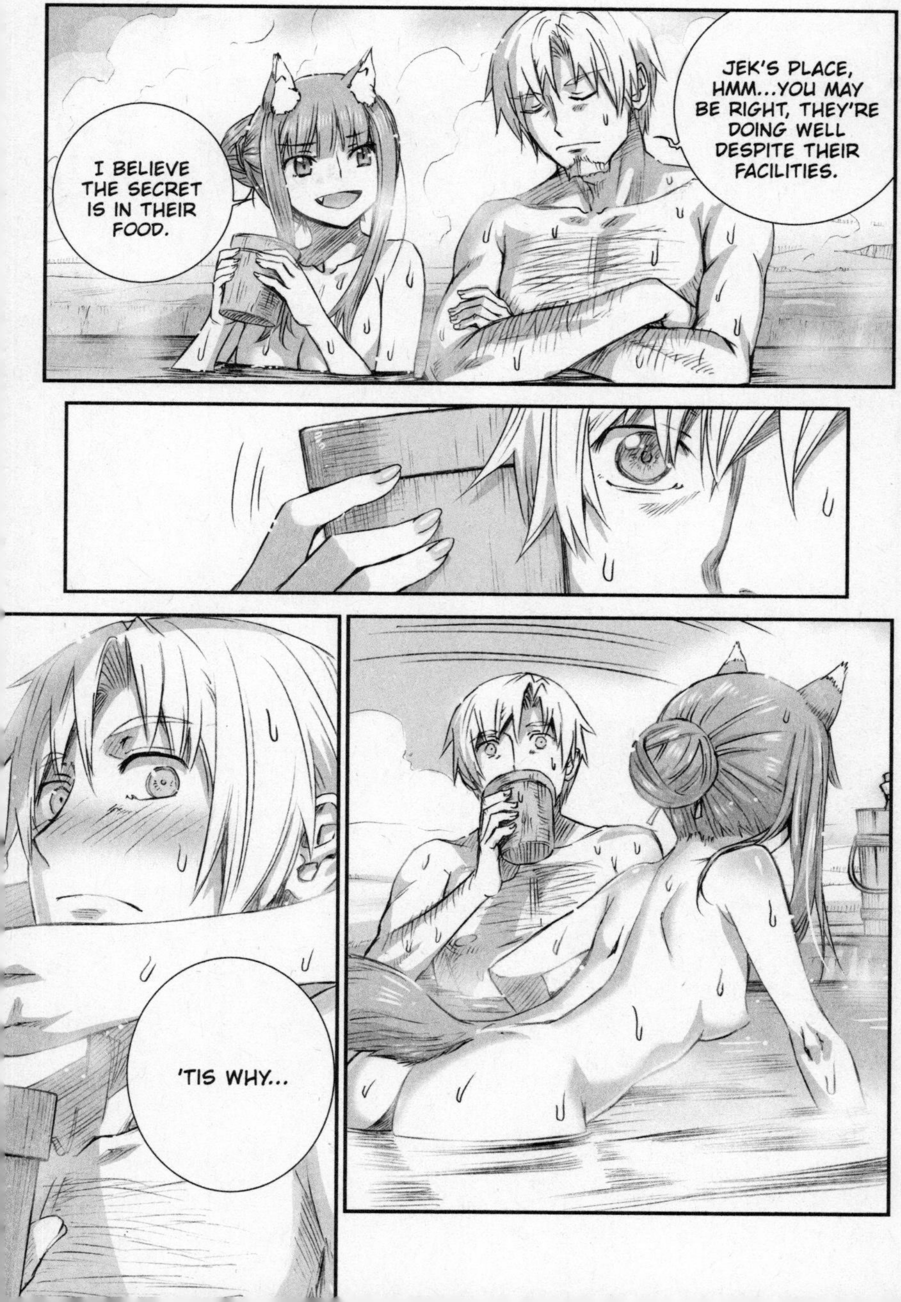
JEK'S PLACE, HMM...YOU MAY BE RIGHT, THEY'RE DOING WELL DESPITE THEIR FACILITIES.
I BELIEVE THE SECRET IS IN THEIR FOOD.
'TIS WHY...

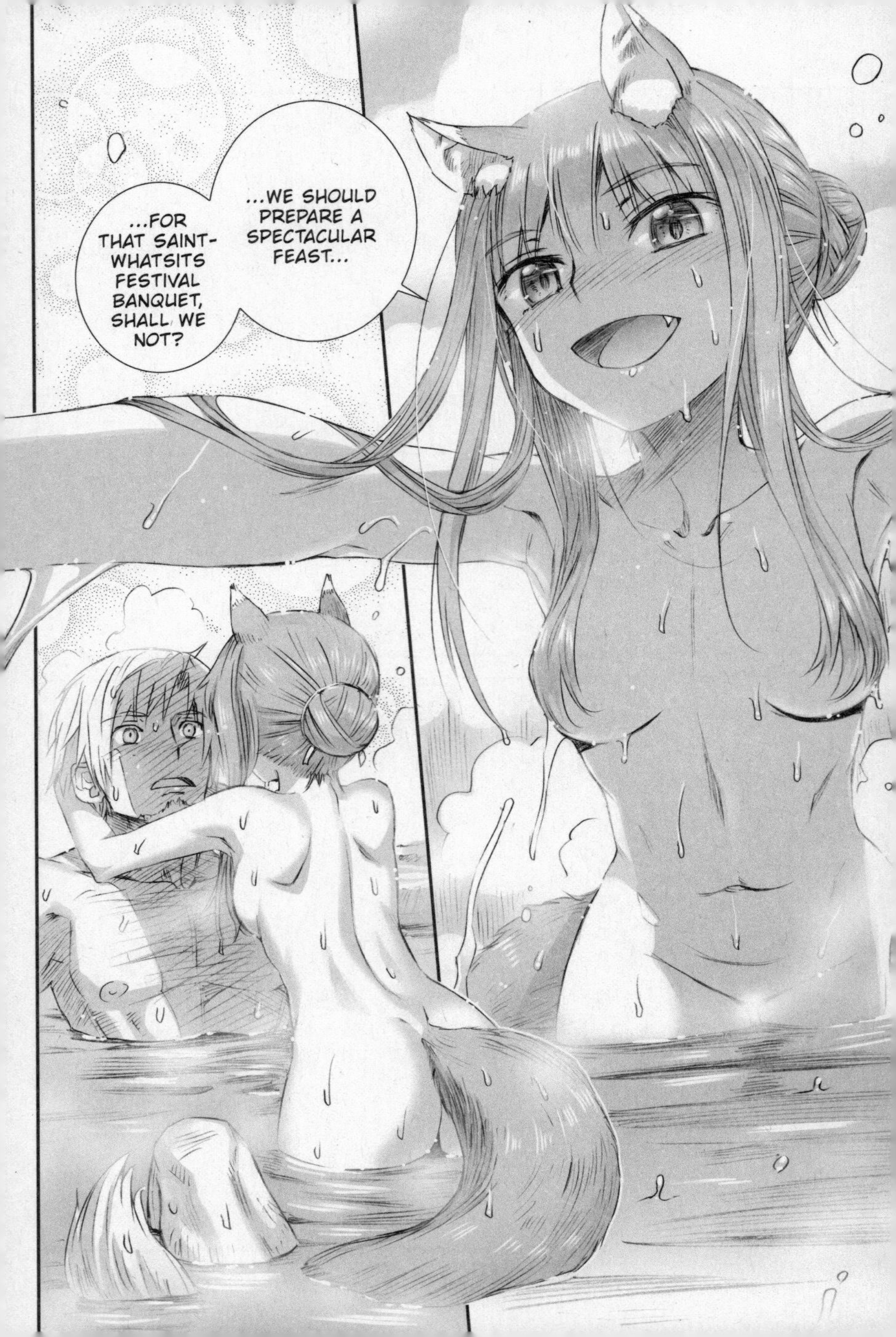
...WE SHOULD PREPARE A SPECTACULAR FEAST...
...FOR THAT SAINT-WHATSITS FESTIVAL BANQUET, SHALL WE NOT?

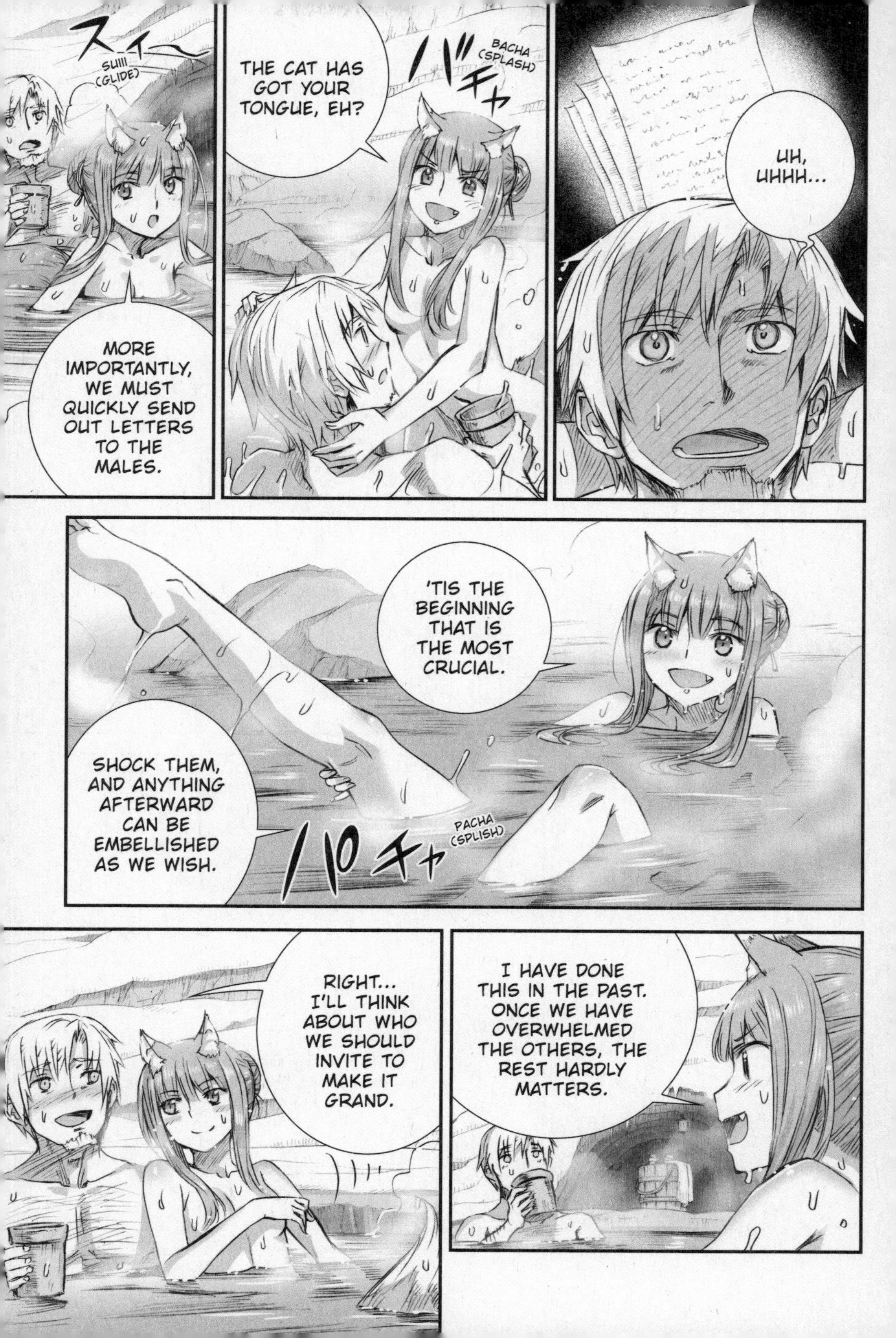
UH, UHHH...
バチャ
BACHA (SPLASH)
THE CAT HAS GOT YOUR TONGUE, EH?
スイー
SUIII (GLIDE)
MORE IMPORTANTLY, WE MUST QUICKLY SEND OUT LETTERS TO THE MALES.
'TIS THE BEGINNING THAT IS THE MOST CRUCIAL.
SHOCK THEM, AND ANYTHING AFTERWARD CAN BE EMBELLISHED AS WE WISH.
パチャ
PACHA (SPLISH)
I HAVE DONE THIS IN THE PAST. ONCE WE HAVE OVERWHELMED THE OTHERS, THE REST HARDLY MATTERS.
RIGHT... I'LL THINK ABOUT WHO WE SHOULD INVITE TO MAKE IT GRAND.

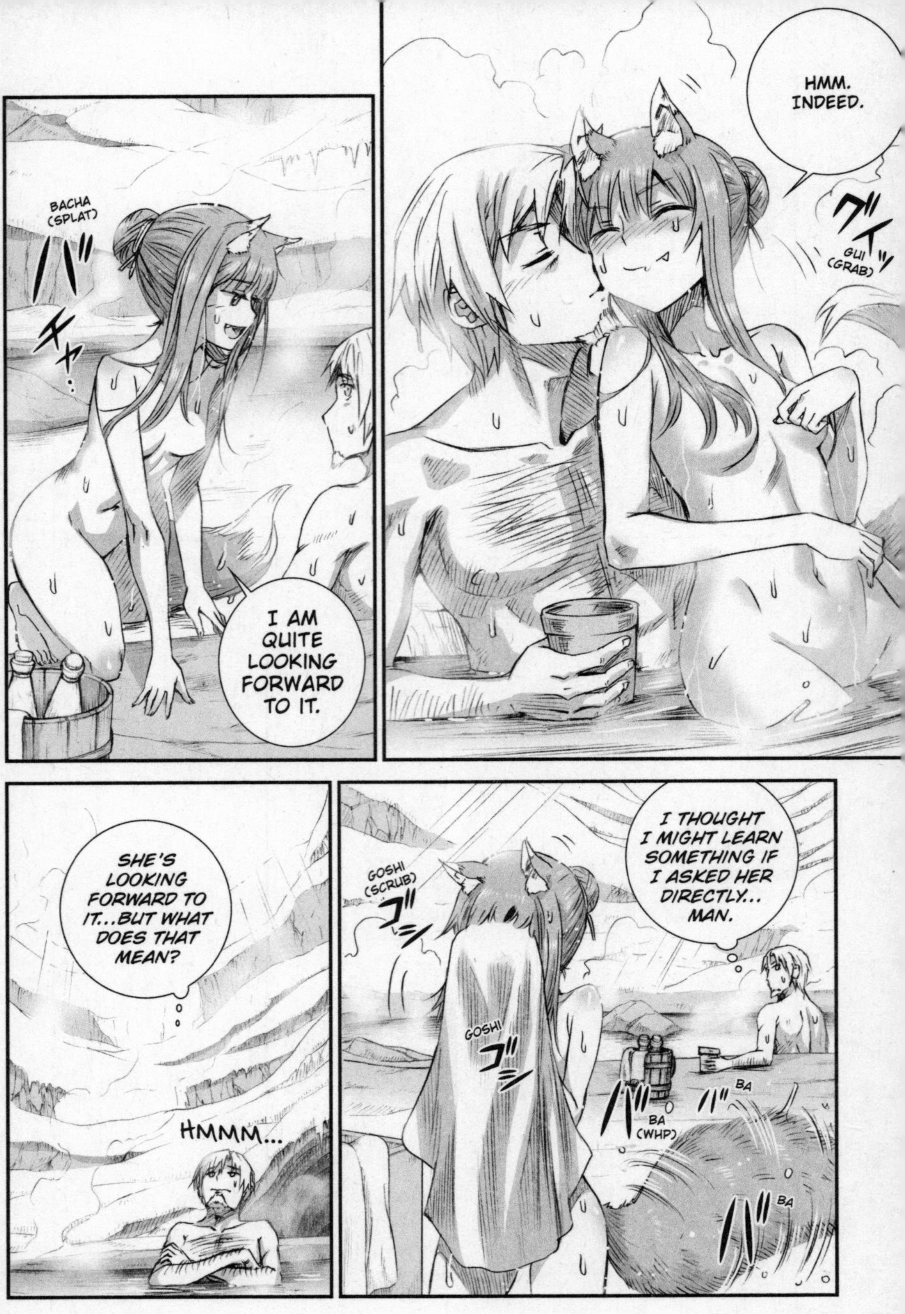
HMM. INDEED.
GUI (GRAB)
BACHA (SPLAT)
I AM QUITE LOOKING FORWARD TO IT.
I THOUGHT I MIGHT LEARN SOMETHING IF I ASKED HER DIRECTLY... MAN.
GOSHI (SCRUB)
GOSHI
BA
BA (WHP)
BA
SHE'S LOOKING FORWARD TO IT...BUT WHAT DOES THAT MEAN?
HMMM...

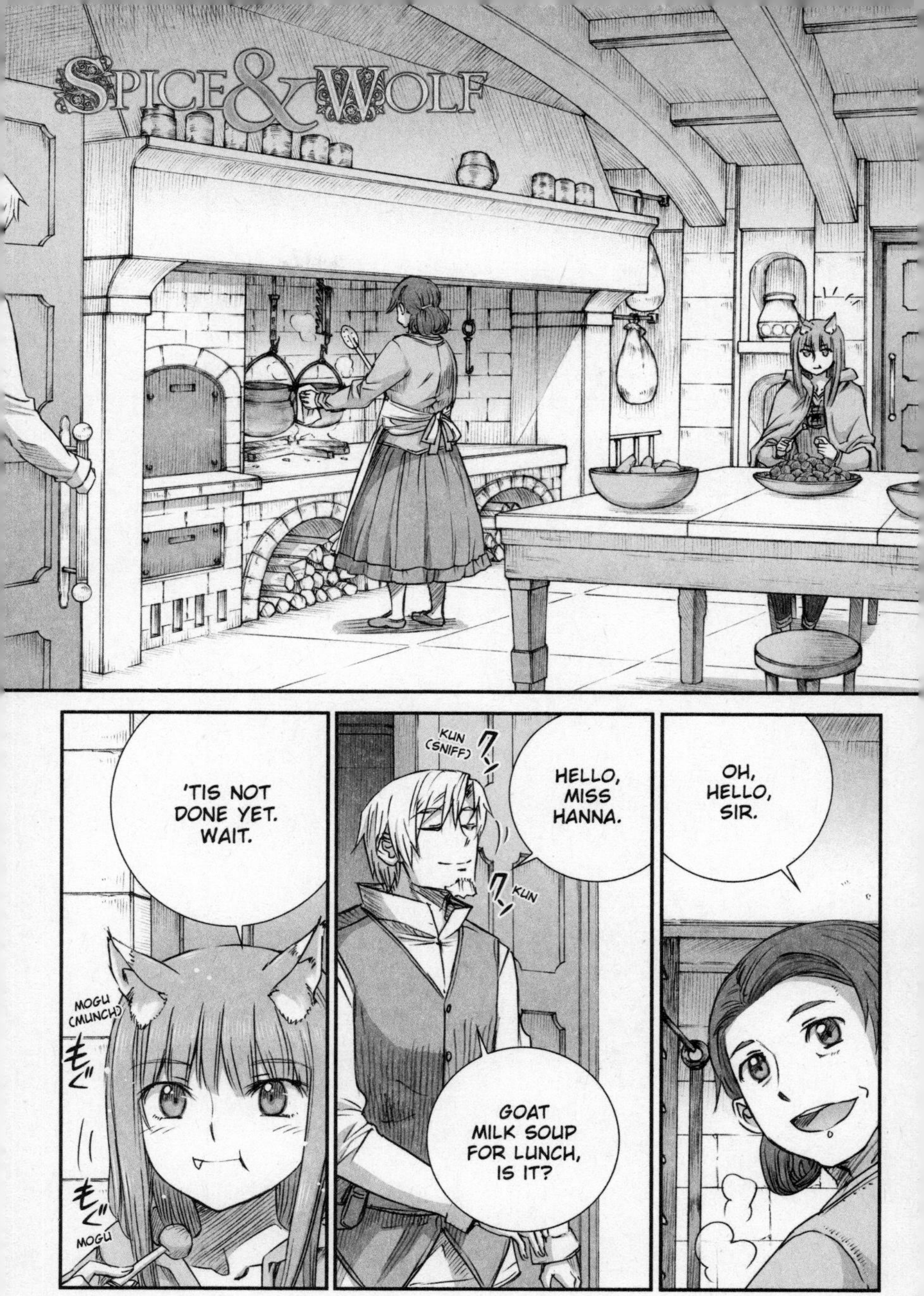
SPICE & WOLF
OH, HELLO, SIR.
KUN (SNIFF)
HELLO, MISS HANNA.
KUN
GOAT MILK SOUP FOR LUNCH, IS IT?
'TIS NOT DONE YET. WAIT.
MOGU (MUNCH)
MOGU

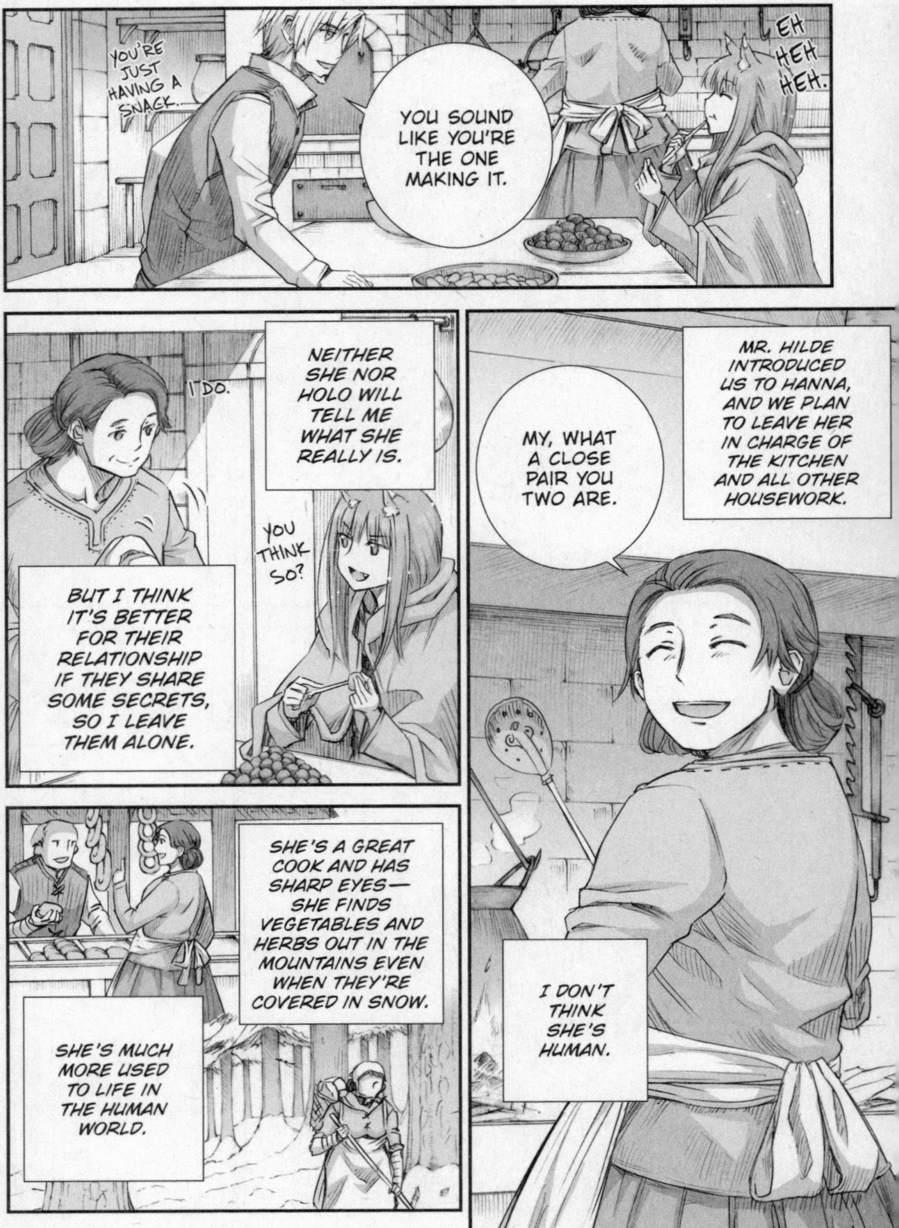
EH HEH HEH.
YOU SOUND LIKE YOU'RE THE ONE MAKING IT.
YOU'RE JUST HAVING A SNACK...
MR. HILDE INTRODUCED US TO HANNA, AND WE PLAN TO LEAVE HER IN CHARGE OF THE KITCHEN AND ALL OTHER HOUSEWORK.
MY, WHAT A CLOSE PAIR YOU TWO ARE.
I DON'T THINK SHE'S HUMAN.
NEITHER SHE NOR HOLO WILL TELL ME WHAT SHE REALLY IS.
I DO.
YOU THINK SO?
BUT I THINK IT'S BETTER FOR THEIR RELATIONSHIP IF THEY SHARE SOME SECRETS, SO I LEAVE THEM ALONE.
SHE'S A GREAT COOK AND HAS SHARP EYES—SHE FINDS VEGETABLES AND HERBS OUT IN THE MOUNTAINS EVEN WHEN THEY'RE COVERED IN SNOW.
SHE'S MUCH MORE USED TO LIFE IN THE HUMAN WORLD.

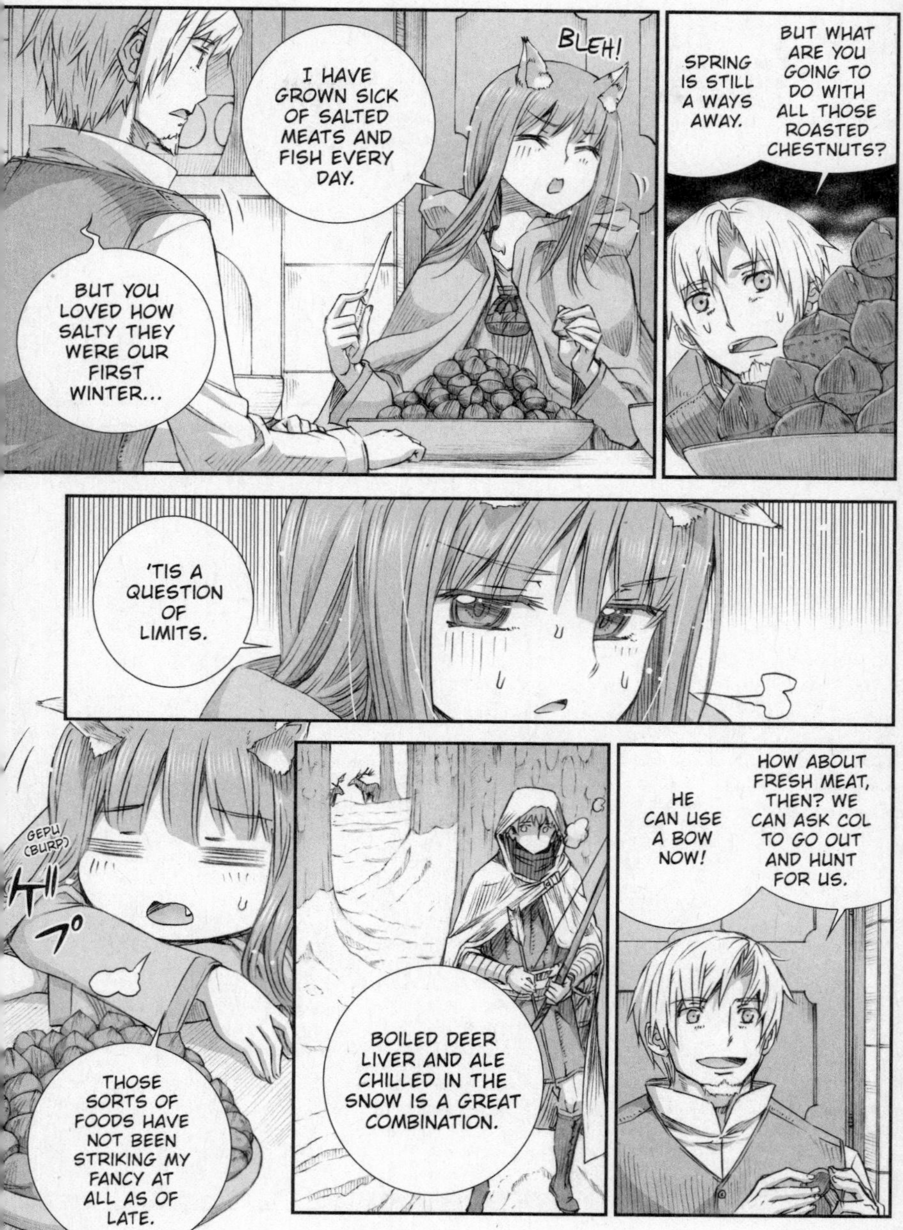
BUT WHAT ARE YOU GOING TO DO WITH ALL THOSE ROASTED CHESTNUTS?
SPRING IS STILL A WAYS AWAY.
BLEH!
I HAVE GROWN SICK OF SALTED MEATS AND FISH EVERY DAY.
BUT YOU LOVED HOW SALTY THEY WERE OUR FIRST WINTER...
'TIS A QUESTION OF LIMITS.
HOW ABOUT FRESH MEAT, THEN? WE CAN ASK COL TO GO OUT AND HUNT FOR US.
HE CAN USE A BOW NOW!
BOILED DEER LIVER AND ALE CHILLED IN THE SNOW IS A GREAT COMBINATION.
GEPU (BURP)
THOSE SORTS OF FOODS HAVE NOT BEEN STRIKING MY FANCY AT ALL AS OF LATE.

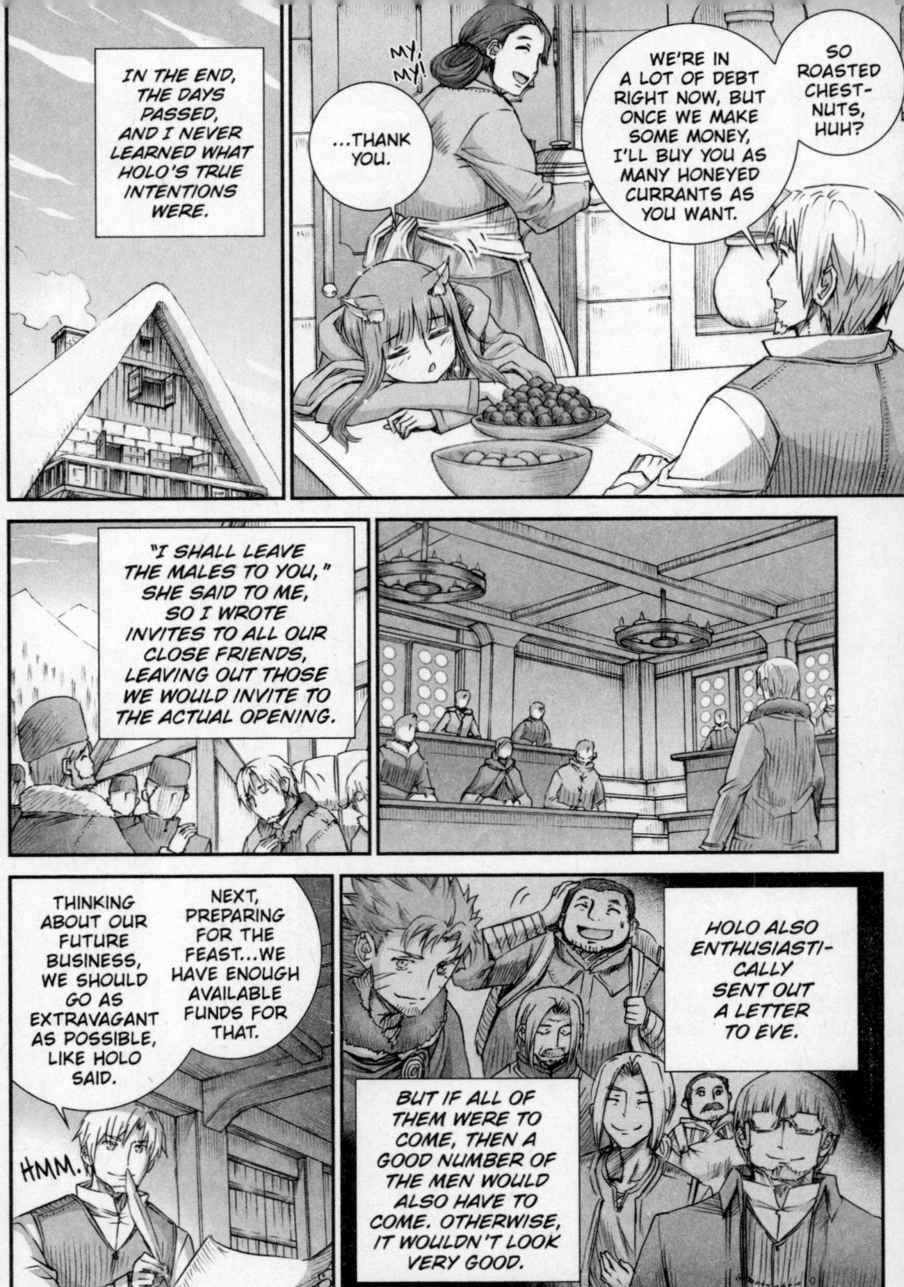
SO ROASTED CHEST-NUTS, HUH?
WE'RE IN A LOT OF DEBT RIGHT NOW, BUT ONCE WE MAKE SOME MONEY, I'LL BUY YOU AS MANY HONEYED CURRANTS AS YOU WANT.
MY, MY!
...THANK YOU.
IN THE END, THE DAYS PASSED, AND I NEVER LEARNED WHAT HOLO'S TRUE INTENTIONS WERE.
"I SHALL LEAVE THE MALES TO YOU," SHE SAID TO ME, SO I WROTE INVITES TO ALL OUR CLOSE FRIENDS, LEAVING OUT THOSE WE WOULD INVITE TO THE ACTUAL OPENING.
HOLO ALSO ENTHUSIASTI-CALLY SENT OUT A LETTER TO EVE.
BUT IF ALL OF THEM WERE TO COME, THEN A GOOD NUMBER OF THE MEN WOULD ALSO HAVE TO COME. OTHERWISE, IT WOULDN'T LOOK VERY GOOD.
NEXT, PREPARING FOR THE FEAST...WE HAVE ENOUGH AVAILABLE FUNDS FOR THAT.
THINKING ABOUT OUR FUTURE BUSINESS, WE SHOULD GO AS EXTRAVAGANT AS POSSIBLE, LIKE HOLO SAID.
HMM.

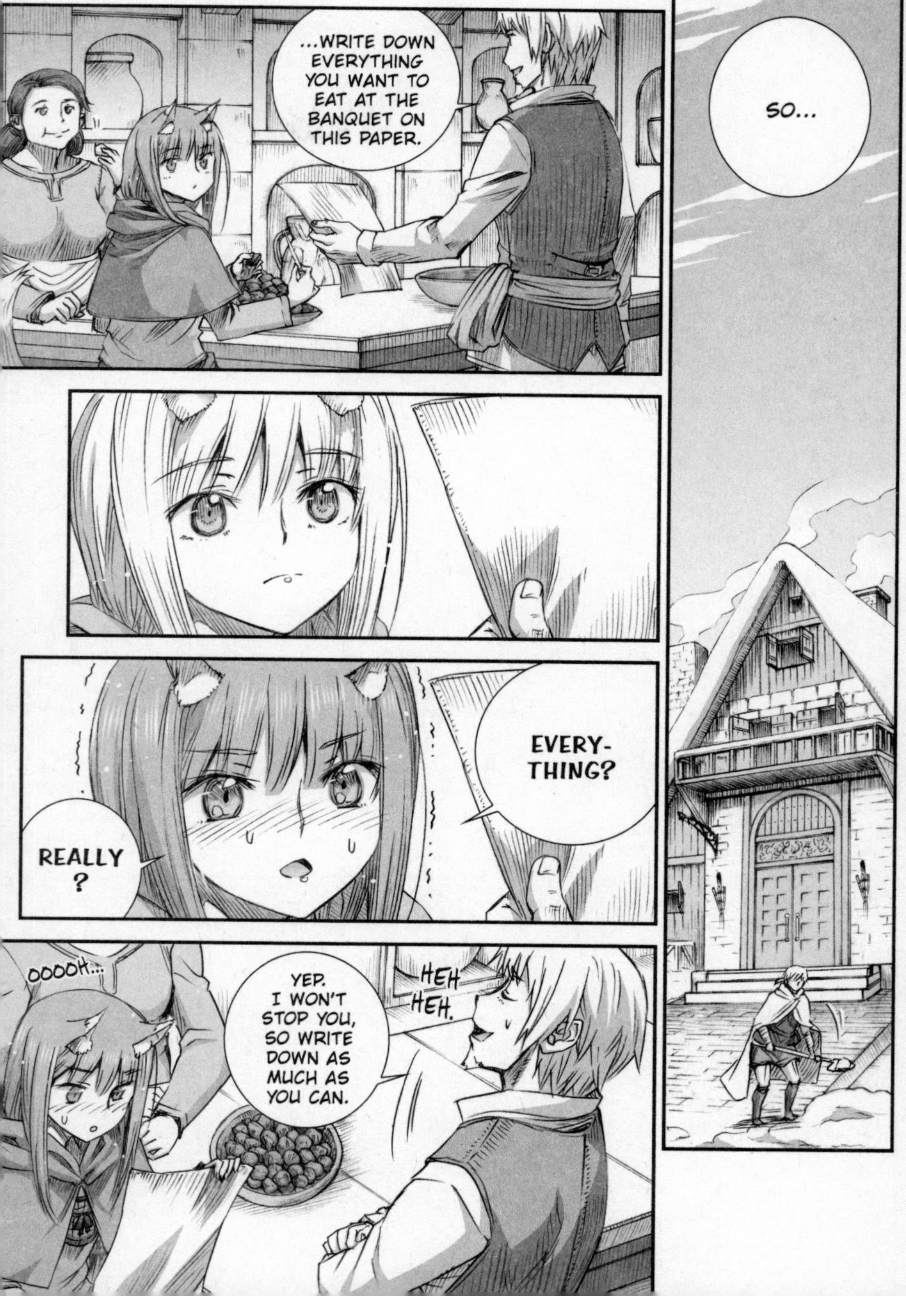
SO...
...WRITE DOWN EVERYTHING YOU WANT TO EAT AT THE BANQUET ON THIS PAPER.
EVERY-THING?
REALLY?
HEH HEH.
YEP. I WON'T STOP YOU, SO WRITE DOWN AS MUCH AS YOU CAN.
OOOOH...

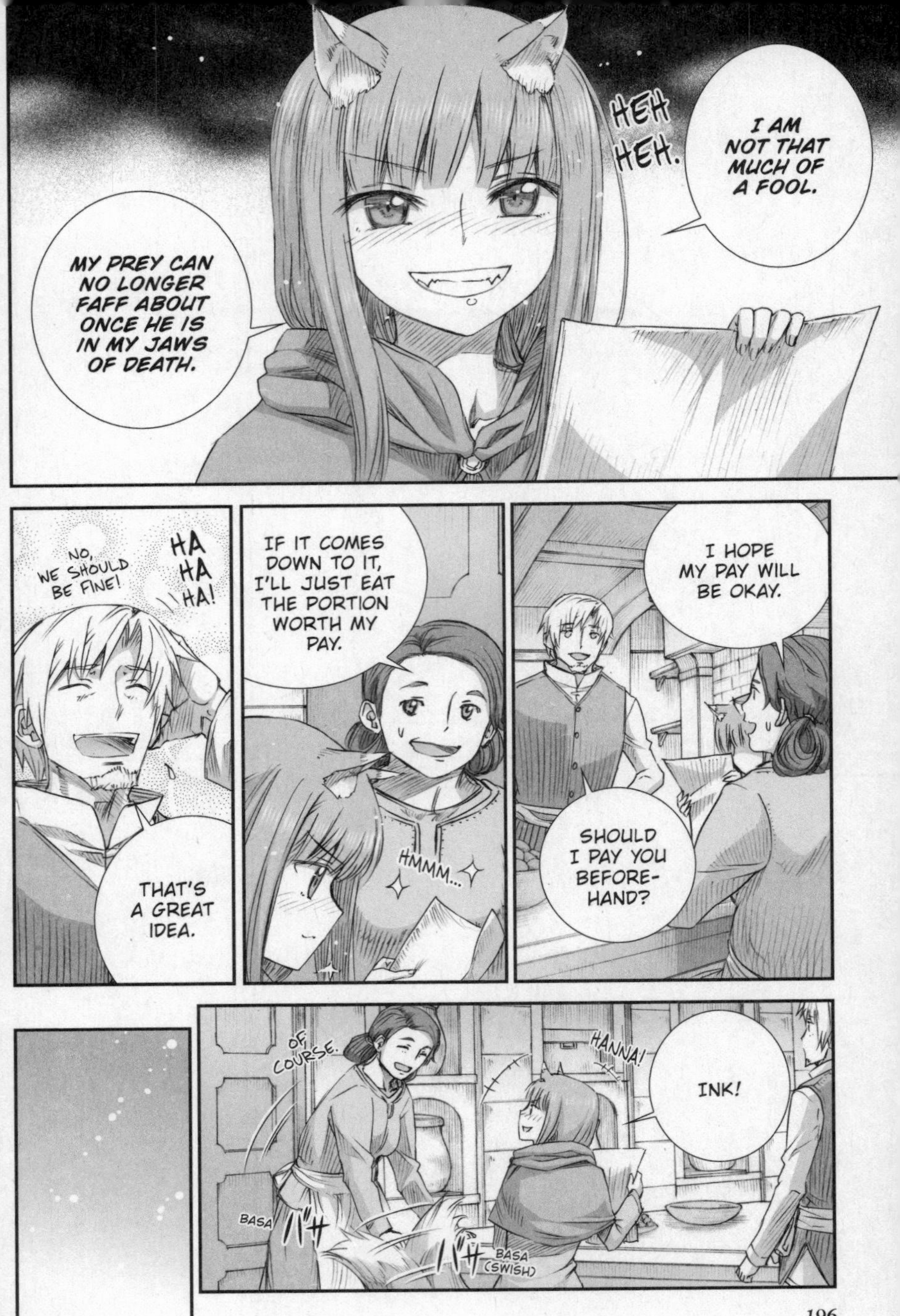
HEH HEH.
I AM NOT THAT MUCH OF A FOOL.
MY PREY CAN NO LONGER FAFF ABOUT ONCE HE IS IN MY JAWS OF DEATH.
I HOPE MY PAY WILL BE OKAY.
SHOULD I PAY YOU BEFORE-HAND?
IF IT COMES DOWN TO IT, I'LL JUST EAT THE PORTION WORTH MY PAY.
HMMM...
HA HA HA!
NO, WE SHOULD BE FINE!
THAT'S A GREAT IDEA.
INK!
HANNA!
OF COURSE.
BASA (SWISH)
BASA

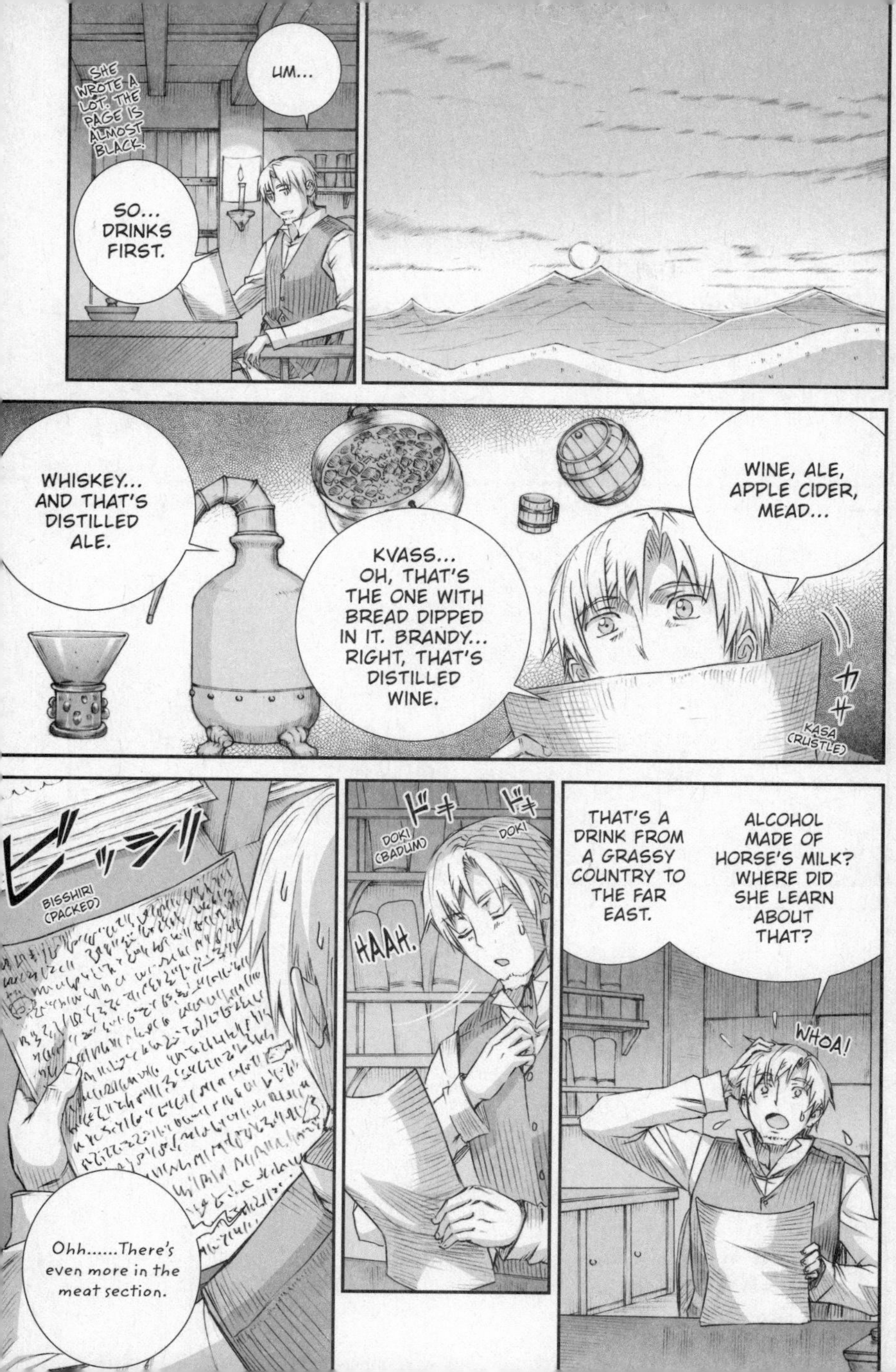
UM...
SHE WROTE A LOT. THE PAGE IS ALMOST BLACK.
SO... DRINKS FIRST.
WINE, ALE, APPLE CIDER, MEAD...
カサ
KASA (RUSTLE)
KVASS... OH, THAT'S THE ONE WITH BREAD DIPPED IN IT. BRANDY... RIGHT, THAT'S DISTILLED WINE.
WHISKEY... AND THAT'S DISTILLED ALE.
ALCOHOL MADE OF HORSE'S MILK? WHERE DID SHE LEARN ABOUT THAT?
THAT'S A DRINK FROM A GRASSY COUNTRY TO THE FAR EAST.
WHOA!
ドキ ドキ
DOKI (BADUM)
DOKI
HAAH.
ビッシリ
BISSHIRI (PACKED)
Ohh......There's even more in the meat section.

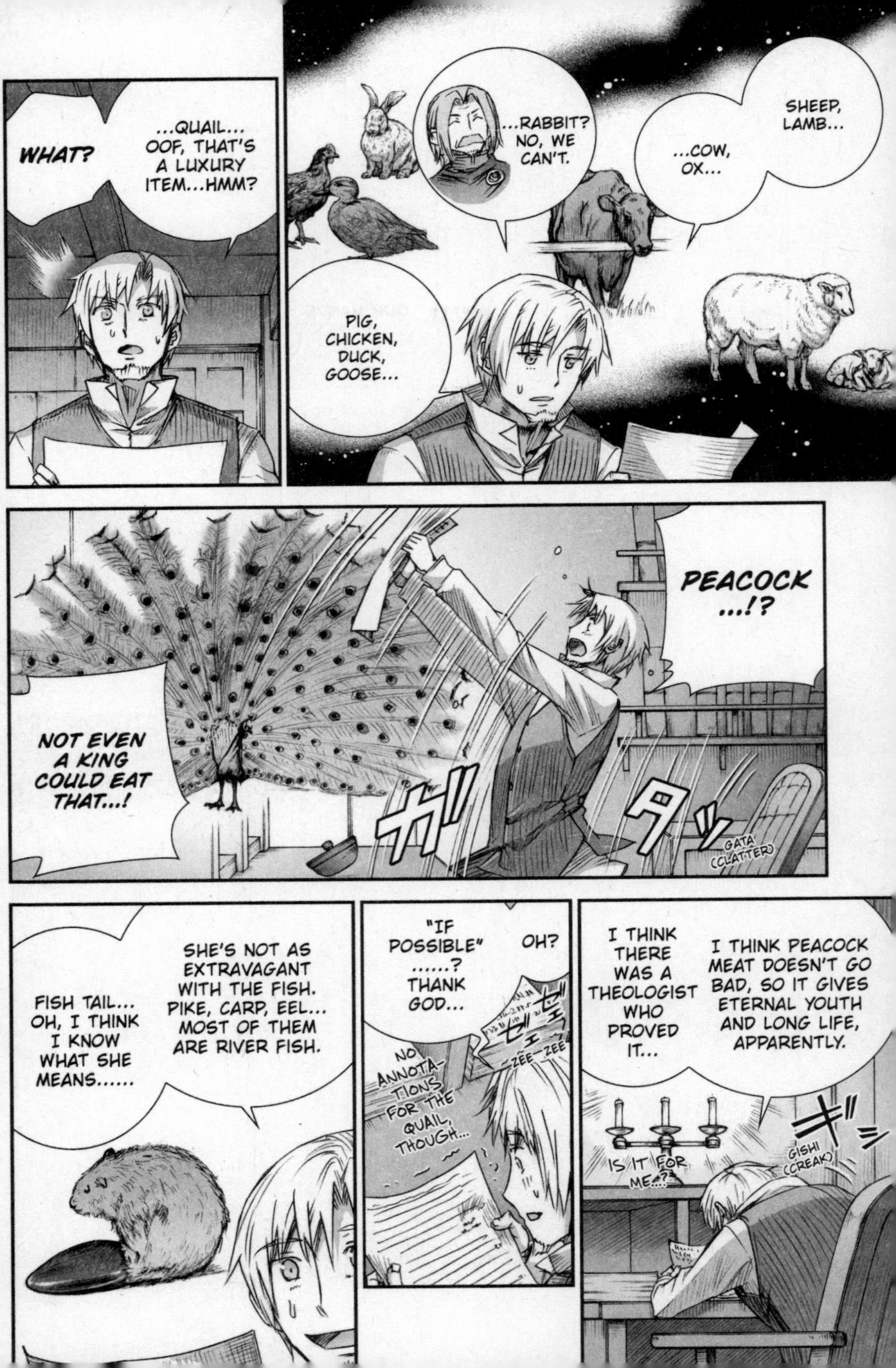
SHEEP, LAMB...
...COW, OX...
...RABBIT? NO, WE CAN'T.
PIG, CHICKEN, DUCK, GOOSE...
...QUAIL... OOF, THAT'S A LUXURY ITEM...HMM?
WHAT?
PEACOCK ...!?
GATA (CLATTER)
NOT EVEN A KING COULD EAT THAT...!
I THINK PEACOCK MEAT DOESN'T GO BAD, SO IT GIVES ETERNAL YOUTH AND LONG LIFE, APPARENTLY.
I THINK THERE WAS A THEOLOGIST WHO PROVED IT...
GISHI (CREAK)
IS IT FOR ME...?
OH?
"IF POSSIBLE" ......? THANK GOD...
ZEE ZEE
NO ANNOTATIONS FOR THE QUAIL, THOUGH...
SHE'S NOT AS EXTRAVAGANT WITH THE FISH. PIKE, CARP, EEL... MOST OF THEM ARE RIVER FISH.
FISH TAIL... OH, I THINK I KNOW WHAT SHE MEANS......

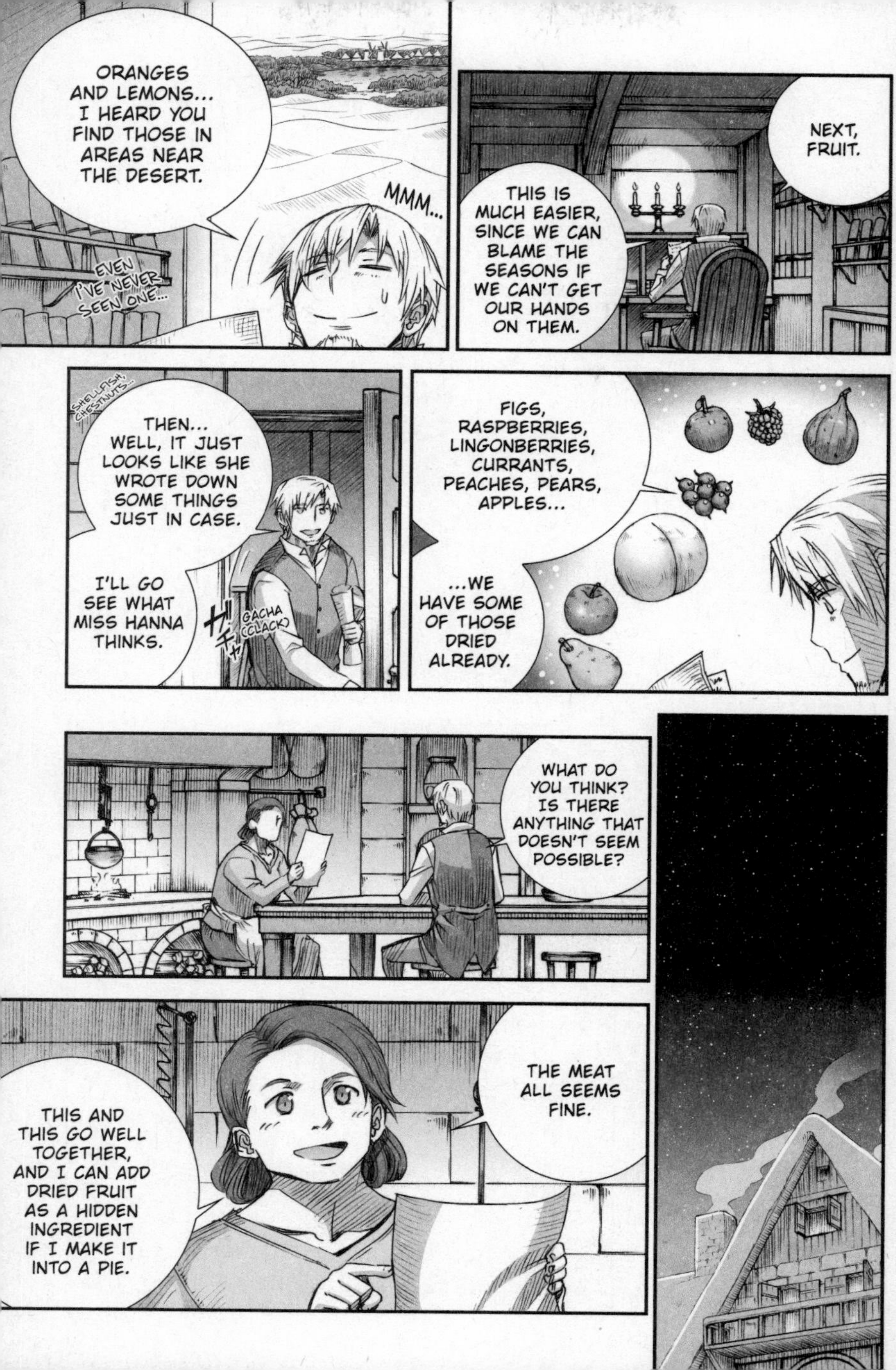
NEXT, FRUIT.
THIS IS MUCH EASIER, SINCE WE CAN BLAME THE SEASONS IF WE CAN'T GET OUR HANDS ON THEM.
ORANGES AND LEMONS... I HEARD YOU FIND THOSE IN AREAS NEAR THE DESERT.
MMM...
EVEN I'VE NEVER SEEN ONE...
FIGS, RASPBERRIES, LINGONBERRIES, CURRANTS, PEACHES, PEARS, APPLES...
...WE HAVE SOME OF THOSE DRIED ALREADY.
SHELLFISH, CHESTNUTS...
THEN... WELL, IT JUST LOOKS LIKE SHE WROTE DOWN SOME THINGS JUST IN CASE.
I'LL GO SEE WHAT MISS HANNA THINKS.
GACHA (CLACK)
WHAT DO YOU THINK? IS THERE ANYTHING THAT DOESN'T SEEM POSSIBLE?
THE MEAT ALL SEEMS FINE.
THIS AND THIS GO WELL TOGETHER, AND I CAN ADD DRIED FRUIT AS A HIDDEN INGREDIENT IF I MAKE IT INTO A PIE.

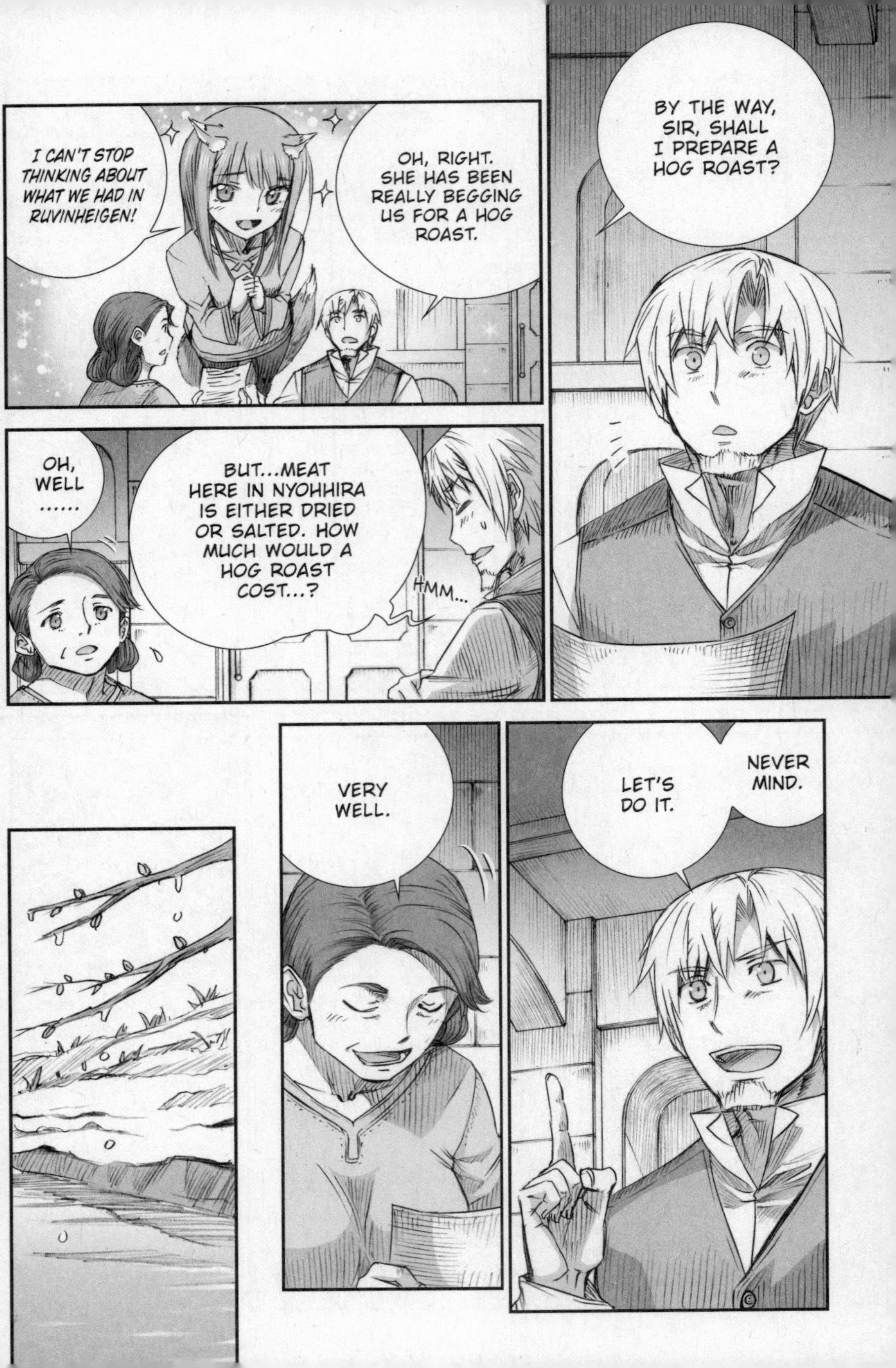

BY THE WAY, SIR, SHALL I PREPARE A HOG ROAST?
OH, RIGHT. SHE HAS BEEN REALLY BEGGING US FOR A HOG ROAST.
I CAN'T STOP THINKING ABOUT WHAT WE HAD IN RUVINHEIGEN!
HMM...
BUT...MEAT HERE IN NYOHHIRA IS EITHER DRIED OR SALTED. HOW MUCH WOULD A HOG ROAST COST...?
OH, WELL ......
NEVER MIND.
LET'S DO IT.
VERY WELL.

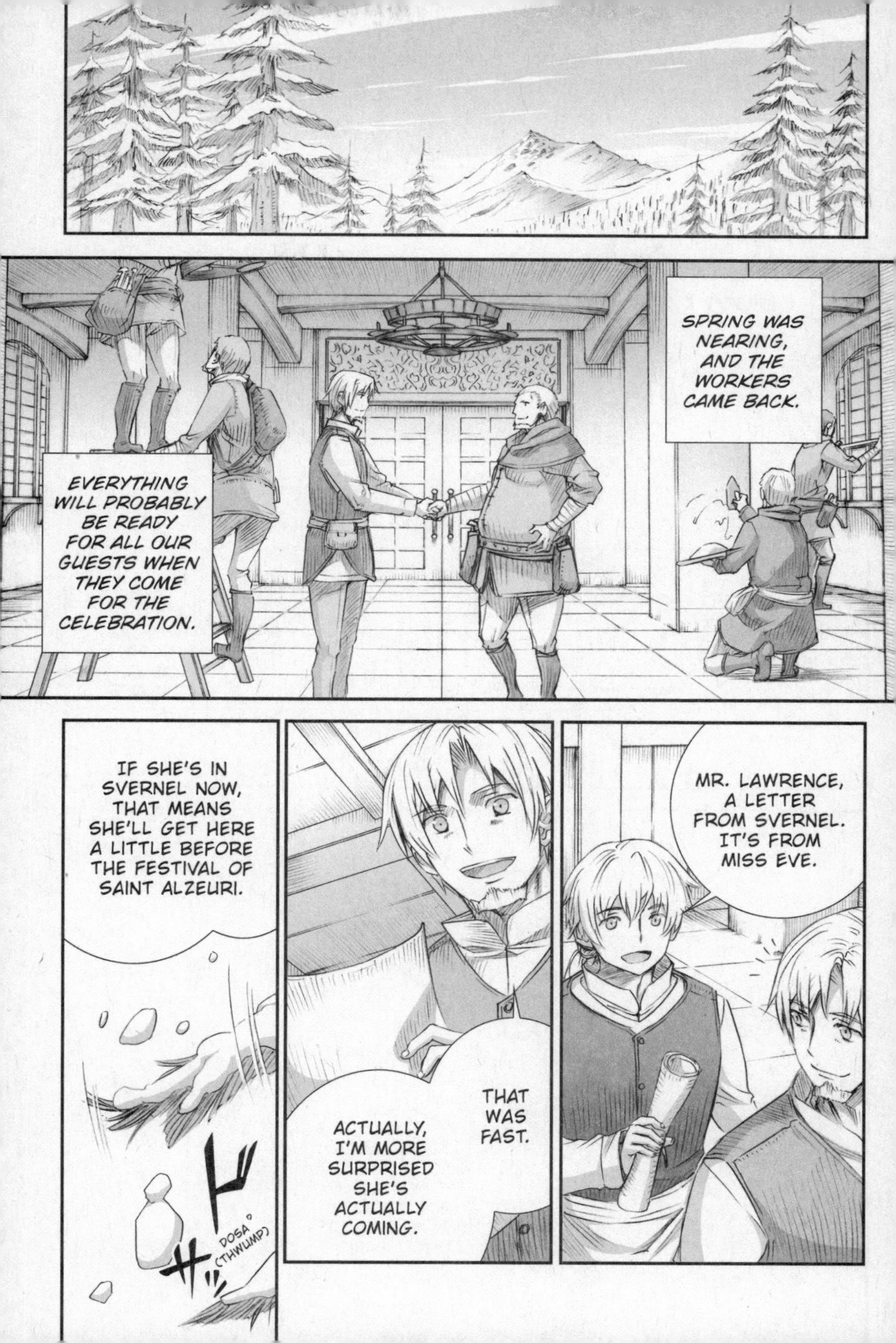
SPRING WAS NEARING, AND THE WORKERS CAME BACK.
EVERYTHING WILL PROBABLY BE READY FOR ALL OUR GUESTS WHEN THEY COME FOR THE CELEBRATION.
MR. LAWRENCE, A LETTER FROM SVERNEL. IT'S FROM MISS EVE.
THAT WAS FAST.
ACTUALLY, I'M MORE SURPRISED SHE'S ACTUALLY COMING.
IF SHE'S IN SVERNEL NOW, THAT MEANS SHE'LL GET HERE A LITTLE BEFORE THE FESTIVAL OF SAINT ALZEURI.
DOSA (THWUMP)

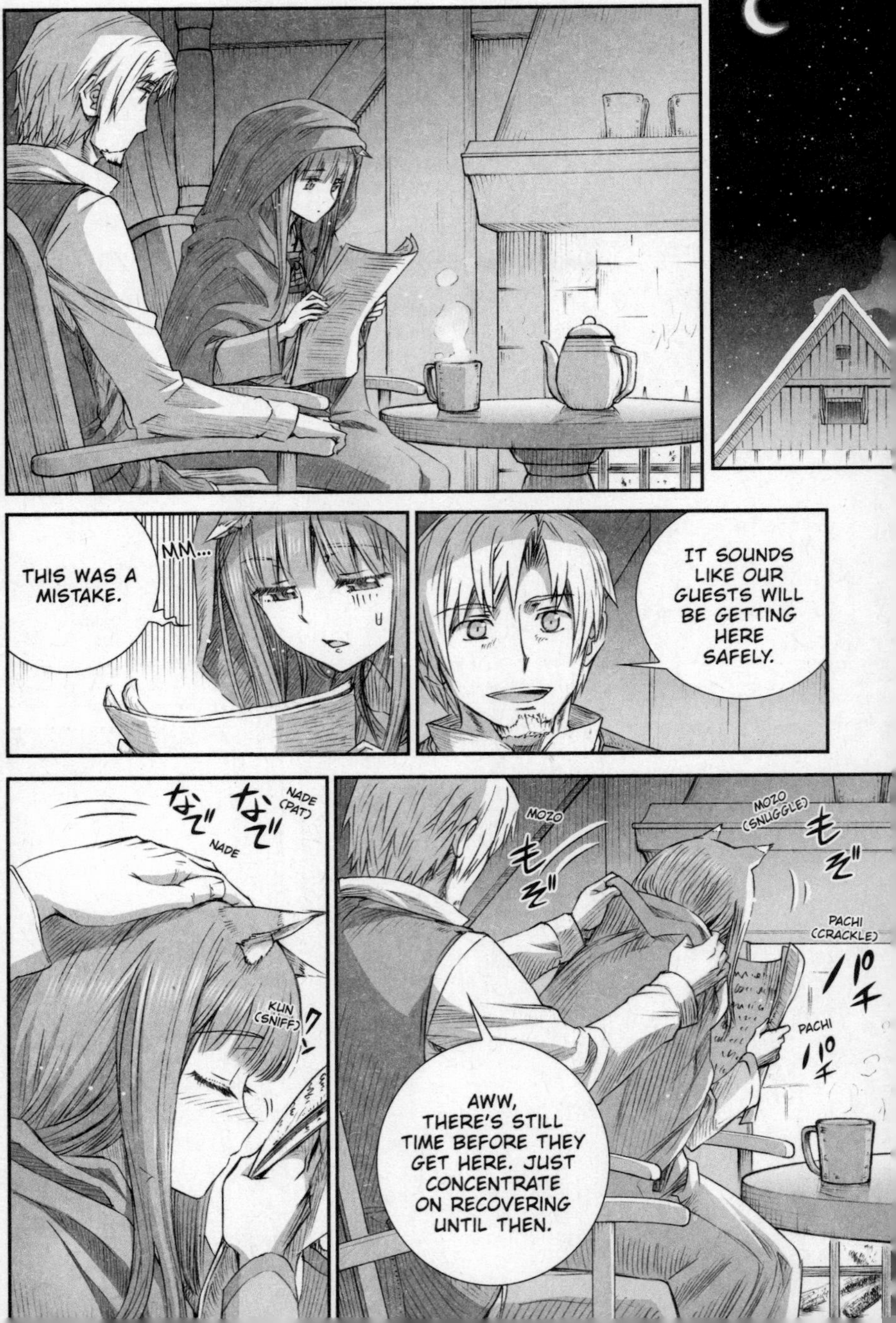
IT SOUNDS LIKE OUR GUESTS WILL BE GETTING HERE SAFELY.
MM...
THIS WAS A MISTAKE.
MOZO (SNUGGLE)
もぞ
MOZO
もぞ
PACHI (CRACKLE)
パチ
PACHI
パチ
AWW, THERE'S STILL TIME BEFORE THEY GET HERE. JUST CONCENTRATE ON RECOVERING UNTIL THEN.
NADE (PAT)
なで
NADE
なで
KUN (SNIFF)
クン

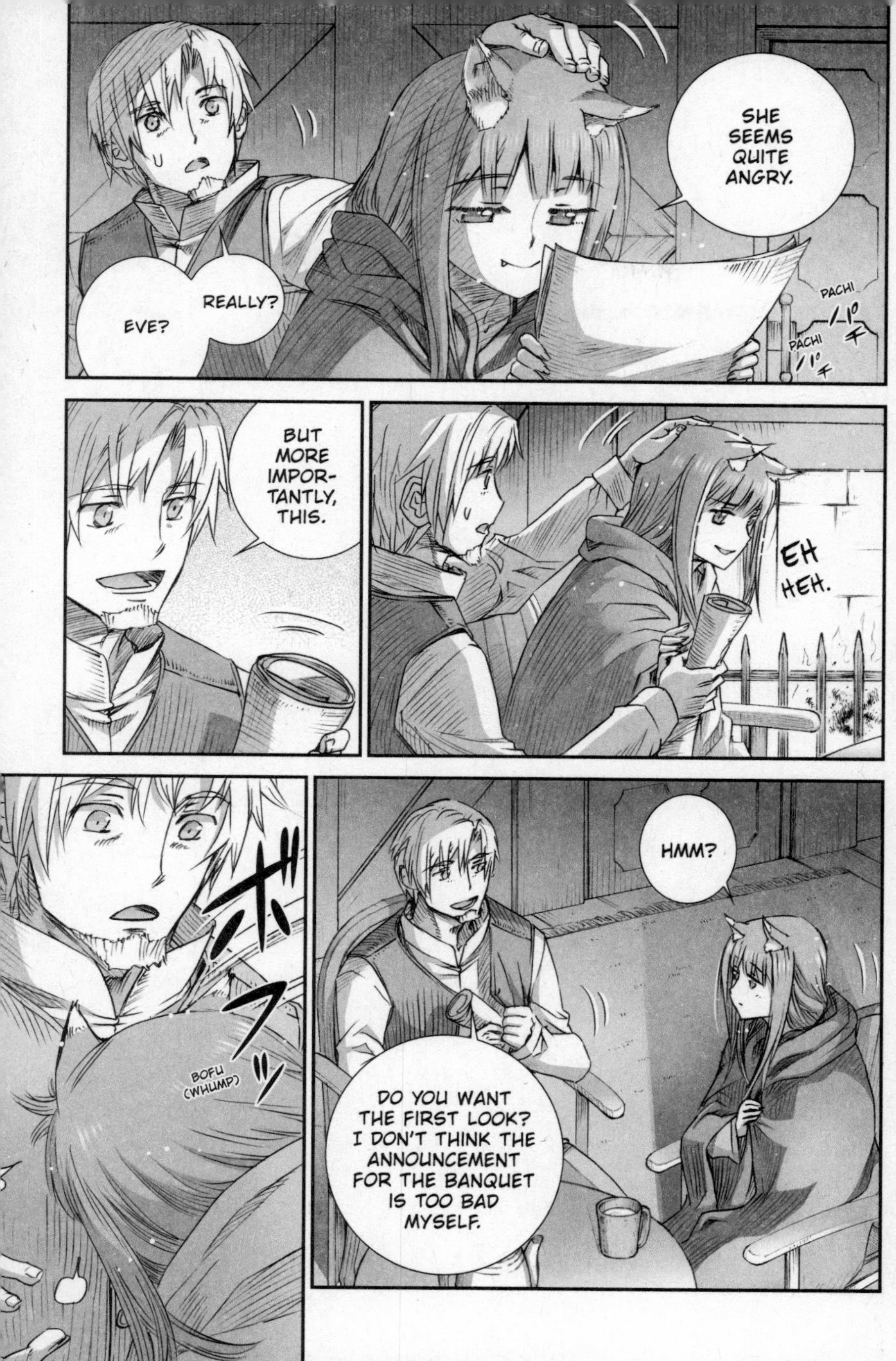
SHE SEEMS QUITE ANGRY.
REALLY?
EVE?
PACHI
PACHI
EH HEH.
BUT MORE IMPORTANTLY, THIS.
HMM?
DO YOU WANT THE FIRST LOOK? I DON'T THINK THE ANNOUNCEMENT FOR THE BANQUET IS TOO BAD MYSELF.
BOFU (WHUMP)

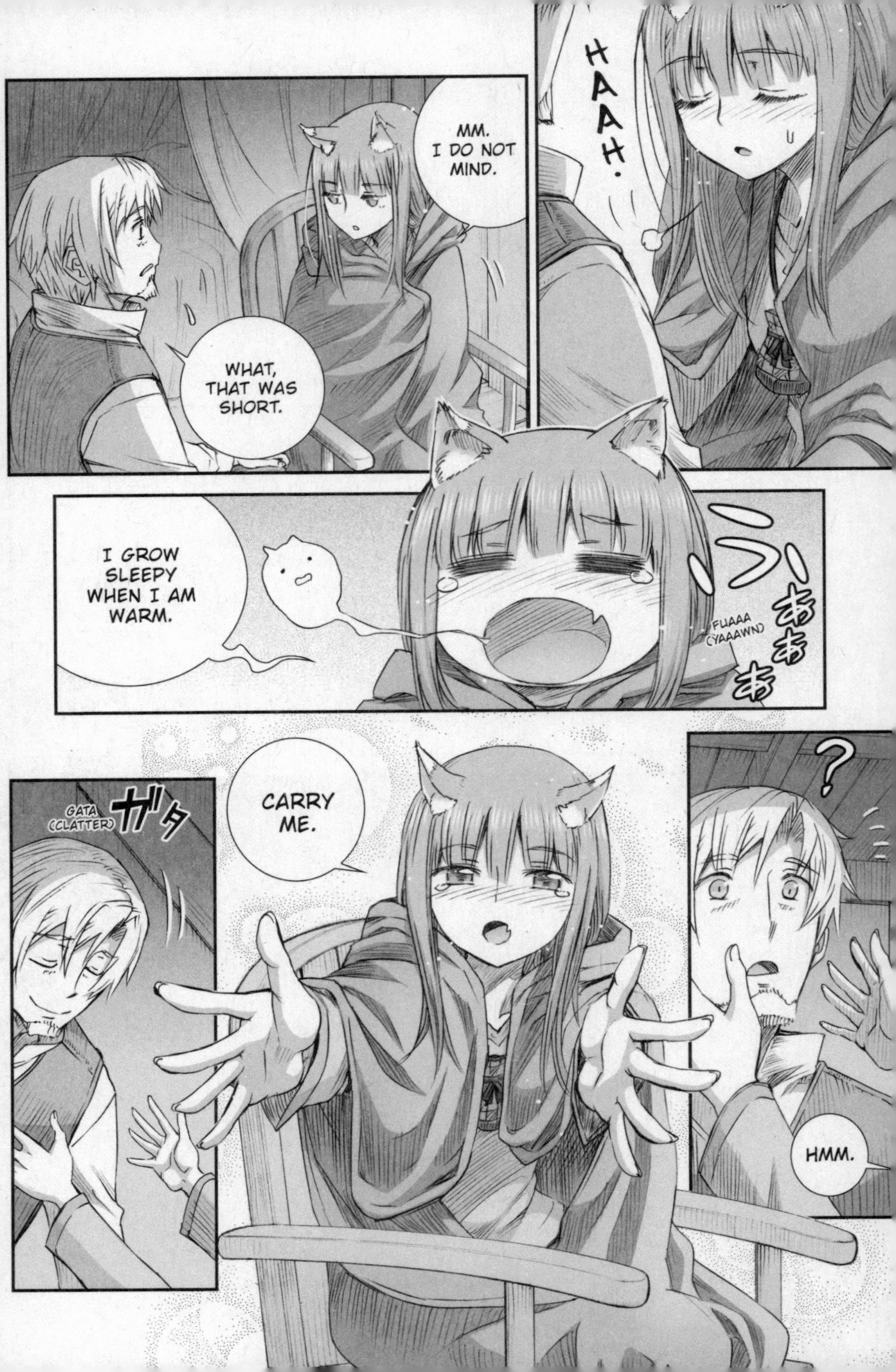
HAAH.
MM. I DO NOT MIND.
WHAT, THAT WAS SHORT.
ふぁあああ
FUAAA (YAAAWN)
I GROW SLEEPY WHEN I AM WARM.
?
HMM.
CARRY ME.
ガタ
GATA (CLATTER)

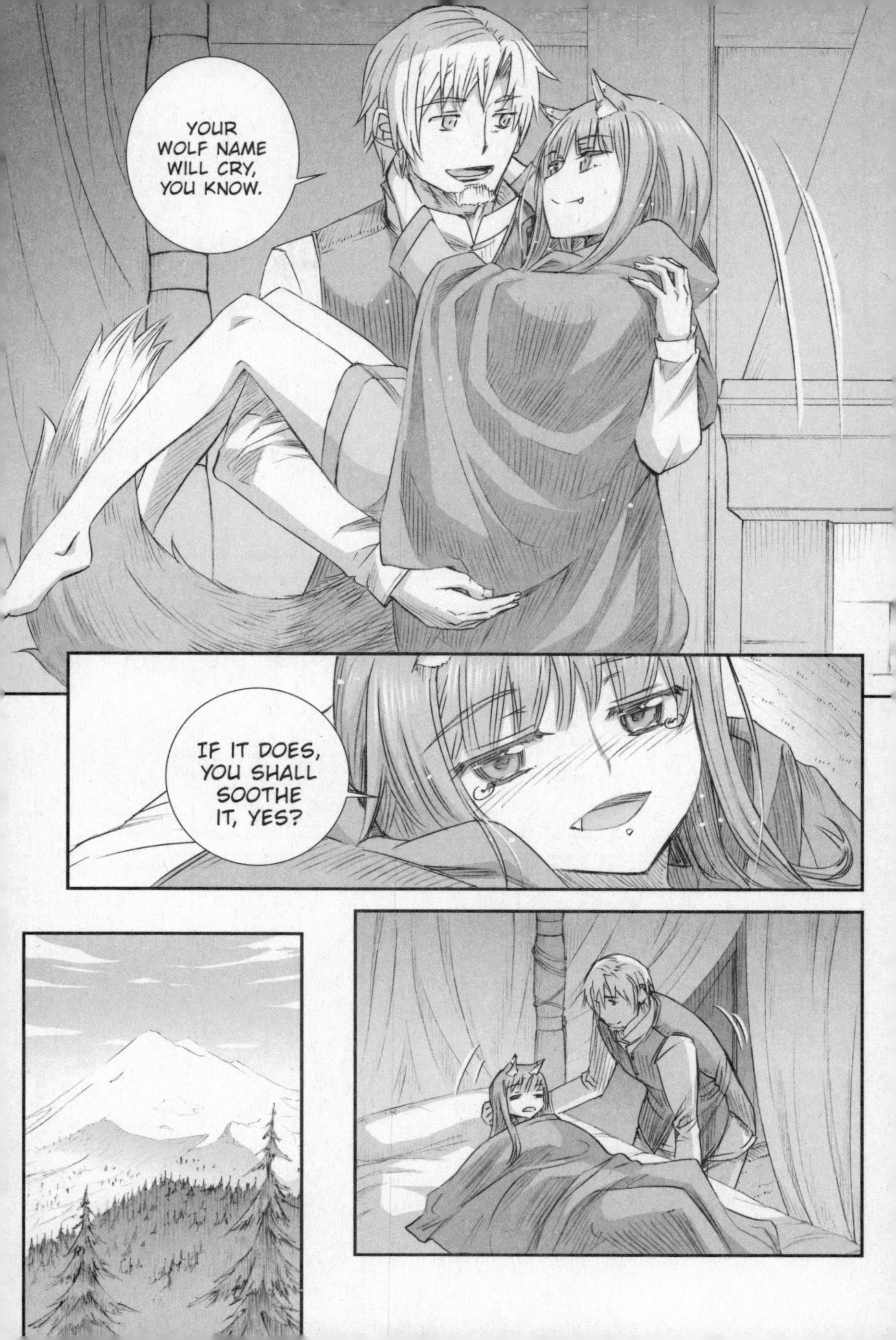
YOUR WOLF NAME WILL CRY, YOU KNOW.
IF IT DOES, YOU SHALL SOOTHE IT, YES?

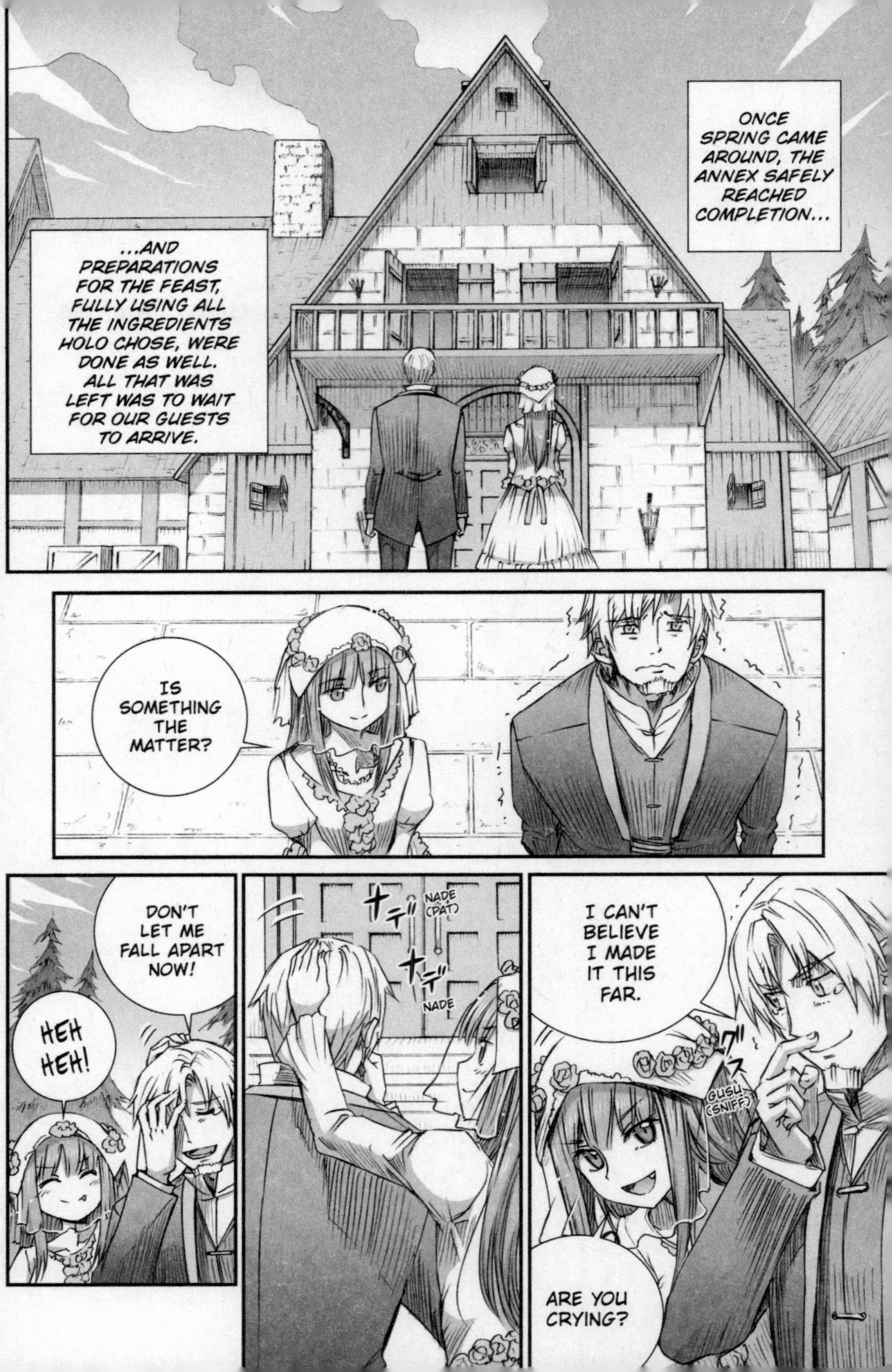
ONCE SPRING CAME AROUND, THE ANNEX SAFELY REACHED COMPLETION...
...AND PREPARATIONS FOR THE FEAST, FULLY USING ALL THE INGREDIENTS HOLO CHOSE, WERE DONE AS WELL. ALL THAT WAS LEFT WAS TO WAIT FOR OUR GUESTS TO ARRIVE.
IS SOMETHING THE MATTER?
I CAN'T BELIEVE I MADE IT THIS FAR.
GUSU (SNIFF)
ARE YOU CRYING?
NADE (PAT)
NADE
DON'T LET ME FALL APART NOW!
HEH HEH!

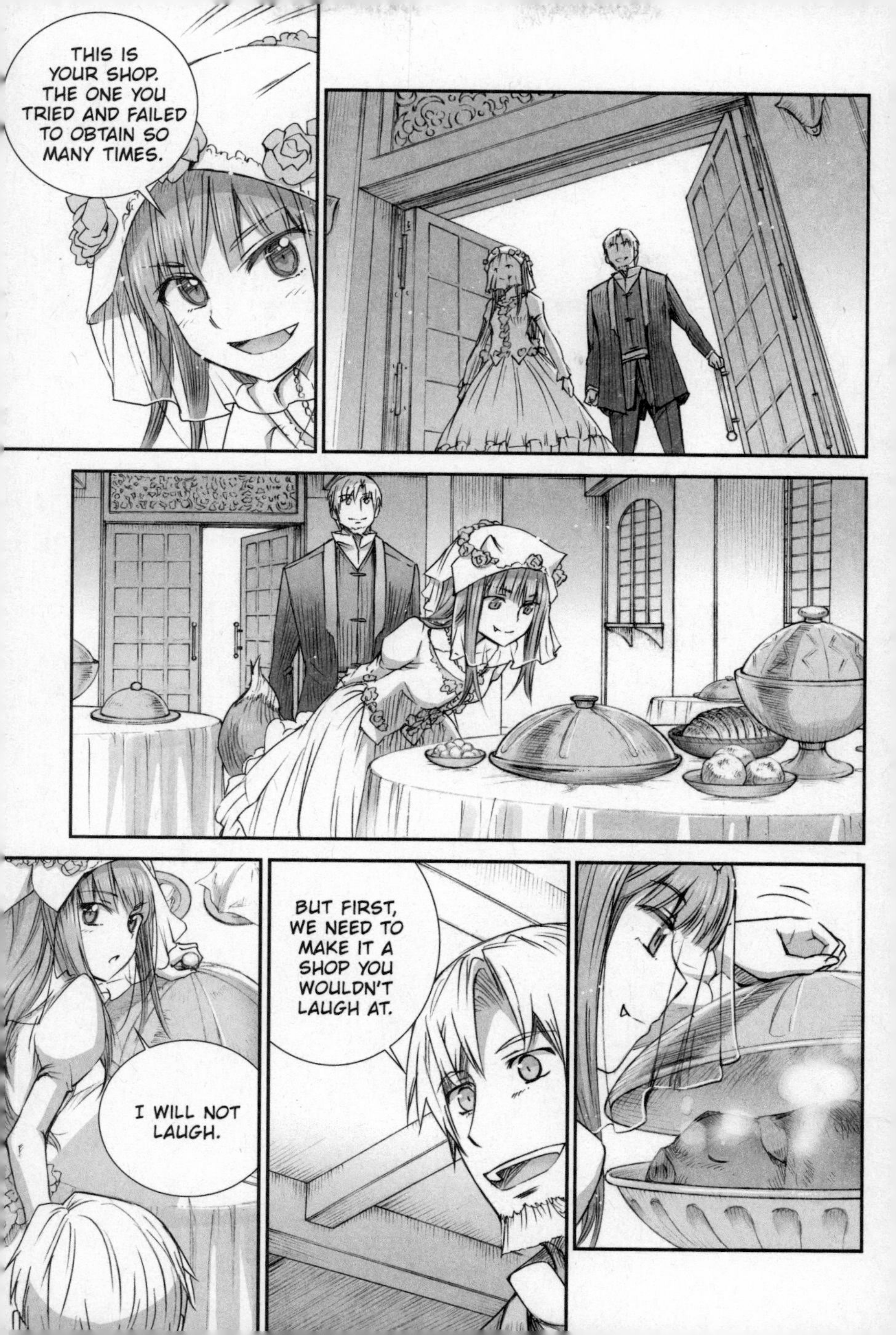
THIS IS YOUR SHOP. THE ONE YOU TRIED AND FAILED TO OBTAIN SO MANY TIMES.
BUT FIRST, WE NEED TO MAKE IT A SHOP YOU WOULDN'T LAUGH AT.
I WILL NOT LAUGH.

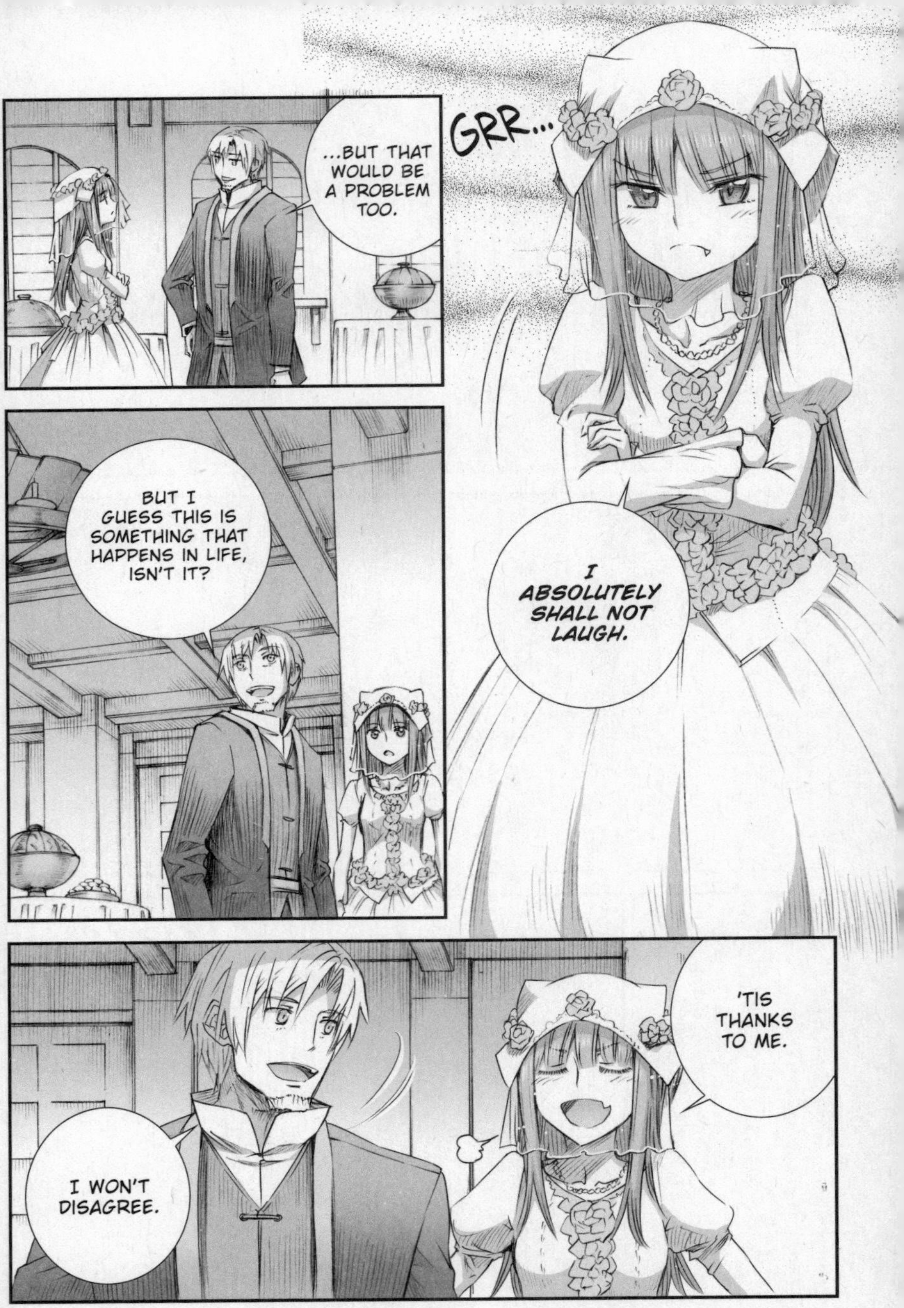
GRR...
I ABSOLUTELY SHALL NOT LAUGH.
...BUT THAT WOULD BE A PROBLEM TOO.
BUT I GUESS THIS IS SOMETHING THAT HAPPENS IN LIFE, ISN'T IT?
'TIS THANKS TO ME.
I WON'T DISAGREE.

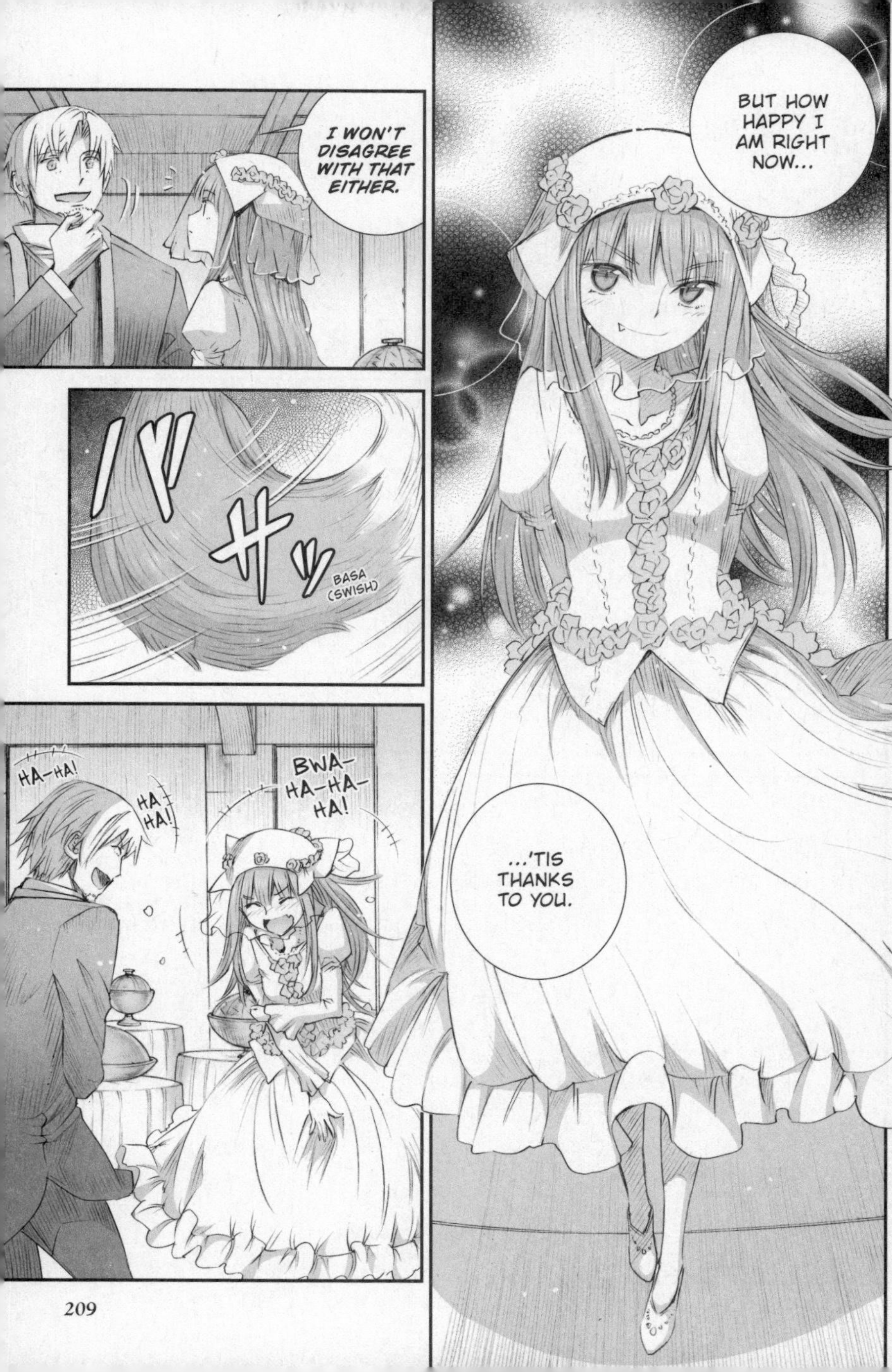
BUT HOW HAPPY I AM RIGHT NOW...
...'TIS THANKS TO YOU.
I WON'T DISAGREE WITH THAT EITHER.
BASA (SWISH)
BWA-HA-HA-HA!
HA HA!
HA-HA!

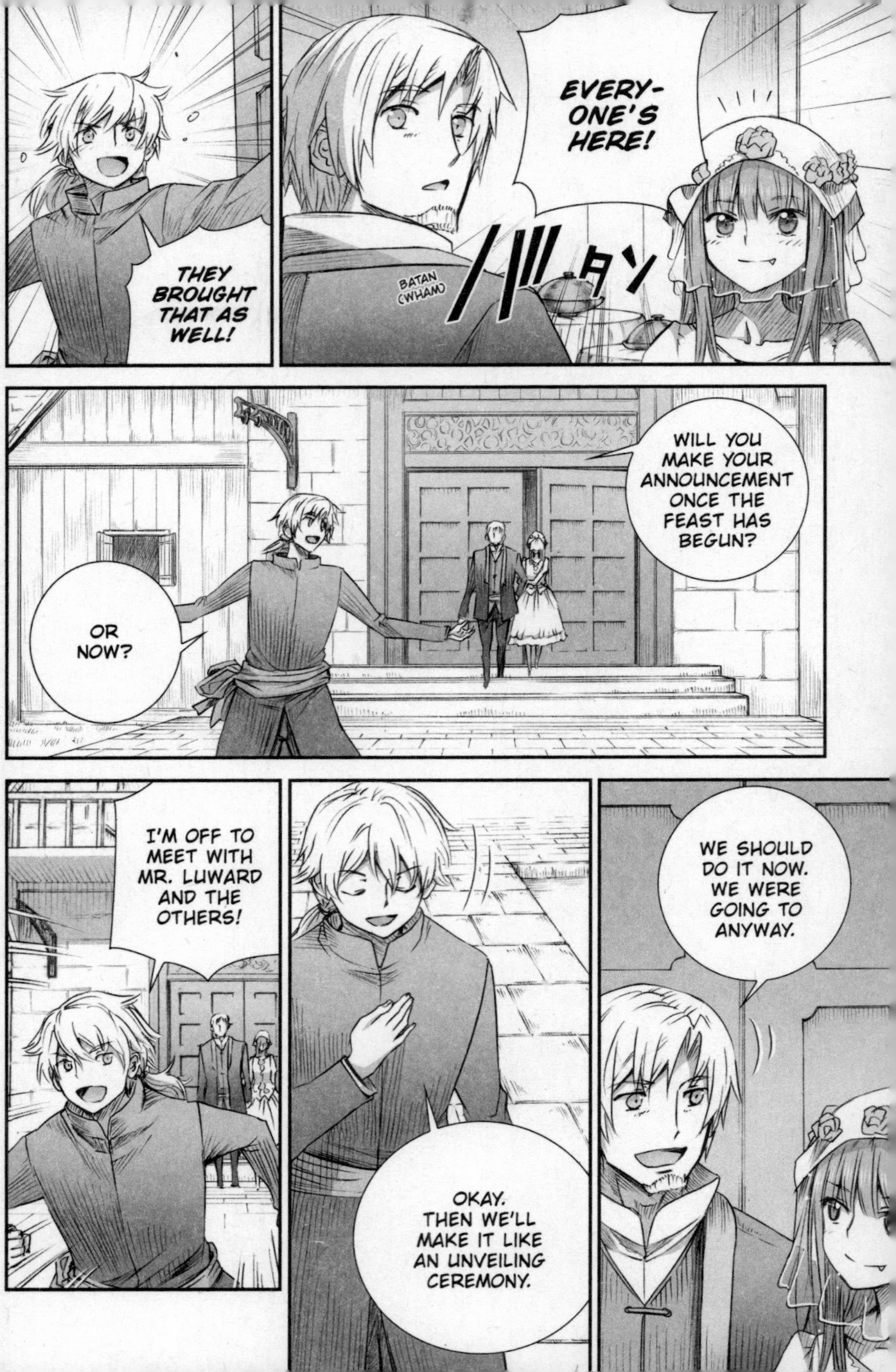
EVERY-ONE'S HERE!
バタン
BATAN (WHAM)
THEY BROUGHT THAT AS WELL!
WILL YOU MAKE YOUR ANNOUNCEMENT ONCE THE FEAST HAS BEGUN?
OR NOW?
WE SHOULD DO IT NOW. WE WERE GOING TO ANYWAY.
OKAY. THEN WE'LL MAKE IT LIKE AN UNVEILING CEREMONY.
I'M OFF TO MEET WITH MR. LUWARD AND THE OTHERS!

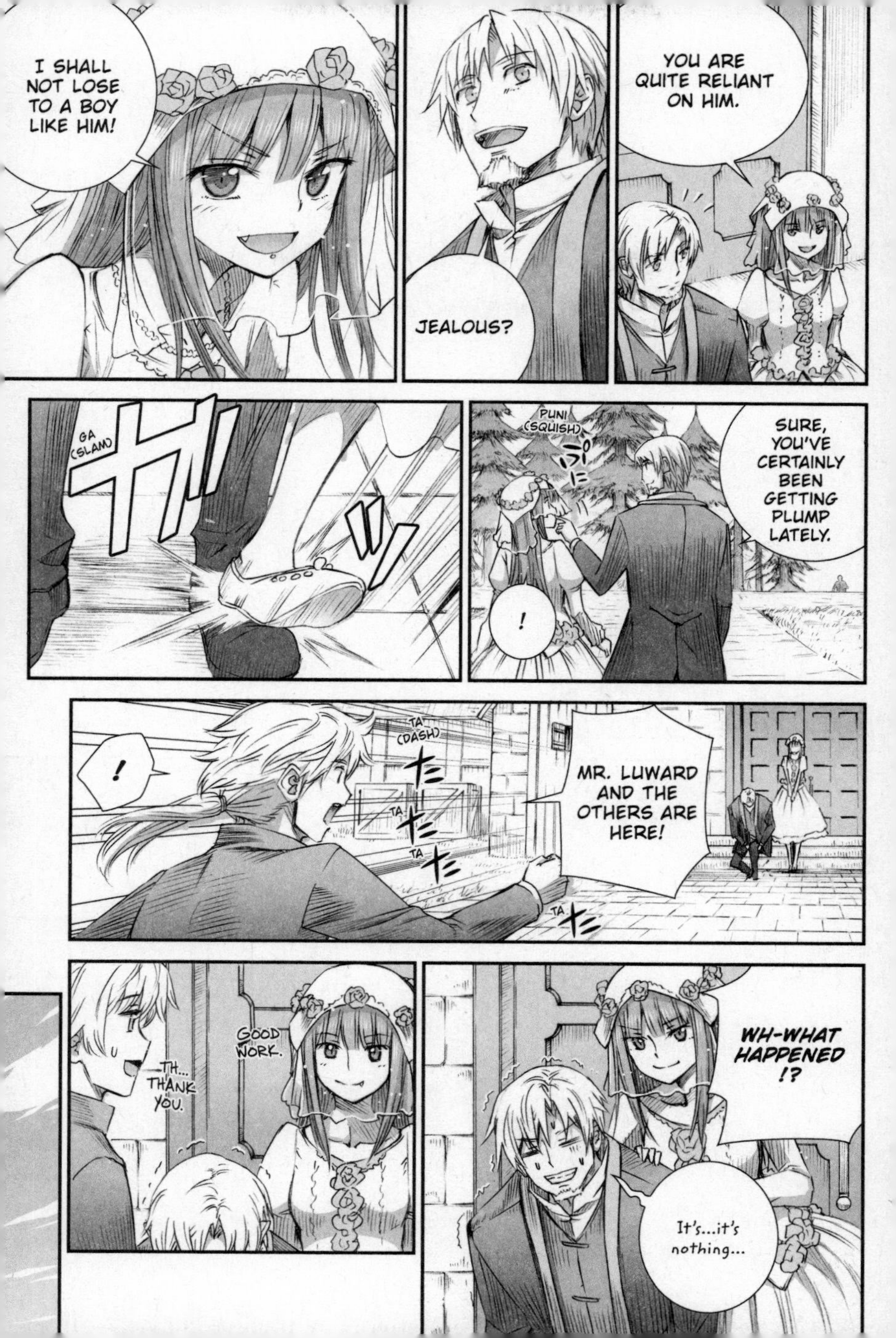
YOU ARE QUITE RELIANT ON HIM.
JEALOUS?
I SHALL NOT LOSE TO A BOY LIKE HIM!
SURE, YOU'VE CERTAINLY BEEN GETTING PLUMP LATELY.
PUNI (SQUISH)
!
GA (SLAM)
TA (DASH)
MR. LUWARD AND THE OTHERS ARE HERE!
TA
TA
TA
!
WH-WHAT HAPPENED!?
It's...it's nothing...
GOOD WORK.
TH... THANK YOU.

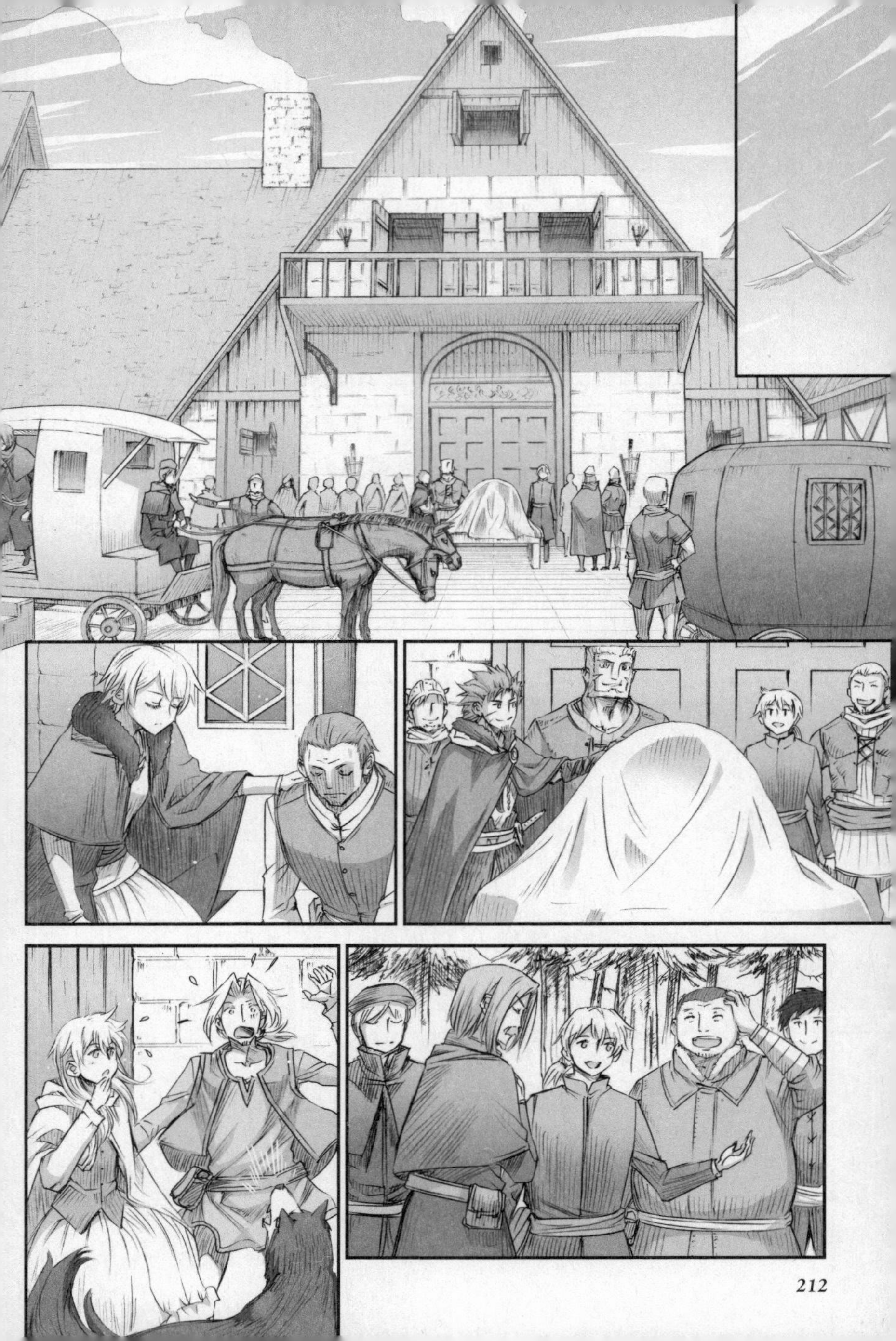

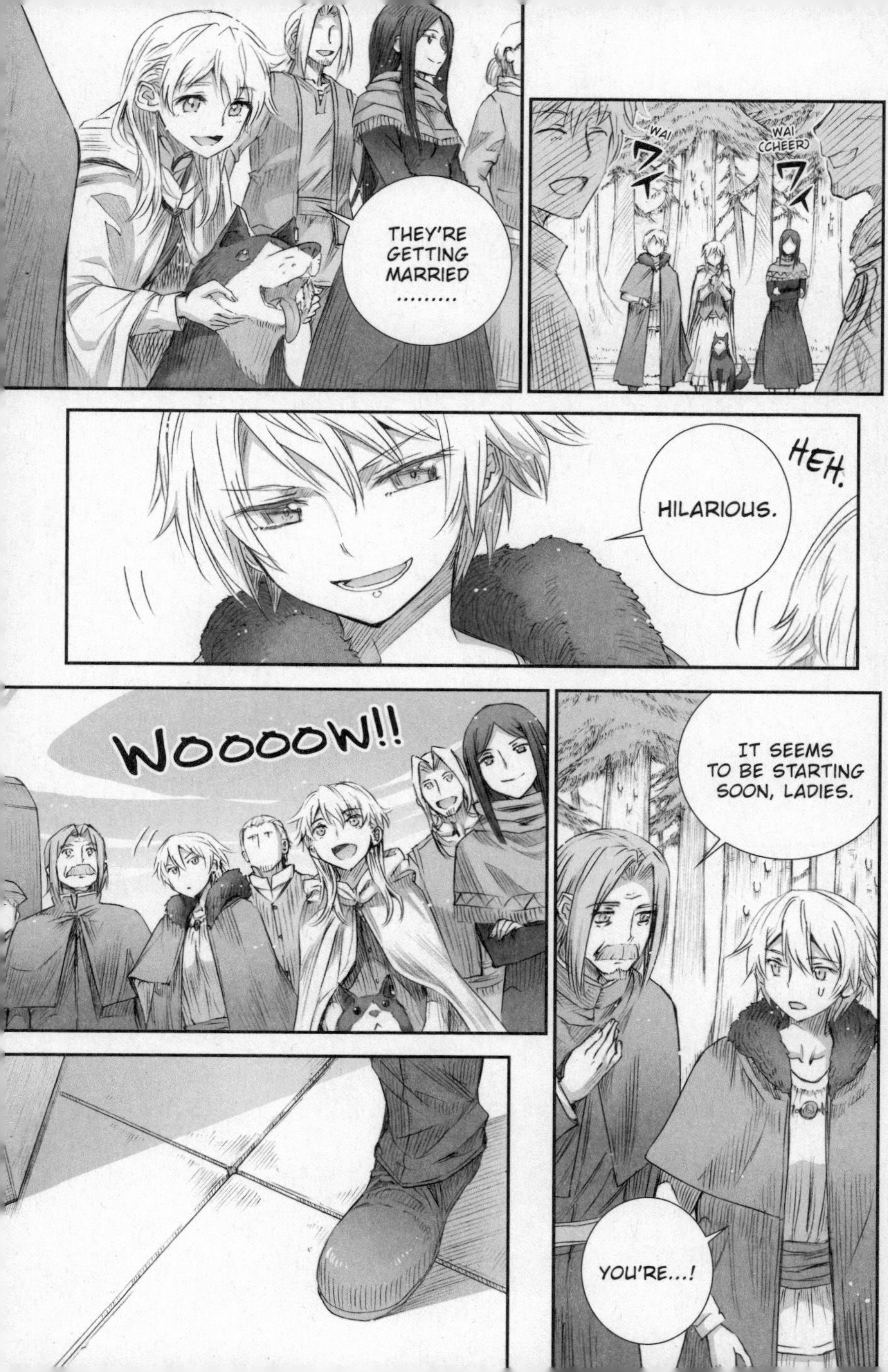
WAI (CHEER)
ワイ
WAI
ワイ
THEY'RE GETTING MARRIED ....
HEH.
HILARIOUS.
IT SEEMS TO BE STARTING SOON, LADIES.
YOU'RE...!
WOOOOW!!

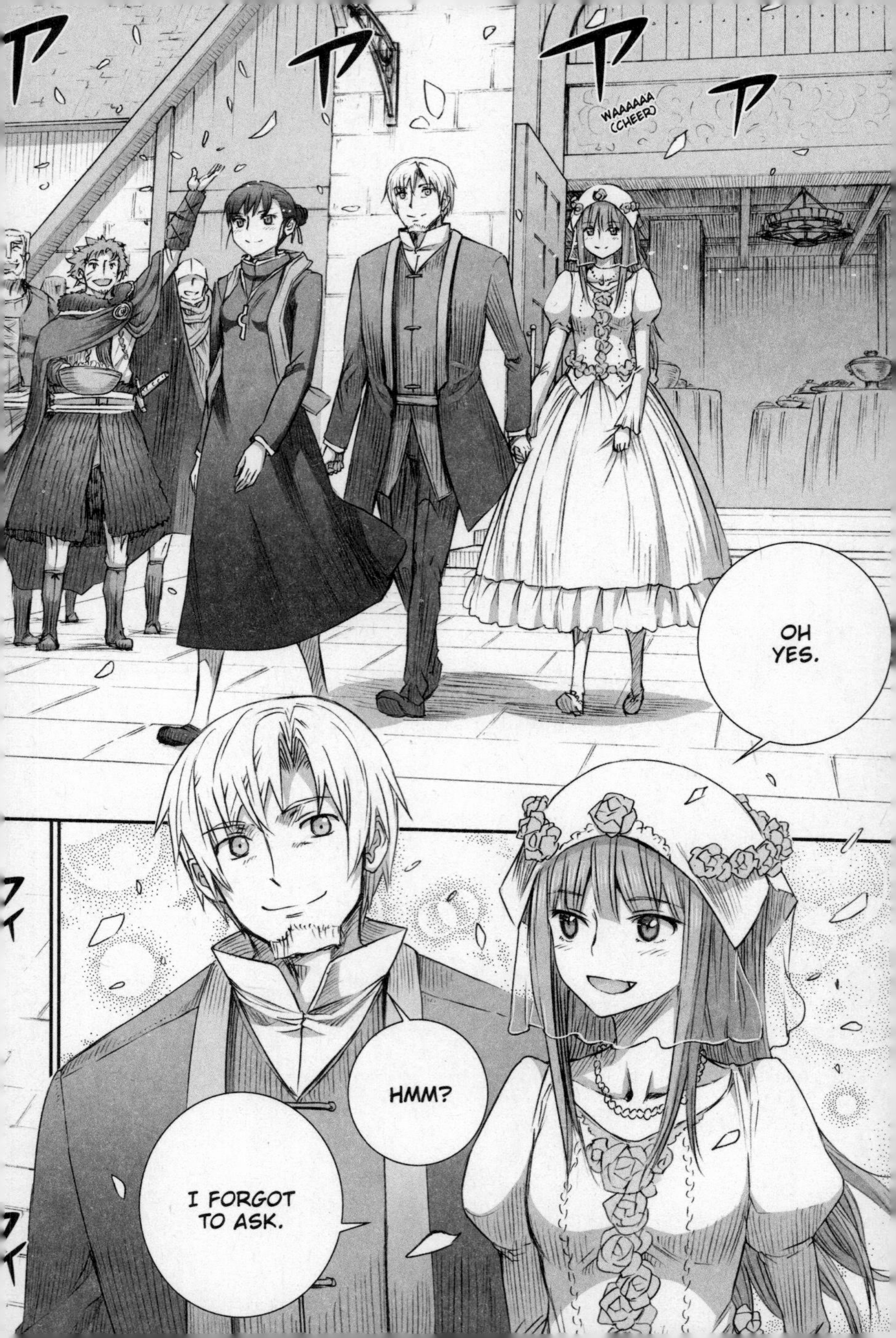
ア
WAAAAAA (CHEER)
ア
ア
ア
OH YES.
HMM?
I FORGOT TO ASK.
フイ
フイ

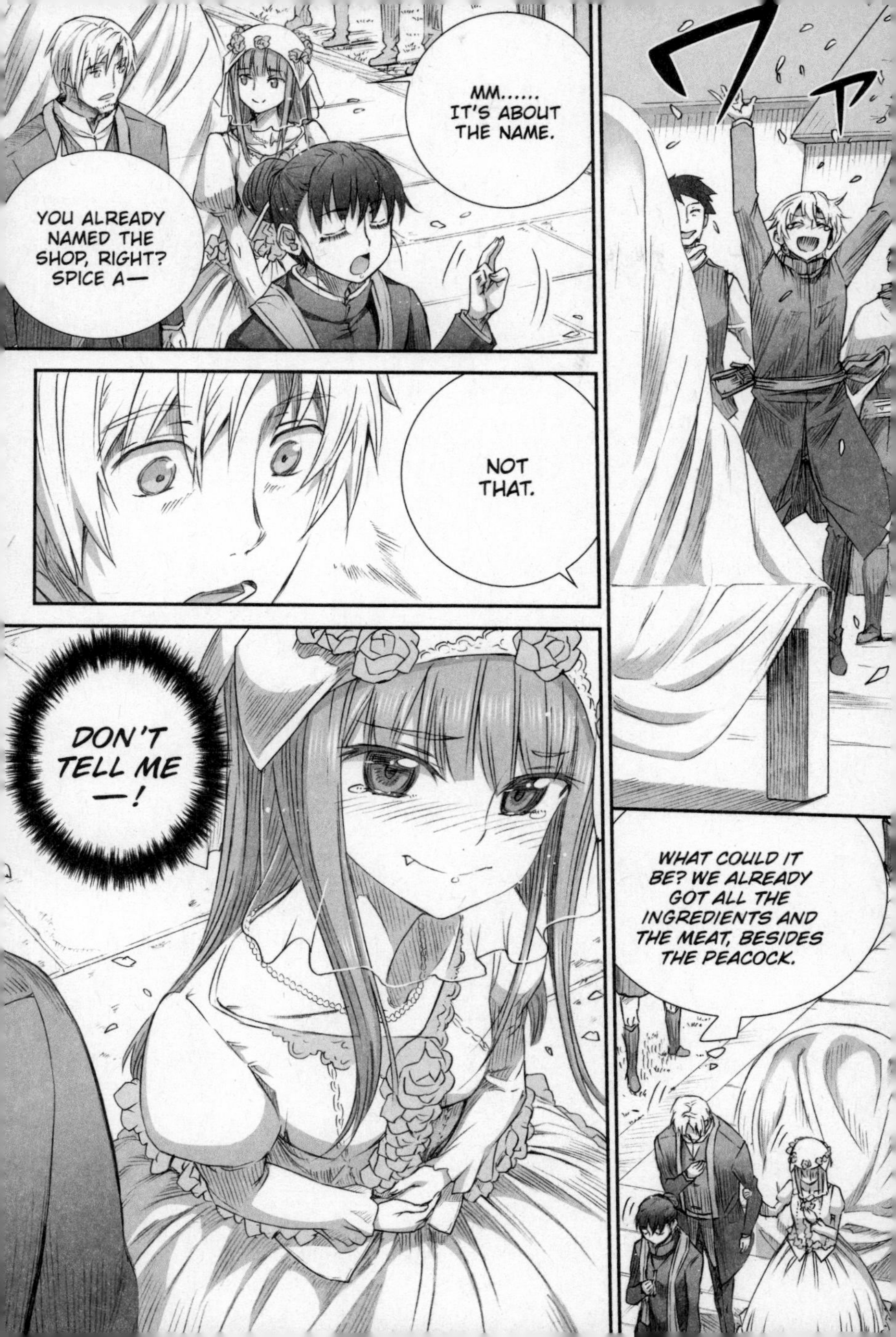
ワァ
WHAT COULD IT BE? WE ALREADY GOT ALL THE INGREDIENTS AND THE MEAT, BESIDES THE PEACOCK.
MM...... IT'S ABOUT THE NAME.
YOU ALREADY NAMED THE SHOP, RIGHT? SPICE A—
NOT THAT.
DON'T TELL ME —!

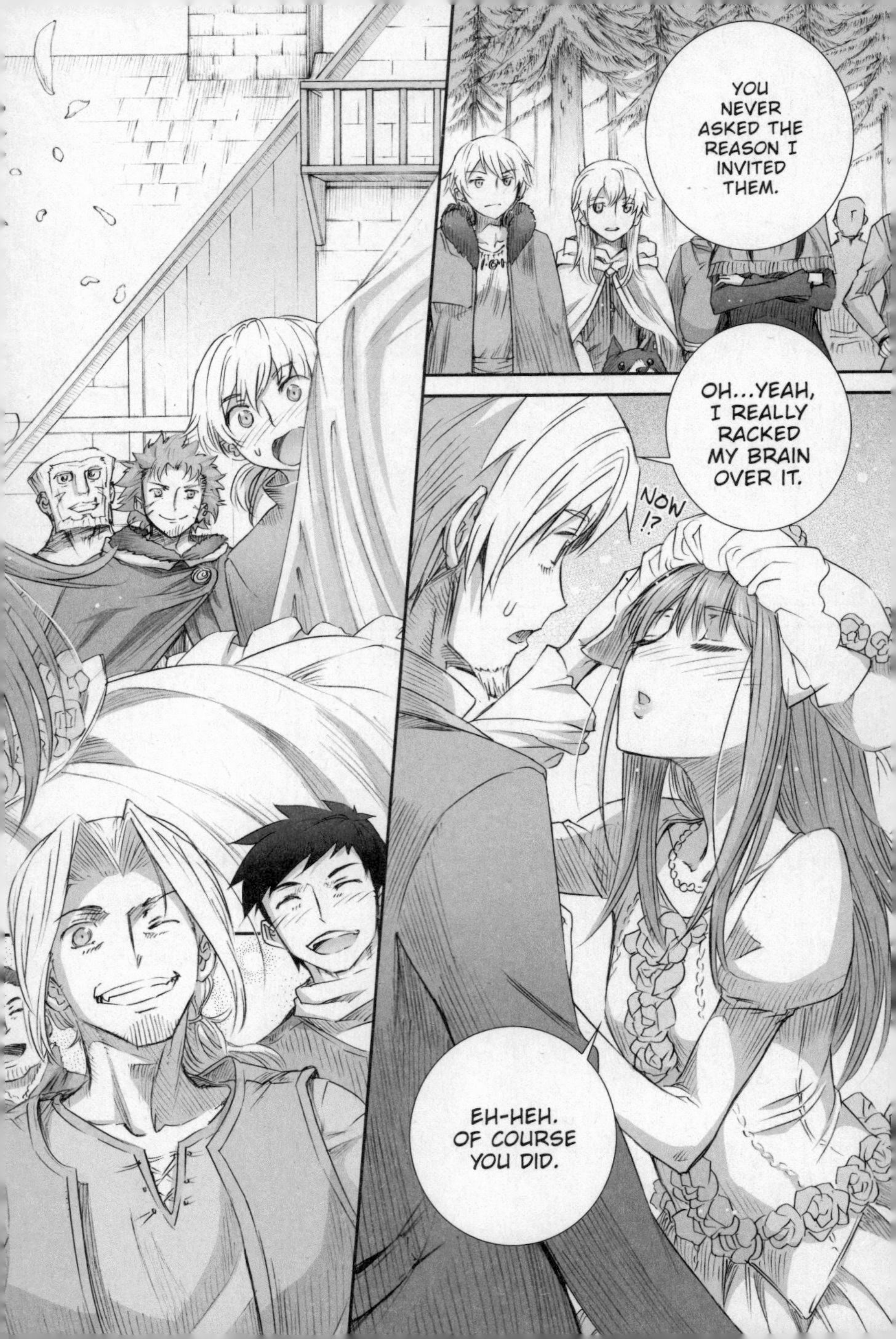
YOU NEVER ASKED THE REASON I INVITED THEM.
OH...YEAH, I REALLY RACKED MY BRAIN OVER IT.
NOW!?
EH-HEH. OF COURSE YOU DID.

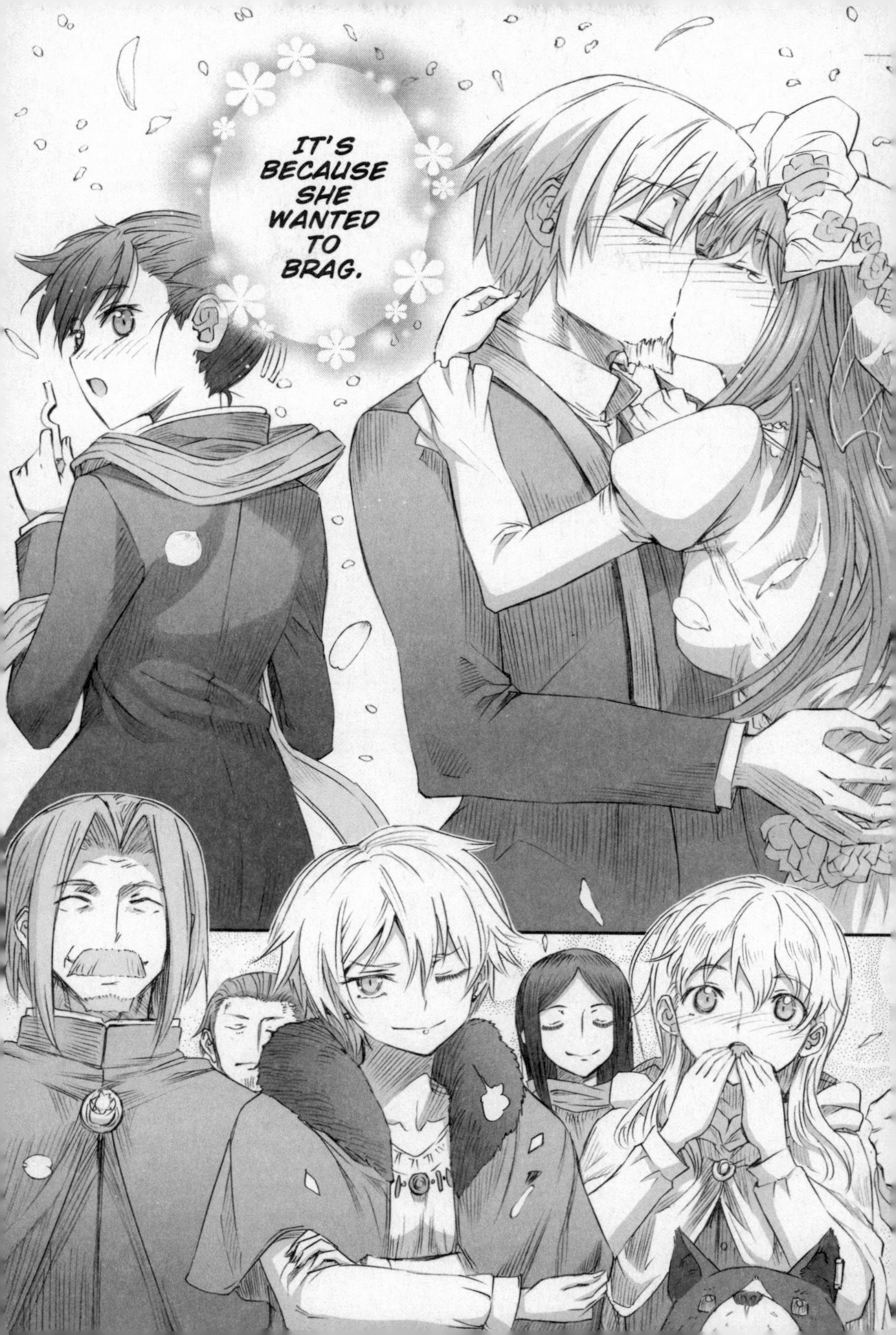
IT'S BECAUSE SHE WANTED TO BRAG.

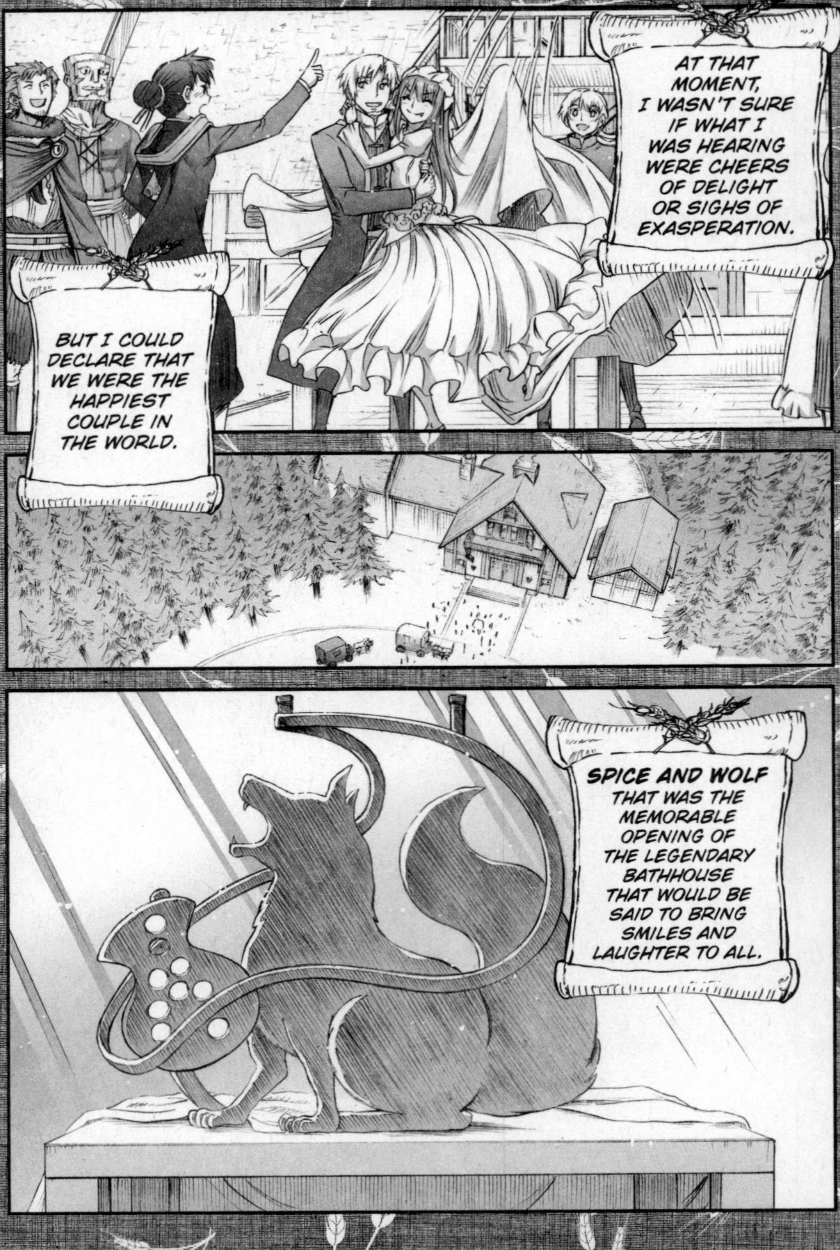
AT THAT MOMENT, I WASN'T SURE IF WHAT I WAS HEARING WERE CHEERS OF DELIGHT OR SIGHS OF EXASPERATION.
BUT I COULD DECLARE THAT WE WERE THE HAPPIEST COUPLE IN THE WORLD.
SPICE AND WOLF
THAT WAS THE MEMORABLE OPENING OF THE LEGENDARY BATHHOUSE THAT WOULD BE SAID TO BRING SMILES AND LAUGHTER TO ALL.

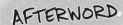

AFTERWORD

HELLO, THIS IS KOUME KEITO. I'VE FINALLY FINISHED DRAWING ALL ONE HUNDRED CHAPTERS OF THE MANGA VERSION OF SPICE AND WOLF OVER TEN LONG YEARS. I GIVE MY THANKS TO THE ORIGINAL AUTHOR, HASEKURA-SENSEI, AND EVERYONE WHO SUPPORTED HIM.

THE STORY IS STILL ONGOING, ACTUALLY, SO PLEASE TAKE A LOOK AT HASEKURA-SENSEI'S WOLF AND PARCHMENT. FINALLY, I DECIDED TO MAKE ONE OF HASEKURA-SENSEI'S ORIGINAL SHORT STORIES FROM HIS ILLUSTRATION COLLECTION INTO A COMIC.

I HAVE DECIDED THAT THIS IS AS FAR AS MY GOALS GO. I WOULD BE DELIGHTED IF YOU READ IT.

THANK YOU FOR YOUR READERSHIP FOR TEN LONG YEARS!

KOUME KEITO

Special Thanks!!

PRIVATE MR. OKAMOTO
MR. TENTSU TOI
MR. YAKKUN
MR. N-TA
MR. HIRATA ORIGUCHI
MR. A
MR. YUU

2018.1.21

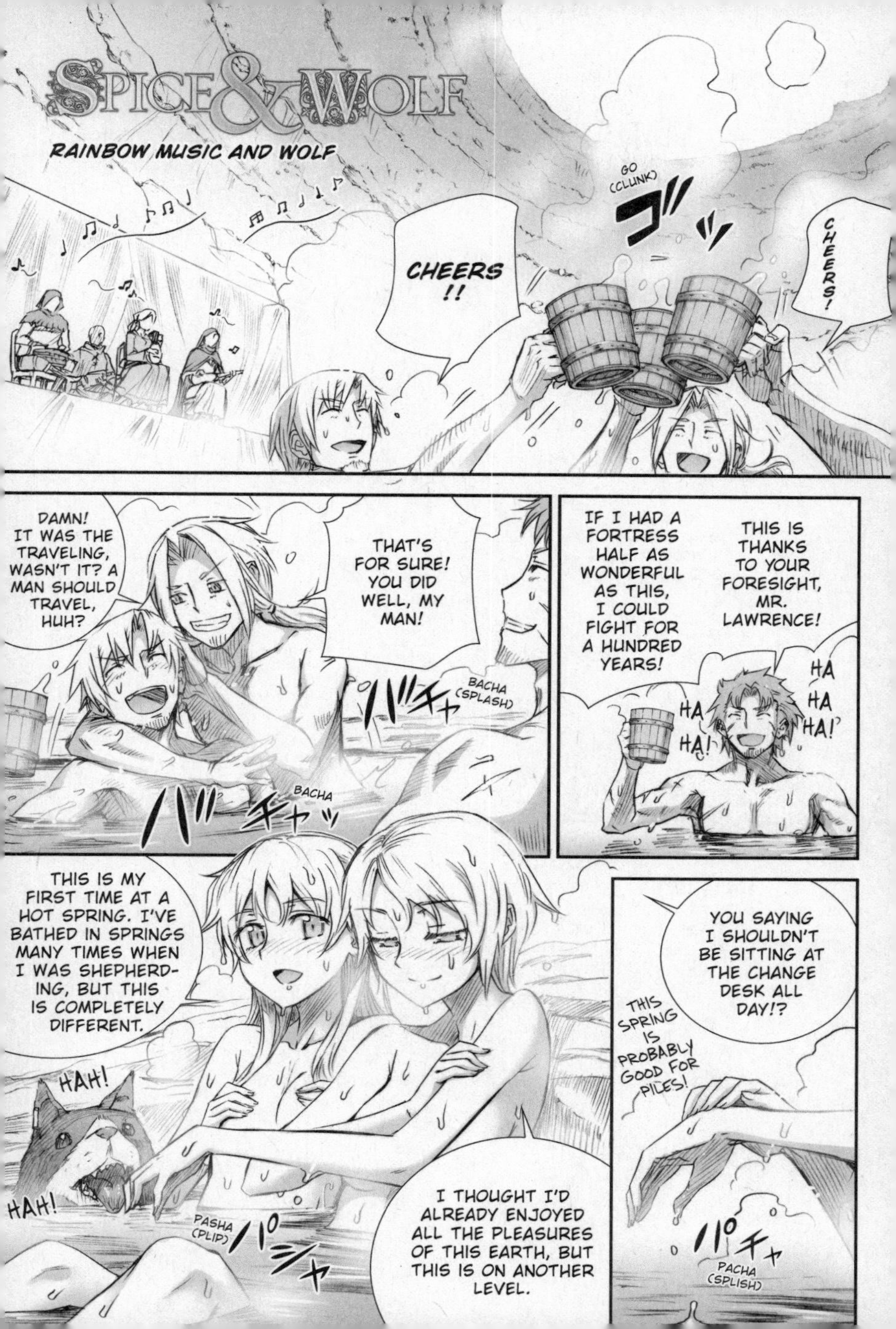
SPICE & WOLF
RAINBOW MUSIC AND WOLF
CHEERS!
GO (CLUNK)
CHEERS!!
THIS IS THANKS TO YOUR FORESIGHT, MR. LAWRENCE!
IF I HAD A FORTRESS HALF AS WONDERFUL AS THIS, I COULD FIGHT FOR A HUNDRED YEARS!
HA HA HA!
HA HA!
THAT'S FOR SURE! YOU DID WELL, MY MAN!
DAMN! IT WAS THE TRAVELING, WASN'T IT? A MAN SHOULD TRAVEL, HUH?
BACHA (SPLASH)
BACHA
YOU SAYING I SHOULDN'T BE SITTING AT THE CHANGE DESK ALL DAY!?
THIS SPRING IS PROBABLY GOOD FOR PILES!
PACHA (SPLISH)
THIS IS MY FIRST TIME AT A HOT SPRING. I'VE BATHED IN SPRINGS MANY TIMES WHEN I WAS SHEPHERD-ING, BUT THIS IS COMPLETELY DIFFERENT.
I THOUGHT I'D ALREADY ENJOYED ALL THE PLEASURES OF THIS EARTH, BUT THIS IS ON ANOTHER LEVEL.
HAH!
HAH!
PASHA (PLIP)

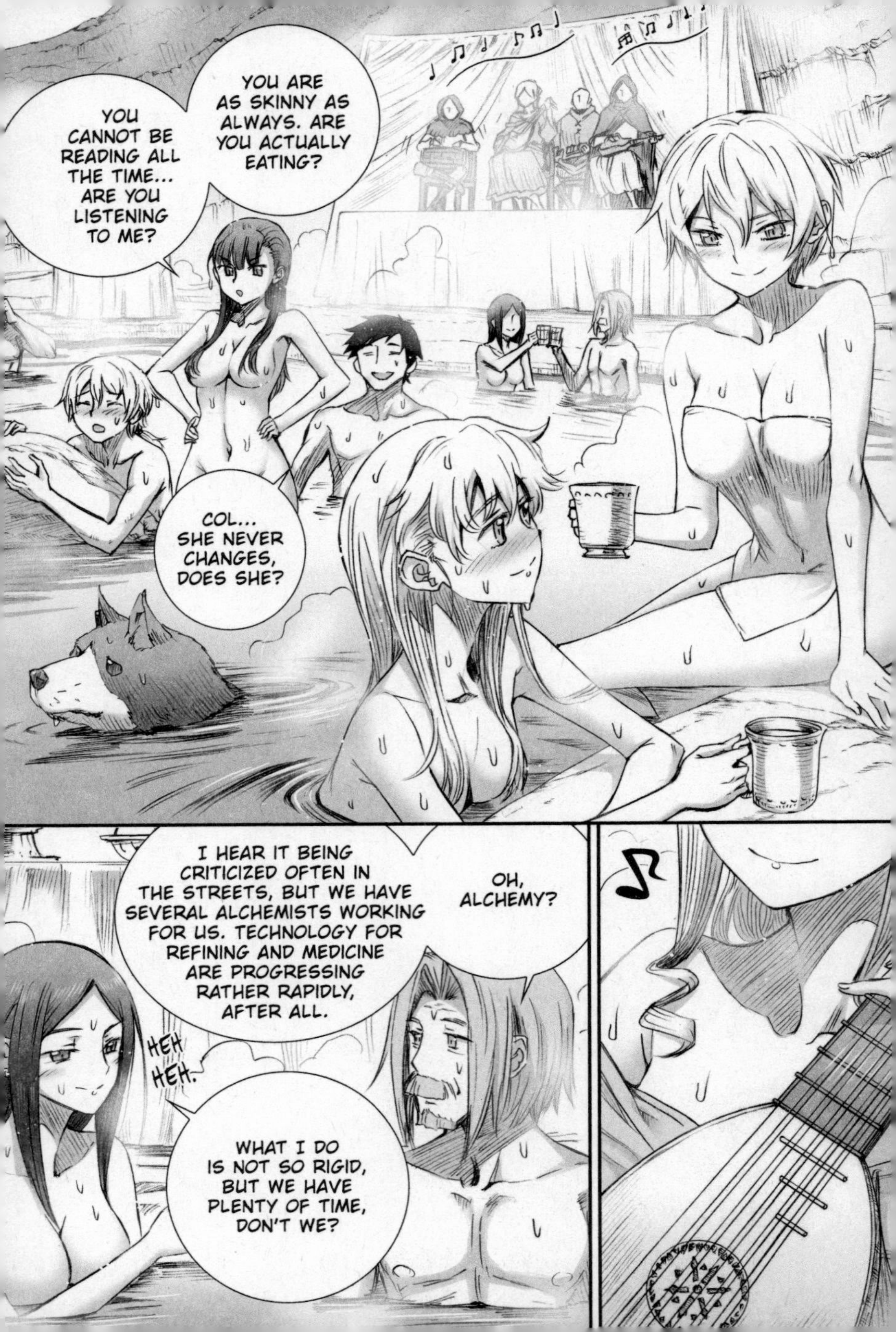
YOU ARE AS SKINNY AS ALWAYS. ARE YOU ACTUALLY EATING?
YOU CANNOT BE READING ALL THE TIME... ARE YOU LISTENING TO ME?
COL... SHE NEVER CHANGES, DOES SHE?
OH, ALCHEMY?
I HEAR IT BEING CRITICIZED OFTEN IN THE STREETS, BUT WE HAVE SEVERAL ALCHEMISTS WORKING FOR US. TECHNOLOGY FOR REFINING AND MEDICINE ARE PROGRESSING RATHER RAPIDLY, AFTER ALL.
HEH HEH.
WHAT I DO IS NOT SO RIGID, BUT WE HAVE PLENTY OF TIME, DON'T WE?

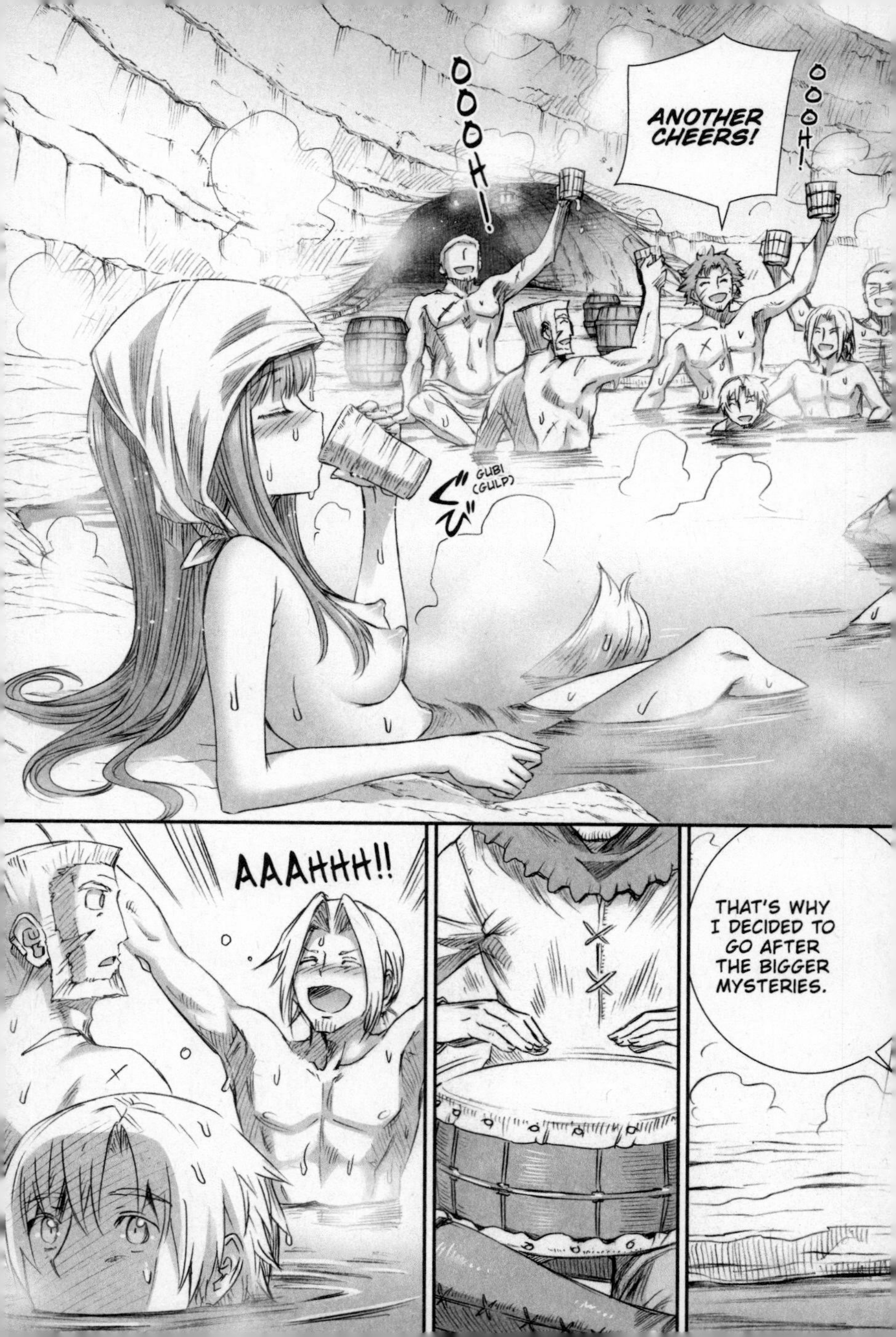
OOOH!
ANOTHER CHEERS!
OOOOH!
GUBI (GULP)
THAT'S WHY I DECIDED TO GO AFTER THE BIGGER MYSTERIES.
AAAHHH!!

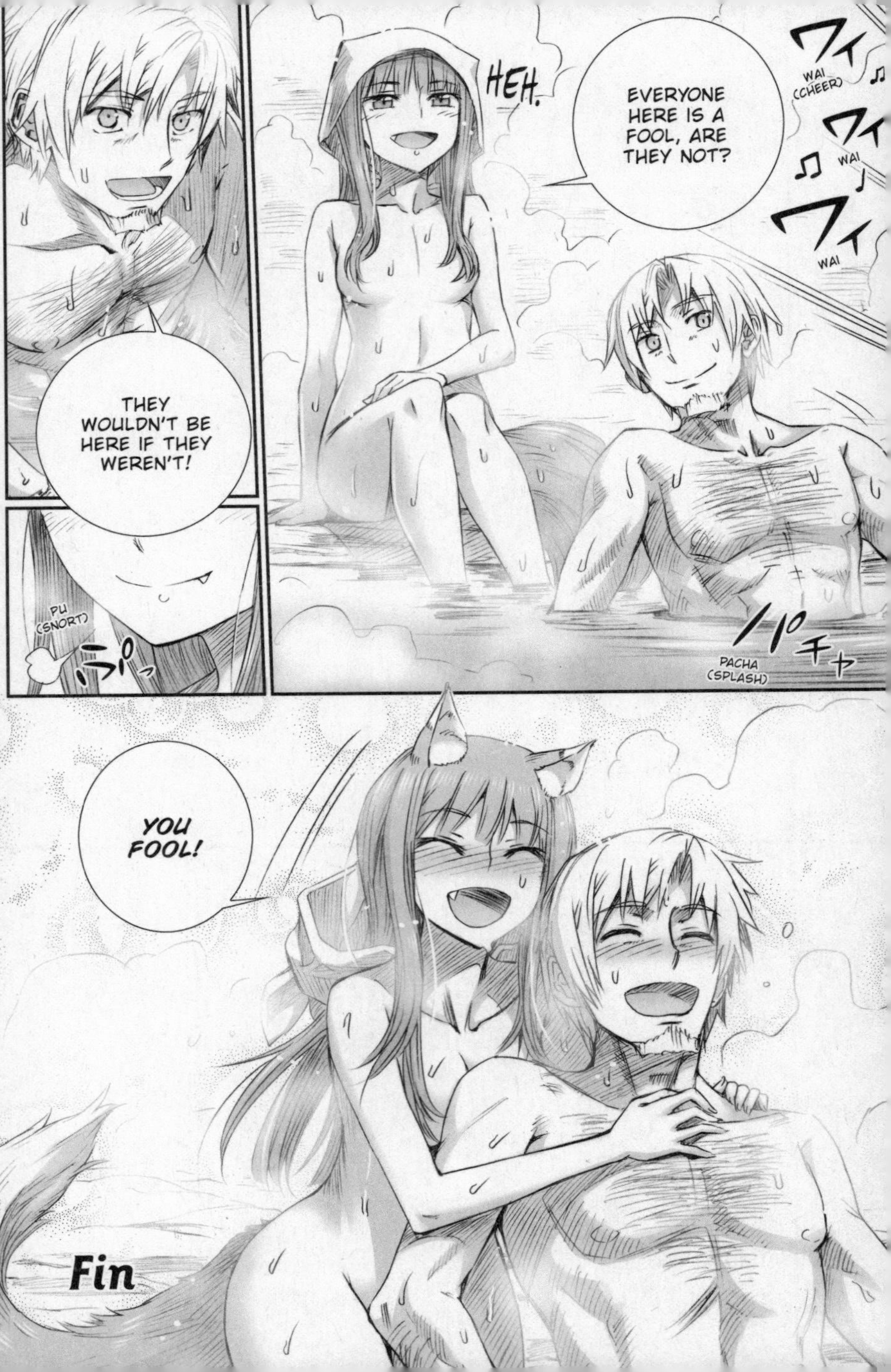
ワイ
WAI (CHEER)
ワイ
WAI
ワイ
WAI
EVERYONE HERE IS A FOOL, ARE THEY NOT?
HEH.
パチャ
PACHA (SPLASH)
THEY WOULDN'T BE HERE IF THEY WEREN'T!
ぷっ
PU (SNORT)
YOU FOOL!
Fin

KEITO KOUME-SENSEI,
CONGRATULATIONS!
PARTWAY THROUGH YOUR WORK,
I STARTED ENJOYING IT NOT
AS THE ORIGINAL AUTHOR
BUT AS A READER. AND SO
AS THIS JOURNEY COMES TO
AN END, I FEEL EVEN MORE
DEEPLY MOVED THAN I DID
WHEN I FINISHED WRITING
IT ON MY OWN. YOUR UNIQUE
TOUCH AND PORTRAYAL OF
EVEN THE SMALLEST OBJECTS
GAVE DEFINITE DEPTH AND
WIDTH TO THE WOLF
WORLD. THERE IS NO
GREATER HAPPINESS
I CAN ASK FOR AS THE
ORIGINAL AUTHOR THAN HAVING
SUCH A LONG SERIES
BE DRAWN WITH
SUCH GREAT
PASSION
UNTIL THE
VERY END.
THANK YOU
SO MUCH!

KEITO KOUME-SENSEI,
CONGRATULATIONS ON FINISHING
THE *SPICE AND WOLF* COMIC! AS ONE OF
YOUR READERS, I WAS TRULY HAPPY TO
WATCH YOU BREATHE LIFE INTO THE WORLD
AND STORY OF *SPICE AND WOLF* FOR OVER
TEN YEARS. I BELIEVE THAT I FELT LIKE HOLO
AND LAWRENCE'S JOURNEY WAS STILL
CONTINUING DESPITE HOW THE ORIGINAL
NOVELS WERE ALREADY COMPLETED WAS,
WITHOUT A DOUBT, BECAUSE OF KOUME-
SENSEI'S COMICS. I FINALLY FELT LIKE
THEIR JOURNEY HAD REACHED AN END WHEN
I SAW THE WEDDING SCENE IN THE LAST
CHAPTER, AND I COULD SQUARE THOSE
FEELINGS AWAY (EVEN THOUGH THERE WILL
BE A START TO A NEW TALE...). I FEEL SO
TOUCHED RIGHT NOW THAT MY WORDS AREN'T
REALLY COMING TOGETHER—I'M SORRY.
   I PRAY THAT WE CAN SEE YOUR HAPPY
         HOLO AND LAWRENCE AS
         THEY SPEAK FONDLY
         OF EACH OTHER AGAIN
         ONE DAY. YOU HAVE TRULY
         CREATED SOMETHING
         WONDERFUL. THANK
         YOU SO MUCH!!

SPICE & WOLF 16

ISUNA HASEKURA
KEITO KOUME
CHARACTER DESIGN:
JYUU AYAKURA

TRANSLATION: JASMINE BERNHARDT

LETTERING: KATIE BLAKESLEE

OOKAMI TO KOUSHINRYOU Vol. 16
©ISUNA HASEKURA/KEITO KOUME 2018
FIRST PUBLISHED IN JAPAN IN 2018 BY
KADOKAWA CORPORATION, Tokyo.
ENGLISH TRANSLATION RIGHTS ARRANGED WITH
KADOKAWA CORPORATION, Tokyo,
THROUGH TUTTLE-MORI AGENCY, INC., Tokyo.

YEN PRESS
1290 AVENUE OF THE AMERICAS
NEW YORK, NY 10104

VISIT US AT YENPRESS.COM
FACEBOOK.COM/YENPRESS
TWITTER.COM/YENPRESS
YENPRESS.TUMBLR.COM
INSTAGRAM.COM/YENPRESS

FIRST YEN PRESS EDITION: DECEMBER 2018

YEN PRESS IS AN IMPRINT OF YEN PRESS, LLC.
THE YEN PRESS NAME AND LOGO ARE TRADEMARKS OF YEN PRESS, LLC.

THE PUBLISHER IS NOT RESPONSIBLE FOR WEBSITES (OR THEIR CONTENT) THAT ARE NOT OWNED BY THE PUBLISHER.

LIBRARY OF CONGRESS CONTROL NUMBER: 2015956856

ISBNs: 978-1-9753-2799-6 (PAPERBACK)
       978-1-9753-8307-7 (EBOOK)

10 9 8 7 6 5 4 3 2 1

WOR

PRINTED IN THE UNITED STATES OF AMERICA